FLIGHT FEVER

L'essayer c'est tout
  —IGOR I. SIKORSKY

Flight Fever

JOSEPH R. HAMLEN

DOUBLEDAY & COMPANY, INC., Garden City, New York, 1971

PHOTO CREDITS

Harry M. Jones; 28, 33, 34, 38, 44, 45, 46, 49

Maine Historical Society; 35, 47, 48, 50

National Air and Space Museum, Smithsonian Institution; 4, 6, 9, 53, 55

Portland *Press Herald-Evening Express*, Portland, Maine; 27, 29, 36

United Press International; 1, 2, 3, 5, 7, 8, 10, 11, 12, 13, 14, 15, 16, 17, 18, 19, 20, 21, 22, 23, 24, 25, 26, 30, 31, 37, 39, 40, 41, 42, 43, 51, 52, 54, 56

Wide World Photo; 32

Library of Congress Catalog Card Number 69–12201
Copyright © 1971 by Joseph R. Hamlen
Printed in the United States of America. All Rights Reserved
First Edition

To Cyrilla with love

Contents

FOREWORD

Flight Fever is a loving remembrance of my youth. It was born at Grand Beach, Maine, many years ago where my grandfather and grandmother invited my brother and me to spend cool summers in their modest compound overlooking the ocean while our parents kept our winter home ready in Little Rock, Arkansas.

Grand Beach was an exciting place for children and adults in 1927, but especially for children. Flying was still a novelty. In past years we children had gazed in awe as our idol, Harry Jones, flew off the beach with passengers in his biplaned Stinson. That year we had an added attraction—the heroic ocean flyers. Lindbergh and Chamberlin, who had flown the Atlantic in the late spring, visited us—the boyish Lindy swooping down to the sand in his silvery little *Spirit of St. Louis*, and the slender Chamberlin arriving planeless, for *Columbia* was still abroad with her owner. Then came *Pride of Detroit*, *Old Glory*, *Royal Windsor*, and *Dawn* to fill out our thrilling summer.

For remembrances of days at the Beach, I thank my Uncle Jim and Aunt Eleanor, my brother Bill and my cousins who were "we" in my story, Rear Admiral Robert J. White, USNR (Ret), Joseph Snow, and Robert Longfellow, who were all a part of those days.

I thank also my old friend Harry Jones who has furnished me with pictures together with all of his flying memories from 1912 on. He has provided me with vivid factual and technical information which is invaluable to a history.

The remainder of my story was done from research into books on the era, and magazines and papers of the day. It was reinforced by gracious assistance from Rear Admiral John Jay Schieffelin, USNR (Ret), the late Major General Robert Gilpin Ervin, USAF (Ret),

John Hay Whitney, John M. Lockwood, René Lefevre (who was to fly the Atlantic himself in 1929), Arthur Shreiber, and the personnel of the National Air and Space Museum of the Smithsonian Institution, Washington, D.C.

I would also like to thank Chauncey Stillman for lending me the beauty and peace of Wethersfield Farm while I worked on the original manuscript, and Martha Thompson for her translations and her interview of M. Lefevre.

The book, however, would not have been a book without the help of Miss Margaret Stoddard. "Mug," whom I have known as long as I can remember, cajoled, cut, reasoned, scissored and pasted with me and without me until my mass of remembrances was an acceptable whole. I will never be able to thank her adequately.

Finally, my grateful love goes to my wife, Cyrilla, for her patience, to my mother for her encouragement, and to my daughter Mary for her confidence. She always said, "Daddu, I like your book!"

For those who remember the days of which I write, I hope it portrays an accurate history; for those who were born later, I hope similar exciting memories have been or will be theirs in the years to come.

New York, N.Y.
October 15, 1970

FLIGHT FEVER

PROLOGUE

New Year's Eve

1. It was cold and wet in Times Square on New Year's Eve. The traditional crowds were soaked by a fine, wetting rain as they flocked from theaters and night clubs to welcome in the new year in the vicinity of the Times Tower.

Some had come from Fred Stone's musical comedy, *Criss-Cross*, playing at the Globe Theatre; others from seeing the movie version of *What Price Glory?* with Victor McLaglen and Edmund Lowe; and still others from the perennial favorite, *Abie's Irish Rose*, in its fifth year at the Republic Theatre on West 42nd Street.

The night clubs, too, were jammed, despite the fancy prices. There was a $40 cover charge at Club Anatole on 54th Street and at Roger Wolfe Kahn's exclusive Le Perroquet de Paris. The hotels were more reasonable. At the Plaza, 2500 people were entertained at $10 per customer, while the Astor, in the heart of Times Square, had a mere $7.50 cover. Dancers with comic hats inched around the packed floors to rhythmic tunes such as "Clap Yo' Hands," "Do-Do-Do," and "I Know That You Know"—the top hits of the day. Drinkers were less covert than usual, for Prohibition Administrator Chester P. Mills had informed his agents that any work they did this night would be purely voluntary.

It had been a good year, and, only yesterday, Alfred E. Sloan of General Motors had issued a statement predicting an even more prosperous new year, a prediction backed by the fact that General Motors had closed at 155½ in the final trading of the year on the New York Stock Exchange.

As the lighted ball on the Tower dropped slowly, tolling the last seconds of 1926, the gay cheers of the vast crowd grew to a roaring welcome to 1927 amid the familiar strains of "Auld Lang Syne."

The year 1926 had been one of the gayest years of the Jazz Age.

There were the frolicking steps of the Charleston and the Black Bottom. There were the short skirts and bobbed hair, the Stutz Bearcat, raccoon coats, bootleggers and speakeasies. Boys and girls said "Welcome, sucker!", "Twenty-three skidoo!", read about George F. Babbit and the Great Gatsby, sang "Who?" and the wistful, "Remember," and reveled in the romantic movie roles played by Rudolph Valentino and lovely Clara Bow.

The summer had been long and hot, exciting and sad. The world applauded when Gertrude Ederle swam the English Channel in 14½ hours, and wept profusely when the adored Valentino died suddenly. Those in the United States followed the morbid details of the trial of Mrs. Eleanor Mills and the Reverend Edward Hall for the murder of Mrs. Mills's minister-husband in New Brunswick, New Jersey, but the investors among them forgot the crime swiftly, when General Motors shares leaped 12½ points in value in one day to close at 213½.

Abroad, the government of President Elias Plutarco Calles of Mexico had stirred the world on August 1, by imposing laws bent on curtailing the influence there of the Roman Catholic Church, while, in Nicaragua, President Adolfo Díaz accused his political opponent, Juan B. Sacasa, of attempting to overthrow his regime with the aid of "that tyrant, Calles!" and appealed to U. S. Secretary of State Frank B. Kellogg for immediate military aid.

Broadway had glittered. Lovely Marilyn Miller was nearing the end of a sensationally long run in Jerome Kern's *Sunny*, at the New Amsterdam Theatre and Gertrude Lawrence was delighting audiences at the Imperial Theatre in George Gershwin's *Oh, Kay!*

In sports, it had been a year of upsets. Heavyweight boxing champion Jack Dempsey went down to defeat from the clever fists of his Shakespeare-quoting challenger, Gene Tunney, before a rain-soaked throng of 102,000 in Philadelphia, while at Forest Hills, Henri Cochet of France defeated America's redoubtable Bill Tilden to win the United States Tennis championship; and the mighty Yankees of New York lost baseball's World Series to the St. Louis Cardinals, as the venerable Grover Cleveland Alexander came on to strike out Tony Lazzeri with the bases loaded, while the great Babe Ruth was thrown out stealing to end the final game.

The boom continued in the business world. In New York, Judge Elbert H. Gary, Chairman of the Board of U. S. Steel, flanked by board members J. P. Morgan and George F. Baker, announced a record stock bonus of 203,321,000 shares, to be paid to Steel's 86,000 holders of record. The bonanza attracted countless new investors, and caused yet another upsweep in market prices—U. S. Steel, naturally, setting the pace with an advance of 4⅝, to climb to its all-time high of 160½.

Leaders everywhere struggled with problems which were dimmed in importance by the fireworks of the Roaring Twenties. New York City's Transit Commission strived to maintain the nickel subway fare, President Nicholas Murray Butler sought to raise $60,000,000 for his Columbia University, and in far-off China a young general by the name of Chiang Kai-shek commanded the Cantonese forces in a war of unification of his country, while at the same time fending off a threatened infiltration of his forces by Michael Borodin, the Russian adviser to the Cantonese government.

President Calvin Coolidge, despite the embarrassing Teapot Dome scandal, had so far but one problem to disturb his placid stewardship—that of a growing and restless annoyance by the people with a controversial law, the 18th Amendment.

2. Only a very few celebrating the passing of the old year had an inkling of the excitement that would mark the new year.

Instrumental in setting the scene for the events to come in 1927 were the well-meaning intentions and patriotic fervor of a well-known Franco-American restaurateur. It was a significant but little publicized event which took place in New York City, and which would have an important bearing on future ocean flights.

Back in 1919 Raymond Orteig, the well-to-do owner of the plush Brevoort and Lafayette Hotels in New York, offered a prize of $25,000 "to be awarded to the first aviator who shall cross the Atlantic in a land or water aircraft (heavier-than-air) from Paris or the shores of France to New York or from New York to Paris or the shores of France, without a stop." The offer further stipulated that contestants would file a sixty-day notice of intention prior to take-off—a requirement that was subsequently waived.

The offer was communicated without fanfare to Augustus Post, secretary of the Aero Club of America, and it was accepted promptly and made public; however, little notice was taken of it, due possibly to the successful flight of Alcock and Brown to Ireland a month later.

Orteig was the classical success story. He was raised humbly in a little village in the south of France at the foot of the Pyrénées, and before he was twenty came to New York in the late 1880s where he supported himself as a bellhop at the Brevoort on lower Fifth Avenue. It was not long before he owned, not only the Brevoort, but another hotel, the Lafayette, both of which he transformed into gay and popular hostelries, with superb cuisines, so as to give Americans a touch of his beloved France. The two hotels became landmarks in New York and were home for the many young French and Allied airmen during World War I, then in the United States for training, and as the years passed, served as the plush and exclusive hostelries for Americans and Europeans with discriminating tastes. Thus it was that the humbly born Mr. Orteig became rich and famous, and this attractive and urbane gentleman sought now new interests to stimulate his active mind. The hallowed days of individual combat during World War I, when Fokkers, Spads, Sopwith "Camels," and Nieuports tumbled about the air in unforgettable "dogfights," fired his imagination, and it was not long before he had developed an undying interest in aviation, along with unrelenting hopes for its future.

His prize offer was communicated without fanfare to Augustus Post, secretary of the Aero Club of America, and it was accepted promptly and made public, though little notice was taken of it, for the eyes of the world were on Newfoundland, where British aviators, released from their wartime duties, were preparing to make a challenge for a prize offer of 10,000 pounds (then $50,000), made originally in 1913 by the London *Daily Mail* to the crew of the first airplane to fly the Atlantic, non-stop, in either direction, in under 72 hours. No doubt the British challenge fired up Orteig's French patriotism and led to his offer, for he saw no reason why French flyers should not share in the glory; had it not been the great Louis Blériot, a Frenchman who, in 1909, had led the way for the world when he made the first substantial over-the-water flight in history, across the English Channel from Calais to a little field beyond the Dover Cliffs? But it would be eight long years before a challenge would be made for his prize.

In that first postwar springtime of 1919, Orteig followed, with interest and envy, as the British flyers readied themselves for their assault on the perilous Atlantic.

At the same time, and totally unconnected with the *Daily Mail* prize offer, plans for a flight of U.S. seaplanes to Europe via the Azores were being made at the Naval Air Station in Rockaway Beach, New York. By early May three big four-engined Glenn Curtiss-designed flying boats, NC-1, NC-3, and NC-4 (NC-2 had been destroyed earlier in a hangar fire), under the over-all command of Commander John H. "Jack" Towers, (later Admiral Towers of U. S. Navy Air Force fame in World War II) had by chance joined two of the British crews, already hard at work in Newfoundland. The American boats were moored at Trepassey Bay Harbor on the southern tip of the Avalon Peninsula. Sixty miles to the north, near the city of St. John's, were based the two British crews on rough-hewn farm fields four miles apart: Harry G. Hawker, the handsome young test pilot, and Kenneth Mackenzie Grieve, the navigator, in their single-engined Sopwith biplane *Atlantic*, and Hawker's old friend and instructor, baby-faced Frederick P. Raynham and his navigator C. W. F. Morgan, with their Martinsyde biplane, *Raymor*. The British crews were competing for the cash prize, and, though Commander Towers's group had no intention of racing, for their flight was to be made in easy stages to Plymouth, England, with a flotilla of destroyers blanketed along their route, the imagination of the postwar world would not have it. Everywhere people talked of who would be the first to get across.

Though the Hawker and Raynham crews had been ready since early April, the combination of bad weather, dances at the Bally Hally Golf Club, and gay, late soirées at St. John's Hotel Cochrane (despite the recent enactment of prohibition legislation) combined to keep them grounded, and it was the Americans who got away first on May 16. After a harrowing overnight flight, NC-4, commanded by Albert C. "Putty" Read, loomed out of the gloomy skies over Horta Harbor, the Azores, and landed safely. Commander "Pat" Bellinger's NC-1, piloted by Marc A. "Pete" Mitscher, (later a naval air hero of World War II), and Towers's flagship, were less fortunate, being forced down into the sea short of their goal. The crew of NC-1 was rescued, after bobbing helplessly for five hours in a rough sea, but the flying boat was damaged beyond repair. NC-3, the flagship, was unreported for three days, and just when she and her crew were given up for lost, she taxied proudly into the harbor at Ponta Delgada, Azores, after a 205-mile voyage on the water. Like her sister NC-1, she would not fly again.

On May 18, Harry Hawker, goaded into action by the initial

success of NC-4, took off with Grieve from the dirt strip at his
Mount Perl Farm base and headed for sea after passing gloatingly
over his rival Raynham's base at nearby Lake Quidi Vici. Within
the hour, Raynham and Morgan hopped into their scarlet *Raymor*
and attempted a take-off in a valiant effort to catch both Hawker
and NC-4. The attempt, however, ended in disaster. *Raymor*'s landing
gear buckled under the load, and she slithered in clouds of dust to an
ignominious end. Though neither crewman was injured seriously
Raymor was and did not fly again.

Hawker, too, had his troubles. After flying to the east over the
ocean for eleven hours, his engine heated up and he was forced to
land in the sea, where he and Grieve were picked up by the little
Danish ship *Mary*. The *Mary* carried no wireless, however, and it
wasn't until May 26, when the world had given up hope for the
two flyers, that word was received that Hawker and Grieve were safe.

Meanwhile, two other British crews had put into Newfoundland
in quest of the elusive prize. The first was led by Admiral Mark
Kerr of the British Navy, and he set up camp at a spanking new
airstrip at Harbor Grace, west of St. John's, across Concepcion Bay,
and assembled his giant four-engined, converted Handley Page
bomber. The second was comprised of Captain John "Jack" Alcock
and Lieutenant Arthur Whitten "Teddy" Brown, veteran war flyers
with the Royal Navy. They set up their camp, after a long and
frustrating search, on a cow pasture leased to them by Rupert Lester,
and prepared their twin-motored Vickers Vimy, also a converted
bomber, for their try at the Atlantic.

Before either plane could get off Lieutenant Commander "Putty"
Read, having taken over command of the Navy flight from the
planeless Jack Towers, streaked across the Atlantic from Ponta
Delgada, and landed 9¾ hours later on the Tagus River in Lisbon
to the cheers of a wildly excited crowd lining its banks. The Atlantic
had been flown! On May 31 NC-4 flew the last leg of her planned
trip, landing in Plymouth, England, after covering 3925 miles in a
flying time of 57¼ hours.

The "race" had been won, but the *Daily Mail*'s prize for the
first non-stop flight was still up for grabs. At Lester's farm, as
thousands watched, Alcock and Brown tested their big Vickers
biplane daily. Finally, on June 15, they were satisfied. It was a
bright Sunday afternoon when they climbed aboard, carrying with
them sandwiches, coffee, and a bottle of "medicinal" whisky. The
take-off was perilous, and the heavily laden ship, carrying 8000

pounds of petrol, inched up agonizingly. She made it, and was last seen passing over Cabot Tower on Signal Hill while the boats in St. John's Harbor below tooted a farewell salute.

They flew all night through cloud, violent air currents, and icing, the latter peril forcing Teddy Brown, more than once, to climb out onto the fuselage and chip the ice off the radiator shutters with a jackknife. Once during the horror-filled and blinding night the plane went into a steep, inexplicable spiral, and plunged toward the dark ocean. Alcock was able to right the plane a mere fifty feet over the dark and forbidding ocean.

When morning came the weather cleared and they flew on smoothly. Soon the Irish coastline appeared and it was not long before Alcock was circling over a promising-looking green meadow near Clifden in beautiful Connemara. He let down easily, watching the "green field" sway through his windshield as turbulence rocked his ship gently. When touchdown came, the lovely meadow turned out to be a disguise for a marshy bog. The wheels sank deep into the mire, and the plane came abruptly to a stop and nosed over into the mud. The Atlantic had been crossed non-stop in just over 16 hours, and the names of Alcock and Brown were headlined throughout the world. Within the week they were presented the *Daily Mail* prize by Winston Churchill at a gala luncheon reception at London's Savoy Hotel, and shortly thereafter they were knighted by King George V at an investiture at Buckingham Palace. Sadly, though, the life of Sir John Alcock was not for long; he was killed in December of that same year of 1919 in a plane crash in France. Until he died in 1948, Teddy Brown, who never flew again, paid an annual visit to the Science Museum at South Kensington, London, where the big Vickers biplane stood proudly, and gazed in awesome wonder at the ship that had carried him so far.

Raymond Orteig applauded with the rest of the world the brave achievements of the flyers that spring, though his joy was tempered slightly and naturally by the fact that a Frenchman had not been involved.

3. In the ensuing years, Orteig waited and watched in New York and at his summer home in the valley of the Pyrénées. No challenge was made for his prize, but his faith in aviation was rewarded, nevertheless, as numerous flights were made— some spectacular, which served to tone up both pilot and plane for

the arduous tasks that lay ahead. He knew that sooner or later the challenge would come. Captain Ross Smith and his brother Keith followed Alcock's and Brown's triumph in 1919 by flying from London to Australia in just under thirty days; and Alan Cobham of England did them one better by flying from England to Australia and back, finishing the flight with a flourish by landing on the Thames directly in front of the Houses of Parliament. Orteig followed with pride the exploits of his fellow countrymen, Captain François Coli, a one-eyed war veteran, who was the first to complete a round trip crossing of the Mediterranean in under 24 hours, and who, later, with Lieutenant Paul Tarascon, a one-legged veteran, made a successful flight from Paris to Casablanca. And there was Captain Dieudonné Coste, who, in the middle years of the new decade, drew the raves of the aviation world, by flying non-stop, in his little Bréguet biplane from Paris to Jask, Persia. Portuguese flyers claimed a share of the spotlight, too, when in 1922, Captains Sacadura and Coutinho, flew across the South Atlantic from Lisbon to Rio de Janeiro, a trip that took two and a half months, and required three seaplanes. Later, Captain Ramón Franco of Spain, not to be outdone by his Portuguese neighbors, beat their record by two months, when he flew his hydroplane across the South Atlantic in sixteen days.

Orteig noticed that American flyers were not idle during this time. While many of the thousands of discharged Army pilots bought up secondhand aircraft, and barnstormed throughout the country, eking out a living by flying passengers, wing-walking, and parachute jumping from any available cow pasture, there were others who participated in dazzling flights which foretold the great strides that were soon to be made. In the summer of 1919 dashing young Bert Acosta flew an all-metal plane from New York to California and back—a flight that consumed three weeks in time, but only 59 flying hours. Four years later, as Major General Mason M. Patrick and Colonel William Mitchell, the wartime Air Corps leaders, looked on, Lieutenants Oakley G. Kelly and John A. Macready took off from Roosevelt Field in a converted Fokker D-7 war plane, and landed at Rockwell Field, San Diego, after a non-stop hop of 26 hours and 50 minutes. The next year, Lieutenant Russell L. Maughan, heretofore known affectionately as the airsick pilot, raced the sun across the continent and won by 1 minute, after flying for 24 hours and 48 minutes. In 1924 the United States Army, spearheaded by General Patrick who was determined that his branch would not be outdone by the Navy's effort of 1919, sponsored a round the world flight of Army planes. Young Donald Douglas designed four World Cruisers and two completed the trip in an elapsed flying time of 371 hours and 11 minutes.

While Orteig waited patiently—he was forced to renew his original 5 year offer in 1924, planes, engines and instruments were being developed which would make the quest for his prize, ultimately possible. Abroad, designers such as Sopwith, the Farman brothers, Dr. Hugo Junkers, and Claude Dornier, to name only a few, were flourishing. In America, Anthony H. G. Fokker, fresh from his brilliant wartime career as a designer for the German air force, arrived in America, and soon started on a peacetime aviation career at his new factory at Hasbrouck Heights, New Jersey (now known as Teterboro Airport). Also to American shores came young Igor Sikorsky, in flight from his native but revolution-torn Russia, penniless, to set up shop on a borrowed farm field in Mineola, Long Island. There, with the help of a timely loan from musician Sergei Rachmaninoff, and the hard work of other Russian émigrés, he started again on an interrupted career which would lead him to great heights in the years to come.

4. Igor I. Sikorsky was born into a well-to-do, upper middle class family in 1889 in Kiev, Russia—a family that over the years had given many members to the service of the church, though his father was a prominent Kiev psychiatrist.

He had a mania for mechanics. He built electric motors as a child, and at twelve constructed a rubber-powered helicopter designed to go straight up and down—this at the turn of the century! To young Igor's chagrin though, it wouldn't fly.

His education was varied and spotty. He entered the Naval Academy in Petrograd in 1903, only to resign soon after to study engineering. He spent the revolutionary year of 1906 in Paris, returning to enter the Polytechnical Institute of Kiev in 1907. During these years, his interest in flying continued to grow, and when, in 1908, he was taken abroad by his father and met the famed Count Ferdinand von Zeppelin and the Wright brothers, Orville and Wilbur, the die was cast.

He borrowed money from his sister, Olga, and again went to

Paris to see an exhibition by the greats of the day. He asked questions incessantly of anyone who seemed to have even a remote knowledge of airplanes, and it was there that he received a simple piece of advice that he would always remember *"L'essayer, c'est tout!"* ("Everything is in the effort").

He was in the market for a simple motor to power his latest design, and was advised that an Italian motorcycle builder by the name of Alexander Anzani built the simplest—a 3-cylinder, 25-horsepower engine. It now seems inconceivable, but Blériot made his famous Channel flight with such a motor. Sikorsky scraped up the money and bought a used engine, took it home, and built a helicopter he hoped would fly. He was not yet twenty years old. The machine had two blades, one on top of the other, which rotated at 160 revolutions a minute. But, alas, it wouldn't fly, as the little Anzani was unable to provide sufficient power. In 1910, he followed up with his Sikorsky 2, or S-2, the second in a long line of Sikorsky ships which would include the famed Pan American Clippers. This was a tractor-type plane and Sikorsky flew it safely. It crashed and was demolished on a later test, but Igor was able to crawl away with his feelings and body bruised slightly, but otherwise no worse for the wear. Money became a problem but he was able to get help from members of his family, particularly sister Olga. During the next two years he built and flew the S-3 with its family-financed 40-horsepower motor, the S-4, and the S-5 powered by a magnificent engine with 50 horsepower! In the latter plane, he astounded himself, his family, and his countrymen by flying for one half an hour at 1000 feet. He was promptly awarded the Imperial Aero Club of Russia's license 64, and began to attract a growing attention throughout the country.

In 1911, when he built the S-6A, a three-seater which he flew at the then incredible speed of 70 miles an hour, the Russian Baltic Railroad Car Company became interested in his work, and he was commissioned by them to build a "large" plane. The new cabin plane was ready in early 1913. *The Grand,* as she was called, weighed 9000 pounds and had four 100-horsepower 4-cycle Argus engines mounted in tandem (back to back) on the wing. She was comfortable in the cabin with four upholstered seats and a reclining sofa. She flew on her maiden trip on May 13 with great ease, carrying three passengers. Sadly though, her life was short and came to an abrupt end when an engine was accidentally dropped on her as it was being mounted and disabled her beyond repair. Prior to her

demise, Sikorsky had removed the tandem-type engines and replaced them with four engines in a line on the wing, an innovation
which has lasted to this day.

With the clouds of war gathering over his country and the rest
of Europe, it was only natural that he should turn his talents to
the development of military aircraft. Unlike Anthony Fokker, the
Dutch-born designer of Germany's speedy pursuit ships, Sikorsky
was a pioneer in the development of large multi-engined bombers
heavily armed with guns for protection against attack by fighters.
What he built was, in many respects, an early version of the
American B-17 Flying Fortress of World War II fame.

The first was a transport with the then huge wingspan of 102
feet. It was a biplane, weighed 10,000 pounds, and was powered by
four engines placed between the wings. It had a long snub nose
into which was built an open balcony or bridge directly in front of
the enclosed pilot's cabin. The interior was equipped with electric
lighting, and the cabin was heated by a system connected to the
exhaust pipes. She was christened the *Ilya Mourametz*, and on
February 11, 1914, took off and flew for an hour with sixteen
passengers, a record at the time. The engines were placed so that
mechanics could clamber out a catwalk leading to the wing and
make in-flight repairs on faulty engines. But the most amazing factor
about this amazing plane was that it could and did fly on two of
its four engines. The second *Ilya* was built soon after, adding more
power by substituting 140-horsepower inboard engines to go with
her standard 125-horsepower outboards. *Ilya II* flew from Petrograd to
Kiev and return in 12 hours with Sikorsky at the controls. As always,
the interior was luxuriously appointed, and, during the flight, hot
meals were elegantly served around a dining-room table while the
plane flew evenly through inordinately bad spring weather.

Following the flight, the Russian Imperial Army became exceed-
ingly interested in the work of young Sikorsky and ordered a military
version of the *Ilyas*. Thereupon Sikorsky constructed a huge military
biplane, the *Ilya III*, complete with his now distinctive trademark,
the long snub nose, and thoroughly armed from stem to stern with
machine guns. The plane had a ceiling of 10,000 feet, and was
designed primarily for bombing. Since bomb bays and bombsights
were then unknown, the bombs were dropped necessarily, by hand
over the side. Early in the war, on a bombing raid against German
positions, the pilot, a general by the name of Shidlovski, found
himself under attack by three German fighters, yet was able to bring

the plane home with three engines badly damaged and barely turning over, and with a large section of the right wing shot away. Shades again of the B-17 of World War II. *Ilya Mourametz XV*, with six machine guns strategically placed, was attacked by a flight of four Fokkers. Two of them were shot down by the gunners, but not before two of *Ilya's* motors were shot out. With the remaining two engines, the pilot was able to return safely to his base, two hundred miles away.

Prior to the cessation of hostilities between Russia and Germany, seventy-five *Ilya Mourametz*-type bombers were built. One half were used on missions and the other half for training purposes. In four hundred missions that were flown, only one bomber was lost. Again the hurried pressures of war had caused rapid strides in the development of efficient aircraft, and Sikorsky would put the experience and knowledge he had gained during these harassed years to good use when it came time for him to challenge the oceans.

The Russian Revolution started a new phase in Igor's life. His disenchantment with it became complete when General Shidlovski, whose faith in the *Ilya* bomber had so enhanced young Igor's reputation, was executed along with his son in Petrograd, and all the worldly goods of the Sikorsky family, comprised of real estate and Czarist bonds, were expropriated by the new state. Igor fled to Murmansk, and in March 1918 was able to make his way to London. From there, he moved on to Paris during the summer where he joined many other refugees from the unhappiness that was to them, home.

Paris was a thriving aviation metropolis at the time with the war entering its final stages, and the Allied leaders were forever on the lookout for new ways to shorten the conflict further. Sikorsky's name was known well to the Allied air authorities, and he was soon approached by them with an order for the design of a plane capable of carrying a 2200-pound bomb. In no time he finished the plans for a typical snub-nosed Sikorsky ship, powered by four His-pano-Suiza engines. The plans were accepted, and five planes were ordered forthwith, but the war ended before they could be built and used.

Like many other refugees from the upper middle class of Russia, the war's end found him in rather precarious financial circumstances. Some chose to remain in France closer to home and plying whatever trade their talents would allow. Sikorsky struck out for New York,

1

where he landed March 30, 1919, without funds, but steadfastly determined to carry on as a vital part of the glowing future of peacetime aviation.

5.   In the summer of 1926 at Roosevelt Field in Westbury, Long Island, a huge tri-motored biplane was being assembled under the watchful eye of young Sikorsky.

Two years before, a group of men had formed an organization called the Argonauts for the express purpose of sponsoring a New York to Paris flight in quest of the Orteig prize. They were headed by Robert Jackson, a wealthy manufacturer from Concord, New Hampshire, who resided in Paris; and Colonel Harold E. Hartney, a veteran war flyer, was appointed vice-president and manager of the flight in New York. They had contracted with Igor Sikorsky for the design and construction of the aircraft to be used, reputedly at a cost of over $100,000, and with famed French war ace, Captain René Fonck, to act as pilot at a fee of $250 a week. Captain Homer M. Berry, a friend of Hartney's, was selected as co-pilot, and, at this time, it was understood by all connected with the adventure that an American pilot should be a part of the crew. Captain Berry, it later turned out, was actually only a lieutenant in the Army Flying Services, and had received his "captaincy" from Pancho Villa when he had done a stint with the Mexican rebel during his campaigns.

As the summer of 1926 progressed, Sikorsky's bird began to grow, a huge-bodied, luxuriously appointed biplane with three engines, the center motor located where his snub-nosed bows had given his previous planes such a distinct appearance. When Sikorsky was criticized for the bulk of the body, he replied, "Most people think that a plane should be like an eagle, with a broad wingspan and slight body; but, no, an eagle has a very short range. My plane is constructed like an albatross, with a powerful body and great wings. The albatross flies great distances against heavy winds in all weather, and that is what my plane will do."

Three 425-horsepower Gnôme-Rhône Jupiter motors were ordered from the Jupiter motor factory in France, and arrived at Roosevelt Field in early August together with Georges Honneur, a mechanic, whose duty it was to supervise the installation and make sure that they would run steadily for the 33 hours that Sikorsky estimated would be the time needed for the trip. An improved radio set was put aboard, one guaranteed to operate properly where Hawker's and Alcock's had failed.

The first tests of the big ship consisted of taxiing the plane around Roosevelt Field to the far corners and back. The performance was satisfactory save for an overheating of the wheel bearings, caused by the weight of the craft; accordingly, four extra wheels were added to strengthen the undercarriage, for it was expected that the plane, when fully loaded for take-off, would weigh in the neighborhood of 28,000 pounds! As an added safety measure, it was decided to remove the tail skid and substitute a wheel so as to ease the drag on the moving ship. Workmen were never idle at the Sikorsky hangar at Roosevelt Field during the next weeks, as preparations were rushed for what, all hoped, would be an early take-off.

Meanwhile, Chief New York Forecaster, Weatherman James H. Scarr, with the assistance of James H. Kimball, began to prepare two weather maps daily, covering the North Atlantic area, for the use of Fonck and Berry. They assured the pilots, that providing forecasts for them would involve no difficulty as they received constant weather observations from twenty to thirty ships at sea near the proposed flight route. Fonck's route led tentatively from Roosevelt Field to Providence, Rhode Island; Plymouth, Massachusetts; Cape Breton Island, Bonavista Bay, Newfoundland; then across the Atlantic to an estimated landfall at Cape Clear, Ireland; then on to Falmouth, England; Cherbourg, France; and Le Bourget Field in Paris. The main concern of the forecasters was the almost constant fog that lay off the Grand Banks and the entire Newfoundland coast.

In late August, Sikorsky announced suddenly, when everything appeared ready, that the flight had been postponed for several weeks. It turned out that Fonck wished to replace "Captain" Berry with an experienced navigator, Lieutenant Allan P. Snody, USN. Berry, naturally enough, was upset by his threatened ouster and said that he didn't care how many medals the French pilot had won, but he, Berry, would not be thrown out of the flight without a lawsuit. Dissension in the Fonck group grew until it split the sponsoring Argonauts into bitter, rival camps. Colonel Hartney stood firmly behind his friend Berry while Jackson, the largest investor, backed Fonck. The quarrel became so public that the august New York *Times* found it necessary to intercede, saying editorially that Fonck had a perfect right to select a crew of his own choice. At length,

Berry backed down with the gracious statement that "the success of the flight is more important than my personal feelings."

On September 7, Sikorsky, Fonck, Snody, and an Army contingent took part in a test hop. With the designer at the controls, the big ship rose into the air after a run of 21 seconds which was, to the onlookers, a remarkable feat in that she carried 20,000 pounds, only 7000 less than the estimated load for the Paris take-off. She climbed to 2000 feet in just under three minutes. With his passengers comfortably ensconced on the plush divans and chairs of the luxurious cabin, Sikorsky showed them some more of what his new plane could do. He throttled back on the center engine, and with power coming from only her outboard motors, she climbed 500 feet more in two minutes. The Army observers were awestruck, in that their latest bomber designs were unable to approach such a rate of climb—even with full power. Fonck took over the controls, and flew over Long Island until, fully satisfied with her performance, he slid her easily back onto the turf at Roosevelt Field. All hands were elated over the test, and convinced, at last, that the flight would be a success.

So was Mayor James J. Walker of New York when he participated in the ship's christening the following day. Brandishing a large bottle of mineral water (the traditional champagne being outlawed), he intoned, "I christen you the *New York to Paris,*" and then swung the bottle at a heavy, metal exhaust pipe. The bottle remained intact. The dapper and imperturbable mayor swung then mightily at the metal propeller—twice. The only result was two slight dents in the blade. Finally, a mechanic came to the rescue with a large Stillson wrench, holding it over the exhaust pipe which had proved as impregnable as the bottle. The bottle broke to the cheers of the crowd. "Nothing'll ever sink this ship," cracked the mayor. "Some bottle!" replied a voice in the crowd.

The next day the giant ship flew to Anacostia Naval Base in Washington, D.C., against stiff head winds, and made the trip in two hours, returning to Roosevelt Field the following day. She was pronounced ready, and Fonck commented, "She's everything we wanted her to be!" Last-minute preparations were begun. Two inflatable rubber safety bags were loaded. When blown up—a procedure requiring only seconds—it was claimed that they could float a weight of 6000 pounds. At this time, it was announced also that the plane would carry a hot dinner in a vacuum container, prepared by the chefs at the Hotel McAlpin in New York, which would be served, hopefully still hot, to Robert Jackson of the Argonauts by waiters at the Hotel Crillon in Paris at the conclusion of the flight.

But first the weather, and then a faulty oil system in one of the engines, held them up. Then Lieutenant Snody was mysteriously absent. It was announced that he was ill with bronchitis which had affected his heart. Indeed, he had been ill and was forced to drop out of the crew, his place being taken by Lieutenant Lawrence W. Curtin, also of the U. S. Navy. There were rumors of further changes in the crew, which became a reality when Captain John R. Irwin, the American radioman, withdrew. Lieutenant George O. Noville, who had been the flight engineer on the Byrd expedition to the North Pole earlier in the summer, and presently was serving as automotive and lubricating engineer for the Vacuum Oil Company, was on hand often enough to give credence to reports that he would be a replacement. Even Lieutenant Stanton H. Wooster, USN, who came to the field only to congratulate his friend Curtin on his selection, was mentioned. At last, it was announced that a Frenchman, Charles Clavier, would be added to the crew as radioman. Clavier had joined the French Navy in 1908, where he had been trained as a radio specialist; more recently, he had assisted in the construction of the radio aboard the *New York to Paris*, and seemed, therefore, to Fonck and Sikorsky, to be the logical man to operate it. He was a great favorite at the field during these last days, always jovial and optimistic, desiring only to get to Paris and rejoin his wife and three young children. A few days later, Jacob Islamov, a native of Petrograd, was named mechanic for the flight. Islamov had been graduated from the Russian Naval Academy, after which he completed a tour of duty as a lieutenant in the Czar's Imperial Navy. Only twenty-eight still, he had worked for Sikorsky for three years helping to build the famous *Yorktown*, Sikorski's first successful American-built plane. Now, he wished to get to Constantinople where his aged parents were living in exile, and this seemed the quickest way.

In addition to his duties as co-pilot, Lieutenant Curtin was assigned the duties of navigator, one of which was to operate the "bubble sextant." This instrument, first used by the NC flying boats, had been perfected for their flight by the then young naval lieutenant, Richard E. Byrd, and it enabled a navigator to get a true fix from an artificial horizon when there was a cloud cover.

The night of September 25 was a busy one at Roosevelt Field. Kimball, at the Weather Bureau, had advised Fonck earlier that weather conditions over the North Atlantic were favorable. The floodlights were on at the field as mechanics swarmed over the huge plane. Bathed by the lights and flares that surrounded her, she looked like an enormous dragonfly, shimmering and silvery under the beams. At the rear of the fuselage there was painted a stork in flight, the emblem of the French 6th Pursuit Squadron, Fonck's wartime group. The words *New York to Paris* were clearly visible forward of the stork together with crossed American and French flags. As 2380 gallons of gasoline, sufficient to keep the three engines running for 33 hours, were loaded into her tanks from nearby drums, bringing her weight to 28,860 pounds, Captain Fonck and his crew were taking a last-minute rest. The night was balmy and clear, and as it gave way to the early hours of the new day, hundreds of motorists began to collect at the field as Fonck had announced a dawn take-off. His countrymen had been disturbed by the many delays to the extent that editorials were appearing in the Paris press to the effect that he should either go or call the flight off entirely. But the criticism did not hurry Fonck in his decision to leave. He, Sikorsky, and the crew felt now that all possible precautions had been taken, and that the time was ripe. A fuel-line leak had been discovered and repaired in the afternoon by the ever-watchful Honneur, and he, too, concurred with the decision.

By 5 A.M. a crowd of over two thousand had gathered, excited and expectant; ungainly looking cars of the day, complete with the inevitable running boards, surrounded Roosevelt Field, their occupants staring almost fearsomely at the big plane.

The runway at the field was laid out in an east-west direction to take advantage of the prevailing westerly winds at take-off. At the western end of the runway there was a sharp incline or bank about 40 feet in height. Below the incline was Curtiss Field. At the eastern end of the strip—which was 5180 feet long—was a line of telegraph wires which were to prove such a mental hazard to flyers of the future taking off in heavily laden planes. Beyond the wires was a golf course which stretched out toward the end of Long Island, and to the north lay the waters of Long Island Sound.

The composition of the runway—which was 200 feet wide—was a mixture of sand and clay. Paved runways were not yet in use, principally because of the delicate landing gears of the times. It was thought that the "give" of a dirt strip would serve to protect the frail gear during a bumpy landing or heavily laden take-off. In wet weather, though, the runway became soft and muddy and difficult to move on, as wheels would sink into the mire. Luckily, this night it was dry.

At 6 A.M., as the gray of dawn was beginning to show, Honneur, with the help of a mechanic and an electric starting machine, turned over the engines. Part of the fuel load was in tanks located at the rear of the outboard engines, giving them a cigar-shaped look; they shone under the lights; the name SIKORSKY was spelled out on each in big block letters. As other attendants put aboard supplies of sandwiches, coffee and tea, and completed little last-minute preparations, the engines were run up, one by one, as Honneur's expert ear sought to detect any faulty sound. The plane quivered behind the wheel chocks as each powerful motor let off a blasting roar. Satisfied with the sounds, he closed down the throttles, and the three props turned over idly.

Then Islamov, quiet and confident, appeared, with his white flying suit looming brightly under the lights, closely followed by the jovial Clavier, dressed in a dingy, brown leather jacket. He seemed happy that he would soon be in his beloved Paris and reunited with his young family. A car drove up, and out stepped Captain Fonck, resplendent in his blue French Air Force uniform decorated with its chestful of ribbons. Curtin arrived, accompanied by Chance Vought with whom he had spent the night. Sikorsky, too, was there, nervously overseeing the final inspections.

Quickly, Fonck and Curtin changed into their flying suits. Fonck's flat-topped military hat was exchanged for the more familiar helmet and goggles used by the flyers of that day. A woman stepped out of the crowd, grasped Fonck's hand, and said *"Bon voyage!"*

Fonck saluted formally and replied, *"Merci, madame. Au revoir."*

As they climbed aboard, Fonck and Curtin into the open pilot's compartment behind the center motor, Clavier and Islamov behind them, the cars which had surrounded the field, moved off hurriedly to get positions which would afford a better view of the historic take-off. Other cars, driven by field personnel, sped to the eastern end of the runway and shone their headlights down the field as an aid to the pilot.

Fonck, at the controls, opened the throttles, and the big plane moved heavily toward the starting point at the east end of the field. This end had been selected because of the light westerly wind which blew down. The engines whined, almost protestingly, as the huge ship trundled along. Finally with a burst from the outboard engine, it turned and faced down the one-mile stretch, within which distance it must be lifted off the ground. The crowds lined the field in the semi-darkness, and numbered in the thousands despite the early hour.

Suddenly the engines were opened wide and roared with a fearful din in the early morning calm. The *New York to Paris* started off slowly. At 900 feet she was laboring still with not nearly enough speed to become airborne, and seemed to hit a slight sag in the runway where a road crossed it. In horror, spectators noticed that one of the auxiliary landing wheels situated to the rear of the main gear had flown off. The plane appeared to slue to the left—then straighten—and then slue again. Still, there was not enough speed. Onlookers grew tense; the experts including Sikorsky, frankly worried. On the plane roared to 2000 feet, veering slightly to the left and then straightening. At 3000 feet another rut was crossed, and the right landing gear began to weaken perceptibly under the huge load. Closer and closer came the end of the runway, as the giant, silver biplane moved toward the 40-foot incline which would spell disaster. She was still lumbering along and weaving, but Fonck had not seen fit to cut the power. Perhaps there was still hope. About fifty feet from the end of the strip, the crowd let out a gasp! The right gear had given away completely. Still no reduction in power, and instantly *New York to Paris* cascaded over the end of the runway and disappeared from view down the incline. Her disappearance was followed by ghastly orange flames and black smoke shooting 70 feet into the still darkish sky.

The crowd swept toward the scene. Curtin and Fonck were seen soon, smeared with soot, oil and dirt, clambering up over the embankment. They had been able to free themselves at the last minute, but lost in the funereal furnace were Charles Clavier and Jacob Islamov. They had been trapped in the fuselage when the plane had cartwheeled on her right wing and turned over, with the highly volatile gasoline being ignited by spilling onto the red-hot exhausts of the overstrained engines.

There was an investigation, of course, complete with the testimony of all witnesses. Colonel Hartney, still embittered by Fonck's replacement of his friend Berry, called the French ace "an incompetent" for his failure to bring the plane to a stop when he realized it could not get off. But Fonck was cleared. He explained that the wheels had never left the ground, and that he had never been able to get the speed over 60 miles an hour; that, when the auxiliary gear went, he dared not decelerate too quickly for fear of losing the

entire undercarriage which bore the huge and volatile load; but
he thought he had enough speed to make a safe landing over the
incline. However, when the entire right side of the undercarriage
gave way, it had caused the ship to lean to the right, and the right
lower wing struck the ground, resulting in the cartwheel. The blazing
inferno, witnesses observed, precluded any attempts at the rescue
of the unfortunate Clavier and Islamov. Lieutenant Curtin, for his
part, added that the combined efforts of him and Fonck on the
rudder bars were not sufficient to prevent the heavy ship from sluing
down the runway. The sluing, in turn, prevented any chance for
New York to Paris to attain flying speed.

Fonck and Curtin, though their wish was not to be fulfilled, expressed a desire to try again as soon as a new Sikorsky could be built.
Sikorsky, heartbroken over the failure, returned to his drawing board,
unaware of the aviation triumphs that would come to him in later
years.

The public, stunned at first, recovered quickly, and pondered another disaster being reported in the newspapers—a disastrous hur-
ricane that swept across Florida, in mid-September of 1926, leaving
372 dead and 40,000 homeless on its devastating trip from Miami to
St. Petersburg and across the Gulf of Mexico into Alabama.

At airfields throughout the world, pilots with eyes on the Orteig
prize, and disturbed by the Fonck crash, debated the possible causes
and resolved to profit somehow from the tragic experience.

Though Fonck and Curtin obtained a new Sikorsky within a year,
circumstances prevented them from making a new attempt. Thereafter, Fonck returned to France and lived out a useful life in government service until his death in 1953. Curtin died in a tragic crash of
a seaplane in Central America a few years after his near-fatal experience of 1926.

CHAPTER I

January 1927

1. The new year started quietly enough as radio lovers gathered around their sets to listen to Graham McNamee's colorful description of the Rose Bowl game in Pasadena, California, between Stanford and Alabama, or to hear John McCormack, Rosa Ponselle, and Mischa Elman sing and play to the accompaniment of Nathaniel Schilkret's Salon Orchestra.

It was only a matter of days, though, before the national affairs of the Republic reached the explosive stage. Secretary of State Kellogg lit the fuse by asserting that Mexico was the base of a Red War against the United States. He cited the Mexican President's support of the rebel leader, Sacasa, against President Díaz in Nicaragua, and a resolution of the Third Congress of the Red International of Trade Unions in 1924 which called for a struggle against "American Imperialism" by uniting individual countries of the Americas against it.

A wildly heated debate in Congress followed. Senator James T. Heflin of Alabama accused the Roman Catholic Church of fomenting a United States war with Mexico, while Catholic Senator Tom Walsh of Montana vigorously refuted the charge. Senator William E. Borah, Chairman of the Senate Foreign Relations Committee attempted to mediate by calling for immediate elections in Nicaragua and for negotiations with Mexico. President Coolidge, too, tried his hand at pacification, when, at a news conference, he asked the press to back the government in its foreign policies so as not to give other nations reason to believe that we were divided.

No sooner had that uproar abated than another one stormed on the scene when the Senate, by a vote of 48–33, declined to seat Senator-elect Colonel Frank L. Smith of Illinois, because of moral unfitness—which consisted of unusually heavy campaign expenses. The debate over his seating continued for months on the floor and in committee, interspersed by frequent testimony from Samuel Insull, the utilities magnate, who, it was said, had given utility funds to Smith for his campaign. The issue was resolved only by the death of the colonel many months later.

In Europe all was calm. Britain's Chancellor of the Exchequer, Winston S. Churchill, fresh from a meeting with Benito Mussolini, applauded the Duce for "his triumphant struggle against the bestial appetites of Leninism," and added that he "could not help being charmed by his [Mussolini's] gentle, simple bearing, and calm, detached prose." But, in New York, Italy's exiled professor, Gaetano Salvemini, sounded a sober warning to a Foreign Policy Association meeting, when he denounced the Fascist leader as a "skilled demagogue."

There were other items of interest. It was announced that the public debt in the United States had dropped to $19,612,522.14 for the fiscal year ending in July 1926, and congressional leaders talked of tax cuts; Al Smith was inaugurated for a second term as Governor of New York, and thirty-three-year-old Dan Moody, on the strength of his campaign against the Ku Klux Klan, supplanted "Ma" Ferguson, as Governor of Texas.

From Montreal came the tragedy of the month, as seventy-seven children panicked in a flash fire, and perished at the Laurier Palace Theatre, while watching a motion picture entitled *Get 'Em Young!*

2. The Commanding Officer of the Naval Reserve Field in Squantum, Massachusetts, in the fall of 1926 was an inactive lieutenant commander: short, muscular Noel Davis. He was a pleasant-looking man in his mid-thirties with prominent eyes that were, at the same time, alert and all-seeing, and gave the impression at once of a quick wit possessed by the owner. He had assumed his duties at the air base while studying at the Harvard Law School from which he had recently graduated. He became the first American to announce publicly his intention to fly non-stop from New York to Paris.

His earlier days at Annapolis had amounted to a fabulous tale. He was born in Utah, and his early education was sketchy. Mostly, he learned mining engineering from prospectors in the area. However, he was possessed of a keen mind with a natural talent for mathematics and when he took his exams for the Naval Academy, his scores in that field were so superior that they offset deficiencies in other subjects, and he was admitted. He soon cured those other deficiencies and finished his career as a midshipman at the top of his class.

On graduation, he was made aide to Admiral William S. Sims, and at the start of the Great War was sent overseas as Chief of Staff to Admiral Joseph Strauss who was in command of minelaying activities in the North Sea. He served with distinction and bravery, both during the war, and afterward when his command was charged with the equally hazardous duty of clearing up the mine fields promptly so that peacetime shipping could get under way without delay.

When he returned home, Davis decided on a career in naval aviation and took his pilot training in Pensacola, Florida. On graduation he became Naval Aviator 2944. Davis was a good flyer, but more than that, he studied and so distinguished himself in the techniques of aerodynamics that he was able to write a number of scholarly and widely used books on the subject. His ever-curious mind was not satisfied, and in 1923 he sought and obtained inactive status in order to study aeronautical law, even though there must have been little precedence in the books of the Harvard Law School due to the newness of aviation. By this time, he was married and the father of Noel, Jr. He was able to support his little family during his legal education by occasional mining ventures in Minnesota and by his reserve duties at Squantum.

During 1925 his mind turned to the possibilities of an ocean flight —more particularly, a flight to Paris. But, there was the prior necessity of obtaining an airplane, and even more important, some financial backing. He made many inquiries and talked to many people over a period of months. They listened politely to his carefully stated plan, but always gave him an equally polite but firm "no." At length he was forced to abandon the project for the year, but he kept looking and he kept talking, always quietly, for he did not wish to have the news of his venture reach the public until the arrangements were well on their way to completion.

In the summer of 1926, he ran into a Pensacola friend, thirty-two-year-old Lieutenant Stanton Hall Wooster, Naval Aviator 2731, then being mentioned as a possible co-pilot for Fonck. Wooster, born in Connecticut, had attended Yale for one year, and then transferred to the Naval Academy from which he was graduated in 1917. He served on the battleship *Nebraska* on convoy duty during the war, and, at the Armistice, like Davis, had joined the Naval Air Corps in Pensacola for flight training. "Bob," as he was known to his friends, was a witty, fun-loving soul, and the epitome of the carefree aviator of the day. He was noted for his skill in piloting big planes—which fitted in with Davis's plans. They were well-mated for such a venture —Davis, serious, scientific, and intellectual; Wooster, the gregarious yet skillful flyer.

Davis carefully broached the subject of an ocean flight to Wooster and the latter jumped at the opportunity for he had thought of little else since hearing his name mentioned in connection with the Fonck flight, which was, at the time, in its final preparations.

Davis had his crew and needed now only a plane and some financing. Both were forthcoming shortly. A trip to Washington, and an interview with Major General Mason M. Patrick, Chief of the Army Air Services, opened one door. General Patrick, who had organized the Army Round the World flight of 1924, was filled with optimism over the airplane's long-distance prospects, and was himself planning an Army-sponsored flight over the Pacific for the coming summer. He was sympathetic to Davis's cause and promised to give it serious consideration. Davis left the general's office encouraged, and rightly so, for within a week he had his answer. He would be allowed to buy a stripped-down version of the Huff-Daland Company's Keystone "Pathfinder" bomber, then in production for Army use. Davis, having obtained a pledge of secrecy from Patrick until his plans were further developed, made a quick trip to Bristol, Pennsylvania, where the Huff-Daland factory was located, and introduced himself to Richard F. Hoyt, chairman of the board. Hoyt, a Harvard graduate, had become interested in aviation while serving as first civilian assistant to the Commanding Officer of McCook Field, Dayton, Ohio, during the war, and, though still in his early thirties, had made his mark already in the financial world as a partner in Hayden, Stone Company. He now headed up one of the leading companies in the aircraft industry.

Davis stated his case with his usual clarity, and Hoyt, highly impressed with the comprehensive presentation, agreed to form a syndicate to back the venture. Davis left the office elated. They had agreed to meet soon again to go over Davis's requirements for the ocean flight with Huff-Daland's designer, C. Talbot Porter, who would supervise the renovation of the bomber.

Porter had been busy at the Pennsylvania factory with plans for the conversion of the bomber to Davis's specific needs. More often than not, Davis was on the scene, keeping careful watch over all phases of the work, and offering valuable suggestions and solutions to problems as they arose. Lieutenant Wooster was present also, on occasion, so as to be familiar with the plane he would fly. Construction work on the plane itself was about to commence inside one of the company's large field-side hangars.

The "Pathfinder" was a big tri-motored plane, 44 feet in length. The fuselage and platforms which held the wing motors were of welded steel tubing while the 67-foot wings were of the usual wood framing, but of unusual thickness for the purpose of providing added lift.

The plane was powered by three 225-horsepower Whirlwind engines, one installed in the nose in front of the pilot's compartment, and the other two, well streamlined, mounted on each side of the fuselage on the lower wing. They were capable of driving the ship through the air at 120 miles an hour at full throttle, though the cruising speed was slightly less than 90. The engines, known to the flying trade as the Wright J-5 and to the general public as the Whirlwind, were the creation of Charles L. Lawrence, president of the Wright Aeronautical Corporation. Lawrence, whose interest in engines had grown in him through his years at Groton School, Yale, and the École des Beaux Arts, where he studied aerodynamics for three years, supervised the construction of a powerful, new and light 225-horsepower motor that could run seemingly forever if properly fueled and would be used almost exclusively by the American flyers in their attempts to fly the Atlantic during 1927.

The ship in Army tests had proved that it could fly, and even climb, with only two motors operating, and Porter devised a means by which the fin or stabilizer could be set permanently in the event a motor was lost, thereby relieving the pilot of constant pressures on the rudder controls.

The pilot's cabin was a roomy, open compartment situated in the snout-like nose of the plane. There were two seats, but only one wheel which could be flipped from one seat to the next, depending on who was at the controls. A catwalk on top of the fuselage led to the aft cabin which was to be converted into a stand-up navigation room. The walk was equipped with two tiny hand rails and a wire rope for a safety clip, to lessen as much as possible the hazards of the open walk back. The thought of this did not seem to bother either Davis or Wooster. The designs for the navigation cabin showed a spacious area with a chart table on the right side, and a radio tucked into an opening in the rear. There were other neat and easily accessible holds provided for flares, life rafts, and other emergency equipment. RCA was developing a radio for the flight with a range of 1000 miles, and Davis had placed his order for it with the manufacturer, Westinghouse.

Porter's main design problem was where to place the necessary fuel for the long flight. After study, he decided that the main tank, with a capacity of 900 gallons, should be in the body of the fuselage, slung from its top beams and positioned forward of the navigation cabin, thus closing off the inside passageway to the pilot's cockpit, but the amount of gasoline they would have to carry made any other solution impossible. He and Davis worked out a scheme to equip the large brass tank with a number of partitions so as to prevent the sloshing of gasoline during rough weather. Two hand pumps were attached to the rear of the tank, and only two or three thrusts were needed to send 50 gallons of gas to the three gravity tanks located in the upper wing. The gravity tanks themselves held a total of 600 gallons. The over-all capacity of 1500 gallons, they hoped would give the plane an ample range of 4200 miles.

Another design problem was the undercarriage. Davis and Wooster, as well as Porter, were well aware that undercarriage weakness had been a major contributing cause of the Fonck disaster, and they sought to take special care that it would not happen on the "Pathfinder." Extra strength was planned for the tail skid and wheel supports until the three felt sure that with the anticipated load at take-off the landing gear would be secure.

The Wright Company assigned one of their foremost engine experts, Kenneth J. "Spoons" Boedeker, to supervise the installation and maintenance of the three J-5 engines. Davis and Wooster kept in close touch with him as the powerful motors were built and thoroughly block-tested to make sure of their readiness when the renovations to the plane had been completed. As the winter moved on, Davis appeared to have an edge in preparations over any competitors, except possibly Nungesser and Coli, two Frenchmen whose plane was already under construction at Villacoublay Airdrome outside of Paris.

3.   In the early summer of 1926, a dashing blond Frenchman in his early thirties was given a farewell party aboard a French liner about to sail from New York for Le Havre. As the guests left his stateroom sparkling from quantities of champagne, the passenger, Charles Nungesser, who had ranked as the third

leading French ace in the recent war behind the great René Fonck and the legendary George Guynemer, drew his brother Robert aside and said, "Au revoir; the next time I shall return here will be by air."

Following war exploits, Nungesser had come to America where he had staged, for thrilled thousands, replicas of his air duels in France. The programs advertised his show as "the most sensational air attraction of the age!" The proud Nungesser took a jaundiced view of exploiting his name in this fashion, but justified it, at the time, because he needed the money. Afterward it was on to Hollywood where he made a motion picture called the *Sky Raiders*, and where he married Consuelo Hatmaker, a direct descendant of Sutter of gold rush fame. Attractive and witty with a continental charm to go with good looks and his legendary flying exploits, he was popular and sought after wherever he went in the United States.

Charles Eugène Jules Marie Nungesser was born in Paris in 1892. He was educated at the College of Armentières and later at the School of Arts and Crafts. He taught himself to fly in 1910 while working as a mechanic at La Brayelle Airdrome near Douai. He never had a teacher, but learned rather by watching, questioning, and then practicing in "borrowed" aircraft.

Soon after, this free-spirited youngster picked up and traveled to Argentina, where, until the war brought him home, he led the life of a gaucho—busting broncs, roping cattle, and shooting. He made a reputation as a boxer, when he substituted for a Frenchman against a local Argentinian champion. Though outweighed and battered during the early rounds, the wiry and strong Nungesser came back to knock out his opponent, becoming thereby an idol to the Argentinians who gave him an ovation for his gritty performance.

When the war came in 1914, he was drafted into the 2nd Regiment of Hussars, and, in the first days of the "Great Retreat," found himself surrounded with his battalion at Coucy le Château. With two other infantrymen he set out to break through the German lines to Laon. Their lorry was intercepted by the Germans, and the three barely escaped into the nearby woods. At dawn, they reached a level crossing on the railroad tracks between Coucy and Laon. Nungesser stole down and shut a gate across the tracks. When a German car came along, they fired from their wooded ambush and killed the crew. They then boarded the car, and rode triumphantly through a hail of enemy fire into Laon. For this feat, he was awarded the Military Medal.

In early 1915 he requested and obtained a transfer into the Air Forces. He passed his flight tests quickly, and by July had shot down his first plane. By May 1916 he had accounted for twenty-five German aircraft, and his name was known to every Frenchman. At war's end, he had forty-five enemy planes to his credit, had been mentioned in dispatches fifteen times, was an Officer of the Legion of Honor, and had twenty-eight palms to his Military Cross. In addition, he had been wounded seventeen times—twice seriously. Once, in January 1916, he was pulled from the wreckage of his plane and given up for dead, with fractures of his skull, jaw, and both legs; but incredibly soon he turned up at his airdrome, on crutches, ready to fly again. In between these hair-raising feats he found time to enjoy the company of Mata Hari, and amused himself by feeding the famed spy masses of misinformation.

Nungesser was not the only Frenchman to be bitten by the ocean-flying bug. In the summer of 1925, the first man to register for the Orteig prize, Lieutenant Paul Tarascon, a war ace, had announced his intention to fly to America in a Potez biplane with his old friend Captain François Coli. Almost simultaneously came the announcement that Maurice Drouhin with his co-pilot M. Landry would attempt the same flight in a huge Farman *Goliath*. The weather kept them both grounded during most of the summer, and as autumn came on Drouhin and Landry dropped their plans for the year; Tarascon, this time with co-pilot, a Lieutenant Favereau, crashed while making a long-distance test flight and the plane was demolished while the flyers just escaped with their lives. Now both teams were back at work, planning for a 1927 effort. They were joined also by Captain Dieudonné Coste, another war flyer of renown and skill. Nungesser was not without serious competition in his own country.

Nungesser sought out his friends first at the Air Ministry and explained his intentions. Official eyebrows arched and heads shook negatively, even to this well-known French hero. The country was in the throes of a mild recession. "At this time," he was told, "the government cannot justify the expense and risk of such a venture." Disappointed but still hopeful, he went directly to the offices of Pierre Levasseur, the famous French designer on the Avenue Félix Faure.

Levasseur listened to Nungesser as he explained his need for a plane capable of flying the Atlantic. The designer asked for time to think it over, but Nungesser would not be put off. He was aware of his competition in France and he knew that it would be building up soon in the United States and in other parts of Europe. Levasseur looked at his man. He knew his reputation and he liked his confidence, and his methodical way of planning. They moved on to discuss the type of aircraft that might be suitable. Nungesser expressed his opinion that a hydroplane was too heavy, and that a multiengined craft would require too much fuel, and thus, also, be too heavy. He wanted a small plane that he could fly by himself. Levasseur was taken aback by the audacity of a solo flight, and voiced briefly his objections, but Nungesser seemed adamant. Then an idea struck Levasseur; he'd been building planes for the French Navy with a discardable landing gear attached to a hull-like fuselage, so that in the event of an emergency, the plane would be able to float on water. This sounded good to Nungesser, but he explained that the plane would have to have a range of at least 4200 miles. The designer replied that such a range would pose no problem, but requested some time—as Patrick had done with Davis; for, if the Navy plane was to be used, it would first have to be cleared with the Admiralty.

It was now early October. René Fonck had returned to Paris after his crash to seek engines for the new Sikorsky in which he hoped to try again. Levasseur obtained the necessary consent of the Admiralty without delay, and work was started at once on plans for the modification of the naval plane to make it fit for the ocean flight. Nungesser watched over every last detail with care. Moreover, he studied meteorology, radio (though he would decide not to carry one), navigation, and every known bit of aeronautical information that would help him to succeed. He was determined that his would be no hit or miss junket, and that nothing would be left to chance.

It was this careful approach to the venture that made him reappraise his idea of flying alone. Perhaps Levasseur was right. It would be a grueling flight—over 40 hours into prevailing westerly winds, and his chances of success would be enhanced, no doubt, by having a pilot along who could spell him.

Thus, Captain François Coli joined the flight. He was ten years older than Nungesser, short and dark-haired, with a black mustache. He wore a patch over his right eye, which had been lost as the result of a war injury. Until now, he had been a part of Paul Tarascon's crew, but when the latter's flight plans seemed to be foundering for want of funds, Coli leaped at the chance of joining Nungesser.

Coli was born in Marseilles into a seafaring family, his father and three uncles having served in the merchant marine. Quite naturally, he went to the Naval Academy in Marseilles where he became an expert in navigation—a talent which attracted him to Nungesser. In 1902, he served for a year on the admiral's flagship *Brennus*, and then, he, too, joined the merchant marine, remaining with them until 1912 and reaching the rank of ship's officer. When the war broke out, he, like Nungesser, was in Argentina on family business. He returned at once to France, but found that the Navy had no place for him except as second officer on a hospital ship. Rather than accept such a post, he enlisted in the infantry, again like Nungesser, as a private in the 78th Regiment. He rose quickly through the ranks, and by February 1915 had won a battlefield commission. He was wounded twice, and after a promotion to captain and a case of badly frozen feet, he requested a transfer to the Air Force in January 1918. He became a pilot in May after intensive training, and followed up with a brilliant career as a pursuit pilot. In no time, he was given command of the 62nd Fighter Squadron, "The Cocks." By the end of the war he had been mentioned in dispatches nine times in his short flying tenure, and made an officer of the Legion of Honor. Since, as we have seen, he distinguished himself by making a number of notable long-distance flights—among them his round trip crossing of the Mediterranean, and a non-stop flight from Paris to Casablanca.

As the fall of 1926 turned into winter, the two former French heroes joined forces, and worked incessantly on such problems as fuel consumption, maximum load and balances, routes, weather, emergency equipment, and even food to be carried. There was no little detail that they considered unimportant. They conferred constantly with Levasseur over problems of design, and over the causes of the Fonck crash, which had disturbed them seriously, for they did not wish history to repeat itself on their flight.

At Le Bourget Airdrome, Paul Tarascon, the one-legged war ace, had found a new sponsor, and was trying to get back into the race. He had enlisted the services of a naval aviator by the name of Le Prieur to act as navigator and plans for a monoplane to be named *Oiseau Tango* had been completed by French designers Bernard and Hubert. It was to be a large plane, 37 feet long, with a thick 55-foot wing, and the design called for a weight of 9680 pounds, fully loaded, with a fuel capacity of 800 gallons. The cockpit would be enclosed in the nose of the plane, with an unimpeded view ahead through the spinning propeller. The designers were confident that *Oiseau Tango* would have no trouble maintaining a cruising speed of 115 miles an hour—well above the average for the day. Though construction had not yet begun, the S.I.N.B. Company of Paris had agreed already to build the ship for Tarascon.

Not far away, at Toussus-le-Noble Airfield, the famed Farman Company had started construction on a Goliath type biplane for another contestant, Maurice Drouhin, the celebrated pilot who held the world endurance record for heavier-than-aircraft. The Farmans had chosen, as his co-pilot and navigator, Joseph Le Brix, a decorated veteran of the Moroccan war, and a seasoned flyer in his own right. Their plane *Oiseau Bleu* was to be powered by twin 500-horsepower Lorraine-Dietrich engines, each with a four-bladed propeller, and mounted in tandem fashion on the upper wing. The tandem installation simplified the control of power by the pilots, and operated so that the forward engine pulled the plane while the rear one pushed it. As its trade name indicated, it was to be a huge craft, 54 feet in length, with a wingspread of 80 feet. The lower wing was to stand 6 feet off the ground, with a distance of 12 feet separating it from the upper wing. The blueprints showed a closed cockpit in the nose of the long, slender fuselage, with a semi-octagon of windows, which gave the pilots clear forward and lateral vision. Twelve separate gas tanks were planned, extending the length of the fuselage, which would hold sufficient fuel for 60 hours of non-stop flight, and making the estimated take-off weight in excess of 12 tons! Despite its size, it was a frail-looking plane as its frame began to take shape, but no one seemed concerned, for the three Farman brothers had made their reputation by designing planes, which, though frail in looks, had proved strong and reliable on commercial flights, in all kinds of weather.

There was also Dieudonné Coste, perhaps the most well-known postwar French aviator, who, at the time, was trying to persuade the military authorities to permit him to use a Bréguet Army biplane for a flight to New York. Coste, a war ace, with sixteen enemy planes to his credit, had since been a commercial pilot on Moroccan and European passenger flights, and had only recently won renown by flying from Paris to Persia non-stop. Even before learning of the Army's decision, the Bréguet Airplane Company indicated that they would not sell him the used plane that was within his means, but insisted that he buy a new one for such a hazardous flight that would cause such notoriety. Nevertheless, Coste continued to plan and to hope.

There were still other European flyers rumored to be getting ready.

Frenchmen Favereau (Tarascon's co-pilot in a near-fatal crash in 1925) and Marmier, it was said, were planning a flight from Etampes Airfield to New York in a single-engined biplane; in Belgium word was out that two lieutenants by the name of Medaets and Verhaegen had obtained a Bréguet monoplane for a spring take-off, and there were stories of pilots from Italy, Germany, and Great Britain who were scurrying about in search of financial backing for an ocean adventure. There appeared to be no dearth of competitors for Atlantic honors in this opening month of 1927. The question that was being asked, even now, was who would be the winner?

CHAPTER II

February 1927

1. The heated debates on Capitol Hill between the Hawks and Doves of the day over Mexico and Nicaragua were temporarily interrupted by the memorable events of February 13. On that day, the members of Congress were treated to ringside seats for two fights that erupted among their number, and, as if to be impartial, there was a main event in each chamber. In the Senate, Burton K. Wheeler of Montana and Carter Glass of Virginia squared off after exchanges of "You lie, sir!" only to be separated within seconds by Joe Robinson of Arkansas, the presiding officer; while, in the House of Representatives Congressmen Tinker and Strong, both of Kansas, threw flurries of punches after a heated exchange, until the mild-mannered Speaker of the House, Nicholas Longworth, was able to step in and intervene. A few days later, not to be outdone, Representatives Sol Bloom of New York and Blanton of Texas came to blows during a debate over the District of Columbia's Blue Laws.

It was not as violent elsewhere. Lawrence Tibbett sang the lead on the opening night of Deems Taylor's *The King's Henchman* at the Metropolitan Opera House which was reviewed glowingly as the greatest American opera to date; Bert Wheeler and Robert Woolsey opened at New York's new Ziegfeld Theatre in *Rio Rita*, while Eddie Dowling was delighting audiences with his performance in *Honeymoon Lane* at the Knickerbocker.

Abroad, the new Anglican Prayer Book was introduced in England, and shocked all prospective husbands by dropping the word "obey" from the marriage ceremony; however, the shock was eased somewhat with the requirement that the husband hereafter need only "share" goods with his spouse rather than "endow" her with them, as before.

In France, Auguste Escoffier, the noted chef, boosted the morale of the U.S. gourmets by announcing that he was conducting experiments with new alcohol-free sauces so as to brighten up the foods in "dry" America, but it didn't help those who craved only a cold beer to wash down a pastrami on rye.

2. Early in the month of February, Commander Richard Evelyn Byrd announced that he would attempt a New York to Paris flight in the late spring or early summer. The announcement put to rest a persistent rumor that he was planning to join forces with Lieutenant Commander Davis. Byrd's giant tri-motored monoplane was being assembled gradually at Hasbrouck Heights under the watchful eyes of Tony Fokker, while a short distance away in Paterson, New Jersey, T. Harold "Doc" Kinkaid, one of Wright's engine experts, had been assigned to watch over the construction of the Whirlwind engines.

Byrd and his ever-present friend and pilot, Warrant Officer Floyd Bennett, were being lionized for, on May 9, having been the first to fly successfully over the North Pole. But they were devoting increasing time to the task ahead. Though nothing had been said, there was little doubt that Bennett would be called on to fly the Fokker on its ocean trip. The composition of the rest of the crew remained a mystery. Byrd, however, took time to get in touch with another old friend, Rodman Wanamaker, scion of the Philadelphia mercantile king. Wanamaker, a long-time Francophile, and an avid aviation buff, seemed the ideal man to talk to regarding an Atlantic flight, particularly if it was to terminate in Paris, which was now Byrd's plan. Prior to the war, Wanamaker had formed the American Trans-Oceanic Company for the express purpose of connecting France and America by air. To this end, he had engaged Glenn Curtiss to design and construct the largest seaplane ever built; but the war interfered, the huge ship never left the water, and the company remained inactive.

Byrd's plan for a flight to Paris, solely in the interest of the furtherance of aviation, appealed at once to Wanamaker. The commander told Wanamaker he wanted to prove the reliability of planes and motors, together with the ability to fly through any type of weather. This would entail the skillful use of the latest navigational equipment. He said also that he planned to keep in constant communication with the ground by employing the most reliable radio transmitter and receiver that could be obtained.

By September, Wanamaker was convinced of the value of such a trip, and offered to Byrd all of the considerable resources at his command. Negotiations were entered into for a long-term lease of Roosevelt Field to the newly activated Trans-Oceanic Company; Grover Whalen, the dapper City Greeter of New Yorker was hired as executive vice-president of the company to conduct primarily the public relations for the venture. Yet, for a time, all was kept quiet. The only hint of the impending flight came when Byrd, on October 28, told newsmen at a Bridgeport, Connecticut testimonial to the commander that he expected a New York to Paris flight would be made successfully during the coming year, and that he himself was seriously considering the possibilities of such a flight. Already, at this time, Anthony Fokker had received an order, and had commenced work on a new tri-motored monoplane for Byrd at his Hasbrouck Heights factory.

There was good reason for the easy working relations between Byrd and Wanamaker. Both came from illustrious backgrounds, and shared similar tastes. Byrd was descended directly from Colonel William Byrd, an original James River, Virginia, settler. His father, Richard E. Byrd, was a prominent Winchester, Virginia, lawyer, while his brother, Harry Flood Byrd, barely in his thirties, was preparing himself for an illustrious career as Governor of Virginia and a long-time member of the United States Senate.

The commander's life was adventurous from the start. At the turn of the century, at the age of twelve, he was sent alone to visit a family friend in the Philippines, and displayed an adventurous spirit in his earliest years by deciding to return home in the opposite direction, so as to circumnavigate the globe. He attended briefly the University of Virginia, and then entered Annapolis in 1908. Though weighing but 135 pounds, he quarterbacked Navy's football team in his third year only to break a leg in the game against Princeton. While performing as a member of the gymnastic team, he suffered another badly broken leg. This ended his athletic career and hindered him thereafter. On the eve of America's entry into the war, this injury caused him to be placed on inactive duty.

Byrd was not idle for long. By virtue of his constant persuasion—even harassment of his superiors—he won their consent to enter the Naval Aviation School at Pensacola, Florida, in 1918. Flying had fascinated him since he had been up in an open Curtiss plane in 1914. After a training course, which included a head-on crash with another plane on take-off, he was awarded his wings as Naval Aviator

608 and assigned to Halifax, Nova Scotia, to direct the construction of a U. S. Naval Air Base. It was at this time, actually, in 1919, that he first felt the urge for an ocean flight. He wanted to deliver a plane to France by air to demonstrate good will and American air prowess. He was disappointed, sorely, that he was not included in the crews of the NC seaplanes, and they and Alcock and Brown stole his thunder temporarily. He was, however, a member of the ground staff at Trepassey, and until the last minute hoped against hope that he would be able to fill a vacancy on one of the flights.

Later, when the British dirigible R-38 was being built for the U. S. Navy, Byrd was assigned to fly in her to America. Her sister ship R-34 had made a successful east to west Atlantic crossing, thereby generating a Naval Department interest in lighter-than-air craft. Byrd left for England, happy to be at last a part of a great flying adventure. The day of R-38's final test flight, on which Byrd was to be a passenger, his train from London to Howden (where the huge ship was moored) was late, and he arrived to see her floating majestically away. He, along with the rest of the world, was stunned, hours later, when word was received that she had exploded over the Humber River and was totally destroyed, with all hands lost.

In 1924 Byrd was engaged in setting up a peacetime U. S. Navy Base in Chicago, and trying, at the same time, to include himself in an expedition to the North Pole in the dirigible *Shenandoah* (later destroyed in a storm over Ohio) under the command of Captain Bob Bartlett. Protests from the Congress killed the venture, but Byrd had his new idea—that of flying a heavier-than-air craft over the Pole. Thus his successful venture of 1926 came into being.

Byrd, a slender, classically handsome young man with curly black hair, was still being lionized throughout the forty-eight states and simultaneously was engaged in the enormous amount of detail work that was necessary for his hoped-for flight of 1927. Always articulate, sometimes to the point of verbosity (most likely because of his boyish enthusiasm), he stressed to the public, when the flight was made official, that it would not be a stunt but "a purely scientific probing of the feasibility of aircraft as a means of transportation!"

3.   The story of Anthony H. G. Fokker is similar in many respects to that of his Russian counterpart, Igor Sikorsky. Both were from well-to-do families, both had sketchy educations, and both had a natural aptitude for things mechanical.

Fokker was a Dutchman, known to one and all as "Tony." Born in Kediri, Java, where his father was the prosperous owner of a coffee plantation, he was brought back to Holland as a young boy, and entered school in Haarlem. He was undistinguished as a student, but displayed soon a definite manual talent and imagination by developing a sliding peephole in his desktop under which he placed information that was helpful in answering difficult examination questions. He became adept in the construction of toy trains, and also experimented with gas explosion engines and Bunsen burners which necessitated the tapping of his house's gas line. When the gas bill mounted sharply, his father called a halt; but Tony, ever resourceful, located a neighbor's pipe nearby, tapped into it, and regained his source of supply. When he found that his young relatives were interrupting his work by overly frequent visits to his shop, he was equally resourceful. He discouraged them by electrifying his doorknobs, and then took a ghoulish pleasure in waiting to hear their shocked shrieks.

School was a burden to him, and, he, to his teachers. He was constantly being asked to leave the classroom, which didn't faze him, for it meant that he could work on his latest invention—a puncture-proof tire. At length, he went to his teacher and asked for a two-week vacation so that he could finish it, adding as a part of his argument, that "after all, I've been in the same class for two years!" The request was granted, and the large metal wheel was finished, only to find out that a French patent for a similar invention was already in existence.

His formal schooling ended abruptly after a trip to Paris where he saw, at an exhibition, the thrilling flying machines of the Farmans, the Wrights and Blériot. His ample aptitudes were applied thereafter to his new love—aviation.

After a brief fling at an aeronautical school in Germany, he built his first plane with financial assistance from his father, and flew it in Mainz in 1911. In the ensuing years, he became a famous barnstormer and stunt flyer throughout Europe in planes of his own design and construction. He was only in his early twenties at the time, but he entered and competed in, with success, all of the important European air meets of the day. He became the first man in Germany to loop the loop which he accomplished a short time after the Frenchman, Adolphe Pégoud, did it for the first time in history. Also, of interest, is the fact that Fokker was the first to recommend the use of the color orange on wind vanes and other visual aids for pilots, in

that he had noticed, during his early cross-country hops that it stood
out more clearly than the white which was then in use.

Fokker's early aircraft were distinctive in that he made use of V-
shaped, swept-back wings that did not have ailerons. They were bulky,
made of wood framing, covered with fabric, and attached to a rectangular fuselage of welded tubing. The design proved to be so advanced and efficient for the day, that, at the beginning of the war, he
was persuaded by the Germans to set up shop inside of Germany and
build aircraft for their newly formed air force. His success was instantaneous, and between 1914 and 1918, some 7600 Fokker military
planes were built of which 4300 came from his own factory. There is
no question that he profited handsomely from his ventures, but he
produced planes for the German air force that, for a time, were
slightly superior to their Allied counterparts. He was not content with
conventional designs, but continually experimented. He developed a
speedy, parasol-type monoplane, the D-8, and the famed three-winged
triplane, used so successfully by Baron Manfred von Richthofen and
the Circus, which, though slower, proved to be more maneuverable
in less space than anything in the air at the time. He seemed always
a step ahead of the pack. He was highly respected and so feared by
the Allies that it was learned later that the British Secret Service,
through their agents in Holland, had offered him two million pounds
to go over to the Allied side. The Germans learned of the offer, however, and saved Tony from any decision-making by keeping him a
virtual prisoner for the remainder of the war.

His fertile mind was not confined entirely to the design of planes.
Mounting guns on planes so as to provide maximum shooting efficiency became an increasing problem to both sides, and it was
finally reduced to the question of how to shoot through a whirling
propeller of a fighter plane without shooting the propeller into splin-
ters. Roland Garros, the famed French pilot, came up with the idea
of placing metal strips on the blades so that bullets fired from his
gun which failed to clear, would at least bounce off, leaving only a
dent or two. Fokker, hearing of this, felt that there must be a more
efficient system; and in five days devised the first synchronized machine gun by means of the use of a simple interrupter gear. This
gear permitted 600 bullets a minute to be fired through a propeller
which was spinning 1600 times a minute. Until the Allies came up
with a similar gear, the agile brain of Tony Fokker gave the Germans
another edge during their halcyon days of 1915.

Though the war years were prosperous for his German company, postwar inflation in Germany left him penniless, with only a large idle factory containing vast amounts of equipment to show for his wartime work. Determined and resourceful, the young twenty-eight-year-old Fokker was able to smuggle sixty carloads of precious equipment across Germany and into his native Holland, partly by the use of bribes, and also by the ingenious method of staging a mock anti-smuggling raid on his own train, thereby throwing off customs and military inspectors. With the equipment, he was able to reopen a Dutch business which thrives to this day, and which has only recently turned out a twin-engined jet transport which is gaining wide acceptance in Europe.

Fokker always maintained stoutly that he brought no cash profits out of Germany after the war, and, despite accusations to the contrary, that he paid all taxes that were owing to the German government prior to returning home. As a consequence, he felt that he was fully justified in removing the equipment which, he maintained, was his property.

Meanwhile, he had married the daughter of a high-ranking German general, and he plunged back into aviation on a private, commercial level. In 1919 Fokker entered his latest aircraft at a Paris air show, a move which nearly provoked a national crisis in France. For the French, still filled with the memories of the costly though victorious war, split widely over whether the young Dutchman, who had done so much for the enemy, should be allowed to show his wares. Newspapers and politicians joined the fracas while the population argued vehemently the pros and cons of the issue amid many instances of wild melees. Blériot and the Farman brothers, his fellow designers, defended his side together with war ace Nungesser while the great René Fonck declared vehemently that his presence in France alone, was an outrage to the memory of her dead heroes. The storm abated as quickly as it came on, and the show went on with Fokker planes standing in the exhibition hall alongside the latest French and Allied designs.

Fokker, as the result of the sale to the U. S. Army of a number of his D-7-type planes, came to the United States in 1922, became attached briefly to Dayton-Wright Field in Ohio, and then with the help of the engineering firm of Ford, Davis & Spencer, formed the American branch of the Fokker Company in Hasbrouck Heights, New Jersey, adjacent to an airstrip now known as Teterboro Airport. There the balding, husky, and outspoken Dutchman applied his genius to a giant, tri-motored airplane in its final stages of construction. Its thick wing, 71 feet in length, was the typical Fokker wing, designed for the purpose of greater lift, by creating a vacuum on the upper part of the surface. It was made of wood, and covered with three-ply veneer, ³⁄₃₂ of an inch thick, on closely spaced ribs. It contained gas tanks, but the main tank was suspended from the wing beams, in an area that separated the pilot's cabin from the navigator's compartment. When fully loaded, it was planned that *America*, as she was to be called, would carry 1300 gallons of gasoline, and weigh close to eight tons.

Her three Wright Whirlwind engines would be entrusted with the task of getting her off the ground. Two of the engines were slung from the wing, on each side of the fuselage, and with the aid of a specially designed catwalk extending from a small opening in the fuselage a mechanic would be able to make basic in-flight repairs. The third engine was mounted on the nose of the ship, in front of a glassed-in cockpit. Work on her had reached the stage that there was speculation on how soon Bert Acosta, a Fokker test pilot, would take her up on her first test spin.

Byrd and Bennett alternated now between the Fokker plant and Roosevelt Field, which had been leased by the American Trans-Oceanic Company. The east to west runway was receiving special attention. A westerly take-off toward Curtiss Field was planned because of the prevailing winds, and Byrd felt that it would be helpful to construct an artificial hill at the easterly end of the field, so as to provide the huge *America* with running start. Thereupon, a 25-foot slope was built, complete with a track for the tail skid, to hold the fuselage steady during the initial run. The intention was to tie the tail securely with a heavy rope, run up the engines to full power, then simultaneously, pull the wheel chocks free and cut the rope with an ax, and *America* would streak down the incline, hitting the runway at close to flying speed.

It was at this time that Lieutenant George O. Noville, a bespectacled thirty-seven-year-old, was added to the crew. He was an expert in motors, fuel and radio, and a lifelong friend of Byrd's. During the polar expedition of the past summer, he had been in charge of the Spitzbergen base.

He was known as "Rex" to his friends and was raised in Cleveland where he graduated from high school; afterward he enlisted in the Navy. He was famous for his athletic ability and had distinguished himself as a member of a championship, service football team, and in track as a broadjumper.

Noville was assigned, subsequently, to Columbia University, where he studied aeronautical engineering, and in 1917 was awarded his commission as an ensign. Further training at Pensacola groomed him for war duty, and he joined the Escadrille Candinana, seeing service on the Italian front. On his return to the United States, he became inactive, and took successive positions as Inspector of Aircraft for Stout Engineering Laboratories and the Ford Aviation Division in Detroit.

In 1922, reactivated by the Navy, he was made head of the Labrador Section to aid the Army Round the World flyers, in a gesture of interservice comity. He was a natural for *America's* crew, in that Byrd took an almost paternal interest in his old mates, and treated them, regardless of rank, as loyal and trusted friends.

At the same time, Byrd, along with Tony Fokker, wanted to include the young Norwegian, Bernt Balchen, who had served the polar expedition well in Spitzbergen. Wanamaker, however, demurred, saying that he desired an all-American crew. Fokker, however, was determined to have a pilot of Balchen's ability aboard his creation and prodded Balchen and Byrd. Thereupon, Balchen, a retired Norwegian naval officer at twenty-seven, looked into the possibilities of becoming an American citizen in short order; but the official crew was, thus far, Byrd, Bennett, and Noville.

Despite the fact that the commander denied steadfastly that he was part of any race, and insisted continuously that his flight was solely in the interest of aeronautical science, there was no denying that at this time his state of preparedness was up to that of the acknowledged leaders—Nungesser in Paris and Davis in Bristol, Pennsylvania.

4. Across the ocean at Villacoublay Airdrome, a beautiful white biplane stood in a hangar at the side of the field, as workmen climbed over her putting on the finishing touches under the watchful eyes of M. Levasseur. M. Farret, another French engineer of note, was there also, giving the expedition the benefit of his experience. Frequently Nungesser and Coli watched the work, making suggestions from time to time. Most of all, they were waiting impatiently for the day when they could try *Oiseau Blanc* in the air.

She was a sleek ship, 32 feet long, 13 feet high, with a wingspread of 47 feet 11 inches. It was estimated that when her 450-horsepower Levasseur engine was installed, she would weigh, empty, in the neighborhood of 3500 pounds. But her engine was presently undergoing block tests in a pit at the Chartres Airdrome, to make certain that it could run, without a flaw, for 40 hours. So far the results had been encouraging.

Oiseau Blanc's fuselage was of wood and watertight, for the flyers intended to jettison their sturdy landing gear after they became airborne, and land as a seaplane when they reached their destination. The pilot's cockpit was located directly behind the trailing edge of the upper wing, and directly behind a large fuel tank. The pilot would sit on the left-hand side of the open cockpit behind a three-paneled glass windshield with the navigator to his right and to the rear, but close enough to converse over the roar of the engine.

The two pilots were satisfied thoroughly with their progress, but were restless as they awaited her completion. While Nungesser spent his days haunting Admiral Delcambre, the Chief of the French Meteorological service, on the Avenue Rapp, Coli pored over charts of the North Atlantic, plotting and replotting his course. He realized that *Oiseau Blanc* would be fighting head winds all the way; also, he knew that the ship, though designed for a top speed of 125 miles an hour, would cruise at a little over 100, and this speed would be lessened by the adverse winds; he was further aware that at most the craft could stay aloft for 42 hours. Both flyers hoped, therefore, that by some meteorological freak, they would get tail winds for a part of their journey at least. Nungesser pleaded for this with the weathermen, but Coli had to plan for the worst. He drew three alternate courses: the first, from Cherbourg directly across to the Bay of Fundy, then on to Boston and New York; the second, Cherbourg to Fastnet Rock, off the Irish coast, to the Magdalen Islands in the Gulf of St. Lawrence, and to Boston and New York; and the third, Cherbourg to St. John's, Newfoundland, Halifax, Nova Scotia, and New York. They planned to land in the Hudson River, as close as possible to the Battery. Coli, the old sailor, wished only that they could carry sufficient gas to enable them to tack on the winds, like the sailing ships of old.

Despite efforts at maintaining some privacy during their preparations, Paris became quickly aware of all their doings. Crowds swarmed to Villacoublay. Newspapers and magazines besieged them with questions, and offers for the exclusive story of the flight. Word had spread through France of the impending American flights, and excitement grew as it appeared that their own Nungesser and Coli might win it all. The excitement was less at Toussus le Noble, where Drouhin and Le Brix were getting *Oiseau Bleu* ready, or at nearby Le Bourget, where Paul Tarascon was trying to speed up work on his *Oiseau Tango*. They seemed hopelessly behind; but at Villacoublay it was something else, and all French attention was focused there.

CHAPTER III

March 1927

1. The month of March arrived in customary, windy fashion. In Washington the Congress adjourned its session at the end of a prolonged filibuster so as to circumvent some controversial legislation, and in New York, Babe Ruth and Colonel Jacob Ruppert, owner of the New York Yankees, engaged in an equally long debate before the baseball hero signed a three-year contract at an estimated $70,000 per annum.

Supreme Court Justice Oliver Wendell Holmes celebrated his eighty-sixth birthday by participating in a landmark decision which found that a Texas law barring a Negro, Dr. L. A. Nixon, from voting in a primary election was in violation of the 14th Amendment; while Governor Al Smith of New York, already mentioned as a likely presidential candidate in 1928, was challenged by attorney Charles C. Marshall with the question: "Is the record of the Roman Catholic Church in England, sir, in your opinion, consistent with the peace and safety of the state?"

New York City was beset by perennial problems. The State Crime Commission issued a report, revealing that inadequate housing and a dearth of playground facilities, was the cause of the rise of gangs in the city's slum areas such as the Cat's Alleys, and the Degraw Street Mob; and the State Housing Commission, noting that vacancies in the housing market had reached a prewar level, suggested that the Emergency Rent Laws be suspended in apartments with rents in excess of $15 a room.

There were items of more general interest. Sinclair Lewis's controversial novel *Elmer Gantry*, appeared on bookstore shelves throughout the country, and reviewer Elmer Davis commented succinctly that the book had "struck a blow beneath the Bible belt"; Robert M. Hutchins, at twenty-eight, became America's boy wonder with his appointment as Acting Dean of Yale's Law School; and Bobby Jones won the Southern Open Golf Championship in Atlanta by eight strokes. Naturally, on March 17, New York's Irish paraded proudly up Fifth Avenue to the stirring strains of "The Wearin' of the Green."

Spring was on its way, with her accompanying fevers; but they would not last long for many reasons, one of which being a small dispatch that was hidden in the back pages of daily newspapers on March 1: It announced that one "Captain Charles Linberg" would make a flight from New York to Paris, in July, in a Ryan airplane then under construction in San Diego.

2. From childhood when he saw his first airplane in Minnesota, Charles Augustus Lindbergh was fascinated by the thought of flying. Glenn Curtiss and Lincoln Beachey, the famous prewar stunt flyer, were his idols. The fascination became a passion and resulted in his withdrawal from the University of Wisconsin during his sophomore year in order to enter a flying school in Lincoln, Nebraska. He took to piloting easily, and soon was barnstorming throughout the country in second- or third-hand Jennys, which could be bought for a song. "Slim," as he became known to his fellow pilots, followed the usual barnstormer's practice of carrying passengers, wing-walking, and parachute-jumping to meet his expenses. In the fall of 1923 he sold the plane he was flying then to one of his students, and sat for, and passed, the examination for cadet training in the United States Army Air Services. Then followed a year of intensive instruction in military aviation at Brooks and Kelly Fields in Texas, where among his classmates was Cadet Russell L. Maughan, later of "Dawn to Dusk" fame across the country. On graduation, "Slim" returned to Lambert Field in St. Louis (with the gold bars of second lieutenant in the reserves on his shoulders) and was promptly offered the job as Chief Pilot by Robertson Aircraft, flying the mail. Simultaneously, he enlisted in the Missouri National Guard, where he instructed older wartime pilots in the latest flying techniques. The promotions came quickly, and it was now Captain Charles A. Lindbergh of the Army Reserve.

He was a serious young man, yet he had a quiet humor about him that was ingratiating at once with a new acquaintance. Flying was his whole life. He cared little for the *haut monde* and bright lights.

He owned but one suit. His garb was his flying suit—old army pants, leather boots, and a jacket together with a helmet and goggles.

It was in September of 1926 at an Army Reserve get-together in Omaha that he had bumped into Lieutenant "Gil" Ervin, who had "borrowed" an engine from the Army for designer Donald Douglas's first plane, and who had been assigned recently to fly Hanford Mac-Nider, Assistant Secretary of War, on a nation-wide tour.

"I'm going to fly to Paris," "Slim" whispered to Gil.

Ervin looked at the gangling Lindbergh, unbelieving. "Hope your arms are strong," he laughed, waving his in imitation of a bird.

Lindbergh was deadly serious. He planned systematically. First, he needed money. He thought of the important people in St. Louis who were interested in aviation. There was Harold Bixby, the banker, and Earl Thompson, the insurance executive, both of whom had recently bought planes, and there were the three Robertson brothers of Robertson Aircraft; they were not rich, but they might be able to help. Also, personally, he had a little money saved up.

Such a flight, he thought, would bring prestige to St. Louis, and he decided to base his promotion on the idea of a wholly backed St. Louis flight.

He wasted no time. He went to Thompson with whom he was acquainted. He gave him all the reasons for the flight: the prestige for St. Louis, the promotion of aviation interest, the advancement of America's position in the air world, and the proof of the reliability of modern aviation equipment. But, he explained to Thompson, he would have to raise at least $10,000 for an adequate airplane. Thompson was sold by the persuasiveness of the young pilot. Lindbergh then approached the Robertsons who agreed to help where they could. He always held hope that the airplane manufacturers might chip in with some form of discount for the public relations and advertisement that a successful flight by one of their planes would mean to their business.

He tried the St. Louis *Post-Dispatch*, and they turned him down. They classified the venture as being too risky. He then met with Harry Bixby, the banker. Bixby, though at first cool to Lindbergh's idea of flying alone in a single-engined plane, was soon convinced, and the syndicate was formed. "Slim" was now on the way to Paris.

His mind swirled with plans for the flight. Lists of necessaries were made and remade so that nothing would be forgotten. Of first importance was an airplane. One day, in early October of 1926, he heard that a representative of the Fokker Company was in the

Robertson Aircraft offices. Lindbergh cornered him and asked him the price of a Fokker which would be able to fly the ocean. The reply was a shocking $90,000. Staggered, but keeping a poker face, Lindbergh then inquired about a single-engined Fokker. He was told coldly: "Mr. Fokker wouldn't consider selling a single-engined plane for such a flight."

Early in November, in a specially bought new suit, he entrained for New York and called on the Wright Corporation in Paterson, New Jersey, hoping to obtain a Wright-Bellanca plane. He was ushered into the office of an executive who explained that the Bellanca had been built only to demonstrate the new Whirlwind engine, and, that if he wanted information on the price of such a plane, he had best see Mr. Giuseppe Bellanca.

Bellanca and Lindbergh took to each other at once. The gentle Sicilian answered all the young pilot's incisive questions on the performance of his plane with a directness that "Slim" liked. When he assured "Slim" that his plane could fly for 50 hours without refueling, it became a matter only of negotiation, and Lindbergh returned to St. Louis with his hopes high, for Bellanca told him that he thought the plane could be bought for such a flight. The Wright Company, however, soon threw cold water on his hopes with a terse telegram advising him that the ship was not for sale. He was disheartened further when Bellanca wired him that a new plane would cost $29,000. He turned in desperation to the Travelair Company of Wichita, Kansas, who built a similar-type cabin plane, but they turned him down. As the year ran out, he seemed just a little farther from Paris than ever before.

3. Giuseppe M. Bellanca was slight, gentle, dark-haired, and Italian-born. His interest in flying began when as a child he watched with rapt intent as kites were flown by boys in his native Sciacca, a town overlooking the Mediterranean on the southern coast of Sicily. He soon took part in the sport and in no time bettered the kites made by his less talented friends by cutting holes in them, so as to "bleed the air through," thus improving vastly on their performance.

His father, a thrifty miller, recognizing his son's latent abilities, was determined that he get an education. Young Giuseppe was sent to the local technical high school, and then on to the Royal Institute in Milan, where he excelled in mathematics, and, of all things, debating. One night after a lengthy and losing debate on the politics of the times with a group of Milanese, he happened to pick up a Paris newspaper, and read that someone by the name of De La Grange had remained aloft for 6 minutes in a Voisin airplane. From then on, his debating days were finished, and his new hobby was aviation. He built a "pusher"-type plane, similar to the Wrights', but the results were unsatisfactory. In 1909 he built a biplane with the startling innovation of having the fuselage and tail to the rear of the wings, an innovation which has since become standard to the point of being classical; he always maintained, incidentally, that his was the first of its type. However, hampered by the perennial problem of the day for designers—lack of funds—he was unable to obtain an engine to find out if it would fly.

Bellanca came to the United States in 1910, determined to continue in his work in the land of plenty. His first plane was, depending whether or not one had to fly it or in it, his "famous" or "infamous" parasol monoplane. Old pilots who remember the ship still shudder at the thought of it.

In the spring of 1911 he hired a hangar at Mineola, Long Island, and prepared to test it while aviators shook their heads in collective despair. He said later that "experts gave me fifteen days to live. But this was hopeful to me for it gave me the impression that they thought the machine would at least get off the ground." And it did.

The plane had a parasol-shaped wing—hence the name—with the tail and fuselage jutting out to the rear, opposite in design to the Pusher-type craft then popular. It was powered by a 3-cylinder, 25-horsepower, radial, air-cooled Anzani engine which weighed as much as the later Wright 225-horsepower motors used on the ocean flights. Its successful flights, while nerve-wracking to those who watched below, established Bellanca as an aviation name, of sorts. Clarence Chamberlin, later a successful Atlantic flyer, flew it in 1921, and became one of its stanchest supporters, declaring with admiration "that it could fly itself!"

Bellanca then opened a flying school. During the prewar and war years he taught many young men how to fly, including the late Mayor Fiorello H. La Guardia of New York, and a large contingent of Chinese and Japanese students who were in the United States for that purpose. In addition, he kept building planes, and, in 1919, came out with a two-seater which furthered his reputation by flying, with Chamberlin at the controls, from Hagerstown, Maryland, to Glens Falls, New York, on only eight gallons of gasoline!

In 1921, he moved to Omaha, Nebraska, where, in a garage, he built his first, high-winged monoplane with the distinctive Bellanca struts that were to be his trademark. They consisted of two stream-lined supports that ran from wing to fuselage on each side of the plane, and served a twofold purpose, giving the wing added support, and increasing its lifting surfaces. Another innovation on this plane was the streamlined "wheel pants" which cut down appreciably on the wind resistance of the landing gear. The plane was the marvel of 1922, winning thirteen first prizes in the four meets in which it competed, and it pushed the slender Italian's name into the forefront of aeronautical engineers.

Two years later, he returned to the East and busied himself briefly by building biplanes for the use of the airmail lines. Then he joined the Wright Company in Paterson, New Jersey, who were taking a brief plunge into the field of aircraft construction to implement their thriving engine business. It was there, during early 1926, that he designed and built the famous *Columbia*, which was to play such a prominent role in the new race for the North Atlantic a year later.

Bellanca said that when, as a youngster at home, he expressed the desire to fly, his family answered him always by saying, "If God had wanted you to fly, He'd have given you wings." He added, "But I thought perhaps He gave me brains to devise wings. However, as my first plane rose [the Parasol at Mineola], I said to myself, 'Giuseppe, God may let you know before you get down again what His wishes are as regards flying.'"

4. The new Bellanca monoplane that had been the talk of the aviation world with its stunning air race victories during the summer of 1926 was parked at a field near the Wright Company's plant in Paterson. Giuseppe Bellanca had ob-tained the services of his old friend Clarence Duncan Chamberlin. Besides being a close friend of the studious Iowan, Bellanca recognized him as one of the country's ablest pilots, and felt more secure with his beloved creation in Chamberlin's hands.

Sandy-haired Chamberlin was a member in good standing of the flying fraternity. He had spent his boyhood in England and his adolescence in Denison, Iowa, where his father was a watch repair-man. He learned to fly and received his commission in the Army as a pilot at the end of World War I. When discharged from the service he took to barnstorming. For a while he worked as a mechanic in the Bronx, New York, and then he engaged in the sale of used airplanes until his partner absconded with all the assets. Finally, to make both ends meet, he went into aerial photography, which proved interesting and lucrative for a time. He photographed sporting events from the air and flew the pictures back to New York in time for the early editions. There were other odd flying jobs, too. He was hired by the West Point Cadet Corps in 1922 to fly over the Yale Bowl during a football game, trailing a banner with the words, GET 'EM ARMY!

Once he was hired by a sky-writer to pilot a plane on a very rough flying day, while the writer took care of the advertisement of a new and complicated trade name. After thirty minutes of tortuous climbing in the turbulent air he leveled off at 10,000 feet and motioned to his passenger in the rear cockpit to take over and do his job. Nothing happened. Again Chamberlin motioned and there was no response. Finally, he got a signal to go back down. As they clambered out of the plane, Chamberlin asked with annoyance, "Whatinhell was the matter?"

The sky-writer replied mournfully, "I forgot how to spell it!"

Chamberlin was an early and ardent admirer of Giuseppe Bellanca, and he flew all the Sicilian's early planes for test and sales purposes. He was at the controls of the Omaha-built monoplane with the new struts and wheel pants, when it performed so memorably in the air races of 1922. Therefore, when Bellanca joined the Wright Company, it was inevitable that Chamberlin would go with him as test pilot.

Chamberlin experienced his bad moments. He crashed during a trial run before a race and there were numerous other emergency and crash landings in his career, including one inside the walls of a federal penitentiary! But he survived them all to become one of America's heroes in 1927.

The *Columbia* was similar to the Omaha-built plane of 1922 which had so dominated the air races of that era. It was a high-winged monoplane, 20 feet 9 inches from rudder to cockpit, with a wingspread of 46 feet 6 inches. The wings were supported on each side by two 8-foot struts which ran to the fuselage. She stood only 8 feet off the ground at her topmost part. The pilot's cabin was roomy, with a glass windshield looking forward over her Wright 9-cylinder, J-5 or Whirlwind motor. Directly behind the pilot's seat, and running under it, was a 17-gallon oil tank; back of that and separating the pilot's compartment from a tiny chart room, was a large, piano-shaped, Duralumin fuel tank, from which the 65-gallon wing tanks were filled by the use of an automatic fuel pump. The chart room contained the radio, charts and a sextant, together with a small table and a seat. A triangular window had been cut in the top of the fuselage for the purpose of navigational readings. To get to the chart room from the pilot's cabin required a certain amount of contortion, for it was necessary to squeeze over the "keyboard," as the lowest part of the piano-shaped tank came to be known. The "keyboard" had an auxiliary use during later flights, in that it provided a moderately comfortable resting place for short periods, when well-cushioned with blankets.

Bellanca equipped the plane with a dump valve—a necessity in those days when planes took off with enormous loads. If it became apparent that the plane was not going to be able to sustain flight, a ton of gasoline could be emptied in a matter of seconds, thus minimizing the risk of fire in the event of a crash landing.

The control panel was situated directly in front of the pilot below the windshield. From left to right, it consisted of an air speed indicator, a double-dialed earth inductor compass, an altimeter, a tachometer (indicating the engine revolutions per minute), an oil thermometer, a gas gauge, throttle, and engine switches. From the floor jutted the joystick control. Hanging down from the transparent mica roof of the cockpit was the magnetic compass, and attached to both side windows were brackets for a drift indicator.

The plane had a top speed of 132½ miles an hour, cruised at well over 100, and her low gas consumption at cruising speed won the raves of the pilots during her summer performances.

Bellanca had made one visible change from his 1922 design. He sacrificed the "wheel pants"—a Bellanca trademark along with the struts—for the sake of lightening the ship. She now weighed only 1850 pounds when empty!

At the time of Lindbergh's visit to the Wright plant in November 1926, she had been flying for six months; had been tested thoroughly by the knowledgeable Chamberlin, and had won the Air Races in Philadelphia in late summer, with Lieutenant C. C. Champion, Jr., USN, at the controls.

She was a pretty ship, a lemon-yellow color with silver trimmings, with the name of her designer inscribed on the rudder, and her racing number, 120, on her fuselage.

Bellanca knew she was a fine aircraft and was anxious to test her to the limit; consequently, he, too, was disappointed when the

Wright management declined to allow Lindbergh's syndicate to purchase her for his Atlantic flight, for he was convinced she would make it with ease. However, 120's time would come.

The Wright Company was then under the able direction of Charles L. Lawrance, who had revolutionized the motor industry with his recent design of the air-cooled Whirlwind engine. Bellanca was hired by the company in 1925 to build airplanes for them. Whether the company ever intended seriously to go into the manufacture of aircraft, or whether they were discouraged from it by other manufacturers (who would be customers for their engines), has never been made clear either by private sources or anti-trust lawyers. In any event, soon after Lindbergh's visit to Paterson, Wright made its decision to restrict itself to the engine field and to divest itself of the services of Bellanca and his airplane.

Thus into the picture came a thirty-year-old entrepreneur—dapper, hard-driving, fast-talking, Charles A. Levine. He had grown up in the Williamsburg section of Brooklyn, New York, and his formal education ended with his graduation from P.S. 32. He worked for his father's scrap metal business, but, after two years, tired of it and got a job as an apprentice mechanic with the Morrisant Aviation Company on Long Island. After six months, in which he apparently developed his taste for aviation, his father demanded that he return to the metal business. He couldn't be held down, however—even by parental authority. A year later, at age nineteen, the sharp-witted young man left the family business again and struck out for himself. He enjoyed mechanics and had learned the basics at the aviation company, so it was only natural that he started buying, repairing, and selling secondhand cars. He was a shrewd trader, with boundless energy, and the profits mounted quickly. He sank them into various ventures, including an unsuccessful development of a high speed motor. Despite the failure, his automotive business thrived.

Shortly after, he married the "Belle of Williamsburg," Grace Nova, who was from a prominent Brooklyn family. He'd first met her when she was thirteen, some years before, and had pursued her relentlessly, until, as a rich young man with a future, he won her.

In 1921 he organized the Columbia Salvage Company, which brought up old shell casings and ammunition from war surplus stockpiles. This work took him all over the country, thereby satisfying partially his incurable mania for travel, and, beyond that, it added immensely to his already considerable wealth, enabling him to satisfy another mania, that of driving sleek, high-powered automobiles.

Looking for new fields to conquer, he learned in the latter part of 1926 that the well-known Wright Company was looking to divest themselves of the highly touted new Bellanca monoplane. Levine moved quickly, and soon the monoplane, together with the services of designing genius Giuseppe Bellanca and pilot Clarence Chamberlin were his. He formed another corporation, the Columbia Aircraft Corporation, and opened sumptuous offices on the 46th floor of the Woolworth Building in New York City.

Now, his ideas came tumbling forth. One minute he planned to build large transports; then it would be aircraft for the Army, or perhaps he'd start an airline. First, he realized that it would be necessary to publicize his new little company. Bellanca told him of the young flyer from St. Louis who was planning a flight to Paris over the Atlantic, and desired the use of 120 for the trip. Levine's agile mine grasped quickly the public relations value of such a flight, but he remained curiously silent, thinking apparently of the other ramifications. Such a flight would take long months of planning, and he needed the publicity now. Perhaps a shorter and safer flight, he thought, such as an attempt to break Maurice Drouhin's endurance record, would suit more aptly the current needs of the Columbia Aircraft Corporation, and such a flight could be made with a minimum of risk to his plane and its crew.

5. Lindbergh's plight, meanwhile, was becoming serious. He'd been turned down in his search for a plane by both Fokker and Travelair, and was considering the newer and less well-known companies of Bill Boeing and Donald Douglas. He still yearned most for the Bellanca; he admired the slight, dark-haired Sicilian designer, and felt certain that his plane was suited perfectly for the flight, but the Wright Company had ended, seemingly, any chance of his getting it. It was frustrating to have the backing and no airplane, and his frustrations grew as he read, almost daily, dispatches on the progress of the Byrd and Davis flights. Furthermore, he'd been told that at the Sikorsky plant at College Point, Long Island, work was well under way on a new plane in which Fonck would try again. And, of course, there were the Frenchmen, particularly Nungesser and Coli in Paris.

Then Lindbergh learned of a small airplane company named Ryan, located in San Diego. They were building a much-talked-about monoplane for the use of the Western airmail flyers, and performance reports obtained via the pilots' grapevine were excellent.

Lindbergh telegraphed them asking for a quote on the price of a new plane with one motor which would be capable of flying the North Atlantic, non-stop. Fearing that his telegram would be ignored as having come from a crank if he signed his own name, he signed ROBERTSON AIRCRAFT CORPORATION. Almost immediately, he got an answer to the effect that such a plane could be delivered in four months, for a price of $6000, less the power plant. It was a ray of hope. "Slim" was thrilled, and was on the verge of following up on the offer, when he received another telegram, this one from Giuseppe Bellanca at an unfamiliar address in the Woolworth Building in New York. It contained the exciting invitation to come to New York in that he, Bellanca, believed that his plane could be obtained for Lindbergh's proposed flight. "Slim" dropped everything and took the next train, forgetting for the moment the Ryan Company's proposal. Two days later he stood in the private office of Charles A. Levine, chairman of the board of Columbia Aircraft Corporation. Also present as the lanky 6 feet 3 inch youngster walked in was the familiar figure of Bellanca, and a slender, serious man, who introduced himself as Clarence Chamberlin, test pilot for Columbia.

Lindbergh came straight to the point, telling those assembled that he wished to buy the plane for a solo flight from New York to Paris. He directed some questions on the ship's performance to Chamberlin, who had flown her frequently. Chamberlin was enthusiastic in his answers. Lindbergh then asked Levine how much the plane would cost. The answer was that though it had cost him $25,000, he would let Lindbergh have it for $15,000 in the interest of aviation. But how, he asked, would Lindbergh pay for it? "Slim" named quickly the partners of his St. Louis syndicate, and Levine, impressed, seemed satisfied. "Slim" told Levine that he had not expected to pay that much for a plane, and that he would have to return to St. Louis, to discuss it with his partners. Back he went to St. Louis and directly to the offices of Harold Bixby. Quickly, the banker gave his consent, telling Lindbergh that it was important to have the best equipment available for such a venture. So, it was back to New York to Levine's carpeted office. Lindbergh indicated that the price would be satisfactory and Levine nodded, but then, suddenly and inexplicably, he threw cold water on the deal by saying, "Of course you realize, Mr. Lindbergh, that my company, despite the sale of the plane to your syndicate, must retain final say-so on who will fly the plane, and who will make up the crew."

Lindbergh was astounded. He argued with Levine that he had made it clear from the outset that he was to be the pilot, but to no avail. Levine was adamant.

"You must understand," he said, "that we can't let just anyone fly this plane on such a dangerous venture!"

Lindbergh, infuriated, left the office and returned to St. Louis, emptyhanded and disappointed. Bixby and Thompson bucked up his sagging spirits and advised him to look into the Ryan proposition carefully.

A few days thereafter, Lindbergh pulled up to an old ramshackle barn located on the water's edge in the less fashionable section of San Diego. It served as the modest headquarters of Ryan Airlines, Inc., but from the outside it seemed more like a fisherman's warehouse. There was no airstrip to be seen, only well-used fishermen's nets and equipment, and everything was permeated with a distinctive fishy odor.

He was greeted by B. F. Mahoney, the president—a large jovial man in his late twenties—who escorted him into his office. There they were joined by Donald Hall, the chief designer, and the three took a quick tour of the plant. Outward appearances, as always, were deceiving, for Lindbergh saw many workers hard at their labors on many fuselages throughout the cavernous building, which would soon become Ryan M-1 and M-2 designs ordered by Western airlines for use on the airmail routes. Lindbergh was duly impressed.

It was not long before Hall and Lindbergh were at work on the design of the new plane. Lindbergh, or "Charlie" as Hall called him, gave his requirements, a plane that would be able to carry him, alone, a distance of 3610 miles to Paris without a stop (the exact mileage having been determined by a fast look at the globe of the world in the San Diego Public Library). Hall was astounded when Charlie said that he'd go alone, but, in a way, it relieved him, for it would be possible now to save 300 pounds which would mean the addition of 50 gallons of precious fuel. Hall was even more astounded to learn that Lindbergh wished to sacrifice the weight of such life-saving equipment as a radio and sextant, along with a co-pilot, for the added gasoline that would give him extra range and a better chance for success.

The design took shape rapidly. It was a single-engine monoplane,

modeled along the lines of Ryan's successful M-2. To ensure proper
balance, the main gas tank was placed forward of the pilot's cabin,
which meant that the pilot would have no forward vision. Lindbergh
did not object to this, for he knew there would be no traffic over
the ocean, and he could always, with gentle banks, get good visibility
from his side windows when over land or airfields. Besides, the plans
included a periscope to be placed within easy reach, inside the cockpit.

Within days, the design was completed, and Lindbergh received
telegraphed authorization from Bixby to go ahead with the construction. Mahoney, despite the changes from the standard M-2 design,
and despite the overtime required by Lindbergh's insistence that the
plane be completed within three months, stayed with his original price
of $6000 for the ship. Meanwhile, a 9-cylinder, J-5 motor was ordered
from the Wright Company at a price of $4000. As the building
started, it was expected that the plane would carry 425 gallons of
gasoline, giving it an approximate range of 4100 miles, and providing
Lindbergh a safety margin of 500 miles.

As the days passed, the workers at the Ryan plant, oblivious to
their own personal comforts, worked day and night on the exciting
new assignment, while Lindbergh studied navigation with the help
of skeptical naval officers at Rockwell Field on North Island. He
learned the tricks of a Ryan monoplane on short hops over San Diego
in a company-owned plane, from the Ryan Field at nearby Dutch
Flats. He was, at last, in the running. As he pored over his ocean
maps, planning his course, he decided to sacrifice the safety of the
ship lanes on the southern route, for the shorter, but more desolate
great circle course. He hoped now for an early June departure, and
also hoped that the date would not be too late.

The preparations of American and French flyers in their quest for
the Orteig prize were well known now, and stirred up challenges
from other parts of Europe. Perhaps they would not be eligible for
the prize money, but they wished for fame and glory for themselves and their native lands by being the first to cross the ocean by
air, and land in a major city in the "new world."

6. In England, Captain W. H. Johnson-
Wreford, a young British Army veteran, and a cousin of Britain's
Home Secretary, Sir William Joynson-Hicks, was discussing the pos-
sibility of an Atlantic flight with Captain Robert H. McIntosh,

thirty-two, a British Imperial Airways pilot, with a long experience on the London to Paris run. Their discussions had reached a point where they had been already in touch with the Fokker plant in Amsterdam to order a plane, and designs were being drawn for a single-engined Fokker monoplane which would be named, ultimately, *Princess Xenia*, after the Russian wife of their financial backer. Despite the salesman's refusal to consider a one-engined plane for Lindbergh, this would be one of three such Fokkers that would attempt an Atlantic crossing during the summer.

Also, in England, an adventurous, non-conforming and avant-garde lady, sixty-six years of age, was looking at the Atlantic with envious eyes. She was the Princess Lowenstein-Wertheim, born Lady Anne Savile, and a sister of the Earl of Mexborough. She had been widowed since 1898, when her husband was killed in the Philippines fighting with the Spaniards. Since then, her gay and off-beat exploits had been the talk of London. She was an avid sportswoman. Skilled at skiing and sailing, she had learned to fly early, mainly to transport her to and from the sporting centers of Europe—though she had taken part also in notable distance flights to such far-off places as Egypt. She had developed an injury-proof ski, "anti-seasick pills," and had marched as a militant and effective suffragette. It was only natural that the challenge of the Atlantic would attract her.

She had shared many flying experiences with boyish-looking, twenty-eight-year-old Captain Leslie Hamilton, noted in Europe for his stunt flying, and called affectionately "The Flying Gypsy." Hamilton had served as her pilot on occasion, and in 1925 on a flight from Paris to London the two were missing for 24 hours—only to turn up in an out-of-the-way town in France, after a forced landing.

She turned now to him with her new idea. Hamilton was delighted with it, and together, they enlisted the services of Captain F. F. Minchin, another British Imperial Airways pilot who had recently gained attention with a flight to Africa. Consultations began, at once, with the Fokker Company in Amsterdam regarding the construction of another single-engined plane—a sister ship of *Princess Xenia*—to be known as *San Raphael*. Though the Princess was the sole backer of the flight Hamilton and Minchin kept her role in the venture secret. It was well known that the Princess's family was violently opposed to her flying escapades and would go to any length to stop this latest lark. Thus, her membership in the flight crew was unknown to the public, virtually until take-off time.

Captain Frank T. Courtney, a thirty-three-year-old Irishman, with a covetous eye on his flying competitors, journeyed at this time to the Dornier Factory in Friederichshafen, Germany, to look over the *Whale*, a large flying boat that had flown the Norwegian explorer, Roald Amundsen, home from his recent arctic explorations. Courtney, a racing pilot before the war, had served in the Royal Flying Corps and had won the soubriquet of "Magic Hands" for his delicate touch on the controls. With him were his aviation-interested wife, F. W. M. Downer, twenty-four, an instructor in navigation at the Royal Air Force school at Calshot, and R. A. Little, twenty-seven, a mechanic from Croydon Field in London.

The *Whale* was an all-metal, bi-winged flying boat with an upper wing that spanned 72 feet, and a lower wing that was slightly shorter. She had twin 450-horsepower, Napier-Lyon engines, with four-bladed propellers mounted in tandem on the top wing. They drove the plane at a maximum speed of 125 miles an hour.

The hull was long and broad-beamed, for stability in the water. In the extreme bow there was an open cockpit for the navigator, and slightly aft but forward of the leading edge of the wings was another open cockpit for the pilot and mechanic. The problem that faced them, as they talked over the possibilities for an Atlantic flight with Dornier officials, was the redesign of the plane so as to permit the carrying of, at least, 1000 gallons of gasoline.

Though the flyers from the United Kingdom were well behind their American and French counterparts, there was mounting evidence that the coming summer would be a memorable era in transatlantic aviation.

Back in New York in February, Charles A. Levine thought about the future of his Bellanca monoplane. The only decision that he had reached, thus far, was that she should be called *Columbia*. He realized that he was far ahead in the race for the Orteig prize if he were to compete, for his was the only plane that was ready, presently, to fly. Young Lindbergh's visit and quest had stirred his already active imagination. Perhaps, he thought, he would go himself. That he was not a pilot did not faze him in his reveries. There were many experienced pilots about who would be more than happy to go and take him along. But then came the doubts. There would be dangers, and *Columbia* was a large and valuable investment. If he could show her worth to the world in another way, with a less hazardous flight, it would serve to make his new company just as important in the world of aviation.

Often he would discuss the future of his plane with Bellanca and test pilot Chamberlin without revealing his quandary to them. Both were anxious to have the plane make the ocean trip, and both were confident that it could be done, with ease—but Levine would not commit himself. No doubt, he felt the pressure of time, for, like Lindbergh, he was well aware of the feverish preparations of Davis and Wooster, and Nungesser and Coli, and the steady progress of Byrd. He knew that his lead would be dissipated if he did not act soon, for *Columbia* would require extensive modification to fly the ocean.

At last he came to a conclusion of sorts. He would proceed with the alterations on *Columbia*, with an eye, first, on the flight endurance record then held by Drouhin and Landry of France. If that met with success, there would still be time to think about the Orteig prize. Work commenced forthwith, in a hangar at Curtiss Field, Long Island.

7. March saw the veil of secrecy lifted from the flyers' preparations as first Byrd, then Davis, and finally Nungesser gave specific data as to their plans and various states of preparedness.

Byrd disclosed, for the first time, that Rodman Wanamaker was his angel, to the extent of $100,000; while Davis and the American Legion, in a joint statement, let it be known that the veterans organization was contributing to the expenses of his Paris flight, in order to further aviation and to promote Franco-American relations. It was a natural ploy for the Legion, in that they were holding their annual convention in Paris during the summer. For his part, Davis advised that his plane would be christened *American Legion*. In Paris Nungesser informed the world that his state of readiness was such that he hoped for a take-off sometime in early April.

Lindbergh, in San Diego, was well aware of these announcements, and realized, unhappily, that it would take failures on the part of his opponents if he were to have a chance at the prize. While he continued to get ready for an Atlantic flight with the utmost speed, his mind considered alternatives: possibly a Pacific crossing or even an around-the-world flight in his new Ryan if one of the others were successful before him.

Work on his plane continued rapidly and ahead of schedule—

frequently on a round-the-clock basis. The workers, among whom was a young mechanic named Douglas Corrigan who later would make "Wrong Way" history on a flight to Ireland, took great pride in the exacting task, and the construction was conforming to the blueprints with faithful precision.

"Slim" spent half his time watching the growing plane—which was to be called the *Spirit of St. Louis*. The remainder of his waking hours were spent studying his North Atlantic route. He considered every possible obstacle—icing, fog, winds aloft, and such navigational problems as compass settings and wind drift. He made careful studies of the coastlines of Ireland, England, and France so that they would be recognizable to him. He determined how far Le Bourget Airfield lay northeast of Paris. Nothing escaped his attention. Always foremost in his mind was the disposal of excess weight so as to make more room for fuel. For this reason he turned down a large offer to carry a packet of mail, abandoned any thought of a radio and disposed of all but the essential navigational equipment and aircraft instrumentation. He planned on no personal luggage, only food and water enough for the flight, and a minimum of life-saving equipment in the event of a forced landing at sea. He reasoned that if that happened he would need luck to survive the landing, so why plan for it when the extra weight of rafts and paddles would deprive him of precious gallons of gas. He would place his faith in his motor and his plane.

The reporters began to take notice of him. Since the announcement of his intentions, the wire services in New York had engaged reporters from the San Diego papers to cover his progress, and already they were beginning to pall on him with their presence and constant questions. He realized the easy accessibility to them of the field at Dutch Flats, and, with B. F. Mahoney, sought another farther away from prying eyes on which to test fly the *Spirit of St. Louis* when she was completed. They had their eyes on a long, level strip at an out-of-the-way Army base, Camp Kearney.

New requirements had been issued by the Department of Commerce relating to the licensing of aircraft, and they were brought to his attention. With the help of an old friend from the Army Reserve, he applied, and soon was told that his plane would carry the license number NX-211 on her wing (the N designating the international code for North America, and X denoting experimental).

He planned, still, for a June departure, after a transcontinental hop, with a stop in St. Louis, but the construction was proceeding so fast, and was so far ahead of schedule that he dared hope now that it might be earlier.

8. At Curtiss Field, Levine's Bellanca had, at long last, been committed. She was being modified to challenge the non-stop endurance record of 45 hours and 11 minutes, set by Drouhin and Landry of France in August of 1925, who, in turn, had beaten the old record by Americans, Kelly and Macready on their cross-country hop.

Bellanca, John Carisi, the chief mechanic for Columbia Aircraft, T. H. "Doc" Kinkaid (when he wasn't occupied with Byrd's engines), Clarence Chamberlin, and Leigh Wade were hard at work, as *Columbia* was torn apart and rebuilt for the effort. Extra gas tanks were installed, and other refinements were made on the ship. Wade, one of the Army's Round the World flyers, had been signed in an impressive ceremony to fly with Chamberlin. Levine pulled out all stops to publicize the flight. If the record attempt were successful, Levine told the gathered reporters, it would be merely a prelude to the real goal—a flight to Paris for the Orteig prize; for if *Columbia* could stay aloft for over 45 hours, there would be no reason why she could not make Paris with ease.

As the weekends grew milder, a trek of automobiles containing inquisitive New Yorkers began to wend their way along the road to Mineola to look with wonder at the little plane, and hoping, perhaps, to get a glimpse of the men the newspapers had been saying would fly it. At first, the trek was a trickle of the most inquisitive; but, as spring moved on and the days grew warmer, it would become an ocean of excited, aviation-minded "fans," who would for a time drop their other heroes for the new hero of the day—the ocean flyer. If they were lucky now, they would see the sturdy little yellow monoplane with her glass-enclosed cabin, and 140 painted on her fuselage and NX-237 on her wing, standing in front of her hangar while mechanics, riggers, instrument experts, and the ever-present John Carisi swarmed over her. If they were very lucky, they would see a short test hop, as Chamberlin, Carisi, and possibly Pioneer Instrument Company expert Bryce Goldsborough, took her on a flight over neighboring Long Island. Those on the ground marveled at her speed as she swooped through the air like a pursuit ship, then banked sharply, and landed gently, using only a small portion of Curtiss's short runway. This, indeed, was a plane that could do anything that her designer claimed for her.

Bristol, Pennsylvania, the home of the Keystone Company, was active, too, during these days. The giant 3-motored *American Legion* was being flown by Lieutenant Bob Wooster and Commander Davis on short experimental hops. Wooster was ecstatic with the instant response the plane made to his slightest pressures on the control column. With the throttle wide open, the "Pathfinder" exceeded its top speed of 125 miles an hour, and proved its designer's claim that it could maintain flight, and even gain altitude, with one engine shut down.

The resourceful Davis, besides sharing the controls with Wooster on these flights, engaged himself, also, in the design of a miniature, lightweight sextant which he planned to use on the flight. Radio expert Bock busied himself on a set with a reputed range of 1000 miles, and arranged for the transmitter to operate on a frequency of 45 and 600 meters. Both he and Davis had alerted and made the necessary arrangements with radio stations located at Chatham, Massachusetts, and Louisbourg, off Cape Breton, Nova Scotia. "Spoons" Boedeker was forever tuning and adjusting his beloved Wright J-5 engines so that they would operate at maximum efficiency. In a short hop over Bristol, near the end of the month, he was satisfied completely for *American Legion* had maintained a level flight with both of her outboard engines shut down.

The outside world was little aware of the extent of Davis's readiness, for the papers had given scant coverage to the early test flights. Now, all that remained to be done before take-off were a series of tests with increasing payloads, and others, to determine with accuracy the fuel consumption of the plane. Until now, the big yellow biplane with the crossed American flags on her fuselage had satisfied her pilots and ground staff beyond their best expectations. Davis, Byrd, and Nungesser seemed, at present, to be neck and neck in the race for the prize, and *Columbia*, too, if her owner would commit her definitely to the race.

In Paris, as the month ended, excitement was mounting faster than in the United States, for the papers there followed the progress of *Oiseau Blanc* closely, with headline stories covering every move. The French had been disappointed keenly the previous autumn by the failure of René Fonck, but the plans of the intrepid Nungesser and his navigator, Coli, had revived their spirits and lagging interest.

To them, Nungesser's flying ability, together with Coli to keep him headed properly, more than offset the three engines on the planes of Davis and Byrd. The names of Lindbergh and Levine were, as yet, unknown to them.

9. News of the impending flights by the Americans and French spread to Germany and her flying community reacted as might be expected. Heretofore, they had concentrated on building Lufthansa into a commercial airline that was second to none in Europe. Now, national prestige was at stake and they moved to follow the new trend strenuously, though belatedly.

In Dessau, Professor Hugo Junkers dusted off designs he had drawn up years before for an all-metal, low-winged, cabin monoplane, and set his factory to work in the production of two. The plane, known as type J-33, was distinctive in that it had no outside wires or struts for support. The fuselage, 35 feet long, and the 59-foot wing, were made of Duralumin. The enclosed cockpit was situated above the wing, and to the rear of a Junkers 6-cylinder, 310-horsepower motor capable of generating a top speed of 115 mph and a cruising speed of 97. The pilots sat side by side with clear lateral and forward views, behind a dual control system. Professor Junkers added a thoughtful refinement for the benefit of fatigued airmen, when he arranged for an old-fashioned hammock to be slung aft of the cabin. The two J-33 planes, *Europa* and *Bremen* would play a part in the summer's activities, and *Bremen* would go on to make further aviation history in 1928.

Also, on Dr. Junkers's drawing boards was the design for a giant all-metal, low-winged seaplane D-1230. She was to be 51 feet long, with an astounding wing of 95 feet. The plans called for three Junkers engines to drive her. She was, in many respects, similar to a Junkers twelve-passenger transport already being used by Lufthansa on commercial flights. She, too, would fly during the summer.

The noted designer had a number of flyers on his payroll for the ventures he had in mind for his planes. There were Captain Friedrich "Fritz" Loose, a Czechoslovakian, who had fought as a marine at Jutland, and later taken flight training; Captain Hermann Koehl, thirty-nine, a wartime bomber pilot who had been shot down twice and survived to become Lufthansa's leading night flyer; Cornelius Edzard, twenty-nine, a commercial flyer for the Bremen Air Ship Company; and Johann Risticz, known affectionately as "The Bear," who had won fame as a Hungarian volunteer pilot during the war, and had only recently joined Junkers as a test pilot. Edzard and Risticz would be assigned to *Europa*, while Loose and Koehl would, for a time, be crewmates on *Bremen*, though Loose would be moved later into the command of the flying boat D-1230.

Junkers's plant was not the only German factory at work. The Hamburg-American Line was sponsoring a flight and had engaged the fabled Heinkel Company to build a low-winged seaplane, with a single, high-powered Packard engine for the use of Horst Merz, another Lufthansa pilot, and his crew, consisting of Radio Operator Wilhelm Bock and Navigator Friedrich Rode. They planned a flight to America in D-1220 (D for Deutsch) and would wind up in competition with the Junkers seaplane.

War aces Otto Koennecke and Ernst Udet also threw their hats into the ring. Koennecke, now thirty-five, and most recently a Lufthansa pilot on the Berlin to Munich run, said that he had planned an ocean flight nine years before, to bomb America, but that the end of the war had intervened. The backer of his flight was twenty-eight-year-old Count Georg Solms-Laubech, a close friend of former German Crown Prince Wilhelm who, it was said, was a contributor to the venture. The Caspar Company in Cologne had been given an order for a single-engined biplane, designed by twenty-eight-year-old Reinhold Mewer. The plane would be noted for its lower wing which almost touched the ground, and which, Mewer explained, would enable it to take off with an extremely short run. Udet, meanwhile, had contracted with the Rohrbach Airplane Works for the construction of a large twin-engined flying boat in which he hoped to make a successful assault on the forbidding Atlantic.

Like the English, the Germans were behind the leaders and there appeared to be little hope that they could mount a serious challenge to the French and Americans. The Orteig prize was of little significance to them, though, for it would require a flight from France to America. To bring real glory to the Fatherland would necessitate a take-off from German soil.

CHAPTER IV

April 1927

1. Spring arrived with gaiety and laughter in some quarters. Vincent Youmans's *Hit the Deck* began a successful engagement at the Belasco Theatre in New York, with Louise Groody winning accolades along with the hit song, "Sometimes I'm Happy"; Jeanne Eagels and Leslie Howard were packing them into the Empire Theatre with their new act *Her Cardboard Lover*. For sports fans, the baseball season got under way.

But for Nicola Sacco and Bartolomeo Vanzetti, there were no smiles as Judge William C. Walt, of the Supreme Court of Massachusetts, denied them a new trial for the 1919 murder of a South Braintree, Massachusetts paymaster, and Judge Webster Thayer, the original trial judge, sentenced them promptly, to die in the electric chair during the week of July 10. The decision and sentencing set off massive demonstrations both in the U.S. and abroad on the grounds that the trial judge and jury had been prejudiced by the defendants' radical political beliefs; the demonstrations would increase in number and intensity as the execution date neared.

Nationally, the Hawks and Doves quarreled bitterly over Secretary of State Kellogg's admission that he had provided President Díaz of Nicaragua with arms and ammunition; Governor Al Smith, acting more and more like a presidential candidate, replied to Attorney Marshall's question, by saying that "he recognized no power of the Church to interfere with the affairs of state." At the state level, New York and New Jersey were embroiled in a battle over New York's smoke nuisance and water shortage—and New Jersey's polluted beaches.

There was a clear sign of things to come, when, at the New York offices of the Bell Telephone Company, David Sarnoff of RCA, Gerard Swope of General Electric, Sosthenes Behn of International

Telephone, and William Randolph Hearst, looked with fascination and awe at a little "box" which permitted them to watch, as well as hear Herbert Hoover, the Secretary of Commerce, make a speech in Washington. The scientific age was in full flight!

2. The beginning of April found Byrd's plane completed and ready at Hasbrouck Heights. Actually, she had been flown by Bernt Balchen, acting as a test pilot for Fokker, and he gave pleasing performance reports to the designer. But the crew, for whom she'd been designed, had not as yet flown in her, for Byrd and Bennett had been occupied preparing the artificial hill at Roosevelt. As late as April 8, Byrd had insisted that he was not part of the "race" that was tickling the public's fancy. Again, he stressed that his was a purely scientific venture, to prove the safety and reliability of aircraft on long ocean flights, by the use of the latest and most sophisticated instrumentation. From information obtained on his flight, he planned to prepare charts of the most favorable routes, and obtain valuable meteorological data. Bennett emphasized the lack of desire to race by saying that *America*, regardless of her readiness, would not leave until May 16, when there would be a full moon. As further proof of their intentions, Bennett and Noville, when they applied for passports, gave as their reason for the trip, "for scientific purposes only."

Bennett, in an interview, said that he expected to take off at 4 A.M. so as to be over Paris by midnight the following day. He planned to maintain a speed of 120 miles an hour to Newfoundland—80 mph over the ocean to conserve fuel (hopefully, this speed would be augmented by tail winds), and 100 to 120 miles an hour after reaching the French coast. He was concerned, slightly, by the weight of the plane, and instructed "Doc" Kinkaid to remove the "dust caps" from the motors, thus saving 200 pounds. "I don't expect much dust over the ocean," he said with a smile.

On April 10, Byrd, caught up seemingly in the press-generated excitement over the imminent departures of *American Legion* and *Columbia*, said that he might race after all, though, he added, an early take-off would in no way detract from the scientific reasons for the flight.

April 16 was the day on which the Fokker tri-motor, *America*, was to be tested with her new crew, to determine once and for all whether she was acceptable to them. As was his wont, Tony Fokker was in the pilot's seat for the initial flight at his company's field. Beside him was Floyd Bennett, and directly behind them crouched Byrd and Noville where they could watch the flight more closely than in the navigator's cabin to the rear.

It was late afternoon, on a gray overcast day, when *America* roared down the runway. She carried only enough fuel for a short flight, and her large fuselage tank was empty. The plane rose easily after a short run. For 40 minutes, Fokker put her through the paces to the satisfaction of the Byrd crew still crouched in the forward cockpit. She responded quickly to Fokker's expert touch. Finally, Tony banked her sharply, after circling the field, and glided toward a landing. Fokker has maintained that, because of the lack of fuel in the main tanks which made the ship nose-heavy, he asked Bennett and Noville to go aft; but they declined and the descent continued. Fokker turned to Bennett and asked him then to turn the handle controlling the stabilizer to its lowest position so as to trim the ship, and keep her nose up. This Bennett did, but unbeknownst to both of them, the line jammed before reaching full trim. The big plane glided in and touched down, but the tail would not settle. The ship slid along the ground for fifty yards on its wheels with its tail high in the air as Fokker pulled the control column desperately hard into his lap in an effort to get it down. Suddenly, the ship hit a soft spot in the runway, the tail shot up, and *America* somersaulted to an ignominious stop. Fortunately, Fokker had cut the switches at the last minute, preventing a fire. He was thrown clear of the wreckage, but came up, smeared with oil, from head to foot. Though Byrd was able to crawl free, Bennett and Noville were pinned in by the nose engine which had been pushed back in the crash, and "Doc" Kinkaid and other onlookers had to react fast to extricate them. They were rushed to Hasbrouck Heights General Hospital by ambulance, Bennett with a severely fractured leg above the knee, and Noville, still unconscious, suffering from unknown internal injuries. Byrd, himself, sustained a broken wrist, Dr. Raymond P. Sullivan, summoned from New York's St. Vincent Hospital, gave out the bad news. Bennett would be grounded for at least three months, and Byrd for three to four weeks. Noville, less seriously hurt than thought at first, would be up and around, thankfully, in a matter of days.

America, too, suffered serious damage. Her center engine and cockpit were the principal areas affected together with the tubular steel mounting which supported the engine, and which had pinned both Bennett and Noville at the time of the crash.

Byrd was out of the running as suddenly as he had entered the race. There was some acrimony between Byrd and Fokker over the cause of the crash, but it was soon bypassed as repairs to *America* were begun, while Bennett, Byrd, and Noville began their convalescences.

3. At Bristol, Commander Noel Davis and Lieutenant "Bob" Wooster were exultant over the performance of *American Legion* on test flights. "She handles beautifully," they raved in unison, "responds quickly and easily to the controls, and surpasses our best expectations." They were ready. On April 10, two days before *Columbia* started her endurance flight, Davis and Wooster, together with "Spoons" Boedeker, engineer, Sergeant of Keystone, and radio expert Bock, took off from Bristol and flew to Washington's Anacostia Naval Base in two hours, swooping down to a perfect landing at the base at 5:30 P.M. "She flew beautifully all the way down," said Davis. Wooster and he had shared the flying, and the other three had occupied the navigation cockpit in the rear. She carried a 4000-pound "payload," or about one quarter of her expected load for the Paris trip. She had an ample supply of oil and gas, 200 pounds of baggage, and three extra passengers. She flew at 1000 feet, at an average speed of 80 miles an hour, into a brisk head wind, and landed before a waiting crowd of over 1500 welcomers.

The following day scores of people from the Washington area, including Navy "brass," viewed the *Legion* proudly. Rear Admiral William A. Moffett, Chief of the Bureau of Naval Aeronautics, exclaimed, "She is a perfect ship! I am confident they will succeed!" The remainder of the day was spent in the installation and final check of instruments. A communication was received by Davis from the Beach Nut Packing Company advising him that they would supply him with sandwiches of peanut butter, sliced bacon, and diced beef along with sufficient baked beans for eight days!

Early in the morning of April 12, *American Legion* took off and flew 160 miles to Langley Field, Virginia, in 1 hour and 40 minutes, and four days later, made a 300-mile flight from Langley to Mitchel Field, Long Island, in 3¼ hours. As she flew at 2000 feet under a gray overcast she was sighted by observers over Chesapeake Bay, along the center of the Maryland Peninsula, over Atlantic City, then Barnegat Bay, before she glided into Mitchel Field. The air, Davis said, was bumpy over land, and he noticed a slight tendency for the ship to yaw to the right, but the tendency disappeared in smoother air. Nevertheless, he was pleased with her over-all performance. He had put the large biplane through lengthy cross-country flights, and while not approaching the distance of the flight she would be called on to make, he felt she was well-tested and ready. All that remained were tests in which she would carry a payload closely equivalent to the load she would have to take off the ground en route to Paris. They would be made within a few days at Langley Field.

4. On her return from Mitchel, the *American Legion* was put through a number of load tests. Davis was determined, in his meticulous fashion, to take every precaution before his departure, and to test his big ship thoroughly under every conceivable flight condition.

The test of April 26, scheduled for the early morning, was to be the last before the final take-off from New York. *American Legion* had responded perfectly to all prior tests, and there was no reason to believe that she wouldn't respond as well with a full load of 17,000 pounds. Davis had said confidently to a reporter at the Officers' Club the night before, "I'm sure, we've licked all our problems." Naturally, he felt a certain uneasiness over the enormous weight that would have to be lifted, but he wasn't worried. *Legion's* performances had been too good.

Sally Finney of Washington, D.C., Bob Wooster's fiancée, and Mrs. Davis, along with Noel, Jr., had joined the flyers for the final few days, and were present at the field when Davis and Wooster climbed in the open cockpit at 6 A.M. on a warm Virginia spring morning. Also on hand were Ken Boedeker of Wright, Andy Sergeant, the Keystone mechanic, and F. F. Roberts, a naval mechanic, who had come down from Anacostia. The three engines were started, one by one, and revved up, as the big biplane trembled and thrust against the wheel chocks. Wooster was at the controls behind the windshield with Davis, always alert, beside him. There was not a whisper of wind. The take-off route ran along a smooth, wide field, from hangar-front toward an open space between a dirigible shed and a clump of trees a mile downfield. Mechanics and other personnel spread out along the runway to get a better view. Beyond the line of trees was a series of bomb pits, used by the Army for target practice, and beyond them, a small stream, known as the Back River. Across the river were mudflats which led to the little fishing town of Messick, Virginia; and, to the right, a small strip of green, marshy land, dipping into what appeared to be a deep pool of water, 75 feet wide. The field was considered good for take-offs, with no natural or artificial obstructions in the way.

Wooster opened the throttles, and the big plane started to move laboriously with its burden. The motors whined with an ear-piercing shriek in the still morning as *Legion* strove for flying speed. Ten, twenty, and then thirty seconds passed—and hundreds of feet. She passed the cut-off point, which Davis had planned as the place he would shut down power if he had doubts. Two hundred feet later, the wheels lifted slowly off, while onlookers held their breaths. The big yellow biplane fought her way with patent effort, as she approached the line of trees. She cleared the trees, but she could get no higher. As he passed over the trees, Wooster turned the plane to the right in a shallow bank. *Legion* slipped a little, then straightened; but she wasn't climbing. It then looked as though he was trying to find a place to set her down. Ahead was the green marsh and the pool of water, and the plane was angling toward it. She was now out of control, and losing altitude fast. Everyone on the field could see it. W. J. Forest, a fisherman in a boat on the Back River, saw the big bird in trouble, 500 yards away. He thought it was going to hit him; but Wooster was headed for the green, and, for all appearances, what he hoped was a deep pond beyond. His right wheel brushed the green, his left still in the air. The tail dropped, and the plane began a long, splashing skid across the wet marsh land. With a shower of foamy water, *Legion* hit the pool, plowed to the far side in a swirl of spray, and came suddenly to rest on the opposite shore, with her tail in the air, at a 45-degree angle, and her nose buried in the mud. Fisherman Forest pointed the way as Boedeker, Roberts, and Sergeant, together with Lieutenant McReynolds and Captain Scott of Langley, rushed to the scene by means of a commandeered rowboat and crossed the Back River near the dirigible shed. From the distance, they could see the long furrow dug by the plane in its fatal skid. They could see also that the left wing was smashed, and the center motor looked to be buried in the mire. There was no movement in the cockpit, which was buried under water.

When they arrived, it was too late. Commander Davis and Lieutenant Wooster had died instantly in the wreckage—Davis's head was crushed by the motor, and Wooster's neck broken. The entire fuselage, to the end of the cockpit, was smashed to bits. The wing tanks were ruptured and were still spewing gasoline. Field personnel arrived and helped right the plane. Heartbroken, Ken Boedeker examined the demolished cockpit. He found one switch cut, one partially, and one untouched. It was apparent that until the very end, they hoped they could make it. The aviation world mourned two brave and competent aviators.

The field had been reduced abruptly to Nungesser and Coli, and, perhaps, Drouhin and Tarascon in France, and Levine's *Columbia* in America. Captain Lindbergh's name was heard on occasion, but it was felt that he was too far behind to be considered. It was a strange paradox that the big multi-engined ships, considered by the experts as a safer bet for an ocean crossing, would come to grief so soon—first Fonck, then Byrd, and now Davis. Perhaps the amount of gasoline required for three engines was too much of a burden. In any event, only the single-engined ships of Nungesser and Levine remained in the running, and *Columbia* just the day before, on April 24, had, herself, survived a narrow escape.

5. At Curtiss Field, Mineola, the little silver and yellow monoplane *Columbia* was being tuned up for its 50-hour endurance flight which Giuseppe Bellanca announced would begin on April 11. The main purpose of the flight, he said, would be to determine the plane's capability of competing successfully for the Orteig prize though every effort would be made to bring the endurance record back to America from France. At the same time it was announced that Leigh Wade was being replaced in the crew by Bert Acosta, because, as Bellanca explained, the latter was more experienced with air-cooled engines and with flight conditions in the New York area where the attempt would be made.

Acosta, a burly (210 lbs.), happy-go-lucky man typifying the romanticized "to hell and gone" aviator, was a good pilot, having flown for twelve years. One of his more notorious flights came after a long night in a speakeasy with friend and flyer Lloyd Bertaud. They had ambled unsteadily into the fresh air in the wee hours, and decided to "jazz" (buzz) New York's City Hall in order to set their watches properly from a city timepiece. Jazz City Hall they did with a vengeance, each in his own plane, and in the process waked most of the city's slumbering residents. Irate complaints were heard for weeks. Acosta had been a chief test pilot for the Army during the war in charge of cadet training at Mitchel, Curtiss and Hazlehurst Fields. Greater fame came to him when he finished third in the national Air

Races in 1920, and won in 1921 in Omaha. He was married with two children and was well liked and respected by his fellow pilots. He had the enviable reputation of being able to fly as well, if not better, with a drink or two under his belt.

Acosta, who could spot immediately a defect on any plane that he was testing, had one weakness—the habit of making long, cross-country hops by the "seat of his pants" rather than by compass course. Often, he would seem to be hopelessly lost, but an innate sixth sense would somehow guide him to his destination safely. Once, while flying a VIP east to New York City, his passenger turned to him, and, pointing to a large community passing below, asked, "What is it?"

Acosta looked down, puzzled, thought a minute, and yelled back blandly, "It may be Wheeling, but I think it's Cleveland!" Happily, they arrived at the proper terminal.

In that only a few days remained before take-off, Acosta familiarized himself at once with *Columbia* making short flights over Mitchel, Curtiss, and Roosevelt Fields, and reaccustoming himself to the control of a plane by joystick rather than the control wheel of the Fokkers he had been testing of late.

Tanks of specially "ethylated" gasoline designed to produce added power arrived at Curtiss for use on the flight. Officials at Mitchel and Hadley Fields, the only fields in the area with adequate lighting equipment, agreed to illuminate their fields at night as an aid to the flyers. John Carisi, "Doc" Kinkaid, and others puttered constantly over the ship making last-minute adjustments. Levine was often present, helping where he could and handling the ever-mounting press relations. "No," he said when asked by reporters about the crew for the New York-to-Paris flight, "no selections have been made. Acosta and Chamberlin have been selected as crew for this flight only."

Columbia was moved to Roosevelt Field on April 10, to take advatage of its longer runway; but April 11 was dark and gloomy, with a strong cross wind blowing across the strip. Adverse weather reports for the vicinity caused the flight to be postponed for twenty-four hours, to the disappointment of hundreds of spectators, including Commander and Mrs. Byrd and Lieutenant Noville, who had gathered early in the morning. The forecasts improved overnight, and the cross winds abated, and soon after dawn, *Columbia* was loaded with 385 gallons of "ethylated" gas. Oil was poured into the tanks located under and behind the pilots' seats, and provisions, consisting of beef and chicken sandwiches, soup, milk and water, were stored hastily in the cabin.

At 9 A.M. John Carisi started the engine and warmed it up. Again, a crowd in the hundreds was present. Though the forecasts were favorable, it was a gray, cloudy day. Chamberlin, a slight 160-pounder, and the heavy-set Acosta, appeared and quickly climbed aboard, with Chamberlin at the controls. Both realized that the plane had never flown with such a gas load, as did Levine and Bellanca, and the fact caused a quiet apprehension among Columbia's immediate "family" and the crowd of onlookers. Bellanca and Levine, however, were confident that the experienced Chamberlin, with his intimate knowledge of Columbia, would be able to surmount all difficulties.

Chamberlin cracked the throttle, and the J-5 roared into action, blowing dust into the eyes of the spectators, as he swished the tail around and headed for the eastern end of the runway. Carl F. Schory of the National Aeronautical Association, the official timer, checked his timepieces, as the heavily laden monoplane made its turn at runway's end, and headed into the wind. Then with engine wide open, Columbia started down the runway toward the incline leading to Curtiss Field, where Fonck had crashed—slowly, at first, then faster and faster. The controls began to stiffen in Chamberlin's hand as flying speed approached. At 9:34 A.M. after a run of only 1200 feet, Columbia rose slowly into the air. She had used but a quarter of the runway, and Chamberlin held her nose down to gain adequate speed, so that she was only 75 feet up as she passed over the dreaded incline. But she was aloft, and the spectators below breathed a collective sigh of relief.

Chamberlin nursed her easily up to 2000 feet, then throttled back from 1750 revolutions per minute to 1250, at which rate the engines would consume but five gallons an hour. As they circled over Long Island in the early minutes of the flight, they had their first scare. They were over Mitchel Field when the engine started coughing strangely and came to a stop. Desperately, Chamberlin and Acosta sought the cause, while the former prepared hurriedly for a "dead stick" landing at the Army field. In the nick of time, Chamberlin found that he'd inadvertently hit the gas cut-off valve with his arm or knee. He reopened it quickly, and the engine roared to life again.

They continued to circle over Long Island. Acosta noticed that the oil temperature gauge was not working, but they both laughed at this minor difficulty. They were sitting on the tanks, and could tell very well what the temperature was. As the day wore on, they alternated at the controls. They set up a makeshift bed on top of the piano-shaped tank behind the pilot's cabin, and were able to stretch out and nap briefly on the tank's metal top, which had been softened somewhat by the use of blankets. From time to time, planes containing the press and other dignitaries, came up and flew alongside; the faithful Carisi appeared, looking from the open cockpit of a little biplane, making a firsthand check on his ship's performance. Both pilots settled into a routine, for they knew that they would have to stay up until the morning of April 14 to break Drouhin and Landry's 45-hour record.

After seven hours, they swooped in over Curtiss Field and dropped a message: "Aboard the Bellanca monoplane. 4:31 P.M., April 12. Mr. C. A. Levine, Woolworth Building, New York. Seven hours and all is well. The old Wright J-5 doesn't seem any worse for the wear of the 200–300 hours it has had. Hasn't missed a shot yet."

As the day waned, and turned into a cloudy night, they encountered the discomfort of finding that half of their water supply was unpalatable because the canteens had not been cleaned properly, and when they tried the milk, they found that it had soured from the heat of the oil tanks. They had underestimated, too, their appetites during such a monotonous flight, and, to their dismay, discovered that they had consumed all the sandwiches during the first twelve hours. They would exist for the rest of the trip, on vegetable soup, coffee, four apples and four oranges!

They calculated the time constantly on the four watches they carried. In order to break the record, they would have to stay aloft until 6:45 A.M. of April 14. As each hour passed during the long night, they scratched a mark on a piece of paper which lay between the seats.

The clouds were heavy, and there was a light breeze from the southwest, as they circled, ever wider, over New York City, Long Island, and eastern New Jersey. Now and then, they were able to make out the lights of Hadley Field, or the revolving beacon at Mitchel, which Colonel Benjamin Foulois, the commanding officer, had ordered operative for the flight. It was the night that the Sherry-Netherland Hotel, on New York's Fifth Avenue, caught fire in a spectacular blaze, and the flyers swung over it and watched the flames under the overcast. Chamberlin had, by now, throttled back to 1000 rpm, and the plane still maintained altitude, and, while the fuel was being consumed at a little over the anticipated rate, the supply was sufficient still to ensure a new record.

The second day, April 13, passed uneventfully, as the plane droned on. Again, newsmen, and inquisitive sightseers flew alongside to check on their health and the health of the plane. By now they had settled into two-hour shifts at the controls from the thirty-minute stretches, earlier in the flight, when the plane was heavier and more difficult to handle. Hunger became their chief complaint, and they amused each other during the day, conjuring up menus, and planning their orders when, at last, they would return to land.

At 9:38 P.M., on a clear, moonlit night, they were advised that they had broken Kelly and Macready's American endurance record of 36 hours and 4 minutes, set at Dayton, Ohio, in April 1923. It was a cold night with a fresh wind blowing out of the northwest. Below, at Curtiss Field, the crowds had begun to gather, as word spread that the two flyers were closing in on the world record, and they would reach 5000 miles by morning. The flyers, themselves, tired and hungry, were growing excited by the prospect of the new record, and by the flawless performance of the Bellanca. They concentrated all their thoughts on fuel conservation, as they flew their confining course.

The early pink of dawn changed rapidly into the light of the new day, and, surrounded by aircraft of all descriptions carrying newsmen and photographers, *Columbia* flew into the record books, while the huge crowd on the field cheered wildly. They decided to fly on until the gas gave out. It was a gorgeous, sunlit spring morning as they added hours to their new record. There was a sudden fright, as *Columbia* flew into the sun. "She's afire!" someone screamed with horror; but it was merely the sun's reflection on the plane, and the panic passed promptly as *Columbia* continued on her course.

Just before noon, several Army pursuit ships took off from Mitchel Field. Acosta at the controls and determined to have some fun, opened the throttle, climbed to 4000 feet, and chased the Army ships in mock battle. "Just wanted to see if we had some speed left," he explained later.

At 12:37 P.M. on April 14, the Whirlwind engine coughed, sputtered, and died. The tanks were, at long last, empty. Chamberlin, at the controls, kicked the left rudder, banked, and commenced a long, silent glide into Roosevelt Field. At 12:41 *Columbia* touched down lightly to the cheers of the great crowd. She had been aloft for 51 hours and 11 minutes. The two flyers were acclaimed wildly as they alit from the plane. After cleaning up, they dashed off to the nearby Garden City Hotel where they breakfasted happily with their wives.

Their menus were as follows: Acosta—orange juice, two helpings of oatmeal with cream, four lamb chops with a double order of French fried potatoes, hot rolls and coffee; the lighter-eating Chamberlin— one roast chicken, French fried potatoes, and rolls and coffee. And so to bed.

Levine and Bellanca were exuberant over the performance of the plane and the flyers. "In three days we should be ready to start for Paris," Bellanca said happily. A new J-5 engine was ordered, and it was expected that installation could be completed within 24 hours. In many quarters, the Bellanca became the favorite now to win the prize.

6.   On April 16 Levine returning from a flying trip to Detroit where he had made an unsuccessful bid for the insolvent Rickenbacker Automobile Company, said, with fervor, that the flight to Paris was on, and that preparations would be rushed. "If another plane starts, we'll catch him!" he said with exuberance. However, he threw a bombshell into *Columbia*'s camp by announcing that one of the pilots would be replaced on the flight by an experienced navigator. He indicated, further, that Acosta might be his choice as pilot, when he remarked to the press that "a man like Acosta wouldn't need any undercarriage for a landing." There had been talk of dropping the wheels after take-off, as with Nungesser's *Oiseau Blanc*. Guesses as to who would make up the final crew flew all over in aviation circles; Bryce Goldsborough and Acosta? Bertaud and Acosta? Or Chamberlin and Bertaud? Levine tried to halt the speculation that it was Chamberlin who had been dropped, by saying, "As far as I'm concerned, it can be decided by a flip of the coin."

On Saturday, April 17, the new Whirlwind engine was installed. Bryce Goldsborough of Pioneer Instruments refusing to comment on whether or not he would be the navigator, spent the day putting in three chronometers, an octant, a drift indicator, a turn indicator, and an earth inductor compass. Later, when he borrowed a light plane and flew it around Curtiss Field, rumors increased that he would be the one added to the crew. Meanwhile, Chamberlin and Acosta, paying little attention to the furor, tested *Columbia*'s new engine in short flights over Long Island. Occasionally, they would fly far out over the Sound to get practice flying solely by instruments.

On April 18, Levine tired of the constant speculations, and said that Goldsborough would not be the navigator. He added strangely, that in all probability, it would be a crew of Acosta and Chamberlin. The hard-working Goldsborough completed the installation of the instruments between test hops. The instrument panel was a maze of dials—fourteen in all! Carisi and Kinkaid busied themselves screwing eighteen new spark plugs into place. There was an abundance of fuel on hand, ready to be put aboard on a moment's notice, if the makeup of the crew were settled finally.

On April 28, there was yet another bombshell from Levine's office when it was announced that Lloyd Bertaud had been chosen navigator of the *Columbia*. The announcement added that either Acosta or Chamberlin would serve as pilot. Levine said, further, that he would not make a final selection until the last minute in order to keep both pilots hard at work, and interested in the flight. "Both men," he told reporters, "will appear on the field in flying togs, and their names will be written on slips of paper. One slip will be drawn, and that man will be the pilot." The new turn of events threw the pilot community, as well as the Bellanca camp, into consternation. What was Levine thinking of? He'd broken up a good crew, experienced at flying the Bellanca, that was presumably ready and anxious to leave. It was hard to understand his reasoning. Bellanca, too, was upset, but on different grounds. He was concerned about weight, for Acosta weighed 210 pounds, and Bertaud was ten pounds heavier. He openly espoused the cause of the 165-pound Chamberlin, but Levine would not be moved, and stuck by his original statement. Acosta, unaware of developments until he ran into his old friend Bertaud at the field was unperturbed, and he carried on with Chamberlin as if nothing had happened. "We are going ahead with our preparations, both Chamberlin and myself," he told reporters stoically.

Lloyd Wilson Bertaud, born in Alameda, California, was now thirty-one years old. He was a big, burly, pleasant-looking man with a large shock of sand-colored hair. At age twelve he amazed his home town by building a glider, and flying it off a cliff at Alameda Beach. To everyone's wonder, it traveled 1000 feet before crashing, but young Lloyd escaped, unhurt. A few years later, he entered flying school at Ingleside Beach, California, where he was lucky enough to be taught by the great Lincoln Beachey. He was licensed in 1914 at the age of eighteen, and began, at once, barnstorming throughout the United States and Canada, with famed lady-flyer, Katy Stinson. When the U.S. entered World War I, Bertaud, like so many other pilots, became a civilian instructor at fields throughout the country. After the war, he joined Eddie Stinson, Katy's younger brother, in barnstorming, and the relation culminated in their 25-hour record-breaking endurance flight of 1922.

He tried racing planes, and, in 1920, won a race in Kansas City by flying an Ansaldo at the then dazzling speed of 172 miles an hour. The following day he finished third behind Bert Acosta in a race to Omaha.

With prize money he saved over the years, he built a flying boat to carry passengers from Atlantic City to New York. This venture was unsuccessful, so he tried another. He selected a wife, Miss Helen Lent, and was married by the Flying Parson, the Reverend Belvin Maynard, in a much-publicized ceremony while flying over New York City. The new Mrs. Bertaud persuaded him to give up flying for a time, but not for long. He was soon back, flying the mail between Cleveland and Hadley Field, New Jersey—a job he gave up to join Levine. He was a fun-loving soul, like Acosta. Among flyers, he had the reputation of an able pilot, as well as a competent navigator —a rarity in days when most flights were made by the proverbial "seat of the pants."

As *Columbia*'s new navigator, he set to work with vigor, determined that the flight should not be delayed further. He decided on a route south of the Great Circle in order to avoid icing, which was prevalent at this time of year, and also, to be near the traveled ship lanes. He maintained that there was no discord between him, Acosta and Chamberlin, and indeed there wasn't. They dined frequently together and giggled secretly over the publicity ploys of their peripatetic employer. "I've known both Acosta and Chamberlin for many years, and they're both great pilots," he said.

A heavy mist hung over Curtiss Field on April 22. Bertaud pored over his maps, and then boarded *Columbia* with Bryce Goldsborough to go over the newly installed navigation equipment. Chamberlin kept his eyes on the North Atlantic weather reports, while Acosta arranged for the delivery of a new high-powered radio for use on the plane.

On April 24, the Brooklyn Chamber of Commerce, of which Levine was a member, offered a $15,000 prize to the crew of *Columbia*, if the flight was successful. Ralph Jonas, the chairman, said that it had been decided to offer the prize because of the "magnificent feat" in setting the endurance record. Simultaneously, it was announced that the plane would be christened officially the next day by Eloise Levine, the owner's nine-year-old daughter. Chamberlin, in a test hop, flew

Columbia out to sea, off Patchogue, Long Island, until a stiffening head wind forced him back to Curtiss Field where he found a large crowd had gathered, anticipating a possible take-off. But Levine, present at the field, had no comment on a departure time, thereby increasing the excitement and anticipation. That *Columbia* was ready, there was no doubt. Bellanca said she could go on an hour's notice, but Levine remained, uncharacteristically, silent.

7. April 24, the day for the christening of *Columbia*, dawned clear and bright at Curtiss Field. Crowds assembled from New York and Long Island early, though the ceremony was not scheduled until 4 P.M. They brought picnics, and gaped at the airplanes parked about the field. Many stared at *Columbia* as she sat in splendor outside her hangar. The fever had struck the public, and by early afternoon Curtiss had the look of a prosperous fairgrounds.

At 4 P.M. the notables arrived, led by Mr. and Mrs. Levine, the Chamberlins, the Acostas, the Jonases, the Bertauds, and dignitaries from the city of New York and Nassau County. Young Eloise Levine, a petite left-hander, stood on a small footstool at the nose of the plane and broke the beribboned bottle of ginger ale (with which she was drenched) over the nose amidst a burst of applause from the thousands of onlookers. Flash cameras exploded everywhere. Following the ceremony, Chamberlin and John Carisi boarded the plane, taking with them Grace Jonas, fifteen, and Eloise. The motor was started, and, with Chamberlin at the controls, *Colombia* soared skyward. Though it was not clearly visible to those on the ground, expert eyes noticed with horror that something had given away on the left side of the undercarriage during take-off, and that the left wheel of the ship was dangling aimlessly. It turned out later that a pin in the left shock absorber had sheared off as the plane took its last bounce before becoming airborne, causing the front strut to drop out of its fuselage fitting, leaving the left wheel wobbling uselessly below; but Chamberlin, Carisi, and the girls—flying happily over Curtiss —were oblivious to their peril. It was obvious to those on the ground that the damaged wheel could bear no weight, and that an ordinary landing by an unaware pilot would result in disaster.

Dean Smith, a veteran pilot on the field, jumped quickly into the cockpit of his Curtiss Robin, while mechanics swung his prop. Another mechanic grabbed a spare wheel from the side of a hangar, and hopped into the forward cockpit. Smith opened the throttle, and the little biplane tore down the field, and climbed rapidly in pursuit of the stricken *Columbia*. As Smith maneuvered his plane alongside of the Bellanca, the mechanic in the front seat held the wheel aloft, pointed to it vigorously, and then pointed to the undercarriage of *Columbia*.

Aboard, Chamberlin thought at first that the antics in the Curtiss Robin were a joke, but, at length, he understood. "Guess we've lost our land gear, John," he said to Carisi, who sat alongside him. Meanwhile, another plane, piloted by Everett Chandler, flew beside them, with the pilot gesticulating wildly to make sure that Chamberlin was aware of his plight. By now, they knew only too well, and Carisi already was hanging out of the cockpit, feet first, to try to learn the extent of the damage, and to make repairs, if possible. It was no use.

Chamberlin turned to the girls and said, "One of our wheels is loose. When we come down, we may turn around, or turn over, and get jarred up a bit, but I won't let you get hurt."

The girls, already a little airsick, were cured suddenly, but remained calm. Carisi crawled then behind the "piano tank" and released 350 pounds of sand that were aboard as ballast. Eloise went aft with him, on Chamberlin's instructions, to keep the weight in the rear. Carisi braced himself, his back against the rear partition, two-thirds of the way to the rudder, and held Eloise firmly in his arms.

Up front, Grace Jonas sat alongside of Chamberlin in the co-pilot's seat. He told her to take his seat pad, and hold it in front of her face. "When we come in," he said, "use your other hand to brace yourself against the instrument panel."

On the field below, excitement spread as word of *Columbia*'s difficulties became known to the huge crowd. Bellanca was heard to mumble, "To hell with the Paris hop, so long as they get down safely." Casey Jones, the manager of the field, arranged hurriedly for fire-fighting equipment and for an ambulance. A huddle among the expert flyers came up with the opinion that Curtiss Field was too bumpy for such a precarious landing, and pilot Ed McMullen, with the word *MITCHEL* chalked on the side of his yellow biplane, took off in chase of the Bellanca. Chamberlin got the idea, and banked *Columbia* toward Mitchel Field. He took his final precautions in the event of a crash. He opened the cabin windows, so that he and Grace might be thrown clear if something went wrong. Then, he circled the Army field until he saw the "trouble wagon" and the ambulance race up to the landing area from Curtiss.

He put *Columbia* into a steep bank and pointed toward the strip, sideslipping to lose speed. Thirty feet above the ground, he banked *Columbia* gently to the right and brought her lightly down on the sound right wheel and the tail skid, with her right wing barely off the ground. As she slowed, the left wing dropped, the damaged wheel gave way, and *Columbia* ground-looped and came to a stop, facing up the runway, in a cloud of dust. Crew and passengers jumped happily from the cockpit, none the worse for wear.

New York papers printed extras describing Chamberlin's "sensational" landing. Chamberlin knew it had not been a difficult procedure; but the papers speculated on whether it would influence Levine away from Acosta and toward Chamberlin in the selection of a pilot for the Paris trip. The speculation was academic, however, for four days later Acosta resigned from the flight with a letter to Levine. "I cannot help," it said in part, "but realize that the 60-pound difference in weight between Clarence and myself, gives him an advantage that can materially advance the possibilities of success, and for that reason, I wish to withdraw in his favor." Chamberlin and Acosta dined together at New York's Lambs Club the same evening, and Chamberlin commented on Acosta's withdrawal letter by saying, "It must have been difficult to write that!"

What happened, we'll never know. We do know that Bellanca was heavily in favor of Chamberlin because of the weight differential, and because of his experience with Bellanca planes; and we know that Levine leaned toward Acosta. In truth, perhaps the landing did tip the balance, or did it?

Meanwhile, navigator Bertaud was causing problems in the Levine-Bellanca entente. Besides preferring the longer route over the ship lanes, he was in favor of carrying a radio. Chamberlin and Bellanca disagreed. They reasoned that the radio was too weighty and presented, also, a fire hazard, with the possible emission of short cicuit sparks. Furthermore, they felt that its presence might have a bad effect on the operation of the compasses. As for the route, Chamberlin preferred the Great Circle, so that he might get a chance to check the plane's performance, thoroughly, up to Newfoundland, before heading to sea.

Levine sided with Bertaud on the radio, as he had a contract with the American Newspaper Alliance for an exclusive story of the flight, and it included in-flight reports; besides, he wanted to avoid the criticism of failure, to take all precautions if the plane was forced down at sea. While the argument went on, the radio was installed and removed, then installed again, and again removed. Pioneer technicians grew more irked at the necessity of having to compensate the compasses after each installation, and Levine equally irked at their $75 charge for so doing.

Two days of work were required to repair the damage to the undercarriage and wing at Mitchel Field. *Columbia* was flown back then to Curtiss, where the broken wing strut which had been spliced by a cabinet maker, was examined thoroughly and pronounced stronger than ever. A new dump valve was installed, permitting the instant disposal of 234 gallons of gasoline and oil, and serving, also, as a means to seal the tanks for use as floats. "Spoons" Boedeker, back from the late Commander Davis's camp at Langley, joined Kinkaid and Carisi, to attach double gas lines to the carburetor as a precaution against clogging. The lines were wrapped with care in tape, and other minor adjustments were made to the engine, as the plane received what many thought was a final check prior to the take-off. Andy Sarini, Tom Blainey, Ben Zabora, Jack Rapp and Peter Brooks were among the ground crew who swarmed over *Columbia*, testing every fitting and bolt. Bellanca, impatient, declared that she was ready, but, when possible dates were suggested, Levine always shook his head. Perhaps his doubts were returning, for he gave no reasons. Finally, on April 30, when a new earth inductor compass was installed, he explained the delay: three new radios had been ordered and each would have to be tested prior to any decision on which one to carry.

CHAPTER V

May 1927

1. The Mississippi River welcomed the month of May in a devastating fashion by overflowing its banks in violent floods, leaving thousands homeless and causing damage in the Southwest estimated in millions of dollars. Aid in the form of money, food, and other supplies was poured into the stricken area, and entertainer Will Rogers, with Casey Jones as his pilot, flew on to raise the spirits of the afflicted.

In the nation's capital, the U. S. Treasury Department announced a reduction in the size of paper money—an economy, said Secretary Andrew W. Mellon, that would save American taxpayers $2,000,000 a year. At the same time the Department announced, by way of a reminder, that the Federal tax liability to the winner of the $25,000 Orteig prize would amount to $1233.75.

In the world of entertainment, the theater management on Broadway advertised that a cough drop would be given to all those who watched Norma Talmadge play the title role in the movie *Camille*; Janet Gaynor and Charles Farrell, without the benefit of audience medication, won acclaim for their performance in the silent film *Seventh Heaven*; comedian Charlie Chaplin had his troubles, for his estranged wife, Lita Grey Chaplin, served him with papers, demanding $1,250,000 for a divorce settlement.

Elsewhere, people discussed the lurid details of the Judd Gray-Ruth Snyder murder trial being conducted in New York, read Louis Bromfield's Pulitizer Prize-winning novel *Early Autumn*, or perhaps, were lucky enough to have money on H. P. Whitney's Whiskery, when it won the 53rd Kentucky Derby at Churchill Downs.

The aviators waiting to take off on Atlantic flights were the victims of "one upsmanship," perpetrated by a young mechanic from Kiev, Russia, Ivan Fedorof. He announced that he would make a

15-hour flight to the moon in September in his 72-foot hybrid, airplane projectile, which, he said, would be propelled by a series of
"gas explosions!"

2. In England and Germany, preparations
for summer flights were advancing, though not fast enough to have
any bearing on the race at hand. At the Junkers factory in Dessau,
construction was proceeding on two low-winged monoplanes, and a
seaplane for the use of Captains Koehl and Loose, and Cornelius
Edzard and Johann Risticz. Captain Koennecke's Mewer-designed biplane was being assembled at the Caspar plant, while Ernst Udet's
seaplane took shape under the supervision of Rohrbach workers.
The Heinkel and Fokker factories were hard at work, as well, on a
seaplane for Horst Merz, and two monoplanes for Captain McIntosh and Princess Lowenstein-Wertheim, respectively. At Friederichshafen, Captain Courtney had purchased Dornier's *Whale*, and
oversaw renovations to prepare it for an Atlantic flight. He expected
to be ready in June.

At Villacoublay, Toussus le Noble, and Le Bourget near Paris,
the *Oiseaux Blanc, Bleu,* and *Tango* stood, poised seemingly to
start. Nungesser and Coli at Villacoublay had been conducting weight
tests to determine the speed and climbing abilities with various loads,
of their white biplane. After flying her to an altitude of 18,000 feet
on April 19 with her tanks filled to three-fourths capacity, they
landed, satisfied that there was little *Oiseau Blanc* could not do,
and they announced that they would leave for New York on April 24.
The statement silenced, temporarily, the French press, already out-
spokenly impatient over their delay. A new Levasseur motor, having
been thoroughly block-tested at Chartres Airdrome, was installed.
Instruments from a Fairchild plane at the field were transferred
hurriedly to the *White Bird*'s panel to take the place of a set
which had been ordered but had not arrived. The course was decided.
It would be the Great Circle, and called for the plane to strike the
American continent at Cape Race, Newfoundland, and then proceed down the eastern coast of the United States to Boston and
New York.

The emblem of the Hussars of Death, Nungesser's wartime regiment, was painted on the right side of the fuselage, below the cockpit, along with the tricolor. It consisted of a black skull and cross-
bones beneath a coffin with candles alongside. Nungesser explained

the morbid emblem. "A strong heart doesn't fear death even in its most morbid aspects," he told inquiring reporters. He told, also, of his commanding officer's greeting to him after he escaped through German lines to Laon in 1914. "You are a Hussar, and you drove a car of death. You are a Hussar of death!" the officer had said.

In Paris the excitement had reached a point that bets were being made on who would be the winner. Word of Byrd's mishap had reached the French, and he was no longer in the running; Bertaud and a pilot, as yet unselected were favored over Davis, in view of *Columbia*'s recent endurance performance, but Nungesser had the backing of the majority, because of Coli's navigational prowess. At cafes and restaurants, theaters, the Metro, and in the streets, all talk seemed to be of the impending flights. Drouhin and Tarascon were no longer considered serious contenders, as word spread that their preparations had bogged down for a variety of reasons; and, though the Belgian flyers had arrived recently at Le Bourget with their Bréguet, they did not appear ready to pose a serious threat to the leaders. It was *Oiseau Blanc* against *American Legion* and *Columbia*. Then came the sad word of the Davis tragedy. It was hard to believe, and while it reduced the field further, it cast a pall of gloom over the city. No doubt, it was this news that prompted Nungesser to defy the mocking and insulting French press—now daring him to go, as they had done previously with René Fonck. He postponed the flight again, saying that he would not leave until both he and Coli were certain that there was nothing left to be done in the way of preparations. Among other things, they awaited ideal weather conditions—a tail wind, for at least part of the way, a condition that weathermen considered most unlikely. When not flying, or exercising with weights and medicine balls to keep fit, physically, they continued to haunt the meteorological office, waiting and hoping.

3. At Villacoublay, *Oiseau Blanc*, likewise, stood waiting, poised like a hungry seagull while Nungesser waited for the ideal weather conditions. He was peppered constantly with questions wherever he went: "Are you ready?" or "Will you make it?" or even, "Are you really going?" As the wait grew longer, the questions became irritating.

"It's a hard flight," he would answer. "I've prepared for it for many months, and I do not intend to take off until I am as certain of my plane, and as certain of the weather as is physically possible. I am not inscribed for the Orteig prize [for like Lindbergh, he had not filed his entry within thirty days of take-off, a requirement that would be waived], and I just want to add to the long list of glorious achievements of French aviation."

The press and the public, impatient at his delay, kept hammering at him, but he would not be moved.

On May 3, with a large crowd present at Villacoublay, Nungesser and Coli took *Oiseau Blanc* up, and made a five-hour test hop to Chartres and back. On landing, they appeared pleased with the ship's performance, and announced that it was "not more than a question of days" before take-off. They were confident of their smooth-running engine, and waited, now, only for the weather— 50 hours of clear skies, and a few hundred miles with favorable winds.

At 3 A.M., on the morning of May 4, an unlikely accident came close to ending the flight and destroying *Oiseau Blanc*. A light bulb in her hangar fell to the ground, exploded on the cement floor, and ignited 200 liters of petrol, stored near the plane. There was an instantaneous and spectacular blaze, and only quick work by alert mechanics who were busy adjusting the ship's instruments, saved her from destruction. They shouted for help, and within seconds, the plane was wheeled to safety, outside. Portions of her lower wing had been burned, but Levasseur, on the scene promptly, said that repairs would only take a few hours. All that was needed was to cover the burned portion with varnished silk, as there had been no structural damage. Above all, he added, it would not delay the flight, now scheduled for May 16, the date of the full moon. French weather headquarters, in a long-range forecast, had advised the flyers that the best weather outlook over the North Atlantic could be expected between May 14 and May 20. This information, together with the damage of the plane, had a calming effect on the press and public alike, and outcries for an immediate take-off lessened.

As Levasseur had indicated, repairs to *Oiseau Blanc* were completed by daybreak, and, when Nungesser and Coli arrived at the field, she was ready to fly. She was loaded to three-quarters capacity, and another round trip to Chartres was completed without incident. There was no difficulty in taking off from Villacoublay's short runway, and the two flyers never appeared more confident, fit, or ready. After landing in the early afternoon, Nungesser completed arrangements to fly the plane to Le Bourget, within a few days, for the final take-off. Le Bourget was chosen because of its 2-mile runway, which, it was hoped, would give *Oiseau Blanc* ample room to get her heavy load into the air. Nungesser, wary now of press and public criticism, shared his plans only with Coli and Levasseur. He would not be pinned down to an exact departure date. All that was known was that *Oiseau Blanc* would take off from Le Bourget, and she was still at Villacoublay, heavily guarded against the hordes of spectators from Paris. Nungesser announced that he would not fly any more load tests. It was his feeling that the plane would either get off the ground or not, and he didn't intend to challenge fate more than once.

May 5 and May 6, a Thursday and Friday, were taken up with short hops in the Paris area, testing every control and navigational instrument for last-minute flaws. While on the ground, they kept a constant vigil over the North Atlantic weather, despite weak wireless reception from reporting stations in Greenland and Newfoundland. Nungesser bade unobtrusive farewells. He dined on home cooking with his aged mother at her small apartment near the Place de la République. He didn't have to tell her his departure was imminent. She had seen him go too many times before. But she said nothing, for he had always returned safely. He had been separated from his wife for many months, and though she had visited him briefly in the early part of the year, she had now returned to the United States. Louis Blériot, who had flown the English Channel eighteen years before, wished the flyers luck, and told them there was no reason why they shouldn't succeed.

All Paris was alive again with excitement. The pilgrimage to Villacoublay continued around the clock, and roads were jammed with cars for no one wanted to miss a thing.

On Saturday, May 7, it became known that *Oiseau Blanc* would leave for Le Bourget. At 6 P.M. Nungesser and Coli took off to the cheers of the crowd at Villacoublay. It was almost as though they were really going. The little white plane circled over Paris while final checks for defects were made. Once around the Eiffel Tower, and then back to Le Bourget, they flew, where thousands had gathered already, despite the dark thunderheads on the horizon. A gentle bank to the right into the wind, and *Oiseau Blanc* slipped softly to the ground. As she taxied toward her hangar, the huge crowd broke the police lines and surged toward the moving plane. It required fifty soldiers with fixed bayonets to return the spectators to safety behind the lines. The throng continued to mill around, restless and excited, and undiscouraged, though soaked by a severe thunderstorm that broke suddenly over the field. A fresh detachment of seventy-five soldiers, also with fixed bayonets, guarded the airplane, and kept the overly curious at a distance, while mechanics worked feverishly on her in what seemed to be final preparations. Nungesser and Coli themselves had been whisked back to Paris by a cordon of police, where they went directly to weather headquarters. The French Embassy in Washington had been instructed to cable U.S. weather observations, but the reports were skimpy, thereby preventing a thorough route analysis. While they were at weather headquarters, they learned that the French naval ship, *Eveille*, had been sent to Plymouth, England, to gather weather data, and was now reporting favorable conditions with very light winds. There were reports of fog off Newfoundland, but then there was always fog off Newfoundland. Finally, a late report arrived, and Admiral Delcambre, the director of the Meteorological Bureau, glanced quickly at his maps and beamed happily while lightning flashed and thunder boomed outside.

"These conditions are only local," he said. "You'll have five hundred miles of favorable wind, and you'll have to wait a long time for that to happen again."

It was up to Coli to decide, for he was the navigator and experienced mariner.

"How about it?" asked Nungesser.

"We're off!" said Coli, and the two repaired to Nungesser's apartment for a few hours of sleep.

At Le Bourget the rain had let up and the stars appeared. It was a warm night, and still the crowds surged out from Paris. Many had come from the theater, or other entertainment in Montmartre or Montparnasse, and were dressed in evening clothes. Some brought along picnic lunches, and bottles of good wine and champagne. They were prepared for an all-night stand if necessary. It resembled a large garden party, with little groups clustered about Le Bourget's vast field. Maurice Chevalier, Mistinguette, and Georges Carpentier were only a few of the notables present. It was in the main an orderly crowd, but the soldiers had been heavily reinforced, just in case, by a large number of poilus with steel helmets and carrying guns with fixed bayonets.

Oiseau Blanc was in her hangar to the side of the take-off area. Petrol was poured into her tanks from nearby drums, and the pungent odor was wafted out over the crowd. They knew it wouldn't be long now. Food was loaded, just enough for the flight in the interest of weight: dried fruit, vegetables, and other tabloid foods to be cooked on a small stove by means of canned heat; caviar, sardines, bananas, cold coffee, kola drinks, and a bottle of cognac. The collapsible dinghy was dispensed with, along with the sea anchor, to lighten ship. The only safety equipment was the water-tight flying suits which the flyers would wear, and a fishing line, with which Coli laughingly said he would catch cod—at Cape Cod. They would carry no radio, but there was a flashing light under the fuselage, set to flash the letter "N" automatically in Morse code for identification by ships at sea.

All night long the crowds continued to arrive. Police reported roads leading from Paris clogged with cars at 2 A.M., Sunday, May 8 —in France, the feast of Jeanne d'Arc. At 3 A.M. *Oiseau Blanc*, silvery-white in the rays of the searchlights, was wheeled out of the hangar onto the field, as onlookers cheered loudly. Minutes later, Nungesser and Coli appeared, amid more cheers, still dressed in street clothes. Nungesser, Levasseur, and several mechanics proceeded to make a thorough last-minute check of the plane—every part of it. Nungesser climbed in the cockpit and checked all the contents and instruments. It would be too late when over the Atlantic. Out he got, and took a last look at the outside of his trim ship. Under the lights, the name *LEVASSEUR* stood out dramatically on the rudder. He and Coli went into a small room off the hangar where they were given a massage and an injection of caffeine by Nungesser's personal physician. It was nearing 5 A.M., and already chief mechanic Carol had started the engine. Inside, they could hear the even roar as Carol opened the throttle. It was deep and steady, and there wasn't the trace of a missed beat. Then, Carol throttled back, and the sound died, though the aluminum propeller turned over jerkily, gleaming under the artificial light.

Quickly, the flyers dressed, and as they appeared again on the field, there was yet another cheer. There was the poignant good-bye of lovely Madame Coli as she embraced her husband tenderly, with tears rolling down her cheeks. Levasseur kissed both pilots, and there were many handshakes from well-wishers.

"*Allons!*" said Nungesser finally, and he climbed in behind the controls. After him went Coli, his black patch clearly visible over his missing eye. Nungesser pulled down his goggles, signaled, and the mechanics pulled away the wooden wheel chocks. *Oiseau Blanc* trundled to the leeward end of the 2-mile fairway and, with a resounding blast from the motor, turned into the wind.

The eastern sky was beginning to dawn, ever so slightly, but to the north there were flashes of lightning and distant rolls of thunder. Four small planes, propellers spinning, stood ready to take off, to accompany *Oiseau Blanc* to the coast. They carried the press, and some old flying friends of Nungesser and Coli.

A deafening roar reverberated about the field as the white biplane started up, slowly at first, then faster, and faster. The huge crowd stared anxiously—their noise drowned out by the high-pitched scream of the straining motor—300 yards, then 600, and 1000. *Oiseau Blanc* lifted slightly—then sank back. On she roared. Would she make it? Nungesser had said that he'd cut the switch if not airborne at 2000 yards, and that mark was approaching now. Finally, at 1750 yards, she rose heavily in the air. It was 5:17 A.M., Paris time, as the first Orteig prize contestant got away.

Oiseau Blanc was 50 feet up, and struggling for altitude as she passed over a ravine at the end of the field. Slowly she climbed to 700 feet and headed toward the Seine, twisting and turning to avoid the hills in the vicinity. During her battle for altitude, a following plane saw the landing gear drop free, as Nungesser sought to lighten his ship in her desperate fight to remain airborne.

With four planes surrounding her, watching her gallant struggle, she passed over Merilan at 5:55 A.M. and Mantes at 6:05. By then, Nungesser had coaxed her with the aid of a light breeze from the west to a height of 1200 feet. *Oiseau Blanc* then veered north slightly, passing over Rouen and Bac de Candebar. She struck the coast at 6:45 A.M., near Etretat, and headed to sea over a rough ocean, between Etretat and Fécamp. The accompanying planes dipped their wings in salute and turned back. Their last sight of *Oiseau Blanc*, looking so little and frail below them, was as she headed bravely and alone over the gray ominous Atlantic.

Reports of the Nungesser take-off were received instantly in New York, and plans were started for a gala welcome to the flyers under the direction of Grover Whalen, on temporary leave from his Byrd assignment. Prior to his departure, Nungesser had cabled Captain René Bouygée, president of the French War Veterans of New York, that he would land in the North River, between the Statue of Liberty, and the French Line's Pier 57, where the liner *De Grasse* was berthed. It was arranged that the committee boat *Mecom* would dock at the Battery at 9 A.M., EST, May 9 (the estimated time of arrival was 2 P.M. EST, and 8 P.M. Paris time). Aboard would be Mayor Jimmy Walker of New York, Commander Byrd, Grover Whalen, Robert Nungesser, and other notables from the city and state. Colonel Foulois, the Commandant of Mitchel Field, assigned five Army pursuit ships to fly up the coast, meet *Oiseau Blanc*, and escort her in. Lloyd Bertaud, Chamberlin, Leigh Wade, and other aviators, made arrangements to take off when word was received that the French flyers had reached the coast of Maine. There were also plans for a large air armada from Teterboro Field. It was an expectant and optimistic New York that spent May 8 awaiting word from the daring ocean pilots.

When the news reached *Columbia's* headquarters, it was taken calmly. Bellanca commented that "if the French flyers were successful, *Columbia* likely will not try the flight." Chamberlin was skeptical of their chances. Said he: "Our weather reports show bad ocean weather for three or four days. In the face of this, I don't see how they can make it, but I wish them luck, and the best of it!" Bertaud declared that their success "depended on a good break in the weather. If they get it, they should be here in 40 to 45 hours." He added that *Columbia* had, still, a day of preparation ahead before take-off. Levine said flatly that there would be no purpose in the flight for *Columbia*, if Nungesser and Coli were successful.

Paris and all of Europe remained alert all day, May 8, waiting for any word of the flyers. There was a reliable report that she had been seen by a ship at 10 A.M., near Fastnet Rock, off the coast of Ireland, speeding westward. The flyers, who had accompanied them to the coast, estimated their speed at 115 miles an hour, after the wheels were dropped—15 miles per hour above cruising speed; but "Doc" Kimball in New York gave out the gloomy prediction that they would strike 25-mile-an-hour head winds in mid-Atlantic, and that these winds would increase in velocity as they neared Newfoundland.

Newfoundland and Nova Scotia were on the alert. Cape Race, during May 8, reported heavy northeast winds with snow flurries. Every field and wireless station on the Atlantic coast, waited vigilantly for news and/or sightings.

In Paris, arrangements were made to notify the public of the flyers' success, by firing a cannon off near the Invalides, and it would be confirmed, thereafter, by smoke bombs dropped from Army planes flying over the City. Throughout the day, masses of people crowded around bulletin boards, outside the newspaper offices, waiting for word—any word. When none was forthcoming, they consoled themselves with the thought that the flyers were by now in mid-Atlantic over the clouds and invisible to ships below. They weren't expected in New York, in any case, until tomorrow evening, May 9, Paris time. As night fell, the crowds, tired, dispersed slowly, and went to bed to rest up for the big day ahead.

May 9, at New York Harbor, dawned gray and misty. From the Battery, where crowds began to assemble as early as 7 A.M., it was barely possible to make out the Statue of Liberty. From time to time the mist turned into a fine, soaking rain. The dignitaries were led by Grover Whalen. Nungesser's brother, Robert, from Washington, stood talking to Leigh Wade, late of the Bellanca crew, while peering hopefully through the murky gloom. Nearby, a hydroplane rolled easily in the gentle swell of the harbor. It was one of the ships that would go up to meet *Oiseau Blanc* when reports of her approach were received.

Mist swirled about the tall skyscrapers, and umbrellas were seen everywhere. It was a strangely silent crowd, expectant yet far from exultant, that looked skyward into the dark, scudding clouds. At Pier 57, a suite had been prepared aboard the *De Grasse* to which the flyers would be taken for food and rest. The crowds increased as the morning passed, and lined the rails at harborside, watching and waiting. At 11 A.M., Robert Nungesser, Wade, and other members of the welcoming committee, joined Whalen on board the flag-bedecked *Mecom* while she cruised down the harbor to clear a landing spot for *Oiseau Blanc*. The flyers were expected around 2 P.M., but it was estimated that they had sufficient gas to stay aloft until 6 P.M. New York time.

Suddenly, the crowd noise increased, and there was a sporadic handclapping. A report had been received that *Oiseau Blanc* was sighted off Cape Race, Newfoundland, at 10:10 A.M., a short time before. Then came a report that she had been sighted over St. Pierre-Miquelon, an island off the southwestern coast of Newfoundland, at 9 A.M. by an American destroyer.

At the Battery, the crowds became noisier and gayer; in Paris, there was delirium; but, ominously, there was no confirmation of these sightings when the early editions of the New York afternoon papers hit the streets.

Nevertheless, preparations for the arrival intensified. Police launches 1, 8, and 9 of the Marine Department of Aviation under the command of Captain John Redden were readied for their duties in the foggy harbor; now, Bedloes Island and the Statue of Liberty were hidden completely in the mist. All ears began to strain for the sound of a motor, and, from New York to Portland, Maine, planes of all types prepared to take to the air to welcome the Frenchmen. Weather reports from Cape Race reported fair skies with strong westerly winds—conditions which would not hamper them overly on their trip down the coastline.

Noon came—then one o'clock, and finally, 2 P.M. The crowds stared into the gray mist, eager for the sight of the *White Bird*, or the sound of her engines; but, so far, there was nothing—only fog, thick and quiet, and the uncomfortable fine and drenching rain.

In Paris, it was early evening. The city had been thrilled by reports of the sighting of *Oiseau Blanc* over Cape Race, and they waited breathlessly, on the avenues, in cafes, and in front of newspaper offices, for further word. Then it came—an "extra," hot off the presses of *La Presse*, with banner headlines proclaiming THE ATLANTIC IS CONQUERED! The story told of a smooth landing on the glassy surface of New York Harbor, and of wild greetings by New Yorkers to the tired but happy flyers. The flyers' families were told. Coli's mother in Marseilles, said joyously: "I knew they would do it!" Frenchmen everywhere were elated. Cheering crowds poured onto the streets, embracing and celebrating as though it were already Bastille Day. Soon, they heard the booming salvo from the cannon at the Invalides, and minutes later, an airplane appeared overhead, dropping smoke bombs. It was the confirmation signal! It was true! Nungesser and Coli had done it!

Alas, though, in other newspaper offices in Paris, worried editors sought desperately to get definite word from New York of their arrival. It was not forthcoming. *La Presse* had gone to press with a story "from a usually reliable source." Outside, unaware of the cruel truth, the happy crowds danced in the streets.

In New York, the crowd was quiet, downcast, and wet, as 3 P.M. passed with no further word. Then came a flash from the U. S. Navy Department that they had been seen off Portland, Maine, at 2:53 P.M. At 3:30 there was a report from the Naval Station at Portsmouth, New Hampshire, saying a white plane without wheels had been sighted, flying south off the Isle of Shoals. Surely, this was a reliable sighting, and hope returned. No doubt, now, it was *Oiseau Blanc*.

The same watchful waiting was going on in Boston which, also,

was covered by fog. Crowds had gathered at the high vantage
points—on the balcony of the Custom House tower, the flats of
East Boston, and in other tall buildings of the city. They were
aware, as well, of the report from Portsmouth, but when 4 P.M.,
and then, 5 P.M. arrived without sight or sound of the ship, hope
began to wane. Then, the chilling word was received that the sightings, reported earlier from Portland and Portsmouth, were erroneous.
There had been a white plane without wheels—to be sure—but, it
was a Coast Guard amphibian, which had taken off at 1:30 P.M.
from Rockland, Maine, and been forced down by the weather at
4:30 P.M. off Rockport, Massachusetts.

In New York, when the fog began to lift at 4 P.M., anxiety was
felt by the large throng. When they heard of the mistake in the
reports from Portland and Portsmouth, hopes dimmed rapidly, and
were kept alive only by the knowledge that *Oiseau Blanc* could
have landed elsewhere, or come down at sea, and been picked up.
Though die-hards remained long past the 6 P.M. deadline, most
onlookers left the scene to continue the vigil in the warmth of their
homes, where further news would be available over the radio.

In Paris, when the deadline passed, newsmen could wait no longer
and put out the shocking word to the celebrating crowds that "no
confirmation has been obtained of the flyers' arrival in New York,"
while New York papers carried the stark headline, OISEAU BLANC
OVERDUE.

The Parisians couldn't believe the news at first; when it sank in,
they became bitter and unruly at what they felt was an intentional
deception. They seized all available copies of *La Presse*, and burned
them. They booed and demonstrated wildly. A feeling came over
them that the Americans were responsible, somehow, for their plight,
and a great mob stormed the offices of the Paris *Tribune*, on the
Avenue de l'Opéra. Fortunately, Albert Jaurrett, the advertising
manager, who spoke French fluently, was able at last to quiet them.
It had been a cruel hoax, and the mob, aroused, had sought a
scapegoat.

In America, the morning of May 10 arrived without provable
news. Reports and rumors flew about wildly. They had been seen
at St. John's, Newfoundland, at 5 A.M. yesterday, and off Isle au Haut,
in Penobscot Bay, Maine, at 10 A.M. As usual, there was no verification.

The liners *Mauretania* and *Republic* docked in New York but
could report no sightings of the aircraft. A flurry of excitement

occurred later in the day, when, what was termed a positive report, was received to the effect that *Oiseau Blanc* had been picked up by the SS *Cameronia*, 1000 miles off the Irish coast, but a quick wireless message was received from Captain Gemmel, her master, saying: "Sorry, have not sighted Nungesser airplane." A similar report spread, and a like answer was received, involving the liner *Aquitania*. People seemed to be clutching at straws of hope.

As May 10 came, and went, without word, Paris gave up, although Levasseur's statement that the plane would float for a week if her tanks had been emptied quickly, gave to some, the hope that the flyers would be picked up at sea. Had not Commander Rodgers of the U. S. Navy stayed afloat in the Pacific for nine days in 1925? And there were Hawker and Grieve in 1919. But there was real anguish. The Mesdames, Nungesser and Coli, so thrilled hours before, were in tears, but, as the papers said, "we're brave and full of faith" that the men would be found.

The Chamber of Deputies was in an uproar over the false story of the safe arrival, and many members blamed American rumors. There were also statements made that U.S. weather information had not been made available to the flyers, and they served to whip up anti-American feelings. This caused U. S. Ambassador Myron T. Herrick to cable home and advise Washington that, in view of the disaster, and resulting disappointment to the French, caution should be exercised by American flyers thinking of making a flight to France.

In the United States, aeronautical authorities at Massachusetts Institute of Technology were skeptical about the plane's ability to float. They said that without pontoons the weight of the engine would force the plane under within a few hours at most. On May 11, Levine issued a statement that *Columbia* would take off on the 14th; Ambassador Herrick's warning did not perturb him, for he was sure that the Frenchmen would be found by then.

The days and the weeks went by without word. There were many rumors and stories; hundreds from Newfoundland to Boston reported hearing the plane. A farmer working in a field one mile from Harbor Grace on May 9 at 9 A.M., heard an airplane overhead. He had not heard of either Nungesser or Coli prior thereto. Soon, many others in Newfoundland came forward, and presented stories to Sir Patrick McGrath, president of the legislative counsel of Harbor Grace. John Stapleton, seventy-one, a retired battery man with a cable company, had heard an engine noise in the air that morning, as had Mrs. Lily Hinton, wife of the manager of the Imperial Cable Company, while she did her housework. Mrs. Elizabeth Munn heard it as she fed her chickens, and Patrick Moriarty, nineteen, who was with Stapleton, heard it for ten minutes. All were convinced that the plane had at least reached the Harbor Grace area.

Later, a Sergeant Roberts, at Concepcion Bay, told of hearing a drone, followed by a blast on that Monday morning, and there were lobstermen who reported seeing a white airplane over the Bay of Fundy, headed west. Volunteer expeditions were formed at Harbor Grace and other localities to search the less inhabited parts of Newfoundland, in the event that the flyers had made a forced landing.

So far, the Newfoundland residents had reported only engine sounds, but now came forward Anne Kelly, aged seventy, of Otterbury, west of Harbor Grace. She said she had been gardening Monday morning, when she heard a loud noise, looked up, and saw two "white birds" going south. She, too, had never heard of Nungesser and Coli, and it was surmised that the two birds might have been the double wings of a biplane. Ebeneezer Peddle, fifty-six, and his son, James, eighteen, of Bear Cove, one mile east of Harbor Grace, testified that they were working in the fields at 9 A.M., heard a noise, and saw "a large white machine in the air."

Did Nungesser and Coli, in fact, get to Newfoundland? Extensive searches by land and air turned up nary a clue, nor did similar searches in Nova Scotia, Labrador, and Quebec. In the middle of the month, Rodman Wanamaker, through Grover Whalen, offered a reward of $25,000 for Nungesser and Coli "dead or alive."

In France, bitterness reigned still. General Marie Victor Duval wrote in *Figaro*, that "efforts like Nungesser's advanced neither sport nor aviation." French and American naval vessels which, up to then had been scouring the Atlantic, put into port sadly, reporting no trace of plane or crew. A seaplane, the *Jeanne d'Arc*, piloted by U.S. flyers, P. Sydney Cotton and Cy Caldwell, continued a vain search of Nova Scotia and the eastern section of Newfoundland, between St. John's and Placentia Bay, financed by Daniel Guggenheim, of New York.

There were other reports as the summer arrived. Flares were sighted in June from the Quebec mountains, north of Saint-Germain; 10,000 handbills were dropped at once over the area, saying "Make an effort to signal with smoke in the daytime, on the shores of large lakes or rivers, whose course you should follow. If possible, signal 2 hours after sundown for 15 minutes." Nothing came of the effort.

Sometime thereafter there was an exciting report that the men had been found in the Laurentian Mountains, along the Shipsa River. One Blair, employed by the Price Lumber Company, wired: REPORTED HERE, NUNGESSER AND COLI FOUND. The terse message caused a quick wave of elation in Quebec which as quickly subsided, when the rumor proved false. Investigation later disclosed that the flares were the lights of a Quebec powerhouse, and Mr. Blair, when confronted, admitted inventing his story for no apparent reason.

An interminable number of bottles containing purported messages from the French flyers began to wash ashore, a phenomenon that was to continue for years. The first of such bottles was picked up on May 18 on a beach near Falmouth, England. It contained the message: LANDED 75 MILES LAT. IRELAND. ENGINE TROUBLE. W. H. NUNGESSER. FINDER PLEASE COMMUNICATE WITH H. LAUSERNE, R.A.F. SECRETARY AIR ATTACHÉ FRENCH EMBASSY, LONDON. A quick check determined that the French Embassy had never had an employee by that name. Another was picked up off the Gaspé Peninsula saying, "We are without food, off Harbor Grace. Nungesser and Coli. Lat 75 Lon 45." The obviously incorrect position showed quickly the cruel falsity of the note. Later, there was one found near Halifax, saying, simply, in a crude scrawl, "Nungesser Coli Help!" Many others were picked up during the summer, a few so realistically contrived that they were taken to Madame Nungesser for a possible verification of the handwriting. They turned out to be the work of cranks. The Gaspé area received a flurry of them in August, and the bottles were identified subsequently as being those of a Quebec wine dealer. The last bottle, purportedly from Nungesser and Coli, was recovered on the Dutch coast in 1934.

In 1961, a lobsterman, hauling his trap from the waters of Casco Bay, off Portland, Maine, brought up a corroded instrument panel which was identified as being very similar to the one carried by *Oiseau Blanc*.

How far they got, we'll never know. Some are convinced that they flew, at least, to Newfoundland. Others feel that they plunged into the ocean shortly after leaving the French coast.

The provable facts are scanty. *Oiseau Blanc* was seen leaving France near Etretat, flying smoothly, and there is a reliable report that she was sighted over Fastnet Rock, off the Irish coast, still going well. We know no more, for the Atlantic is a jealous guarder of secrets.

We can only remember that on the morning he took off, Nungesser turned to his friends, and said, "In the event we don't make it, I want you to know that we took no unnecessary risks, and did everything we could to make this flight successful."

Their brave attempt has become legendary in aviation circles. Those who remember ponder still over their fate. During that summer, and in the ensuing years of pioneer ocean flying when memories were fresh, numerous ocean pilots dropped wreaths, flowers, and other mementoes, in mid-ocean in commemoration of their gallant effort.

4. At Curtiss Field, New York, there was much activity in the Bellanca camp. Now that the question of the plane's pilot had been clarified by Acosta's resignation, Chamberlin busied himself with continuous test flights on *Columbia*. He determined that he was able to get 10.8 miles to the gallon at 127 miles an hour, and he experimented further with fuel consumption at varied throttle settings. Bertaud, meanwhile, worked on problems of navigation. He talked to René Fonck, at nearby College Point where he was supervising the construction of his new Sikorsky, and the French pilot warned him of the difficulties in picking up the French coast at night. He talked to Giles Steadman, navigator of the Cunard liner *Leviathan* who backed his decision to stay in the ship lanes south of the Great Circle route, telling him that, in the event of trouble, he could count on a ship every 50 miles all the way across. He and Chamberlin agreed, finally, that they would fly down Long Island Sound, leave land at Westhampton, thence to Nantucket, and straight across the ocean, hitting France on the northern coast of Brittany. They hoped to make landfall on the French coast in daylight, pick up the Seine River at its mouth, and follow it in to Paris.

The radio set was also agreed on and installed. It was designed by A. D. Cardwell, built by Matthew Hanson, had a sending range of 150 miles, and could receive messages from points up to 300 miles away. However, to the dismay of Chamberlin and Bellanca, it required a generator on the right wing strut, which would reduce the air speed by 5 miles an hour. It needed, further, a 200-foot antenna, which would trail the plane! They resisted strenuously the inclusion of these accessories, arguing that they would impair, seriously, the chances of a successful flight, in that they would cut down substantially on the cruising range.

The weeks-old dispute continued for another 24 hours, with

Chamberlin and Bellanca pitted against Bertaud and Levine. Then workmen were seen removing the radio which had just been installed. Bellanca, victorious, announced that a small, battery-operated emergency set, with a transmitting range of 25 miles, would be carried instead.

Rumors about the Nungesser-Coli flight were constant. One swept Curtiss Field on May 6 that they had taken off. It proved unfounded. Lindbergh, too, was rumored to be racing east, and ready to leave within 24 hours after arrival. Yet *Columbia* continued with her methodical preparations. Crew members test-fired her Very pistols and parachute flare guns, and Bertaud communicated constantly with "Doc" Kimball at the New York Weather Bureau, who reported storms over the proposed course. Bertaud was concerned, also, by the fact that *Columbia* carried no lights, and he hoped, aloud, that the French would clear a path for the plane if it so happened that it was dark when they hit the coast. The French were cooperative. They announced that the airfield at Cherbourg would be lighted, and that five fields, leading from there to Calais, would be outlined with flares, to help them get their bearings. Bertaud was notified, too, that a powerful searchlight near Le Bourget would be on, and that its beam could be seen from the coast, and would serve to guide them to Paris.

There seemed no reason for further delay of *Columbia*. At times, during the first week in May, there were reports of bad visibility, or adverse winds to hold them up. But when the weather was favorable, there was no comment. It was a dark mystery to the thousands of tourists, who made the daily trek to Curtiss Field, watching and waiting.

Oiseau Blanc's departure caught the *Columbia* by surprise. Bellanca, Chamberlin, and Bertaud were disappointed. *Columbia* stood poised to leave, but was grounded still on orders from Levine. There was talk of canceling the trip if the Frenchmen were successful. Work virtually ceased as the vigil for *Oiseau Blanc* continued.

On May 10, with the Frenchmen long overdue, word spread that *Columbia* would take off the following day, at 1 P.M. Activity surged again at her hangar at Curtiss Field. Bryce Goldsborough and Maurice Titteringham of Pioneer Instruments were seen making final compass adjustments to compensate for the radio, then scheduled to be included, and Mrs. Bertaud and Mrs. Chamberlin prepared a tasty assortment of foods for their husbands. A small crowd at the field in the late afternoon watched as John Carisi climbed into

Columbia, and took her up into the overhanging fog to test the newly set instruments. The plans were to take the plane over to Roosevelt early the next day for the take-off, but Levine, late in the afternoon, stepped in again, following Ambassador Herrick's warning from Paris. He announced that the flight had been postponed until May 14, in the hopes that by that time word would be forthcoming on the fate of Nungesser and Coli.

On May 12, however, a new and exciting development threw the seemingly unchallenged Bellanca group into a turmoil, for two new contestants appeared suddenly on fields in Long Island. From out of the west in the late afternoon, came the silvery monoplane, the *Spirit of St. Louis,* piloted by young Captain Charles A. Lindbergh, to settle easily on the turf of Curtiss Field. About the same time, there arrived over Roosevelt Field, Commander Byrd's large Fokker *America,* rebuilt in part, and ready to go.

The two arrivals caused Bellanca to announce a take-off at 5 A.M. the following morning, but the announcement was rescinded after an evening conference between Levine, Bellanca, Bertaud, and Chamberlin at the Garden City Hotel. The reason given was a reported low pressure area over the Grand Banks, but the underlying cause for the new delay was hidden for a time, purposely.

A violent disagreement had erupted again in *Columbia's* camp. Bertaud learned that Wanamaker had made arrangements for the financial security of the families of Byrd's crew, in the event of disaster. His and Chamberlin's contracts with Levine contained no such proviso. Secondly, Bertaud was incensed by the provision stating that all prize moneys would be split fifty-fifty, between Columbia Aircraft Corporation and the crew. Finally, as an airmail pilot, he objected to a paragraph of the agreement which provided that he would work for Columbia Aircraft for a term of one year after the flight.

A long and stormy conference was held on May 15 at the Garden City Hotel. Both pilots were represented by counsel, Clarence W. Nutt, for Bertaud, and Senator Charles C. Lockwood, formerly Levine's attorney, for Chamberlin. At one point, Bertaud stormed out of the meeting, saying, "I'll be damned if I'll work for Levine for a year! I may want to do something else!" But this was a minor point. Bertaud wanted the prize money for himself, and financial security for his wife Helen. At length, Levine relented, and it was agreed that new contracts would be drawn up the following day.

Bellanca, at first, remained out of the controversy, remarking that,

"I have only one enemy now, and that is the Atlantic Ocean. Mr. Levine is just as enthusiastic as I am, and merely wants to prove that our plane can cross the Atlantic." The latter part was in response to attorney Nutt's charge that Levine was trying to delay the flight until someone had succeeded, so that he wouldn't have to risk *Columbia*.

The next day, after all had seemed settled, the battle flared anew. The night before it had been agreed that the pilots would receive all the prize money, and that the one-year employment proviso would be waived. Additionally, it was understood that the flyers' wives would receive $50,000 each, in the event of the death of their husbands; but the new contracts, when produced provided for $12,500 of insurance for Chamberlin, and only $5000 for Bertaud; even more objectionable to them was a new provision giving Levine, in his sole discretion, the right to withdraw either plane or pilots at any time in consideration of a payment of four-weeks expense money. Heated words were exchanged over the new "agreement." Samuel Hartman, an attorney brought in to represent Levine, asked Bertaud why he had signed the original contract.

Bertaud retorted, "We were forced to, or we wouldn't go!"

The area of dispute broadened. It became known that neither Acosta nor Chamberlin had been compensated for their endurance flight. Levine explained this, airily, by maintaining that they had done it for "the glory of it," and, he added, Bertaud should maintain a like spirit about the Paris flight. Ralph Jonas, also present, and Chamberlin and attorney Lockwood, all remained curiously neutral and silent, leaving Bertaud and Nutt to combat Levine and Hartman. Suddenly, the bitter fight turned to the question of the radio, and Levine shifted his position, now, to side with Chamberlin and Bellanca, agreeing with them that it would be too weighty, and a potential fire hazard. Bertaud was furious, for, by this time, he, too, had made an agreement with North American News Alliance to do a story of the flight, including on-the-radio reports!

The battle reached a climax when attorney Hartman reproduced the new contracts for signature. Bertaud refused flatly to sign, as did Chamberlin, on the advice of counselor Lockwood. Bertaud charged that Levine had welched on his agreements of the night before. Levine asked him to withdraw from the flight. Bertaud refused and countered with a threat of legal action. The meeting was adjourned in the wee hours after Bertaud had offered to buy *Columbia* at a price to be determined by independent appraisers, to which Levine rebutted with a demand for $25,000. As the tired, angry men left the smoke-filled hotel room, *Columbia* seemed fated to remain, forever, on the ground. Levine, as he climbed into his car to return to his Belle Harbor, Long Island, home, joshed that he would give $25,000 to fly with Lindbergh, to which the latter replied, laughingly, in the next day's papers, "I'll try and figure out a place to put him!"

The next day the controversial radio was removed finally from *Columbia* at Bellanca's insistence, and with Levine's newly won approval. It was estimated that the removal would add 200 miles to the plane's range, and once again, Bryce Goldsborough was summoned to readjust the compasses. Bertaud when questioned said that though he would have preferred having the radio, its removal would not deter him from going along. Goldsborough joined with Bellanca in his relief over its removal, as he had noticed that the presence of the radio was interfering with the performance of the earth inductor compass. Significantly, Bertaud was not aboard later in the day when *Columbia* made two test flights. In the co-pilot's seat was none other than Charles A. Levine, riding as a passenger.

On May 17, Levine announced that he was looking for a new navigator. Bertaud countered by instructing his attorney to draw up injunction papers, restraining the *Columbia* from taking off without him. At the same time, he read a letter to a gathering of reporters, addressed to Levine. It was a masterpiece, and a well-aimed blow, in the battle between the two men for public sympathy. "I did not enter this flight," it said, "because of money. I did it because I desire to do my part in making aviation history, and because aviation is my life's work. Appreciating as I do the spirit of the donor's prize money, I will accept none for myself, but will donate it to the families of Commander Davis and Lieutenant Wooster, comrades of mine, who died in attempting the flight that I am trying so hard to go on. However, if you insist, I will relinquish to you or your company my share of the prize money. I will not accept one dollar from you or your company for this flight, except for my expenses which I would be glad to pay myself if I were financially able to do so. Although I have asked for protection for my wife in the form of insurance or its equivalent, she does not ask for it and will not accept one dollar." He went on to reiterate his offer to buy the Bellanca monoplane, at a price to be agreed upon.

Levine, now irate, answered Bertaud by saying that he had consulted with Bernt Balchen with regard to flying with Chamberlin.

Balchen, then with Byrd's camp, declined to be considered in the hopes of being added to Byrd's crew.

Bertaud, on May 18, obtained a temporary injunction against Levine and Columbia Aircraft, which was signed by Judge Mitchell May. Argument for a permanent injunction was scheduled for May 20. Whereupon Levine called a peace conference for that evening at his home at Belle Harbor. Bellanca, present at the meeting, wryly congratulated Bertaud on "his ability to land with such glowing success in the newspapers." Nevertheless, it had been Bellanca, anxious for his plane to get started, who was responsible for the conference. The unpredictable Levine changed his tune and agreed that Bertaud would not be replaced, and Bertaud, for his part, agreed to withdraw the injunction papers. All appeared to be sweetness and light between the two, when Bertaud told the press: "An amicable discussion was had at which all differences were satisfactorily adjusted." The conference began at 11:15 P.M., and ended at 2:15 A.M. The tired but happy little Bellanca sighed, "I'm awfully glad that the thing has been practically settled." Lawyers and litigants trudged wearily home, ready to return to their respective duties.

However, the peacemakers were stunned the next day when Levine issued the curt statement that "Bertaud was released three days ago, and now appears to be trying to get back into my good graces. I will fight the injunction, and I will expect the flight to be made with some other pilot than Bertaud, as soon as the weather permits. And," he added significantly, "I already have a pilot in mind to replace Bertaud."

Bertaud pressed his claim before Judge May on the 20th, represented by counselor Nutt. Judge May tried, without success, to reconcile the parties, and then heard argument from both sides. The case was dismissed, and the judge's opinion said, in part, that the original contract had been repudiated by Bertaud, and that "the new negotiations did not constitute a waiver of the repudiation." The injunction was denied, and Bertaud was out of the crew. Levine had won after all. For a time, Bertaud returned to his Cleveland-to-Hadley Field mail run, disappointed, but confident that another chance would come. And come it did before the summer was out.

Chamberlin, in the meantime, had kept quiet. To be sure, he wanted to be a part of any new agreement, but his place was assured, in that he was supported solidly by Bellanca, and later, Levine. But who would go with him? Speculation was rife. Balchen was mentioned still, despite his reluctance. So was young Lieutenant Charles Fields, an Annapolis graduate with 1000 flying hours, but Levine would say only that "my new navigator will not be announced until just before the start." But, when would *Columbia* go? She was ready, with *NEW YORK TO PARIS* painted proudly on her fuselage, standing idle and waiting. Giuseppe Bellanca's patience was virtually gone. He was tired of the waiting, the constant bickering, and the ever-changing crew. He knew his plane could make the flight; he had done everything to expedite the take-off including an unpleasant mediation in an impossible dispute—which had proven a failure. The quiet, dark-haired little genius didn't understand the flamboyant and vacillating personality of the dynamic Levine. He didn't want to. All he wanted was to see his designing ability fulfilled by the successful Atlantic flight of his plane. Now the wish seemed further than ever from realization.

CHAPTER VI

The Lone Eagle

1. At the Ryan Company's plant in San Diego, work on Lindbergh's monoplane, *Spirit of St. Louis,* was in its final stage. Mahoney, the young president, had instructed that work on other orders should be suspended, and all efforts concentrated on the Paris-bound plane. Donald Hall showed the way, as he directed the entire work force in an all-out attempt to finish the ship quickly, and it looked now as though the *Spirit of St. Louis* would be ready to fly at the end of the month.

"Slim" painstakingly plotted maps in 100-mile segments, a distance he expected to cover on each hour of flight. He planned to navigate by dead reckoning, and despite warnings that he might drift off course, he was convinced that he would be safe, for, as he answered the experts at Rockwell Field, it would be hard to miss the entire European continent! He decided definitely to dispense with a sextant for the simple reason that he could not fly the plane and operate it at the same time.

The instruments and emergency equipment he thought important enough to carry, arrived. The equipment was stored temporarily, and the instruments were assembled and installed with speed and accuracy by the Ryan crew. They, too, felt a part of the race, as they read the daily dispatches from the camps of the other crews. They felt a part of history, and everyone rushed, but with care, for they were all aware that one misplaced bolt could spell disaster.

Plans still needed to be made for gasoline—Lindbergh hoped in vain that it would be provided by an oil company without cost for the cross-country flight to New York via St. Louis. He thought about the weather, and a myriad of other details. He wanted all preparations complete, insofar as was possible, by the time his plane was ready to be tested, for then his thoughts would be on the Ryan, alone.

He read of Chamberlin's endurance record, and of Nungesser's statement that he would leave on April 24. All he could do was to keep
working with all possible speed, and hope.

The great day arrived when the *Spirit of St. Louis* was to be
moved to Dutch Flats, the Ryan Company's test field. The fuselage,
silvery and shimmering, was loaded aboard a waiting truck together
with the 46-foot wing—which had to be squeezed through the doors
as it was longer than any of Ryan's previous designs. The number
NX-211 stood out clearly, painted in large block figures on the right
tip. Workmen gathered around with a look of nostalgia as their
"baby," now complete except for assembly, left the nursery for the
last time.

The plans called for the early tests to be held at Dutch Flats, and
the later ones, involving loads, at the long, level strip on the remote
Camp Kearney Army base. Lindbergh picked the Army base mainly
to avoid the increasing number of newsmen and inquisitive onlookers,
but also, to take advantage of the bigger field when he would be flying
the *Spirit of St. Louis* weighted down heavily with gasoline.

On April 28, the plane, shining in the bright sunlight, stood
ready for her first test flight. Lindbergh climbed into his cramped
cockpit and looked around. Above was a rectangular skylight type of
window, which, together with the two fuselage windows on each side
of him, constituted his only means of view. He had no forward
vision, only an instrument panel in front of him, containing nine
dials. It was a tiny little "office," but it was adequate. All was ready.
The mechanic turned the propeller three times, and then, with a
violent kick and swing, pulled the prop through, and the powerful
engine caught at once, and roared into action as "Slim" opened the
throttle. The wheel chocks were removed, and he taxied downfield
into position, turned, and took off. The plane rose easily and fast, and
he circled, first over the Ryan factory, and then out over Rockwell
Field, to show her off to those on the ground. She responded instantly to his touch, and her immense power was something he'd
never felt when flying the DHs and Jennys with their old Liberty
engines. He tried her out in banks and stalls, and she reacted normally and efficiently. He dropped to 1000 feet and opened the throttle wide, and watched delightedly as the air speed indicator needle
inched up to 128 miles an hour. He eased back on the stick, and she
zoomed up to 3000 feet, where, in order to get a "feel" of the new
plane, he proceeded to put her through every known flying maneuver.

He was encouraged as he brought her back to a gentle landing on the strip at Dutch Flats. Don Hall met him as the ship rolled to a stop.

"Charlie," he said with pride, "it only took you 6⅛ seconds to get off the ground!" They walked off the field together, happy over the performance, but talking, already of slight adjustments to correct the minor flaws that Lindbergh had detected; but neither saw any reason why plane and pilot could not be in New York, ready to take off, in two or three weeks.

2. Early May, for Lindbergh, was spent in the thorough flight testing of the *Spirit of St. Louis*. She was put through every type of maneuver, to check carefully both speed and structural strength as well as climbing ability. Methodically, he kept charts on her performance, and he and designer Hall at the end of each day examined them to see where adjustments were needed and improvements could be made. It was noted by Lindbergh that stability wasn't one of the plane's strong points, but Hall explained the fact, by pointing out that he had retained the standard-sized tail assembly of the Ryan M-2, while adding to the design's wing surface. He added that it was done to save construction time. Lindbergh wasn't concerned with the lack of stability. He could handle the ship so long as the motor ran and she remained airborne. His main worry was to get her off the ground with enough fuel to reach Paris.

The vital load tests were begun at the parade grounds at Camp Kearney, away from prying newsmen and spectators. Speed tests over a marked course had been successful. At times, the indicator touched 130 mph, which was more than satisfactory, and the revolutions per minute reached their maximum of 1950. Throttled back to 1500 rpms, the plane was able to maintain a speed of 96 mph, which pleased the young pilot.

The weight tests proved equally successful, as he took off from the long field with an added 50 gallons on each hop. He found that the *Spirit of St. Louis* rose quickly every time, using only a few more yards of runway with each load increase. After a test with 300 gallons aboard (the plane was scheduled to carry 425 on the Paris flight), Lindbergh called a halt, though Hall wanted to try 350. "Slim" didn't want to jeopardize the whole flight by trying to land with such a load on the moderately bumpy field. Like Nungesser he didn't want to tempt fate more than once. True, his plane had gotten off the ground with 300 gallons in 28 seconds (Nungesser's final take-off had taken 48), but he felt that his undercarriage had absorbed a beating, both at take-off, and on landing. It was also true that he'd have to lift off a heavier load on his way to Paris, but in all probability the runway would be smoother, and he'd either make it or he wouldn't; when he arrived in Paris, there would be no problem, for the plane would have but a few gallons remaining in her tanks.

"Slim" was now ready. Nungesser and Coli were listed officially as missing. What a combination of circumstances, he thought. Out of all the planes, only the Bellanca was still in the running. His immediate plans were for an overnight flight to Lambert Field, St. Louis, and, hopefully, after a night's rest, a flight on to New York for the big attempt. He worried about banquets that might have been planned in St. Louis. The flight was a city project, after all, and he'd have to abide by the wishes of his backers with respect to them. But he hoped he'd be ready to go on quickly, for he knew Bellanca's plane was ready to go.

The weather across the country on the morning of May 10 was favorable, with a low pressure area moving eastward from the Pacific Coast, leaving in its wake, strong tail winds. Lindbergh packed his few belongings in a battered suitcase. They included one business suit for use in St. Louis and New York. He dropped in and said good-bye to the men at the factory who had worked hard and long for him. They wished him luck. His schedule called for an afternoon departure from Rockwell Field, so as to reach Kansas in daylight early the next morning. He selected Rockwell, rather than the parade grounds at Kearney, because of its relative smoothness, and the length of the runway. He telegraphed Pioneer Instruments in New York to have a representative meet him there, to give his instruments, most particularly his troublesome earth inductor a final check. Then, he made the quick flight to North Island, where, as he said good-bye to his Navy friends, gasoline from a waiting truck was poured into the plane's tanks, until they were filled to one-half capacity—ample for the trip to St. Louis.

He returned to the field and climbed into his flying suit. It was hot under the California sun, but it would turn cold, he knew, during the night. The engine was started and warmed. He taxied into position, gunned the engine, and rose after a short run. He made a wide 180-degree turn to the left and headed east, accompanied for a time by a large convoy of aircraft, carrying friends from Rockwell and the Ryan factory, and, of course, the press.

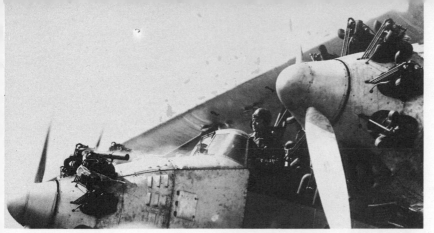

1. René Fonck in cockpit of *New York to Paris*.

2. Commander Noel Davis *(left)*
and Lieutenant "Bob" Wooster
in cockpit of
American Legion.

3. The tragic end of *American Legion*.

4. Captain Charles Nungesser in full uniform.

5. *Oiseau Blanc* arriving at Le Bourget from Villacoublay.

6. Nungesser *(right) and*
   Coli prior to take-off.

7. One of last views of *Oiseau Blanc* as she
heads for the French coast.

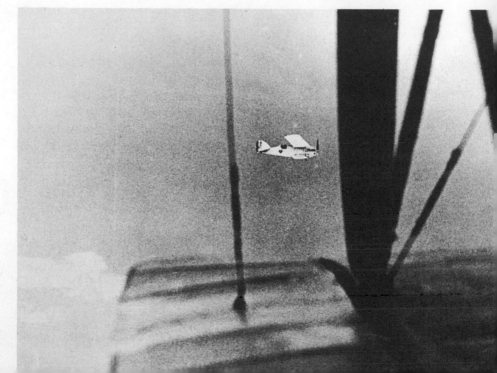

8. The competitors meet at Curtiss Field.
Lindbergh *(left)* greets Chamberlin as Byrd looks on.

9. Giuseppe Bellanca.

10. *(From left to right)* "Rex" Noville, Floyd Bennett, Commander Richard E. Byrd, and Bert Acosta in front of *America* at Roosevelt Field.

11. Tony Fokker, Bernt Balchen, and Commander Byrd perched on *America's* wing.

12. *Spirit of St. Louis* on her way from Curtiss to
Roosevelt Field just prior to take-off for Paris.

13. "Slim" waves from cockpit.

14. German policeman examines *Columbia* after her landing at Kottbus, Germany.

15. Chamberlin *(foreground)* after successful flight. Levine *(in business suit)* walks behind.

16. Chamberlin *(left)*, Levine, and Maurice Drouhin at Le Bourget.

17. Levine, in new white togs, with Hinchcliffe
in cockpit of *Columbia* at Cranwell.

18. *America* in sea off Ver-sur-Mer, France, after forced landing.

The flight in its early stages went smoothly. He was over Arizona as the sun went down, flying at 5000 feet. Below he could make out, barely, the tracks of the Santa Fe Railroad. Later, as darkness came on, he eased the ship up to 8000 feet while scanning constantly the luminous dials on the control panel to make sure that all was in order. They were registering properly. He settled back in the cockpit as the plane sped on through the night.

A sudden sputter and vibration of the engine roused him from the lethargy brought on by the untroubled flight. He looked below. Mountains! A forced landing here, particularly at night, would be disastrous. He glanced at the instrument panel. The fuel pressure was up—but the motor still sputtered and kicked. The joystick trembled in his firm grip. Slowly, the plane began to sink as the engine continued to lose power. He worked the mixture control. The motor still missed. Again, he glanced below. He couldn't make out much in the darkness. He began to circle, and thought of returning to the west for a better landing spot. But as he got lower, miraculously, the engine smoothed out. San Diego was five hours behind him. He decided to go on, and returned to his course. At lower altitudes the sputtering almost ceased, but when it was necessary to climb, occasionally as high as 13000 feet to clear a peak of the Rockies, the coughing and vibrating started again. Soon, though, the Rockies were behind him, enabling him to descend to 6000 feet, as he approached Oklahoma.

The night passed as he flew eastward, the engine running evenly now in the warmer air of the lower altitude, and the early pink in the eastern sky heralding the new day ahead. He flew over Kansas, and soon saw below the winding Missouri River which marked the Kansas-Missouri border. He flew swiftly across the state and finally at 6 A.M. he spotted the familiar outline of Lambert Field. He circled the city of St. Louis, buzzed Lambert Field at full throttle, and slid in to a three-point landing at 6:20 A.M. California time, 14 hours and 25 minutes after leaving Rockwell.

Harry Knight arrived and told a thankful Lindbergh he would be spared the dreaded banquets and celebrations, and that he was free to go to New York whenever he was ready.

He spent the day at Harry Knight's house, and the next morning, at 8:13 A.M., was off again in a clear sky, headed for New York. In a short 7 hours he was circling over the tall buildings of Manhattan. In a matter of minutes, he was over Long Island. He spotted three fields below, two almost adjacent to each other, which he thought must be Curtiss and Roosevelt, and the one to the right, with the greenish-brown hangars, Mitchel, the Army field.

He circled, and, at 5:33 P.M., EST, brought the *Spirit of St. Louis* into Curtiss Field after a flight of 7 hours and 20 minutes. He was greeted immediately by signs of things to come, as photographers, amateur and professional, newsreel cameramen and reporters swarmed around his plane. He was, after all, a newspaperman's dream—young, single, photogenic, and about to fly across the Atlantic Ocean alone. They would make his days in New York miserable with constant questions and requests for pictures, together with fabricated human interest stories and interference into his family life. He disliked it, already, but he would learn to tolerate it.

"Slim" was greeted by "Casey" Jones, the field manager, who showed him the hangar assigned to his plane; then, to "Spoons" Boedeker of Wright, who had been assigned to care for his engine. Lindbergh explained that he had to call Pioneer to arrange for an instrument check, but there was no need, for Boedeker beckoned to a young man, peering already into the window of the *Spirit of St. Louis*. It was Bryce Goldsborough. A representative of Vacuum Oil Company, who had agreed to supply his gasoline, introduced himself, and there were, always, the interminable questions, flashbulbs, the shoving, shouting newsmen, and the giggling young girls, ogling coyly at the handsome young flyer.

A loud noise was heard overhead, and all eyes looked up. "It's the Fokker!" somebody said. Lindbergh was amazed at the speed with which repairs had been made on the Byrd machine, as he watched her bank and settle toward a landing at nearby Roosevelt Field. Another competitor was on the starting line.

The *Columbia* stood in a hangar close by. In the maelstrom and excitement, Lindbergh heard a yell, "Hey, there's Chamberlin and Bertaud!" He didn't see them, for he was rushed off to a press conference.

The young man, in Army khaki pants and puttees, with an open-necked shirt, was then exposed to more questions from a large and inquisitive gathering of correspondents.

"When will you take off?"

"When my engine has been serviced, new compasses installed, and the weather clears."

"Will it be in the morning?"

"I can't answer that. I'll go when everything is right."

There were many other questions, some of a technical nature, regarding his decisions on the radio, sextant, and life raft; others were of an annoying, personal nature, and were reeled off faster than he wanted to think.

"Do you have a girl friend?" "Do you like girls?" "Will your mother come to see you off?" Finally free, though exhausted, he went to the nearby Garden City Hotel for a well-deserved rest.

The next day he caught up on the news of his competition. *Columbia* had not left because of weather and personnel trouble, which, he was told, had nothing to do with Bellanca or Chamberlin, who were champing at the bit to get away. There was no news of Nungesser and Coli, except for a rumor that they'd been picked up at sea. Byrd's Fokker was ready again, as he'd seen yesterday, though Floyd Bennett was still in the hospital and Byrd was walking around with a cast on his wrist. Lindbergh decided on a Roosevelt Field take-off, because of its mile-long runway, longer than either Curtiss or Mitchel. He was assured that he'd have no difficulty in getting permission to use it from Byrd.

The ensuing days were the most hectic of Lindbergh's young life. Crowds of New Yorkers, stimulated by stories in the papers, swarmed to Curtiss Field to see the young curly haired "dark horse" and his plane. On Saturday, May 14, there were an estimated 10,000 people at Curtiss and nearby Roosevelt, with 4000 automobiles parked at random. On Sunday, 30,000 mobbed the fields, and traffic jams of modern-day proportions clogged every road in the vicinity. Reporters and cameramen were always around with their incessant questions and blinding flashbulbs.

"What are you going to do about Ambassador Herrick's warning?" a reporter shouted over the hubbub.

"I'll abide by any advice from the State Department," the youngster replied sagely.

"Can you stay awake long enough?"

"I've been awake for forty hours at a stretch many times," was the answer.

"Slim," realizing the value of good public relations to his backers, remained cool and polite, albeit tired and annoyed by all the commotion. Every edition came out with new human interest yarns on the "Flying Fool" or the "Lone Eagle." The idea men were on the spot, too. One show business entrepreneur tried, in vain, to have a dancer in costume photographed doing a split on the plane's propeller! Mail addressed to him poured in—love letters, good luck letters, crank letters, together with charms of all varieties. He yearned for solitude—

just an hour to himself—but it was hopeless. Dick Blythe, assigned by Wright to stay at his side, was helpful in keeping away the curious and in maintaining a modicum of order in his dealings with the press, but it was hectic and always noisy. Photographers, anxious for special shots, had the audacity to break into the privacy of his room; they were ushered out, politely, swiftly, and very firmly.

There were police assigned to guard him and his plane. Nassau County patrolmen, under the direction of Captain Frank McCahill, were a necessary nuisance to him, but did their job well controlling the huge crowds that surrounded, forever, the *Spirit of St. Louis*.

His mother, Mrs. Evangeline Lodge Lindbergh, a widowed school-teacher from Detroit, arrived to spend a day with him. She wanted to see her son to make sure that he was doing exactly what he wanted, in making the flight. She, too, was engulfed by the crowds and hoopla, and newsmen with their probing questions. The turmoil surrounding her visit became so oppressive to mother and son, that he put her on a train for home, 24 hours later.

On the field, "Spoons" Boedeker, Ed Mulligan, and later Ken Lane from Wright proceeded to overhaul the Whirlwind engine. After hearing from Lindbergh of his engine trouble on the flight east, they decided that it had been caused, most likely, by the cold air at high altitudes, and they installed a carburetor heater. On Saturday, May 14, "Slim" arrived at the field early, to find that his propeller had been removed. The ever-watchful Boedeker and Mulligan had uncovered a crack in the spinner and were awaiting the arrival of a new propeller from Paterson, provided by Wright without charge.

The arrival of Lindbergh had an immediate effect on the rival camps. Electric lights burned all night in *Columbia*'s hangar as Giuseppe Bellanca, John Carisi, and others of the ground crew, raced with final preparations, despite the Bertaud lawsuit being head-lined in the papers. Boedeker and Mulligan, the Wright men, were called on to service her engine, too, and, from time to time, even lent a helping hand to "Doc" Kinkaid at Roosevelt as he worked over the Fokker. They were professionals and gave unstintingly to each crew the benefit of their experience.

Up at the big hangar which housed the tri-motored *America*, Tony Fokker supervised last-minute adjustments, as *America*'s flyers strove to get back into the race. Bert Acosta, recently with Levine, had been added to the crew to replace the injured Floyd Bennett, and made daily test flights. Commander Byrd, Lieutenant Noville, and young Bernt Balchen were always on the scene working, and hoping for an early take-off. Rumors spread to the other camps that Byrd was so nearly ready that he was already loading food supplies, but they were discounted when meteorological reports disclosed bad weather all over the North Atlantic.

There were endless queries over the possible fate of the Nungesser ship from all camps. There had been no word, but there was a report that a Coast Guard boat had picked up a plane's wing off Montauk Point, and was bringing it in for identification.

Despite the crowds, Lindbergh continued methodically with his work. He, too, had heard stories of activity in the other camps, but he was determined not to leave until everything was ready to his satisfaction. Test flights were made with Boedeker and Mulligan to try out the overhauled engine, the new prop, and the carburetor heater. They were of short duration and successful, for the engine purred comfortably, even at higher altitudes. The flights were hampered only by a broken tail skid, caused by a frantic turn after landing to avoid an intrepid photographer lying on the field trying pictures from a new angle.

On Sunday, May 15, with the huge crowd present, "Slim" took Bryce Goldsborough up on several flights, for the purpose of final adjustment to the compass, and to test a new earth inductor compass. Lindbergh prolonged the flight, soaring for extra minutes out over Long Island, despite the crowded cabin, to get a few minutes of respite from the maelstrom on the field below.

Commander Byrd paid a special visit to Lindbergh's hangar and extended a courteous welcome, during which he not only offered the use of Roosevelt Field to Lindbergh, but agreed to exchange weather information. The photographers learned quickly of this informal get-together and the two rivals were forced to pose stoically, and interminably, for pictures. The photography was interrupted only when an enterprising newsman spotted Chamberlin, and corraled him as well.

On Monday, Lindbergh stole off again, this time climbing the hill to Roosevelt Field where he proceeded to examine every foot of the runway for depressions and bumps, and for firmness. The softness and narrowness of the prepared strip, he thought, could have been improved upon, but it was long enough to give the *Spirit of St. Louis* an excellent chance at getting off with its heavy load which had now become heavier by 150 pounds. He had found out that his tanks held, actually, 25 more gallons than had been planned, so that his total fuel capacity would be 450 gallons. He calculated, though, that the plane hadn't burned much oil on the cross-country flight, so he could eliminate 35 pounds by carrying only 20 gallons of oil instead of 25.

He returned to the field to find his friend, and now rival, Bellanca, who greeted him warmly, offering also to exchange weather information and to help him in any way he could. Again, there were the photographers and the endless explosions of flashbulbs as the little Sicilian-born designer and the tall, young airmail pilot clasped hands, with smiles frozen on their faces.

Someone found a kitten, which gave birth to another "human interest" story. The kitten was placed on the wing of the plane, and "Slim" posed, patiently alongside. A rash of stories followed, accompanied by the blown-up photos, which played up an animal-loving Lindbergh, who would carry as a mascot on his flight a gentle little kitten! Despite these stories, which he considered ridiculous, Lindbergh had respect for many of the reporters—particularly, Russell Owen of the New York *Times*, with whose help he negotiated an agreement for the exclusive story of his flight with the *Times*. Naturally, "Slim" had obtained prior approval for the arrangement from Harry Knight in St. Louis, and he was pleased, for it would enable him to repay some of the investors' money.

The weather over the North Atlantic was reported unfavorable as the week progressed. On Wednesday, May 18, he took the advice of Wright's Dick Blythe and traveled into New York to neet James "Doc" Kimball, the noted forecaster, at the U. S. Weather Bureau. Kimball, Michigan born, attended the University of Virginia, and had been in New York with the Weather Bureau since the 1890s. He was one of the leading meteorological experts in the country. He was gracious and friendly to the young flyer, and spread his sparsely plotted North Atlantic maps over a broad table. Together they pored over them, Kimball pointing out the various low pressure areas, and heavy fogs and rains that dotted his course. He apologized to "Slim" for the scanty information on the map over the Great Circle route, explaining that all of his ocean weather data came from ships at sea, in the ship lanes, situated south of his route. But Kimball promised to keep careful watch on conditions, though he advised against an immediate take-off. Lindbergh returned to the field, disheartened, and yet relieved over the reports—depressed because he couldn't go, and relieved that *Columbia* and *America* wouldn't, in all probability, take off either. He busied himself with another thorough inspection of his plane— and ended up by removing six heavy batteries which provided the power to illuminate his cockpit and instrument panel. It would save weight, and, besides, he thought, the lights were too bright, and he'd carry a flashlight which would be sufficient.

He was a guest for a late lunch at the home of Theodore Roosevelt, Jr., in Oyster Bay, which was a peaceful and welcome change. He was shown over historic Sagamore Hill, the home of the late President, and given special introductions to Ambassador Herrick and other important acquaintances of Roosevelt's in France.

Thursday, May 19, was overcast with a light rain falling. A check with "Doc" Kimball disclosed that the weather en route to Paris was not much better. A dense fog blanketed Nova Scotia and Newfoundland, and a heavy storm was reported moving in over the western part of France. He wouldn't go today, he thought, and accepted, gladly, when Dick Blythe came up with some seats to the evening performance of Florenz Ziegfeld's musical, *Rio Rita*. The papers were filled with stories on the personnel battle in *Columbia's* camp. Commander Byrd had remained mum of late, though there were the constant rumors he might be ready to go. B. F. Mahoney, Ryan's president, just off the train from San Diego, arrived at the field, and with "Slim," Ken Lane, and Dick Blythe drove over to the Wright plant in Paterson to spend the afternoon in comparative quiet, away from the crowds. There was little left to be done to the plane save the final loading. She was as fit and ready as she could be made.

It was raining as the four headed for the Ziegfeld Theatre in New York in the evening. They were a relaxed group, for take-off did not seem to be imminent because of the weather. One of them was singing "The Ranger's Song" from *Rio Rita* as they drove along glistening and wet 42nd Street on their way to the theater. Suddenly Lindbergh, who had been quiet, suggested they drop into the Weather Bureau, just in case. They found "Doc" Kimball bent over his maps, sketching in artistic isobars. He greeted them warmly, with an eager look on his face, for he had hopeful news—the weather over the North Atlantic was clearing, and there appeared to be an excellent chance of clear skies and moderate to strong tail winds along a good portion of the route. Forgotten at once was the theater, as the foursome raced back to Curtiss Field. On arrival, Lindbergh glanced toward the Bellanca hangar to see if they'd heard the news and were getting ready. He could see no lights, and no signs of activity. The Fokker's christening was scheduled for the next day, so he felt he was safe from a Byrd challenge. In no time, Boedeker and Mulligan appeared and joined Ken Lane in a final check of the Whirlwind while other attendants prepared to load the little plane to capacity with the precious oil and fuel that stood in large metal drums, around the hangar. How would he get to Roosevelt Field? He couldn't risk flying in the rain, darkness, and mist that hung heavily over Long Island. He ordered that the fueling be de-load would be suicidal.

After all final preparations were attended to, it was well past 11 P.M., and Lindbergh returned to the Garden City Hotel to try and snatch a few hours' sleep. He'd get none tomorrow night. He left orders to be awakened at 2:30 A.M. He slept fitfully, being wakened once by a well-intentioned, though thoughtless well-wisher. It was 2:30 in no time. He got up, dressed, and drove quickly to Curtiss Field where he noticed that the fueling had begun. He was told that a way had been found to tow the plane up to Roosevelt Field. It was raining still, and pitch black out with the lights reflecting on the wet pavements, as the fueling continued, and Lindbergh made a last check of his cockpit. He'd carry only five chicken sandwiches and a canteen of water. There'd be enough time to eat in Paris, and food would just make him sleepy. Anyhow, he'd discarded the Army chocolate rations after tasting them. They were not very appetizing.

At 4 A.M. the fueling was complete. A tarpaulin was placed around the engine of the *Spirit of St. Louis*, and her tail assembly was tied to the back of a truck. Slowly, she was towed off, tail-first with rain falling on her shimmering fuselage, toward Roosevelt Field. Lindbergh, before following her, made a telephone call to New York for a final weather check. The Bureau reported local showers, but clear weather en route. The latest observations showed Chatham, Massachusetts, clear with no wind: Cape Breton and Sydney, Nova Scotia, clear weather with a light westerly, and St. John's, Newfoundland, clear with a temperature of 40 degrees and moderate westerly winds. Good old "Doc" Kimball! He'd hit it on the head. Lindbergh would have perfect weather up the coast, and would be able to get accurate bearings over Newfoundland before heading over the ocean, and the westerly flow of air would add to his cruising speed.

3.   It was daybreak. The *Spirit of St. Louis* stood at the west end of Roosevelt Field, only yards from the embankment leading down to Curtiss. She was pointed east, headed down the long, one-mile runway of clay and sand, which was soft and soggy from the all-night rain. The wind was light and variable. Earlier, it had blown from the east, but just before daybreak, it had shifted, and now came in on the tail of the plane, but not strongly enough to change the direction of the take-off. Yet Lindbergh, now seated in his cramped cockpit, and bundled up in his flying suit and helmet, wished that he had a strong head wind to help his heavy ship off the soft field. She was carrying 5135 pounds. He glanced out of the cockpit into the slipstream of his idling engine. He noticed the wheels had sunk several inches into the wet clay. Around stood a group of spectators including Fokker, Bellanca, Boedeker, Lane, Mahoney, Blythe, and other friends and workers. Mechanics stood braced against the struts to help the plane get its initial momentum.

It was still gray and drizzling, and the watchers stood under a vast tent of umbrellas. The young pilot leaned out again, and looked down the runway. At the end, he could see the telephone wires he would have to clear. He couldn't help wondering if the plane would lift off and get over them. He noticed that his tachometer registered 30 rpm low as he ran up his engine, and the plane rocked against the restraining wheel chocks, but Ken Boedeker had said that it was natural in damp weather. He checked his instrument panel; the dials indicated that all was normal. He took another quick look down the runway and noticed the little pools of rainwater that had gathered. The *Spirit of St. Louis* would have to splash through them, he thought, and they would slow her, but there was no time left to wonder. Outside waited the mechanics and engineers, the policemen and friends who had served him so well. He strapped himself in, pulled down his goggles, waved to the men to pull the wheel chocks clear, and opened the throttle wide. He was, at last, on his way.

The heavy plane began to move. He watched the mechanics,

straining mightily, as they pushed at the wing struts. It seemed hopeless. The engine whined, as if to protest against the back-breaking load. The stick wobbled uselessly in his hand. Then he noticed objects passing by his cabin window with more speed. The plane was moving faster. Water splashed up as the wheels sped through the little pools. At 2000 feet he eased back slowly on the tightening control stick. The plane lifted, and then sank back, but it was gaining momentum. At 3000 feet she lifted off again for a few feet, and then settled back. She was almost flying, but the runway was getting shorter. At 4200 feet, with 800 feet remaining, she was airborne—ten feet up and then fifteen feet, as the dreaded telephone wires rushed toward her. Up she inched, motor roaring. The wires flashed by, a bare twenty feet under the fuselage. He would make it now. There'd be no crash, he thought with elation. Slowly she continued her climb, as the golf course slid by underneath her. Almost 200 feet of altitude had been gained painfully, sufficient to avoid the tree-topped hillocks in the vicinity; he pointed her nose at Long Island Sound, gray and gloomy in the distance under the heavy overcast.

On the ground, meanwhile, spectators watched breathlessly as the silvery monoplane lumbered slowly and heavily down the runway. They could make out SPIRIT OF ST. LOUIS painted in black on her pointed nose, as mechanics, pushing at the struts, ran with her for almost 100 yards. She was moving so laboriously, they thought, she'd never make it. Then, one by one, the mechanics dropped off as she picked up speed. Mahoney, Boedeker, Lane, Blythe, and others of the ground crew eyed her nervously as her wheels sluiced through puddle after puddle. Finally, she appeared to be off—then she was down—then off again. Once more she hit the runway, but more lightly this time. At last, over three-quarters of the way down the field, she rose slowly. She'd never clear the wires, they worried, but she did. At their distance, it seemed so close that they could not believe his wheels had not at least touched. They watched her as she faded in the distance, with the powerful roar of her Whirlwind lessening to a gentle buzz. The Spirit of St. Louis was on her way to Paris at 7:50 A.M. on Friday, May 20, 1927. The "dark horse" had gotten the jump on his competition.

There were reports of a visual sighting of the little monoplane over New London, Connecticut, at a few minutes before 9 A.M., and she was described as flying low and fast. Shortly thereafter, she was sighted flying over Narragansett Bay, and then, Providence,

Rhode Island, where, it was reported that the weather was clearing; and she was seen over Cape Cod, as she tackled her first over-the-water hop—250 miles to Nova Scotia. It was 10 A.M.

As Lindbergh headed to sea, he flew just above the waves to take advantage of the smoother air; his air speed indicator showed that he was making 100 miles an hour. Already, he felt stiff and cramped in the tiny cockpit, but he knew from experience that the feeling would soon pass. The sun beat down on him through the window on top of the fuselage. He was hot, and beginning to be sleepy. So soon, he thought! What'll it be like tomorrow? He climbed to 1000 feet, in the hopes that the change in altitude and cooler air would reinvigorate him. He cupped his hand in the slip-stream to direct cool air in his face. It helped. On he flew over the endless blue waves. There wasn't a boat in sight—just the water and the sky.

At noon, Lindbergh was sighted at St. Mary Bay on the western coast of Nova Scotia, headed northeast on a course for Newfoundland. For three hours, he was spotted at various points as he flew the length of the peninsula. It was rugged country—lakes, timberlands, marshes, and hills. This would not be a good place for a forced landing, he thought. Ahead he noticed clouds gathering slowly above the low, fair-weather cumulus. He flew on, while the large gray mass came creeping closer. He glanced at his altimeter and air speed indicator; they showed him at 900 feet with a speed of a little over 100 mph. Below, the lakes and ponds were streaked now by a heavy wind blowing out of the west onto the plane's port beam. He would have to watch his course more closely.

The little ship began to bump more violently as she flew nearer the darkening skies in the north. Dark patches like rays extended down from the clouds, pointing up heavy rain squalls. Gone now was the brilliant sunshine, as the plane jounced along in the turbulence. Thankfully, he thought, the ship was lighter than at take-off. He hit, suddenly, the first of a series of squalls—and a second, and, yet, another, each heavier than the last. He gripped tightly on the stick as the plane was buffeted about. Lightning flashed around him; he left his course for a time, and flew around the worst of the weather, weaving in and out of the mushrooming clouds, which soared high, dark, and fearsome around him. Rain sprayed over the wings, and off the whirling propeller, but the sturdy little ship plowed along steadily. Almost as suddenly as they came, the squalls were behind him, and the *Spirit of St. Louis* again shining in the sunlight, flew serenely on her course.

It was midafternoon as Lindbergh flew off the coast of Cape Breton Island, and headed for the tip of the Burin Peninsula, Newfoundland, beyond St. Pierre and Miquelon. He'd been in the air for 8 hours, and was 800 miles from Roosevelt Field. He glanced in a small cosmetic mirror, taped on the instrument panel which allowed him to read the earth inductor compass dial over his head. It had been the only place Bryce Goldsborough could find for it, and the numbers had been painted backward for mirror reading. "Slim" was on course. Below was the rugged shoreline of Cape Breton, rising to steep mountains. They passed quickly underneath him as the *Spirit of St. Louis* fled to her final rendezvous with land at Newfoundland.

He set a course from the Burin Peninsula, which would carry him across Placentia Bay, a narrow strip of the Avalon Peninsula, and across Concepcion Bay, with the idea of flying over the little city of St. John's before darkness set in, so that the people below could see him, and send word back that he had, at least, flown that far. He was over the water once more, and again became aware of how sleepy he was. The feeling had left him over Nova Scotia while he battled the squalls, but the return of the smooth flight over the endless water, together with the bright sunlight streaming in on him, brought back the heavy-lidded lethargy. It became a struggle to keep his eyes open. He squirmed in his seat, stamped his feet, and leaned out into the slipstream. It was no good. He still yearned to sleep. Suddenly, he noticed the blue of the water ahead of him turn white and shiny in the sunlight. He blinked. Had he been asleep? As he came closer, he saw that it was an ice field, spreading out without end. He dropped down close to the surface, and the patches of ice flashed by the plane at a breakneck clip. From time to time, he extended his periscope for a forward view. There was nothing ahead but ice and the sky. He was an hour off Cape Breton now; in another hour, he'd be over Placentia Bay.

It was 6 P.M. as he passed over the hill-ringed tip of the Burin Peninsula, and headed across wide Placentia Bay. He was, at last, over Newfoundland. To his right, the Atlantic Ocean spread out endlessly to the horizon. He was forced to pay constant attention to flying. He knew the *Spirit of St. Louis* wasn't the stablest of planes because of her undersized tail assembly. She had a tendency to climb and veer off course unless strict care was taken with her elevators and rudder. The effort, though, served to keep him awake. Soon, the bleak and mountainous Avalon Peninsula was passing under him. The sun was low in the west as evening approached, and the valleys between the mountain peaks were a shadowy, dark color. It was not long before he flew over the southern end of Concepcion Bay. The sun was setting. He'd been aloft for 11 hours, and was now 1100 miles out. The 100-mile-an-hour average pleased him. The Bay was soon left behind, and the city of St. John's appeared under him; it was built around a great harbor, dotted with wharves and little fishing boats, and surrounded by mountains and cliffs, now purpled by the shadows of evening. He eased the stick forward and dove down on the little community; he wanted to be seen once more before he exposed himself and his little plane to the rigors of the broad Atlantic. Over the harbor he streaked, Signal Hill with its Cabot Tower jutting up to his left; then, his pleasuresome frolic over, he pointed the plane's nose seaward. The trip over St. John's had been expensive, for it had left him 90 miles south of his Great Circle course. He compensated by dialing a new heading into his earth inductor compass. Speedily, the friendly Newfoundland coast faded aft into the gathering dusk, and disappeared into the distance. Now, there was only ocean ahead and almost 2000 miles of it.

He was more confident. He had fuel aplenty, was keeping close to his time schedule, and had a tail wind. Furthermore, the smooth-running Whirlwind hadn't missed a beat. Except for his sleepiness, he couldn't have asked for a less-troubled trip. He noted occasional fog patches as he flew over a large field of icebergs, but nothing to worry about. He'd traveled 1200 miles now; one-third of the flight was over, and all was well.

He kept a careful check on his gasoline consumption. For an hour, he flew on the outer wing tanks, switched to the center wing tanks, and then to the tanks in the nose and in the fuselage. He planned to fly during the night on the latter two, so that if the fuel pump failed at any time later on, he could feed the engine from the wing tanks by force of gravity. A fog bank, heavy and blinding, came upon him. He eased back on the stick, and the *Spirit of St. Louis* climbed from 900 feet to 2000 feet, above the gray layer. He continued his climb to 5000 feet. It was dark out. A few stars were faintly visible in the haze. Directly below the plane was a billowing layer of cloud, rising, forcing the plane to higher and higher levels of escape. He looked at his tachometer; it read 1625 rpms—an economical setting. He knew the tail wind was pushing him along faster than the 90-mile-an-hour reading on his air speed indicator, but he didn't know how much faster; yet he was conserving fuel. The sleepiness had left him in the cool night air. He was alert, his mind now stimulated by the problems of navigation. How much had he drifted off course? Was his earth inductor compass accurate? And there was the ever-present concern with fuel consumption. He was now close to 10,000 feet, and above the weather. He checked his instrument panel again with his flashlight. All was in order: oil temperature, 35 degrees centigrade, rpms up to 1700. It was getting colder, and he closed up his flying suit which he had loosened earlier when under the hot sun. The clouds continued to rise menacingly ahead of him, well above the altitude of the plane. They seemed to be large mushrooms, growing out of a bumpy field of stratus. He circled around them, at first, and then it was no longer possible to avoid them. He plunged in, while the plane jounced heavily in the air currents. He looked outside at the silver wings, as they shook in the turbulence. They seemed almost to be flapping like a seagull's. It had become very cold. He was still flying in cloud, and the controls of the plane began to feel logy. He shone his flashlight onto the struts, and noticed little white shiny streaks on them. It was ice! He would have to get out of the cloud, and down to warmer air. He descended, and continued to fly on, but now he weaved to avoid thunderheads, the airman's most dreaded menace. As he flew lower, the ice accumulation began to thin. It would be gone soon, he hoped.

Drowsiness returned to Lindbergh as the plane droned on. It was clear now, and the cockpit was bathed in moonlight. It became more and more difficult to keep the plane on course as he fought off the temptation to sleep. What he wouldn't give for a comfortable bed and 10 hours with nothing to do but sleep. He let his eyes close momentarily, hoping for temporary relief. It just made it worse when they opened. He knew he couldn't afford the luxury of even a short second away from the dimly glowing numbers in front of him, so quickly did the *Spirit of St. Louis* wander off course. He still bore north, but gradually edged to the east, as he followed the easy curve of his planned route.

At 1 A.M., New York time, he passed the point of no return. It was now closer to Europe in the event of trouble. The air was warmer—almost tropical. There wasn't a trace of icing left, as he

flew through the air, 90 miles an hour, at 9500 feet. The heavy
bank of clouds had receded, too, and only scattered patches flitted
by his cockpit windows. Somewhere to the north of him was Greenland; ahead was the safety of Ireland, England, France, and Paris!
Locally, it was 2 hours later, and the new dawn was near as
the plane droned on. The wild roar of the Whirlwind seemed less
noisy now. The yearning for sleep engulfed his mind. He tried everything to keep his eyes open—staring at the instrument panel, rubbing
his eyes, looking out into the slipstream, and bouncing up and
down in his seat. Nothing helped. His heavy lids kept closing. It
angered him—his inability to control himself. The anger would
revive him, briefly, and then tiredness would take over again. The
plane drifted off course—at times, as much as 10 degrees, before he
became alert enough to bring the nose back to the proper heading.
Sleep! Sleep! How he needed it! Again, he rubbed his eyes vigorously
and slapped his face, stingingly hard, to no avail.

The color of the sky lightened from inky black to gray. He roused
himself from his lethargic stupor. He was on course. The earth
inductor compass needle was centered properly, and the air speed
dial showed that he was making 89 miles an hour. Even the ball
on the bank indicator registered normally—meaning that he was
flying on an even keel at 8800 feet. In the early morning light, he
saw another wall of clouds approaching. He plunged in, while the
plane trembled and shuddered. Then, abruptly, he flew into the
clear, to be greeted by the brilliance of the early sun, and, as quickly,
it was dark again as he flew into another cloud bank. He decided
to drop down to the surface to find out what the wind was doing.
He eased the stick forward and plummeted down, as the air speed
indicator rose to 140 miles per hour. Down he went, and leveled off
at 50 feet. The streaks on the waves showed that he was still
favored by a tail wind. The waves were huge and angry, and greenish-
gray under the cloud layer above. How could anyone survive a
landing in such a sea, he thought. The wind appeared to have
reached near gale-force intensity. All the better, he felt, for it would
push him along that much faster. Then he climbed back up again, as
the cloud lowered to the sea.

He continued to fly blind, surrounded by gray, thick, swirling
cloud, sometimes so heavy that his wingtips were lost in it. Suddenly,
he woke with a start, shocked to find that he had dozed off. He
shot a glance at his altimeter—1600 feet—no real danger. It must
have been only a few seconds, but the thought of what might have

happened jolted him to alertness. Still, the plane plowed through thick cloud. It had seemed an age since he had seen sky or ocean— only a thick, wet gray blanket. A little after 5 A.M., New York time, it was clear for an instant—brilliant blue skies above, and sparkling oceans below. Then more cloud smothered the little ship, but soon, there were patches of sky again. It was but a brief respite, for, almost at once, he plunged headlong into a heavy bank which extended from the seas to the heavens.

He was over 10 hours from Newfoundland, as he flew between layers of scattered clouds, sometimes above them, sometimes below. He dropped to the surface and watched with interest the shadow of his plane flying along the water as the sun played hide and seek with the swiftly moving cumulus above. He rose again to safer flying heights, where flying would require less concentration. Now and then the cloud formations in the distance took on the tantalizing appearance of a shore line, complete with trees, sand, and surf, only to fade into the reality of a misty bank, as plane and flyer closed in on it.

As the early morning passed, he calculated that he was 2300 miles from Roosevelt Field, with only 1300 miles left to Paris. He noted that he had burned 300 gallons of gas during 25 hours in the air, leaving him with 150, more than enough to get to Paris. His mind drifted again to problems of navigation, which he had ignored during his struggle to keep awake. How far had he drifted? Should he compensate by heading north a few degrees, to be sure of hitting Ireland? He flew on, over an ocean which stretched out endlessly. All at once, in the distance, he spotted something, black and shiny, squirming in the ocean. Another mirage? He flew closer. No, it was a school of porpoises. Soon, a gull appeared, gliding gracefully over the water. They were the first two signs of life since leaving Newfoundland.

It was after 10 A.M., New York time, and well into the afternoon, locally. The sun had dropped lower in the sky, and shadows again filled his cockpit. It was cooler. He flew in a kind of fatigued trance, glancing idly at the instruments, and then out at the sea ahead. He was in this state, when, suddenly, he saw a dot in the water ahead. A small boat! Human beings! Then he noticed several others drifting about. It was obviously a part of a fishing fleet. He couldn't be too far from the coast, now. He dove lower and banked over them to get a better view, and perhaps determine their nationality. He noticed a man's head stick out of the cabin of one of them, startled, apparently, by the noise of the plane. He closed the throttle and screamed, "Which way is Ireland?" There was neither answer nor movement from the sailor below, only an unbelieving and stupefied stare.

He was now 1100 feet over the ocean in cool, fresh air. Again, his eye was caught by something—a faint, dark line on the horizon. It couldn't be land, he thought; just another mirage, for he was only 16 hours out of Newfoundland, and he'd allowed himself 18½ to reach the Irish coast. But as he drew closer, sure enough, a shore line began to emerge clearly from the haze, with breaking waves, tall hills, and green fields, beyond. Where was he? Scotland? It was too early to have gone that far. He crossed the coastline, still trying to get his bearings. He was now wide awake and alert. There was no longer any urge to sleep. He saw little farms, dirt roads, and a great bay, glistening below in the afternoon sun. He studied his map, which he spread out on his lap. He located a portion on the map that fit the coastline that moved slowly under him. It was Dingle Bay, and Valencia, Ireland! He was right on target, despite all the deviations of his groggy night at sea. He was elated as he spiraled down for a closer look. Never had land looked so lovely, so green, and so warm as it did now; there were only 600 miles more, and he'd be in Paris—at Le Bourget! It was after 11 A.M. New York time, as he circled over the little Irish town, relieved, and confident now of his chances of success. He looked down, and saw people running out into the narrow streets, waving at him. Surely, the news that he had crossed the ocean safely would be passed on, soon, to America, and to those who awaited him anxiously at Le Bourget.

His tiredness had disappeared as he checked the final segments of his course, leading over the southern tip of England, the Channel, the French coast, and on in to Le Bourget. It was late afternoon, locally, but a good portion of the flight, he thought thankfully, would be made in daylight. He pointed back on course, and in no time the green farms of County Kerry flitted by below him. He switched from the fuselage tank to the one in the nose, planning to let it run dry so that the *Spirit of St. Louis* would not be inclined to turn turtle from forward weightiness, when landing. The weather was clear now, with a few fluffy, fair-weather cumulus spotting an otherwise blue afternoon sky. The wind blew, still on the plane's tail, fresher than earlier, and pushing her faster to her destination. The flight was going smoothly and on schedule.

Suddenly the motor coughed and sputtered and the stick vibrated violently in his hand. It was the first "miss" in 29 hours. He looked down, shaken from his serene confidence. He'd come so far, and now? He thought of his engine trouble, flying east from San Diego. Had the carburetor heater failed? It was too warm for that type of trouble. Instinctively, his pilot's mind thought of a forced landing, but on the water? Could he get back to Ireland? The motor continued to miss badly and lose power fast. The cause was slow in coming to his tired brain. Of course! His nose tank had gone dry! With a quick move, he threw the lever switching the gas flow to the center wing tank, and promptly the Whirlwind roared again, smoothly and powerfully. He opened the throttle slightly and watched the needle on the tachometer flit up to 1725 rpm, and the air speed indicator move to 110. No need to worry about fuel now. He had plenty, enough to go on to Rome, if necessary.

The cliffs of Cornwall loomed ahead, rising out of the sea, and the little towns northeast of Newquay with their houses looking so tiny from the air, crept closer. He dropped down again, easing the stick forward. As in Ireland, he noticed heads upward turned, looking at him, with arms waving in welcome. On he flew, toward the Channel, over soft green Maytime England. Plymouth appeared, and then faded in the distance off the tip of his left wing. Then, below, came the Channel coast, at Start Point, near Dartmouth. Ahead was a 95-mile stretch of water to Cap de la Hague.

The minutes passed fast now for the young flyer as the Channel flashed beneath his wings. Success was easily within his grasp. For there in the distance, glowing in the late sunset, was the coast of France. The glow deepened to a lovely purple as the sun dropped below the horizon. Soon he was over Cherbourg, with its lights twinkling already in the twilight. He checked his course carefully. This was no time for mistakes, no time to relax overconfidently. He set his course across the Bay of the Seine to Deauville, where he hoped to pick up the mouth of the Seine River. In no time the little resort town was under him, while far off his left wing, gleamed the lights of the city of Le Havre. He realized he hadn't eaten since the start. On his panel clock, it was now 4:30 P.M., but 9:30, locally—time for an early dinner back home, and almost proper for Continentals, their time. He drank water from his canteen first, then opened a brown paper bag, took out a sandwich and nibbled at it. He swallowed a few bites, but strangely he wasn't hungry. Perhaps it was the mounting excitement, and the gnawing desire to have it all over safely, and without a hitch.

It was dark out now. Two thousand feet below, blinking lights pointed out little villages as they moved slowly by. In the distance he saw a bright flash of light—coming—going—and coming again in the unmistakable fashion of a beacon. It was one of a series he'd read about, to guide flyers on the London to Paris commercial route. Below him, also, curled the Seine. It would not be long now before he caught the welcome sight of the lights of Paris!

Finally they appeared, at first a faint glow in the sky and then a myriad of little pinpoints twinkling gaily below him as he flew over the western outskirts of the city. Then, under him before he knew it, was the brilliantly lit, majestic and graceful Eiffel Tower, symbolizing most perfectly the great city. He circled it, while he studied his maps for what he hoped would be the last time. Within him was only the nagging worry about a safe landing. It served to temper his elation and sharpen his concentration. He had to find Le Bourget and come in without a mishap. He knew he'd made many more difficult landings, at night, on strange fields. He had been told that Le Bourget was northeast of the city, but it didn't show on his map. He banked and pointed the silver nose to where he thought the field should be. He looked out his window, searching below for anything that resembled an airdrome. He thought that it would be marked by a beacon, but the only beacon he saw was behind him, to the southwest of the city. Possibly he was above the beam. A large area, which was big enough for an airfield, appeared below him. It was surrounded, strangely, by hundreds of little lights, closely bunched. But he couldn't see any other lights that usually rimmed and were the standard equipment at large metropolitan fields. He flew on farther, but seemed to be getting away from civilization. He banked, determined to investigate again the large dark area surrounded by the little lights. He pushed the stick forward gently, and dropped to 1000 feet. It would be simpler to make out things from that altitude. He was wide awake, and alert, now, and concentrating thoroughly. There it was again. He dropped lower. It was an airport. He began to see the hangars loom out of the darkness. The myriad of little lights turned out to be hundreds of automobiles, jammed tightly on roads around the field. It was a huge field, he could see. He went lower, and was able to pick out a wind sock. It was flapping idly, indicating a light wind blowing toward the hangar line on a slight angle. He saw also floodlights

shining over the hangars and a portion of the field. He banked
again and began a trial approach. He closed the throttle, but not too
much, and pointed the nose down. He glanced below him as he
skimmed across the field. It seemed smooth enough, and there
was ample space. He opened the throttle again, climbed, and banked
around for his final approach. His earlier elation had been replaced
now by an intense concentration. It had to be a good landing.
He knew he was tired from 33 hours in the air, but he knew, also,
that it must not affect his landing. He headed into the wind, and
pointed back toward the field. Down he glided, now and then
giving a short burst to the engine to ensure flying speed. The hangars
slid by below. Now the ground flashed, just under his wheels, as he
leveled off. The wheels touched, bounced off for a second, and then
came back down as the *Spirit of St. Louis* sped across the firm
turf—then slower, and slower, and she came to a stop. Lindbergh
had made it!

He gunned the engine, swung the ship around, and began to taxi
toward a lighted hangar.

Ambassador Herrick's worries about the French mood following
the Nungesser-Coli tragedy proved needless during the next few
minutes. The *Spirit of St. Louis* had barely made her turn when
she was engulfed by a sea of hysterical and cheering humanity. The
instant they had seen the little silvery plane touch down, they
surged through the carefully placed police lines and swarmed across
the field—thousands of them. Inside the cockpit, Lindbergh cut his
engine, for fear of doing injury with his spinning propeller. He
was unable to see out as the crowd jammed around the plane,
like human sardines, so closely were they packed. He heard rips,
as souvenir hunters tore pieces of fabric off the fuselage. Dazedly, he
opened the cockpit door and tried to alight in order to protect his
little plane. It was useless. His feet never touched the ground as
he was borne aloft by the excited, happy French horde. At some
point he was rescued by a pair of ruggedly built French pilots.
They half carried, half led him, as they shouldered their way, bit by
bit, through the mob to the comparative quiet and privacy of a small
room in a nearby hangar. He was joined there soon by Ambassador
Herrick, who assured him that the *Spirit of St. Louis* too, had
been rescued, and was now in a hangar, guarded carefully, by the
military. She had been damaged, but only superficially, and was little
the worse for wear.

At 4:15 A.M., Paris time, Lindbergh was in bed at the American

Embassy for his first real sleep in 63 hours. He had touched down officially at Le Bourget at 10:22 P.M., Paris time (5:22 P.M., New York time) after 33 hours and 30 minutes alone in the air.

In Paris, the crowds gathered in front of Le Matin's bulletin board, read a posted report in the evening that Lindbergh had been sighted over Cherbourg. At once, the race was on for Le Bourget, with many failing to make the field on time for the landing because of the miles-long, bumper to bumper traffic jam en route. After the arrival, the city went wild, and not only at the airport. American flags were seen everywhere, and cries of "Vive l'Américain," "Vive Lindbergh!" and "Cette fois, ça va!" echoed throughout the night, as thousands remained on the avenues celebrating. The sporting French, forgetting for the minute their sadness over the loss of their own Nungesser and Coli, let loose with long pent-up emotions in an unforgettable welcome to the young flyer.

In the United States, receipt of the news brought on identical, spontaneous, and electric celebrations. In New York cheering throngs gathered along Broadway, from Columbus Circle to Times Square and as far south as 34th Street. Western Union announced quickly a low-rate telegram of congratulations to "Lindy"; an enterprising bartender, despite prohibition, came up with a recipe for a Lindy Cocktail (equal parts of Kinnalillet and gin; 2 dashes of orange juice, apricot, and lemon peel). At once, models of the Spirit of St. Louis, together with pictures of the flyer, were being hawked at street corners; and, the Wright Company stock rose 5¾ points, to close at 34⅞, on a turnover of 13,000 shares. The excitement did not abate for many weeks.

The acclaim over his feat was worldwide. Newspapers in all languages told of the flight with banner headlines. For the week after his landing, he was fêted in Paris as few had ever been before him. He was given the keys of the city, and on May 25, as 500,000 cheered, he was given the Cross of the French Legion of Honor. He then flew to Belgium, where he was met with another wild welcome, led by King Albert, who made him a member of the Order of Chevalier of the Royal Order of Leopold; finally, it was London's turn, and it was Le Bourget all over again when he landed at Croydon Field. The staid Britishers forgot their customary reserve as tens of thousands cheered him wherever he went. The celebrations were climaxed when he was presented with the Air Force Cross by King George V in London. Meanwhile, messages of congratulations poured in from governmental leaders in all parts of the world. He was, indeed, the new Columbus.

His flight was, in truth, a universal victory, untarnished by national prides, and all nations became one as they paid tribute to the young world hero.

After the reception in England the *Spirit of St. Louis* was flown to Gosport, where she was dismantled, crated, and loaded aboard the United States cruiser *Memphis*, dispatched by President Calvin Coolidge to bring Lindbergh home. He returned to a hectic summer of country-wide celebrations in his honor, beginning with a roaring welcome at Washington, D.C., on June 12, followed in New York, on June 13, by the never-to-be-forgotten tickertape parade up Broadway.

Every community in the United States took part in the summer's lionizations, as "We," Lindbergh and the *Spirit of St. Louis*, flew into fields from coast to coast to be fêted and awarded the honors of the locale. Then it was on to Canada for more tributes, followed late in the year by a spectacular 25-hour, non-stop flight from Washington, D.C., to Mexico City, where President Plutarco Calles led the Mexicans in yet another roaring welcome to the hero. The last trip was of particular importance to Lindbergh, for during his stay he was the guest at the embassy of newly appointed Ambassador Dwight W. Morrow whose daughter, Anne, would become his wife.

In New York, on June 16, Lindbergh was presented with the $25,-000 Orteig prize by Raymond Orteig, at an elaborate party at the latter's Hotel Brevoort in the presence of New York Senators Robert F. Wagner and Royal S. Copeland, Juan Trippe, Grover Whalen, and U. S. Attorney Charles H. Tuttle, among others. When the week-long celebrations ended, "Slim" flew off in the *Spirit of St. Louis* to St. Louis for accolades from the citizens of the sponsoring city.

4. The day before Lindbergh's take-off, the apparent quiet in the hangars of *America* and *Columbia* was misleading.

At Roosevelt Field, Lieutenant George Noville was hard at work supervising the loading of the big Fokker, hidden from view behind closed hangar doors. The rations consisted of five gallons of water (sufficient in Noville's opinion to keep three men alive for three weeks), enough pemmican for six weeks, malted milk, and hardtack! The menu was made even less tasteful by the elimination of chocolate from the diet, for fear that it would create undue thirst. The rations were placed in a large compartment to the rear of the navigator's cabin, and alongside them were carefully stored, two pneumatic rubber boats—the larger of which was 14 feet long and had been thoroughly tested in the East River by Commander Byrd and two friends; fishing tackle, complete with a supply of bacon, to be used as bait. "We chose bacon," explained Noville with a straight face, "because, if the fish don't like it, we can eat it." Also stored was a large sail for the rubber boat, and a huge box kite, for use as an antenna on the boat. Except for the menu, *America* seemed comfortably and adequately appointed for its ocean trip; and to add to the conveniences aboard, workmen had installed recently a system of electric lights for the chart room and cabin, and a telephone, connecting the two.

Below, at Curtiss Field, despite the legal wrangling under way at the Courthouse in Brooklyn, *Columbia's* crew had continued, hopefully, with preparations, in the event Judge May was able to effect a settlement between the two litigants. Hopes were dashed when May dismissed the suit by Bertaud, saying, among other things, "The importance of the contemplated flight of the machine is so evident, that a court of equity, under the circumstances, could scarcely justify the issuance of an injunction."

The take-off of Lindbergh on May 20 shocked both camps, particularly *Columbia's*. Levine issued an immediate statement, announcing a take-off at 4 A.M. on the 21st. When asked about the navigator, he answered rather obtusely, "The man is known only to three people—the man himself, Chamberlin, and Levine." However, Chamberlin told the press, at his own conference, that there would be no take-off; that it was too late to catch Lindbergh anyway, and that the weather reports showed head winds all the way to Newfoundland. Nevertheless, as night came on, still-hopeful mechanics under orders from Levine loaded *Columbia's* tanks to capacity. Bellanca made a statement, also, which further confused the issue. He was dead-set against leaving while Lindbergh was still in the air. He said, wisely enough, "If Lindbergh makes it, there is no need for duplication. At best, it would be a stunt, and there will be other opportunities." The announced 4 A.M., Saturday, May 21, came and went. *Columbia* remained in her hangar.

Bellanca, his patience exhausted by the controversy and delay in *Columbia's* camp, finally had enough. Lindbergh had landed safely; the designer was thrilled and relieved by his success. "It will remain as one of the greatest accomplishments in the history of aviation," he said. However, he was sorely disappointed that his plane had not been given a chance. On the same day he came to a parting of the ways with Levine, "severing any and all connections between Mr. Levine and myself." His failure to settle the bitter Bertaud dispute caused him to add, "Two characters such as Levine and myself should not continue in the same enterprise." Levine, appearing shocked, said, "Due to Bellanca's resignation, the plane will be placed in the hangar, and the New York to Paris flight will be abandoned for the present." Levine bought out Bellanca's share of the enterprise and *Columbia* remained in his control; immediate orders were issued to remove Bellanca's name from the tail assembly, and to paint over the *PARIS* portion of *NEW YORK TO PARIS* on the fuselage, leaving an enigmatic blank as the destination.

A bit of excitement happened the following day as *Columbia*'s tanks were being emptied. A careless smoker dropped a cigarette on some spilled gas, and a bright blaze flared up. Bystanders screamed, fearing that *Columbia* was burning up, and fire-fighting apparatus was summoned hastily from Mineola. But she was safe—well beyond the danger line.

Lindbergh's landing took much of the spotlight off of the remaining planes. The flyers were as one in their praise for him despite personal disappointments at not being first. Said Lloyd Bertaud, "The most remarkable flight ever made, and the most unusual human endurance," and Commander Byrd commented, "I think Lindbergh's feat is one of the greatest individual feats in history!"

The sense of urgency now left the two camps. Byrd's family tried to argue the commander out of making the flight, but to no avail; he was adamant, save for his decision to postpone the take-off until after Lindbergh's return to the United States.

Columbia was still ready, but now with neither crew nor destination. Chamberlin, when questioned, admitted as much when he said, "Yes, it's off. When and if we fly, we'll fly somewhere else than Paris—perhaps, Honolulu."

Levine's misfortunes mounted. He had applied recently to the government for the New York to Chicago airmail contract, but Postmaster General Harry S. New turned him down despite his low bid. The grounds were that some of his past dealings with the Army for war surplus ammunition were now under investigation, and, more recently, because of his much-publicized didoes involving Messrs. Wade, Acosta, Bertaud, and now Bellanca.

May came to a close, with the world still agog over the Lindbergh flight. Crowds arrived in droves, still, at Roosevelt and Curtiss Fields, despite the little that was happening. It was a pleasant week-end drive, and they could at least look at the planes. Across the nation, James D. Dole, the Hawaiian Pineapple King, was barely noticed when he offered $25,000 for the flyer who would win his non-stop race from California to Hawaii. He had hoped to attract Lindbergh, but was not to succeed.

The only other thing that mattered, as June approached, was Babe Ruth's batting eye, which had been temporarily dimmed. "George ain't hittin' even half a lick," an unhappy fan moaned.

CHAPTER VII

June 1927

1. June in the western world was devoted to Colonel Charles Augustus Lindbergh—in London, Paris, and Washington—in Dayton, St. Louis, and Columbus. Thousands upon thousands took part in gala parades as tickertape fluttered down and bands played to the shy young hero. He was worshiped and idolized by Americans, in a fashion known only to them.

Despite the furor, things were happening elsewhere. In far-off China there was a turmoil of a different ilk. General Chiang Kai-shek, having divorced his Kuomintang from the influence of Moscow, now sought peace with Manchurian war lord Chiang Tso-lin and the feudal leaders of the north in an effort to form a common front against the enemy, the Hankow Communists.

The clamor over the fate of Sacco and Vanzetti reached such a fever pitch in the United States and in Europe that Governor Alvan T. Fuller of Massachusetts appointed a committee comprised of Presidents Abbott Lawrence Lowell of Harvard and Samuel W. Stratton of MIT, and Judge Robert Grant of the Commonwealth to review the evidence and give him an opinion on whether the convicted men had, in fact, received a fair trial.

A book was banned in Boston for containing passages "liable to corrupt youth," and author Upton Sinclair rushed to the Hub of the Universe with fire in his eye, in an effort to restore his *Oil* to the bookshelves of that city, while, in New Haven, President James Rowland Angell of Yale, in his baccalaureate sermon to the graduating class, warned them against "materialism," and added that "with some warrant, our age is alleged to be glaringly irreligious!"

With Lindbergh's success, it hardly mattered that Bill Tilden was beaten at Wimbledon, Bobby Jones at Oakmont, and that poor Lizzie Borden, accused of giving her parents an alleged forty whacks, died in Fall River, Massachusetts, aged sixty-eight.

2. Silence and mystery pervaded the atmosphere at Curtiss Field, causing the inevitable rumors to fly. There were rumors of an imminent take-off, which were denied by Levine. There were other rumors that Levine wanted to make a non-stop flight to Italy—for he was an outspoken and avid admirer of Benito Mussolini. Levine was silent, and Chamberlin could not be reached. Suddenly, on the morning of June 2, Chamberlin appeared at the field and took off alone in *Columbia*, headed west. Again, there was conjecture, but it was silenced when the yellow monoplane reappeared over Curtiss in the late afternoon, and settled for a landing. She had spent the day at Teterboro for the installation of a new carburetor heater.

On the afternoon of June 3 a startling announcement was issued by Chamberlin. He would take off at 4 A.M., the next day, on an Atlantic flight, and would fly as long as his gas held out, in an attempt to surpass Lindbergh's distance record. At once the hangar at Curtiss became a beehive of activity as Carisi and the ground crew worked feverishly. It was decided that shortly before the take-off, the ship would be hauled up to Roosevelt Field. At long last, it looked as though Bellanca's ship would have the test for which the little designer had yearned.

"Doc" Kimball had advised Chamberlin that the weather over the Atlantic was favorable, and that he could hope for similar conditions to those Lindbergh had met. All night, until 1:30 A.M., he stayed at Curtiss, under the lights and supervising the loading. The wing tanks and the piano-shaped fuselage tank were filled with fuel. Thirteen 5-gallon disposable cans for in-flight fueling were stored aboard. In addition to 65 gallons in the wing, and 390 in the fuselage, the cans would provide *Columbia* with a total fuel load of 520 gallons. If she could get off the ground, she would be able to fly a long way.

The workmen continued to load: a collapsible raft, with sectional oars neatly folded; Very pistols, flares, safety matches, a flashlight, and lights equipped to glow as soon as they touched water. The rations, stored in the pilot's cockpit, consisted of two canteens of water (the canteens had been cleaned carefully and inspected this time), two bottles of chicken soup, a bottle of coffee, a dozen toasted chicken sandwiches on rye bread, chewing gum, half a dozen oranges, and three tins of U. S. Army emergency rations.

Still, no one knew who would accompany Chamberlin when he left the field at 1:30 A.M. on June 4 to join his wife Wilma at the Garden City Hotel for a few hours of sleep. There was talk again of Lieutenant Fields, but he hadn't been seen of late; also, of Bernt Balchen, who had prepared the navigational charts now on board *Columbia*, though it was known that he still hoped to be included in the Byrd crew. All during the night the lights burned and men worked in *Columbia*'s hangar at Curtiss.

The same evening at the Belle Harbor home of Levine, the doorbell rang, and Samuel Hartman, Levine's lawyer, was escorted into a little study where he sat and chatted alone with his client. Levine, after discoursing over his favorite figure, Mussolini, whom he revered as another Napoleon, told his lawyer that he wanted him to draft a new will, in that he intended to sail the next day for Europe aboard the *Franconia*. He thought it wise to have his affairs in order. The hardworking attorney accomplished the task, somehow, during the evening, and before midnight it had been executed properly. There was no further explanation from his client. Hartman left, and Levine went to bed. When questioned later, Hartman stated that he thought Levine was headed, certainly, for Rome, because "It would be the proudest moment of his life when he shook hands with the Italian premier."

Chamberlin left word to be awakened at 3:30 A.M. He bade goodbye to his wife at the hotel, and Charles Lockwood drove him to Roosevelt Field. When he got there, the plane was in the process of being hauled up from Curtiss by truck. He noticed that there was a light wind blowing from the east, which would mean a take-off from the west, as Lindbergh had done, over the telephone wires and out over the golf course. There was little for him to do, as the plane hadn't arrived. A small crowd had gathered already. They waited, at this early hour despite the pre-dawn pitch-blackness, with expectancy and excitement.

Chamberlin and Lockwood drove to the nearby home of a friend, Mrs. Anne Crowley, where they ate a hearty breakfast of bacon, eggs, and milk. They returned quickly to the field. The crowd had grown and a legion of photographers milled about with their flashbulbs popping incessantly and blindingly in the early light. A newsman asked Chamberlin where the navigator was. Chamberlin replied laconically, "Not here, yet." Kinkaid stood on a ladder, giving the engine a final check. Carisi, ever faithful, crawled all over the plane, checking the structure, the controls, the wheel bearings, and the tires. Chamberlin was told that the plane weighed 5418 pounds —300 more than Lindbergh's. His expression did not change.

At 5:45 A.M. he climbed into his flying suit, while Carisi started the engine and ran it up. It screamed shrilly in the quiet of morning. Kinkaid, ear cocked, nodded with satisfaction. They were ready, but there was still no sign of the navigator. Levine and his wife appeared in the crowd. He was fresh and rested, and wore a business suit with a leather vest. He smiled as photographers snapped pictures. His wife, pretty and dressed neatly, stood alongside him, the picture of happiness and pride. Her husband's plane was going, and there'd be no more of those stories in the papers. He chatted with Chamberlin and Carisi, Lockwood and Ralph Jonas. The crowd milled around. An unidentified man rushed up to Chamberlin with a girl, and said, "Shake hands with my wife!" Chamberlin obliged.

It was just after 6 A.M., and there was daylight. Chamberlin walked a few steps, and climbed into *Columbia*, which stood at the western end of the field, engine idling. Suddenly, Levine broke from the crowd, jumped in, and crouched down in the co-pilot's seat beside Chamberlin, as if he were hiding. No one knew it, but his flying clothes were stored aboard. Carisi, Lockwood, and the crowd stared incredulously. Mrs. Levine screamed, "Stop him! He isn't going! No, he isn't! Stop him!"

Carisi looked at the plane, cursed, and then ran to her, saying, "It's all right. It's only a test run!"

On board, Chamberlin opened the throttle, and the plane started down the field, which had been narrowed by the crowds. Slowly *Columbia* gained speed, but Chamberlin felt her begin to swing like a pendulum, to the right and left. He fought it with his rudder bars, but the crowd had left too narrow a lane, and he closed the throttle and brought the heavily laden ship to a stop. He turned and headed back to the extreme west end of the field. Carisi ran out. The plane turned. Carisi stood on the wheel, screaming profanities at Levine, inside. Again Chamberlin opened the throttle, and the plane started to move, Carisi being blown off by the blast, but still cursing visibly. *Columbia* gained speed, imperceptibly at first. The runway was firm. Chamberlin felt the controls begin to take hold, as the plane now flashed along. She began to buck slightly up and down—a touch by the wheels, and then, by the tail skid. He let her fly herself, and 2500 feet down the runway she was airborne. He held her at grass-top level for another 1000 feet to gather speed, then soared gracefully up over the telephone wires, with ample room to spare, and out over the golf links. The air was smooth, as they headed toward Long Island Sound at 700 feet. It was a bright, lovely morning with the blue water in the distance, diamond-studded by the sun's rays. Chamberlin eased back on the throttle—1750 rpms to 1700, then to 1650, and still the airplane responded strongly. At long last, they were off. Abroad, both Berlin and Rome awaited them. No one knew for sure.

On the ground, as the little yellow monoplane faded in the eastern sky, Mrs. Levine sagged back, sobbing, into the arms of a Captain MacCahill, realizing finally that her husband had gone. Carisi ran over and tried to comfort her, "He's all right," he said. "He'll get there. You should be proud of him! He's a brave boy! A real ball of fire!"

The early editions of the afternoon papers carried word of Levine's ploy. Reporters rushed to get comments from the departed members of *Columbia*'s camp. Said Lloyd Bertaud simply: "I'm surprised to see him go. I hope he has a nice ride." Bellanca was found at the office of his attorney, Fiorello H. La Guardia, and his gentle, but firmly disapproving comment was, "That plane is a part of me. It is like a member of my family—my child, my brother. It would make me wince to have it hurt." Later, he added: "I have never had any doubts, as far as courage is concerned, of Mr. Levine's willingness to fly, and I was not surprised. I was informed of his plans a few days ago, and tried to discourage them; I would have been much better satisfied if Chamberlin had had a good navigator."

Controversy over Levine's act, and the reasons for it, filled the air for days. He was trying to prove his courage, some said, after the newspapers had accused him of being afraid to commit himself or his plane. Others said he was trying to improve his public image after the fiascos involving Wade, Acosta, Bertaud, and Bellanca; still others maintained he was publicity crazy. The aviation community, to a man, thought his going was ill-advised, as he was merely a passenger, unable to help materially with the flying or navigation, and his presence, if in dead weight only, would jeopardize the success of the flight.

Chamberlin later gave his version of the escapade. He said that one night late in May, as he was driving Levine to the Garden City Hotel from his Belle Harbor home, Levine turned to him and said, "If you'll take me along, I'll give you $25,000 myself, and put up $50,000 in insurance for Mrs. Chamberlin."

"Suits me," said Chamberlin; whereupon Levine tore up Chamberlin's contract, and executed two new instruments in the presence of Charles Lockwood and Judge George W. Martin. Additional terms included a salary of $150 a week and one-half of the income from all sources arising out of the flight. Perhaps, it was wind of this arrangement that had disturbed Bertaud, as well as Bellanca. In any event, it was a well-kept secret. Thereafter, unbeknownst to the press or public, Chamberlin said he had made many trial flights in *Columbia* with Levine, teaching him to fly a course with the aid of the earth inductor and magnetic compasses, the turn and bank indicator, and the inclometer. Moreover, Bert Acosta had given him prior instruction, so that he was able to fly the ship evenly when it was aloft, though he had been given no teaching in the making of take-offs or landings. It is apparent that Levine had been thinking of going on the flight for many months.

Columbia cruised along the Sound toward the Connecticut shore. Levine struggled into his flying suit. In so doing, he discovered a roll of bills amounting to $300 in his coat pocket. They had been meant for Carisi. "Perhaps that's why he was swearing," Levine roared almost hysterically, and then he added more soberly, "Think of taking all that money down with me."

The earth inductor compass handle was cranked by Chamberlin, so as to set the course on the dial for New London. He would have to keep the needle on the panel dial pointed at o. If it wavered, the plane was off course. They missed New London by 10 miles, which Chamberlin realized was too big an error. They reset it for Newport, Rhode Island, and again missed, passing over St. George's prep school on the outskirts. They were 5 miles off course this time. Below, they could see the schoolboys out on the vast lawns, waving, as they flew by at a bare 200 feet because of increasing winds aloft. They continued across Plymouth Bay, and over the open water to Cape Cod. Once again, the earth inductor compass failed as they found themselves this time 15 miles off course. Finally the compass failed altogether as the needle flopped aimlessly over the dial. The vibrations from the engine had apparently broken a hair-line spring, which controlled the indicator needle. It was useless. Though they had a magnetic compass aboard, too, the first crisis had arisen. Should they go back? They circled over the Cape while deciding.

"Let's go!" said Levine. "I'd rather go into the water than face those newsmen again!" Levine was furious over the failure of the earth inductor, and cursed Pioneer Instruments violently. After all, the "damned thing" had cost him $1125, not including the charges for various adjustments, as against $50.65 for the magnetic compass on which they would now have to rely. As they changed course and made for Nova Scotia, it became an obsession with him, and the cloudless sky, with pleasure craft sailing on the sparkling ocean below, failed to soothe him, and he raved on.

It was Saturday, June 4, and they had lifted off at 6:20 A.M. At 8 A.M. the people of the town of North Westport, Massachusetts, sighted the yellow plane flying 1000 feet, and at 8:50 she was seen over Marshfield, Massachusetts. She was not sighted again, until 12:06 P.M., when she flew over Yarmouth, Nova Scotia; then, at 1:30 P.M., over Chedabukto Head, at the entrance to Halifax Harbor. At 3 P.M. there were reports of her over Wedge Island, Nova Scotia, flying low and fast.

Back at Roosevelt Field, where the progress reports were received, rapid calculations estimated their time of arrival in Rome, at 9:45 P.M., Sunday night, or, in Berlin, at approximately 8 P.M. No one still knew, for sure, what their destination was, for Chamberlin had said only that he would fly until the tanks were dry. They appeared to be traveling slightly east of Lindbergh's course, and lower than the altitude of 12,000 to 14,000 feet that had been advised by Giuseppe Bellanca.

They had been over the Atlantic, and headed for Nova Scotia for 3 hours. They had estimated that they would hit the coast within that time, and were beginning to worry—perhaps distracted somewhat by the failure of the earth inductor compass on which they had placed so much reliance. But Chamberlin thought it might be the fault of the head wind. Three and a half hours out of Cape Cod, they spotted the welcome coastline in the distance, and soon the houses and harbor of the city of Yarmouth. They were dead on course. Chamberlin took a new bearing, and headed directly up the middle of the peninsula. Like Lindbergh, they found it an unfriendly looking land for aviators, hilly and dotted with lakes. It seemed to them to have a curious brown color for so late in the spring. Trees and water flashed 500 feet below as the plane roared on, the engine smooth and powerful-sounding. Levine busied himself by unlashing the first 5-gallon can of fuel. He attached a hose to the tank and opened the petcock. When the can was empty he threw it overboard. As the flight continued over what seemed an endless Nova Scotia, the wind veered gradually to the southeast from the head winds they had been bucking. It now blew directly across their course. The air was smooth and the weather still clear. Chamberlin turned the controls over to Levine briefly as he tried some hot soup —which tasted good. He bit into a sandwich, which was less than succulent. Possibly, it was the cold toast, or maybe he wasn't hungry. Then, it was back to the controls as Levine seemed to be struggling.

They left the coast and headed for the eastern end of Cape Breton Island off the northwest tip of Nova Scotia. The wind began to veer again until it blew on their tail, pushing them faster toward Newfoundland. They decided that because of reported fog in the St. John's area they would head to sea south of that city. At 6 P.M. they came up on the Newfoundland coast at Trepassey Bay, 15 miles northwest of Cape Race, and 40 miles southwest of St. John's. *Columbia* was at 800 feet, as she circled over the harbor from which NC 4 and her sister ships had taken off in 1919. They took a last look at land and headed to sea, as the long twilight of early summer lingered. It became chilly in the cockpit, and while Levine flew again Chamberlin donned all of his extra clothes; woolen drawers which pulled over his knickers, and a heavy, fur-lined parka over his jacket. He stretched out briefly on the piano-shaped tank, while *Columbia* left land slowly behind, and the sun sank below the western horizon. She was at 2000 feet.

Back in the United States, late editions of the newspapers carried skimpy reports on *Columbia*'s progress. Citizens of Yarmouth reported her flying so low that she had nearly scraped housetops. She was seen leaving Nova Scotia in the vicinity of Seal Harbor, between Liscombe and Canso, and was reported over Trepassey Bay at 6:13 P.M. EST, flying at 800 feet. There, she was said to have dropped to rooftop level. The weather was reported clear from Clarence Cove, 7 miles north of Cape Race, where she was last spotted, disappearing fast over a darkening ocean, on an easterly course. Experts noted that Lindbergh had reached St. John's, 40 miles to the northeast, 31 minutes faster than *Columbia* took to get to Trepassey Bay. Adverse winds were the given explanation.

It was a typical long evening of early summer, as *Columbia* sped easterly in her early hours over the North Atlantic. Below her, were what at first seemed white sails, but turned out to be a field of floating icebergs drifting south. Chamberlin checked his drift against them carefully. The plane, which needed little attention because of her stability, flew virtually by herself in the smooth air. The stabilizers on the tail assembly were adjusted so as to trim the ship into a perfect fore and aft balance, and, as a result, Chamberlin, by attaching a spring device to the rudder bars, was able to fly, sometimes as long as an hour, without touching the controls. Levine, alongside him, was at times pensive and silent, only to break out suddenly into excited conversation, as little things arrested his attention briefly— the chilling weather or a particularly bright star on the horizon.

It was dark now. The chronometer on the control panel pointed to 11 P.M., New York time. Ahead, there appeared little blotches of white with blurred edges—traces of low cloud. Chamberlin eased back on the stick slightly and *Columbia* climbed to get above them. They became more and more frequent as the time passed, and the dark, endless carpet of ocean below often was blotted from view. Then there was a gleam of light from a boat in the distance, approaching quickly underneath the speeding airplane. It was a warm friendly sight to both pilot and passenger. Levine blinked at her with a flashlight. There was no response and the lights faded to the west. Fifty minutes later, more welcome lights gleamed on the horizon through breaks in the clouds. Closer and closer they drew. Levine again blinked his light, and this time there was a response.

"She'll give a report on us," he exclaimed excitedly.

The clouds thickened below them, and rose above them as the night wore on. They were forced to ever-higher altitudes, to stay in the clear. No longer were they able to scan the sea for friendly lights, for they now flew over a heavy undercast, dark and billowy. Up and up they soared, to 12,000 feet, then 13,000, and finally, 15,000. Still, a cloud barrier loomed large and menacing through the windshield. Suddenly they were in it, bumping heavily and able to discern only the motor and spinning prop through the gray blanket that engulfed the little plane.

It was 3 A.M. The outside temperature registered 31 degrees, as they flew on. Both men noticed at once that vision through the windshield was dimming.

"Ice!" thought Chamberlin. He glanced out the port window. The leading edge of the wing was collecting the dreaded particles.

"We'll have to get out of this, quick!" Chamberlin said to the now-silent Levine. He pushed the stick forward, and *Columbia* nosed into a moderate dive, the rushing air whistling through the struts. Early dawn was beginning to lighten the cloud banks as they descended . . . 10,000 feet, 9000, 7000, and 6000. The air was getting warmer.

The ice on the windshield melted, and driblets of water wriggled every which way on the glass in front of them. Still, they went down in a steepish glide, always surrounded by cloud that was so thick at times that the wingtips were invisible; 3000 feet now, and steadily down. There was no break in the cloud. Chamberlin thought of the altimeter which had been set at zero for Roosevelt Field. He knew he had to take every precaution; 1000 feet! he straightened his glide a bit but continued the descent. At 750 feet there were slight breaks, and brief glimpses of a white-capped ocean beneath them.

"At last!" he thought with relief. He had kept his worries quiet for fear of upsetting his passenger.

He leveled *Columbia* at 500 feet. The waves flew by at breakneck speed. From time to time now he opened the throttle wide to keep the spark plugs from fouling with oil. He thought of "Doc" Kimball's predictions, and veered slightly south to find the forecasted clear weather. Sure enough, within an hour, occasional breaks appeared above as the heavy overcast thinned out. The weather warmed perceptibly as they hit what he thought must be the Gulf Stream. All of a sudden it was clear, and the cloud bank faded, quickly, off *Columbia*'s tail. The cabin began to get uncomfortably hot to the men in their heavy flying gear. They stripped off their outer clothing. It felt cooler. Chamberlin reset his course after some quick calculations, for Lands End. It was clear and smooth now with a tail wind as they ate their Sunday-morning breakfast of oranges, chicken soup, and coffee. Neither man felt violently hungry, due, no doubt, to nervous tension.

It was 9 A.M. They were flying at 2000 feet in beautiful clear weather. They could see a minimum of 50 miles in every direction; the motor hummed evenly and they both felt well. Confidence grew in the little cabin. Levine spotted a small steamer in the sea ahead, tugged at Chamberlin's sleeve, and gesticulated wildly. They dove down, and circled her at 200 feet. They saw members of the crew, waving on the deck, but were unable to make out her name. Levine thought she was of Danish or Swedish registry; and then they flashed off on course, exhilarated by the welcome rendezvous.

But greater excitement was in store for them as the morning passed. It was a thrilled Chamberlin who first picked out the four smokestacks in the distance. It was a real ocean liner this time. Closer they came. Chamberlin nosed down, eased back on the throttle and dove on her. They streaked alongside her at the level of her top deck, and zoomed up. Levine made out her name—*MAURE-*

TANIA! Again they sped by the side of the huge ship, her rails jammed with waving passengers, then climbed once more, using the *Mauretania*'s wake as a guide, as they headed back onto course. A quick glance at the shipping news in the New York *Times* of June 4 (which Levine had conveniently brought along) indicated that the liner had sailed from Cherbourg less than 24 hours before. They couldn't be far from the coast if, as they calculated, the *Mauretania* averaged 500 miles a day. The elation of impending success and the thrill of showing *Columbia* off to the hundreds of passengers on the huge liner, gripped both pilot and owner as the *Mauretania* grew smaller and smaller, and finally disappeared over the western horizon.

Within an hour, another boat appeared—at first, a tiny spot on the eastern sea—then growing steadily, until a naval vessel emerged below them. It was the United States cruiser *Memphis*, returning to America with Lindbergh and the crated *Spirit of St. Louis* aboard. Levine wanted to buzz her or jazz her (as it was then called), but Chamberlin shook his head.

"Let's save the fuel," he yelled over the deafening engine noise, while pointing to the gas gauge.

The cabin temperature was a hot 88 degrees by midafternoon.

Levine shouted, "Where are you taking me—Berlin or Rome?"

Chamberlin yelled back, with a grin, "Maybe Spain or Africa, you never can tell if this damned earth inductor compass doesn't work any better!" The needle continued to spin crazily all over the dial in front of them. Chamberlin knew it wasn't to be Rome, for he had promised his old friend Bellanca to save that terminal for a later flight in a new Bellanca-designed ship.

In the late afternoon, a haze appeared ahead, lessening their heretofore unlimited visibility. It thickened steadily until they could see less than 5 miles. A half hour before sunset, another liner hove into view out of the growing obscurity below. They circled the large ship. It was the *Transylvania*. A glance at the shipping schedules showed that they were close to shore, and it was only minutes before they saw in the last rays of the setting sun, low, shining cliffs emerging from the smoky haze ahead. Chamberlin put *Columbia* into a shallow glide and dropped to 1000 feet while he studied the land contours on the charts that were spread out on his lap. It was Lands End! They must have missed the Scilly Isles in the worsening visibility. He circled to get his bearings, and took a course which would lead him over Plymouth. Behind the cliffs, the neat stone walls which separated the green fields of Cornwall crept by in the shadows of early evening. The weather grew thicker and thicker as they flew on. Once again, Chamberlin was forced to put the little monoplane into a climb, to avoid the clouds that rose in front of them. A brief hole in the undercast, later, found them over Plymouth, but it quickly closed and they were forced to climb still higher. A gale-like wind blew out of the northwest, speeding them along on their course. It should be an easy 5-hour flight to Berlin from Plymouth, thought Chamberlin, as he determined that he had at least 10 hours of fuel left in the tanks. He leaned out the mixture, slightly, so as to get maximum power at minimum gas consumption. Now the motor should burn only 10½ gallons an hour.

Darkness surrounded them again and the cloud undercast rose, forcing them steadily up. It was their second night in the air. Levine dozed beside Chamberlin. Chamberlin glanced at the aimlessly gy-rating needle of the useless earth inductor, and then to the magnetic compass which hung in front of him. It too was behaving erratically. It was cold. They had, once more, put on their heavy flying jackets. Higher and higher they flew to get out of the cloud as the plane bounced heavily in the turbulent air. At 15,000 feet, *Columbia* broke into the clear for a moment. The stars shone brightly in the black skies above. But in front of them was more weather, soaring well over their route into the heavens. Again *Columbia* was prodded for more altitude. Chamberlin worried over the lack of oxygen. He felt the controls become sluggish, and the plane wobble in the thinning air. He realized then that he couldn't get over the weather, and decided to wait for daylight. He had plenty of gas. Changing course, he flew 20-minute north-south legs. It was cold and rough, as the little plane was tossed pitilessly about in the stormy skies. Chamberlin guessed that he might be over the North Sea. He was exhausted and cold, but he didn't dare trust the controls to the inexperienced Levine at night, and in these violent air currents. From time to time there was a brief break; once he thought he spotted a moving shaft of light; a revolving beacon? Then, it was gone in the rolling, billowing clouds. There was nothing but cloud, tall peaks and deep valleys of it, and the ever-present bouncing and jouncing—the rapid ascents and the breath-taking descents of the little plane as she fought out the storm. He was too tired to think of navigation, and had only the energy to keep *Columbia* on an even keel throughout the perilous night.

The light of dawn came at last, and Chamberlin waked the dozing Levine.

"See what you can do with her for a while. I've got to get some rest."

He unbuckled himself and slid out of his seat, as Levine took over. He climbed up onto the familiar bed atop the fuselage tank, but he wasn't to be there for long. The inexperienced, though ever-willing Levine, lost his bearings in the thick weather. Soon *Columbia* was nose-up in a stall, and then off, sharply, on her left wing, into a steep and dizzy spiral. Levine was laughing wildly, apparently unaware of the danger, when Chamberlin was thrown back into the cabin by the abrupt bank and dive. He struggled back into the pilot's seat. The wings shuddered as the plane plummeted down. The oscillating rudder whipped the rudder bars violently at his feet. The needle on the altimeter spun swiftly around the 100-foot calibrations. He struggled desperately to get control of his ship. The air speed indicator passed 160 mph—its highest point. At last, he was able to smother the rudder bars, and pulled her out of her weird dive. Soon *Columbia* was flying levelly at 4000 feet after having dropped from 17,000 in only a few seconds. Levine explained that he thought he was near the Harz Mountains in Germany, and was trying to clear them!

Chamberlin was determined to find out where he was, and dropped *Columbia* slowly through the blinding cloud. With the aid of the questionable magnetic compass, he had tried to return to course just before the dawn. It was now daylight. At 3000 feet the clouds appeared to thin out, as the flyers could see fleeting openings. He took the ship down farther, and at 750 feet they suddenly caught sight of water below, and then land! In front of them, in the rain and gray mistiness, were eerie, orange lights; maybe the blast furnaces of the Ruhr, Chamberlin thought, optimistically. Perhaps it might be Essen, and the water they had passed might have been the Rhine River. Levine thought that it looked like the vicinity of Bremerhaven, which he had visited recently. They both agreed that they must have had divine guidance to be over land, at all, after the night they had been through.

Presently they saw flares shooting skyward off to their left. Chamberlin swooped low. It was an airport, and it was not long before he could make out the name DORTMUND on a hangar roof. He saw a crowd of workers staring up. He cut his throttles, and flew barely 15 feet above them, as he leaned out of the cabin and screamed in his best German, "*Nach Berlin? Nach Berlin?*" They appeared to have heard him, and pointed. It was 4:30 A.M., locally, as *Columbia* left Dortmund. Her gas supply was dwindling, but at least she was over land.

Meanwhile, in New York, the expected report had been received from the *Mauretania*. *Columbia* had passed over her at 11 A.M., New York time, June 5 (3 P.M., locally). She flew at 150 feet, so that the passengers aboard could make out her markings, clearly. At the time of the sighting, *Mauretania* reported that she was 340 miles off Lands End. *Columbia* was, they reported, flying high over Padstone, Cornwall, at 8:45 P.M. (3:45 P.M., New York time), and was heard over Boulogne, France, for a time around midnight, seemingly flying in a circle. Later, the hearers said, the sound faded on a course that indicated a heading for Cologne.

Mrs. Chamberlin returned from Long Island to the Hotel Biltmore in New York when she heard that they had made landfall. She was thrilled and relieved. At the Levine home in Belle Harbor excitement took the place of the long period of anxiety. Mr. Nova, Levine's father-in-law, and treasurer of Columbia Aircraft, pad and pencil in hand, figured that they had 16 hours of fuel remaining as they left Plymouth, England. Grace Nova Levine, having learned from Lockwood that Berlin was the probable destination, cabled her husband, c/o U. S. Ambassador Jacob Gould Schurman: FOLLOWING YOUR FLIGHT WITH PRAYER, LOVE, PRIDE, AND CONFIDENCE. LOVE FROM FAMILY. CABLE PROMPTLY. WILL LEAVE TO MEET YOU.

Isaac Levine, Charles's proud father, said, "Charlie's is a greater feat than Lindbergh's!"

When questioned as to what he meant, he replied, with glowing and parental pride, "Well, it's Lindbergh's business to fly. He sort of had to go. But Charlie didn't have to go. He just went!" The elderly Mr. Levine admitted that he'd spent a sleepless night.

When Mrs. Chamberlin was told how *Columbia* had flown over the *Mauretania*, she said happily, "How I wish I'd been aboard that ship! I can see him leaning out, and waving to all those people"; and, in his home town of Denison, Iowa, Chamberlin's mother, beaming with joy, said, "I'm not worried in the least. I was worried before he left, but not now!"

As it became more and more evident that Berlin was the intended destination, Mrs. Chamberlin and Mrs. Levine, together with Mrs. Lockwood and Samuel Hartman, made hasty preparations to sail for Bremerhaven the following day aboard the liner *Berlin*.

The *Columbia* flew on in the rain, just under a 2000-foot ceiling.

After 65 miles, the weather began to clear fortunately, for ahead of them loomed Levine's dreaded Harz Mountains. Chamberlin skirted them skillfully rather than climb over them. The fuel problem was becoming acute, and as the needle on the gauge neared the empty mark, Chamberlin kept his eye peeled for a suitable landing spot. Neither of them was sure of their exact position, because of the weather and the faulty compasses. Levine demanded that they fly on until the last drop of fuel was gone.

Chamberlin replied, "You're the doctor. It's your plane, but I'd hate to bend it up trying to get a few more miles."

He asked Levine to climb over the gas tank and brace himself in the rear of the navigator's cabin, for he feared the plane would be nose-heavy on landing, because of the empty tanks. No sooner had Levine clambered aft than the motor sputtered and wheezed and barked to a stop. Chamberlin glanced below quickly and made out a likely field that looked level and clear. From 2000 feet it appeared smooth and hard. He pointed *Columbia*'s nose downward—after banking gently into the wind. He was ready to bring her in again, dead stick. Closer and closer, the grown field bobbed ahead of him through his windshield. Lower, he glided, and he was over the end of it. He eased back on the stick to level out, as, what looked like wheat stalks, swept below the undercarriage. *Columbia* touched down to a three-point landing, and bounced heavily through a rough field. Chamberlin kicked her into a ground loop to avoid an onrushing fence, and brought her to a stop, after 43 hours in the air. *Columbia* had traveled 3905 miles—295 more than Lindbergh. The time of touchdown was 6:05 A.M. (1:05 A.M., New York time), June 6, 1927.

Levine jumped out onto the field, first. Chamberlin followed, unsteady and unable to balance himself properly after the long flight. He looked up and saw a wildly elated Levine, hopping and skipping about like a prize fighter jumping rope.

It was a half hour before anybody arrived. Then they saw a middle-aged woman and two boys come across the field. Levine tried his German, but soon found that it was understood better in New York than in Germany. They were able to understand, at length, that they had come down on a farm outside the village of Mansfeldt, 4 miles from the town of Eisleben, in Saxony. In halting German, well punctuated with gesticulations, the flyers explained that they needed gas. One of the boys caught on, said, "*Ach! benzol!*" and dashed off through the fields to get his bike in order to fetch 90 liters from Eisleben. Chamberlin wanted, also, a map of the local area, but neither of them could think of the word and no amount of charade-playing could get the idea across to their hosts.

Both men wanted to fly on to Berlin as quickly as possible, for they felt that by now a huge crowd must be waiting for them. It was not long before a truck drew up, carrying 20 gallons of fuel, but the only means of transferring it to *Columbia*'s tanks was by the use of a quart-sized coffeepot with a curved spout! The procedure took well over an hour. By then, fifteen or twenty of the more curious local gentry had gathered and stood around gaping wondrously. Levine grabbed a paper bag, scribbled hastily on it the details of the flight, and persuaded ten of them to attest to a certification of the time of landing.

It was now 9 A.M. and the sun was warm in a cloudless sky. It took Chamberlin half an hour to start the engine. He had to do it by hand, as the inertia starter had been removed to save weight. Exhausted from the flight, he was forced to pull the propeller through again and again, without result. Finally the motor caught as the tired pilot neared a collapse. He and Levine climbed aboard, took to the air, and headed hopefully for Berlin. Once airborne, there was a difference of opinion as to the whereabouts of the city. The differences were settled in an unlikely fashion: when Levine flew, he pointed in the direction he thought correct; when Chamberlin took over, they flew another course. As a result, they veered east of Berlin, and an hour and a half later, found themselves again out of gas, 6 miles beyond the airfield at Kottbus. Realizing their predicament too late, they turned back and headed for the field, but the engine died, and Chamberlin was forced to make yet another dead-stick approach into another smooth-looking brown field. Once more Levine squeezed himself over the gas tank, into the rear cabin and took hold. The plane settled easily, but this time Chamberlin had not been as lucky in his emergency choice, for when they touched down, the wheels sank deeply into a soft mire, and the plane stopped with a jerk, and nosed over, breaking her propeller. The jolt was such that every loose article in the cabin cascaded over Chamberlin's head and shoulders. Levine freed himself, first; rushed to the forward part of the plane and peered in the cabin, worried. There sat Chamberlin, covered with powdered milk, soup, assorted chocolates, and other items, cursing, "Whatta helluva landing!"

Crowds arrived faster from the nearer town of Klinge, but the alert Mayor of Kottbus beat his counterpart to the punch and the two flyers were whisked to the Hotel Ansorge, but not until they had ordered a new propeller and some big wheels to extract them from the mud. They were determined to make Berlin.

The news of the two landings traveled fast, and, in no time, airplanes by the dozens flew in from fields in the general vicinity. Within 2 hours, a plane from Tempelhof Airdrome in Berlin landed at Kottbus, carrying a propeller which had been taken off a Heinkel plane with a Wright engine. Other planes bore journalists from all over the continent, including Dorothy Thompson of the New York *Evening Post*, and Arthur Mann of the New York *World*. Little Kottbus suddenly became the boiling center of the aviation world.

The flyers returned to the field to supervise the repairs to *Columbia*. The new propeller was attached, and, rather than risk a take-off from the muddy field, it was decided to tow her to a soccer field nearby. When this had been accomplished with the use of a truck and some strong-backed German helpers, they returned to the hotel. Chamberlin was exhausted—too tired even to eat. He drew a hot tub, sank in, but, alas, there was no soap. So he wrapped himself in a huge bath towel, curled up on his bed, and slept soundly.

The indefatigable Levine accepted an invitation to dine with the Mayor of Kottbus, and it was a splendid table he sat down to. The menu consisted of hors d'oeuvres, crab soup, fried eels, roast goose, and beer.

"I'm sorry we don't have this at home," he gratefully told his host as he finally retired to bed later in the evening.

At Tempelhof in Berlin, thousands of patient spectators camped for the night to await the flyers' arrival the next day.

Congratulatory messages from government leaders poured in to the harassed telegraph office at Kottbus, some addressed to Chamberlin, alone, and some, to both. There were cables from President Calvin Coolidge, Secretary of State Frank B. Kellogg, and Secretary of War Dwight F. Davis. There were many from Great Britain, as the English were thrilled by Chamberlin's English ancestry; and, while the world acclaim did not equal that which greeted Lindbergh, it was more than substantial.

From the aviation world came laudatory statements from Commander Byrd, Elmer Sperry, Igor Sikorsky, Charles L. Lawrance, and René Fonck, now poised in New York for a new try in his new Sikorsky-built *Ville de Paris*.

Said Fonck: "Wonderful lads are Chamberlin and Levine, and it was a wonderful performance!"

Giuseppe Bellanca's comment was guarded, though there was no question that he was thrilled over the success.

"I admire his courage," he said of Levine, "but I'm sorry he went, because I feel sure that if Chamberlin had a competent navigator aboard, he wouldn't have strayed from his course, and the plane would have easily made Berlin." He picked this time, also, to announce through his attorney, La Guardia, that he was organizing a company to build multi-engined planes to carry "not less than forty passengers to Europe," and within days the Bellanca Aircraft Corporation was in existence. Though he would build other fine aircraft, he was not destined to play a large part in the ocean passenger flights of the future.

Chamberlin and Levine, thoroughly refreshed, arose early the next morning. Overnight, a celebration had been planned for them by the citizens of Kottbus. At noon they were marched down the cobblestoned main street to a flag-bedecked City Hall in front of which a large cheering crowd had gathered. At the last minute the harried town fathers discovered that there was no American flag. There was a great scurrying about, until someone came forward with a large banner, he claimed, was the Stars and Stripes. It was run up the flag pole, with haste, and, much to the embarrassment of the reception leaders, they found that it contained only thirty stars and no stripes at all! The omission was forgotten, however, in the gaiety of the occasion. Led by the mayor and other dignitaries, there were innumerable speeches, and loud, martial strains of music. Chamberlin and Levine were presented with the keys to the city, and the festivities closed with a brassy rendition by the town band of the *Star-Spangled Banner*, and *Deutschland Uber Alles*.

The flyers were then escorted to the soccer field, where *Columbia* stood ready. A local mechanic swung the propeller for Chamberlin, and the Whirlwind caught immediately. Chamberlin ran her up, to test the Heinkel prop. It would make only 1350 rpms, but, Chamberlin, impatient, felt that there was sufficient power to get them to Tempelhof. Late in the afternoon, with the crowd cheering and waving, *Columbia* took off without difficulty on the short flight to Berlin, accompanied by a fleet of twenty planes. At 6 P.M., the little yellow plane landed at Tempelhof, before 100,000 wildly excited Germans screaming *"Hoch! Hoch!"* in a unison salute to their heroes. The flyers were rescued from the crowd, and taken to a hangar, where they were greeted by Ambassador Schurman, and, shortly thereafter, they were whisked off to the embassy to rest up for a triumphant, official welcome from Berliners.

The next days were hectic. There was a monster reception in Berlin, led by President Paul von Hindenburg, with the inevitable flag-waving crowds, bands and speeches, as the smiling aviators were acclaimed by hundreds of thousands. Hindenburg cabled a flowery message of congratulation to President Coolidge. There were innumerable press conferences.

"Will you fly back?" Chamberlin was asked.

"Yes, on a boat!" he replied laughingly.

Both agreed that they had comparatively little trouble over the Atlantic and that the worst part of the flight had been on the second night, after they had reached land. "We were completely lost," admitted Chamberlin.

Levine was loquacious and expansive. Simultaneously, he hinted that *Columbia* would make the return trip, announced that he would invest $2,000,000 in an airline to Europe and told of plans for an immediate tour of Europe in *Columbia*, including stops at Vienna, Rome, Madrid, London, and Paris. He was unrelenting in his public criticism of Pioneer Instruments and its earth inductor compass. Charles Colvin, president of Pioneer, came to his company's defense from New York, and charged that Levine was critical only because he didn't want to pay for the equipment.

He said, further: "The compass can't run wild. One of its characteristics is that it runs or it doesn't; besides which, Levine wouldn't let Goldsborough give it a final check-out."

After an inspection of the instrument in Paris by a Pioneer agent, Colvin accused the flyers of disconnecting it out of stupidity. The bitter exchanges continued for many weeks.

Reporters surrounded Mrs. Chamberlin and Mrs. Levine, as they boarded the *Berlin* at 12:30 A.M., June 7, together with Mrs. Lockwood and Samuel Hartman.

"Of course, I'll forgive him," said Mrs. Levine, with regard to her husband's abrupt departure. "I'm the proudest woman in the world!"

Mrs. Chamberlin was equally proud. "I'm simply thrilled," she said with tears in her eyes. "That's all I can say."

Chamberlin and Levine, after their gala reception in Berlin, flew *Columbia* to cities throughout Europe—Munich, Vienna, Budapest, Prague, Warsaw, Berne, and, finally Paris. They were met at each stop with tumultuous welcomes from huge crowds, and elaborate ceremonies in their honor. They were joined by their wives, who were fêted as well. The shy, retiring Chamberlin was exhausted by the unceasing furor; Levine appeared to revel in it. He talked constantly of the return flight, while Chamberlin, seemingly reluctant to make the attempt, refused to be committed. The combined strains drew the two men apart, and led them on separate ways when the schedules of the day did not require a joint appearance. As it turned out, Chamberlin and his wife would return to New York by ship in early July, while Levine would remain in Europe for the summer, cutting a wide, and often controversial swathe.

While the splendid flight of *Columbia* did not generate the electric and spontaneous response from the world as Lindbergh's, the teetotaling Chamberlin did equal "Lindy" in one respect, by having a cocktail named after him. Its ingredients: 65 percent vodka, 25 percent dry sherry; 10 percent Dubonnet, and two dashes of Angostura Bitters!

CHAPTER VIII

The America *and* Bird of Paradise

1. At Roosevelt Field, the giant *America* was undergoing her final load tests. On the day after Lindbergh's landing in Paris, the plane was christened in a flowery ceremony by the daughters of Rodman Wanamaker. Despite the excitement at Le Bourget which had permeated America, a large crowd was on hand for the occasion. Speeches were made by representatives of New York City, the armed forces, the ubiquitous Grover Whalen, and the courtly Commander Byrd and his crew.

The first days of June were quiet. Only *America* was seen on test flights over Long Island—two or three a day—usually with Bert Acosta at the controls and with Kinkaid and Goldsborough, more often than not, aboard, testing the instruments, and listening intently for any false sound out of the Wright engines. On one occasion, the keen ear of Kinkaid caught a sound of faulty valves in the center motor, which he adjusted forthwith; when a run-up disclosed that the rpms had fallen off drastically, no time was wasted. A new engine was installed. On another occasion, as the big ship was trying a take-off, the right axle froze, but the skillful Acosta, again at the controls, was able to bring the ship to a stop without further damage.

The load tests followed. With Acosta as the pilot, *America* lifted easily into the air carrying 13,600 pounds, after a run of but 1000 yards. Soon after, she went up as easily with 14,500 pounds, and with Harry Guggenheim and "Doc" Kinkaid as passengers. Byrd's statement that *America* wouldn't go until Lindbergh had returned home, appeared to be all that was deterring her.

On June 7, with Bert Acosta flying her, she took off quickly carrying the pilot, three mechanics, and a ballast of sand and water—all totaling 15,500 pounds. Without using the ramp, she rose into the air after a run of only 2100 feet, and climbed speedily to 1000 feet, where, on instructions from Acosta, the ballast was dumped to lighten the strain on the undercarriage at landing. After the flight, it was announced, to no one's surprise, that Bernt Balchen had been added to the crew, as relief pilot. Balchen, a twenty-seven-year-old, blond Scandinavian, was born in Norway, the son of a well-known surgeon. He attended public schools, and at eighteen joined the Norwegian army, only to resign two years later. He then entered the Norwegian Naval School for training in engineering, surveying and aviation, and was graduated in 1924 with the rank of lieutenant. He was put in command of a polar search party in 1925 to look for the missing Arctic explorers, Roald Amundsen and Lincoln Ellsworth, and later accompanied Amundsen on his polar expedition in the dirigible *Norge*. It was at this time that he met Byrd, who was planning his polar flight, and the young Norwegian was so useful to the commander at Spitzbergen that he became thereafter one of the Byrd "gang." Though shy, he was well-liked in flying circles, and pilots took delight in imitating his singsongy, accented English. He was known to be a capable navigator, as well as a good pilot— talents which would complement Acosta's vaunted flying abilities. He was the only bachelor in the crew.

Despite the successes of Lindbergh and Chamberlin, the crowds still flocked to Roosevelt Field. They watched *America* make brief flights to test out the radio; they watched Bernt Balchen fly her, often with Bryce Goldsborough aboard to check the instruments. The Pioneer expert paid particular attention to the controversial earth inductor compass, which had become a cause célèbre since *Columbia*'s flight. The public dispute between Levine and Colvin was in the headlines, and Goldsborough wanted to make certain that the compass operated properly this time.

One June 13, the fabulous day of Lindbergh's tickertape parade up Broadway, Byrd issued a statement saying that *America*'s destination would be Paris, and Paris only, in reply to a cable from Levine, suggesting that he and Chamberlin, in *Columbia*, accompany *America* on a return flight to the United States. Chamberlin, when questioned, had no comment.

"Doc" Kimball, at the Weather Bureau, was busy charting four maps a day for Byrd. The weather was not promising, as a low pressure area hovered over the eastern Atlantic. Nevertheless, *America* was loaded, partially, with fuel for the trip; it was explained that

the remainder would not be put aboard until the big ship had
been hauled up to the top of the ramp just prior to the take-off.

One June 17, Kimball reported two storm centers over the Atlantic,
one 1000 miles west of Scotland, and the other covering an 800-
mile area southeast of Newfoundland. His maps were produced
by radioed observations from fifteen ships as they crossed the Atlantic. The messages were forwarded to him by receiving stations of
the Radio Corporation of America.

The following day, Saturday, the storms at sea still prevented a
take-off. There were reports of heavy fogs from Cape Cod to Sable
Island, and thick clouds extending from Halifax east over the ocean.
Bryce Goldsborough spent the day tinkering and making final adjustments on the earth inductor, until it worked to his satisfaction.

On Sunday, "Doc" Kimball reported extremely bad ocean conditions. Rain and fog swept the seas off Newfoundland, and ships in
the Atlantic told of rain and a heavy cloud cover from midocean
to the Irish coast.

There was a restlessness around the Byrd hangar on Sunday—both
among the crew and the thousands of spectators who milled about.
America, filled with 300 gallons of gas out of the 1300 she would
carry on the trip, stood with her nose jutting out of the hangar
door. Suddenly, there was a stir from the crowd when a man appeared on crutches with a plaster cast on his right leg. It was
Floyd Bennett, accompanied by Dr. Raymond P. Sullivan, on a
short outing from St. Vincent's Hospital. Byrd and the rest of
America's crew greeted the injured pilot warmly.

"By George!" said Byrd, "I never thought I'd see you out here!"

Then, in answer to questions from reporters as to future plans
for his old friend, Byrd said firmly, "Certainly, Bennett is going to
the South Pole with me when I go, either as second in command or
as co-commander!"

Noville, nearby, explained to other newsmen that he planned to
transmit radio messages every 2 hours during the flight. He said
that the radio, which weighed 241 pounds excluding the antenna,
had been designed by Malcolm P. Hansen of the Naval Research
Laboratories. The antenna was composed of copper wire, nearly 100
yards in length and weighted at the end. It was operated manually
by reeling it in or out, as the occasion demanded, and when in use,
it would trail far behind the flying plane.

The day went on. "Doc" Kinkaid puttered with the engines as he
would continue to to do until take-off time. Bert Acosta commented

on a published story which said that Mexico planned to claim him as a native son, if the flight were successful.

"I hope they have a good time in their celebration," he said laughingly, "but the truth of the matter is that my father was Castilian Spanish, and his people were among the earliest settlers in California. My parents never went to Mexico, and my mother was Martha Blanche Snook from Emporia, Kansas!"

Before returning to the Garden City Hotel for the night, Byrd again checked the weather. A depression was still centered over the mid-Atlantic with low clouds and rain; but the upper winds, in which he took a great interest, were blowing from the west, off the Irish coast, at 50 miles an hour at 2000 feet, and up to 80 miles an hour, at 18,000.

As if to reassure the public that his flight was to be no mere stunt, he announced again that it was his intention to chart the safest air route to Europe. He said he intended to run the plane like a ship.

"The best route might be the southern end of a low area," he added, "or perhaps a storm area which produces heavy westerly winds."

He had a 600-mile leeway in his cruising range, which would enable him to vary his course to a certain extent.

The next days, *America* remained on the ground, secure in her Roosevelt Field hangar. On June 24, a low was reported extending from Nantucket to Newfoundland, halting the preparations, which had included towing the plane, tail first, to the top of the ramp. She was taken from her hangar at 8:30 P.M. as dusk was settling and a crowd of 2000 murmured with anticipation. Movie newsreel cameramen and photographers bustled about, taking what they thought might be last-minute shots of the plane. Bert Acosta climbed in the pilot's seat, with "Doc" Kinkaid alongside him. The three engines were started, one after the other, and roared into action. Each was run up, and thoroughly tested, as pilot and engineer listened with care—then were shut down. They could detect no flaws.

The huge plane had been dragged up the incline by the use of a steel cable and tackle, and at the top of the hill had been tied securely by the tail, with chocks under its wheels preparatory to the "run-ups."

Afterward, Acosta left for the Garden City Hotel for what appeared to be his last night's rest before the take-off. The crowd, however, remained curious and expectant. At 9 P.M. a storm broke over the field with winds gusting up to 60 miles an hour. The crowd scattered and took shelter. Patrolmen and mechanics raced across the field to the floundering *America*, which was being buffeted menacingly by the heavy gale. They held the tail down, while "Doc" Kinkaid lashed the elevators firmly in an "up" position. Still, the gusts swept over the big wings, threatening to pull *America* loose from her moorings. Kinkaid came to the rescue again; rushed to the cockpit, and sat working the ailerons, so as to stabilize the ship until the storm abated. It was a close call for *America*. Meanwhile, Byrd had received the bad weather news, and, at the hotel, announced a further postponement of the flight.

2.   While the Byrd party waited interminably for an improvement in weather conditions, another race was developing for the first to make a non-stop flight over the Pacific Ocean to Hawaii. The first attempt to fly to Hawaii had been made in the summer of 1925 by Commander John "Jang" Rodgers, Naval Aviator 2 in a large PN-9 flying boat. The plane failed to arrive in Hawaii on schedule. The days went by as hope waned. On the ninth day after taking off, Rodgers and his crew were picked up by an American submarine, drifting several hundred miles off the island of Oahu. They had been forced by lack of fuel to land in the sea, following a flight of 1841 miles. Tragically, Commander Rodgers died in an airplane crash less than a year later.

Major General Mason Patrick, who had authorized Noel Davis's use of an Army plane, was anxious to celebrate his imminent retirement with one final achievement. For many months, he had been busy planning a non-stop flight sponsored by the Army from California to Hawaii. In this connection he obtained the use of a Fokker-built, Army tri-motored airplane powered by three Wright Whirlwind engines. She was painted olive drab, with a red and white striped rudder, and was named *Bird of Paradise*.

To fly her, he enlisted twenty-nine-year-old Lieutenant Lester J. Maitland, a veteran of the aviation section of the Army Signal Corps. Maitland had enlisted in it in 1917 after completing high school in Milwaukee, Wisconsin.

Maitland had flown all types of planes at Army fields throughout the country. In 1923 he was assigned to speed-test a new Curtiss-designed racer, which he flew at 244 miles an hour. He finished second in the Pulitzer Trophy race of 1922, and was known for his ability to handle any type of plane, under almost any circumstances. General Patrick was convinced that he'd picked the ideal pilot.

As navigator for *Bird of Paradise*, he selected Lieutenant Albert F. Hegenberger, a thirty-two-year-old, Boston-born, MIT-educated member of the Army Flying Service. Hegenberger had served for a number of years as Chief of the Instrument Service of the navigation section at McCook Field, Dayton, Ohio. He was an experienced navigator, and had been an early user, and was an advocate of, the now maligned earth inductor compass. It would be his task to navigate the plane so that it would not miss the 317-mile-long chain of Hawaiian Islands after a flight of 3000 miles. A miscalculation on his part of 7½ degrees would spell disaster. It would require even more accuracy to hit the 46-mile long island of Oahu, where their destination, Wheeler Field, was situated.

Patrick, satisfied with plane and crew, added a new feature to ocean flying. He arranged to have a 10-kilowatt transmitter set up on the California coast with a sending range of 1000 miles. A similar installation was built on Paia, the Island of Maui, which would transmit signals toward the California shore. Thus came into being the forerunner of the now-common "beam," for it was planned that the transmissions would serve as a radio guide for the crew. The device had been developed by Hegenberger's group in Dayton.

Two 90-foot antenna masts were constructed at each station, from which triangular loop aerials were suspended. On take-off both beacons were to start flashing signals seaward. If the plane remained on course, or in the "T" zone, the signals "A" and "N" would be heard simultaneously over the plane's receiver. If the plane veered to the left, or south, the signal "N" would be heard alone, and vice versa.

In addition to the beam-receiving equipment, the plane was scheduled to carry an earth inductor compass, a bubble sextant, and smoke bombs, to assist in the calculation of drift. It was planned that *Bird of Paradise* would weigh 13,300 pounds, fully loaded, and would carry 1040 gallons of gasoline, sufficient for thirty hours of flight.

On June 23, Maitland and Hegenberger made final preparations at Rockwell Field, San Diego, for a flight to Oakland, California, which was to be their departure point. Maitland, tall and sandy-haired, and the shorter, balding Hegenberger, were seen supervising the stowing of supplies under the hot California sun, for they did not intend to remain long in Oakland.

At Bay Farm Island Field, near Oakland, a new 7200-foot runway had been completed. On one end stood a shiny, silver Travelair monoplane named the *City of Oakland,* powered by the now-redoubtable Whirlwind engine. The wings jutted out evenly from the top of the fuselage, and there were two open cockpits for pilot and navigator. She was originally designed as a six-passenger ship for commercial use, but had been purchased for $10,000 from the Pacific Air Transport Company by San Francisco realtor, Edward Moffett, who had the necessary renovations made in order to become the first to back a successful non-stop flight over the Pacific. For several weeks, thirty-four-year-old veteran pilot, Ernest L. Smith, and his navigator, Charles F. Carter, had been conducting tests of their speedy little plane from the Army's Crissy Field in San Francisco. The Army, however, had refused them permission to use the field for the take-off, and the plane, only recently, had been dismantled partially and trucked over to Bay Farm. Two or three test flights and minor adjustments were all that remained before they would be ready.

On June 25, Maitland and Hegenberger flew from Rockwell Field to Crissy, and the following day, *Bird of Paradise* joined the *City of Oakland* at the end of the long runway at Bay Farm Island. The field soon became the Roosevelt Field of the West, with crowds flocking from all over the Bay area to stare at the two planes which were parked within feet of each other, while workers swarmed over them in the usual, last-minute preparations. They presented a colorful spectacle—the huge olive-drab tri-motor and the sleek little monoplane.

"Like the tortoise and the hare," mumbled an astute observer, as he peered curiously into the two machines. Major General Patrick, Major Delos Emmons, the Commander of Crissy Field, and others in the Army retinue, inspected the Fokker with care. General Patrick had contributed much to the cause of long-distance flying during his tenure as Chief of the Air Corps, and he was bound to have his last venture a success.

Despite the Army's refusal to Smith for the use of Crissy, a friendly rivalry sprang up between the service and civilian crews. Never did they take their eyes off the other, lest one sneak off first. Little remained to be done. Both planes made final test flights on June 27, and the large crowds, sensing the imminency of a take-off, lingered around the field until late in the evening. At Wheeler Field, located on a high mountain-bounded plateau outside Honolulu, there was also a feeling of imminency, as plans were rushed to welcome the flyers.

Those who remained at Bay Farm Island Field that balmy Monday evening saw gas trucks under the glare of searchlights move toward the *Bird of Paradise,* and workmen commence the 5-hour fueling of the large wing and fuselage tanks. Maitland and Hegenberger retired at 9 P.M. for a night's rest on orders from General Patrick.

It was cloudless and warm when dawn came on June 28 at Bay Farm Island. Spectators streamed to the field early, to join those who had remained all night. By 6:30 A.M., it was estimated that there were more than 20,000 behind the guard ropes which had been set up 100 feet from the planes. Mechanic E. J. Rivers led a crew of workmen, as they gave *Bird of Paradise* a final tuning while, close by, other workmen swarmed over the little Travelair. The crew of *City of Oakland* had taken due notice of the fueling of the Army ship during the night, and accordingly had given instructions for their ship to be ready.

Maitland and Hegenberger arrived at the field at 5:30 A.M., already suited up, accompanied by General Patrick and other officers. They watched intently as work was done on their plane. A naval officer stepped out of the crowd and talked to Hegenberger. He was Lieutenant Byron J. Connell, the pilot of Commander Rodgers's PN-9, which had failed in its Pacific Ocean attempt two years before.

"I wish I were going with you," he said plaintively.

Mr. and Mrs. J. W. Maitland of Burlingame, California, parents of the pilot, were escorted through police lines to join their son in the group that stood around the plane.

At 6:30 A.M., Ernest Smith and Charles Carter rushed up to the *City of Oakland,* startled, apparently, at the readiness of their rivals. They joined with their ground crew, working feverishly to expedite the loading of their little ship. They knew they were behind, but they felt that, with the higher cruising speed of the Travelair, once airborne, they could make up the lost time.

Maitland bade his parents good-bye, and with Hegenberger exchanged farewells with the ground crew and Army officers who surrounded them. The crowd, held back by police lines, murmured with excitement. Ernest Smith looked over his shoulder and hurriedly grabbed another fuel drum.

"God bless you, boys! I hope you make it," said General Patrick fervently, as he shook hands with them both. They climbed into the cockpit; Maitland in the pilot's chair to the left, Hegenberger to his right. Mechanics started the motors, the port, first, then, the center and the starboard. They idled for a few seconds, and then Maitland hit each throttle, consecutively, and each engine responded with a full blast, throwing up clouds of sandy dust behind. Satisfied with the even pulsations, he pulled back on the levers, and there was comparative quiet. The pilot waved from the cockpit, and, at the signal, mechanics pulled the chocks away. Ernest Smith ran over from the *City of Oakland*, smiling, and clasped his hands over his head in the classical, fighter's salute. The three engines growled, then bellowed powerfully, as the huge plane quivered, and started to move down the dry, sandy runway. The swirling propellers blew up small cyclones of dust, and she became hidden virtually from view as she gathered speed. Halfway down the field, her tail rose off the ground. Faster and faster she sped, and at the 6000-foot mark, she rose gracefully into the air. *Bird of Paradise* was seen last by Californians, as she flew west over the Golden Gate, at 7:15 A.M., at 2000 feet.

3.   All attention at the field turned now to the little silver Travelair. The Army had been cooperative in helping the civilian plane. Two days before, they had provided her with a new, light but rugged undercarriage. At this moment, it was learned that *City of Oakland* needed a new altimeter. Captain Bill Royal jumped into a plane and flew over to Crissy Field. He obtained, without delay, an Army instrument, and returned. By 8 A.M., it had been installed, checked, and all seemed ready. Smith and Carter reappeared in flying suits, as last-minute supplies were loaded. Smith climbed in first, and Carter followed into the little open cockpit behind the pilot. The chocks were pulled away, and the 4732-pound monoplane fled down the runway amidst clouds of dust, rose quickly, at the halfway mark, banked, and flew west in hot pursuit of the leaders. The spectators on the ground cheered for the game underdog, as daylight appeared under her wheels at 8:36 A.M.

Alas, though, ten minutes later, the pursuit ended, for the little ship reappeared over the field, banked into the wind, and slipped, gingerly, with her great load, to a gentle landing. The deflector in front of Navigator Carter had broken, and the inrush of air hampered him in his use of the sextant. He tried to attract Smith's attention, but the competitive pilot was too eager in his pursuit of the Army plane. He jabbed Smith in the ribs, leaning forward over the unprotected fuselage. There was still no response. He did it again and again. Finally, the pilot turned, understood the problem, but was reluctant to go back. He motioned, wildly, to the west— out over the Pacific, and tried to shriek over the roaring motor, "Let's go! Let's stay with it!" He pleaded in vain, for Carter was adamant. Sadly Smith turned the silver plane around and headed for home.

Great efforts were made at the field to locate a new shield, while the impatient Smith champed at the bit. One was found, in an adjacent hangar, but it did not fit. Smith, close to tears, begged for permission to go on alone, but wiser heads, including that of his backer Moffett, stopped him. It was too late in the day when a proper-fitting shield arrived, and by the time it had been fitted into place, Navigator Carter declined to go, in that he felt there was no longer any chance to catch Bird of Paradise. In addition, a brisk cross wind had sprung up, making a heavily laden take-off precarious.

Over the Pacific, potentially serious troubles arose almost at once, aboard the Fokker. Within an hour, reception of the signals from the San Francisco beacon faded, and soon were heard no more. The earth inductor compass behaved erratically, and Hegenberger was forced to rely on his skill with the sextant and the magnetic compass to hit the little target that allowed for such a limited margin of error. The most discomforting problem, while not perilous, was discovered when they were 4 hours out. Hunger gripped them, and though Hegenberger searched high and low for the food supply, it was not to be found. They knew it was aboard because they had seen it loaded, but the only thing that turned up was, thankfully, the water, which was found tucked in behind Maitland's seat. Desperately, Hegenberger ransacked the cabin until it looked as though thieves had been searching for jewels, but the food remained hidden. They would have to dine on water!

A little after noon, Maitland pointed the nose of Bird of Paradise upward in a gentle climb, to avoid a cloud layer which had moved in, and to try and escape the effects of a strong wind which crossed their bow. Up and up, they flew, until the altimeter read 11,000 feet. There they found the air smooth, and the winds lighter. But suddenly an alarming bark came from the center engine, and despite frantic efforts by Maitland with the throttle and mixture control, it stopped.

Soon the outboard engines began to roughen, and their revolutions per minute dropped off seriously. The giant plane sagged, then descended slowly toward the rolling sea. At 5000 feet the outboard engines regained an even throb; Maitland struggled still, with the center Whirlwind. He decided that the cause of the trouble was, most likely, icing in the carburetor intake, and he continued his descent to reach warmer air. At 3000 feet, the balky engine kicked and burst into a healthy roar. It didn't miss a beat again.

At 2:30 P.M., San Francisco time, the flyers spotted a liner plowing through the choppy seas below, leaving a foamy wake in her path, and looking for all the world like a child's toy. They were more confident now with the engine troubles over, and they dove down to 200 feet, far under the cloud cover. They could see clearly the passengers on deck, waving vigorously. It was the USS *Sonoma*.

Her radio operator, Coady, later sent the following message: ARMY PLANE PASSED 2:44 P.M. ABOUT 200 FEET HIGH, 32 DEGREES 54 MINUTES NORTH, 136 DEGREES 14 MINUTES WEST. CAME LOW AND NEAR US. EVERYONE LEFT DINING SALOON. PASSENGERS SCREAMED AND SHOUTED AT PLANE. The *Sonoma* reported the weather as being cloudy, with a light rain, and surface winds from the northeast at 30 miles an hour. Those on deck cheered as *Bird of Paradise* disappeared into the western clouds.

The remainder of the afternoon and most of the night was spent flying in the clouds, below the freezing level, to protect the engines. Maitland once took the plane up to 10,000 feet, over the cloud level, to give Hegenberger a celestial reading. They had been on target when they passed over the *Sonoma*, 750 miles from San Francisco and they risked further engine trouble, at the high altitude, to make sure they were still on course; for an error, even though insubstantial, would mean the end. After the readings, Maitland brought the ship down under the ceiling, and flashed over the water barely 300 feet above the waves. On they flew through the dark and moonless night, tiring, and still hungry, but ever nearer their goal.

After 22 hours in the air—it was the darkest hour before dawn—Hegenberger caught sight of a flashing light in the distance. Excitedly, he checked his charts. It was the Kilanea Lighthouse on Kauai Island, the northernmost island of the chain. They were off course, but, thankfully, not fatally. They decided to wait for the sun to rise before making for Wheeler Field on Oahu; and they circled the friendly light for 1½ hours, until the black of night gave way slowly to the rose of dawn.

Thousands stayed all night at Wheeler Field to make sure they wouldn't miss the flyers' arrival. They included the Governor of Hawaii, Wallace R. Farrington, and Major General Edward M. Lewis, Commander of the Hawaiian Department of the Army. Promptly at 7:30 A.M., Hawaiian time, a squadron of Army planes roared off Wheeler Field to find *Bird of Paradise* and escort her in. They disappeared fast into the east under a breaking cloud cover. Just before 9 A.M., as the last of the clouds disappeared, leaving a clear, sunlit sky, *Bird of Paradise* came into sight, at first a tiny dark speck, high to the northeast. "She sneaked in the back way," was the way Hegenberger later put it, referring to his small navigational error.

The big ship lit easily on the runway, to the cheers of the huge crowd. Hungry and tired as they were, Maitland and Hegenberger stepped out of the plane, smiling and happy, and were greeted by roars of "Alohas!" and the traditional wreaths of leis. They had covered the distance in 25 hours and 50 minutes, and there were 250 gallons left in the tanks!

A half hour after they landed, the luckless Army pursuit ships returned, having failed in the rendezvous attempt. One hour after landing, mechancis found the sandwiches, tinned beef, hardtack, and coffee intact and still edible, stored in a box under Hegenberger's seat.

Later in July, Ernest Smith replaced navigator Carter with twenty-nine-year-old Emory A. Bronte on leave as a ship's officer with Moore-McCormack lines, and the author of a well-known book *Practical Navigation*. It was his responsibility to pinpoint tiny Oahu Island. On July 14, they fueled their plane and prepared for take-off.

On the first run, *City of Oakland* struck a depression in the field and slued off the runway, but Smith was able to regain control of the ship and bring it to a stop safely. The second attempt was successful and they headed west over the Pacific. On through the day and the night, they flew, signaling each other over the fuselage during the dark hours by flashlight. Their gas was running low as they closed in on the islands in the early morning, and then the fuel pump failed. Since the wing was on the same level with the engine, it could not be fed by gravitation, and they were forced to pump gas to the engine by hand.

The situation became so desperate that they sent an SOS at 6:15 A.M., and another at 7:45 A.M. on July 15. "We are going to land in the sea. Send help. We have a rubber raft."

Land was sighted, however, and the flyers settled for a crash land-

ing in the trees at Molokai, 60 miles southeast of Wheeler Field, at
10:46 A.M. Honolulu time, after 25 hours and 36 minutes in the air.
They were safe and unhurt, though disappointed over the end of
the trip, which had resulted in the destruction of their plane.

4. At Roosevelt Field, on June 25, reports of
cold weather and icing conditions between Nantucket Island and
Cape Sable sent gloom throughout *America*'s camp. Anthony Fokker
hovered around his creation, and said, "Well, she's ready. What more
can I do?"

The day was spent working on the ship. The word PEACE was
painted under her fuselage window, and AIRMAIL was written under her stabilizer, as Byrd had been sworn in as the first transatlantic, airmail pilot. In an interview at the field, he said that his
course would be slightly south of the great circle—Halifax, south of
St. John's to avoid the worst of the fog area, across the ocean,
where he hoped to make landfall at Bray Head, Ireland (west of
Valencia), Plymouth, Cherbourg, and Paris. Amid all the planning,
he found time to travel to New Haven, Connecticut, where he was
presented with an honorary Master of Arts degree from Yale University.

With a crowd of spectators surrounding them, "Doc" Kinkaid,
Balchen, and Noville attached two extra fuel lines to each engine, as
a safety factor, in the event of a clogging. Other workers busied
themselves with the radio, which had been moved to a small cubby-
hole under the fuselage tank, just aft of the pilot's cockpit. This
would be Noville's office, with the dump valve and manual gas
pumps, close at hand. The radio would use a wave length of 690
meters, which caused comment in that it was close to the International Distress wave of 600 meters.

Balchen checked the control cabin carefully; the instruments, the
dual control wheels, the three long-handled throttle controls, and the
shorter spark levers. Crowds continued to surge around the large
hangar, with AMERICAN TRANS-OCEANIC COMPANY painted
over the entrance. Late in the afternoon, Lieutenant Lawrence W.
Curtin, Fonck's co-pilot, landed in a sleek, new Sikorsky amphibian.
Bert Acosta, who had just come to the field, remarked wryly, "Gee,
I wish we had one of those!"

Rumors floated about that tests of Byrd's radio transmitter disclosed that it had a sending range of only 15 miles. Noville denied

it, hotly. Nerves were getting frayed by the long wait—both those of the crew and the public, but still the crowds came. The crew retired to the Garden City Hotel in the late afternoon to grumble over the weather and to get to bed early—just in case.

It was Sunday, June 26. The take-off had been canceled abruptly at 3:30 A.M.; a local storm reduced the field to a quagmire. Grover Whalen and Kinkaid inspected the runway at midnight and had sunk up to their ankles in the mud. Otherwise, conditions seemed good, with favorable weather from Newfoundland to Ireland, and only scattered thunderstorms up the coast to Nova Scotia. However, the violent electrical storm and torrential rains at the field killed all hopes, because *America*, with its 14,500-pound load, would need a firm runway to get off. Nevertheless, Tom Mulroy, engineer on Byrd's arctic ship *Chantier*, Ross Gardner, and nineteen-year-old volunteer Herbert Armstrong, continued to gas the ship despite the postponement with their wet slickers shining under the field lights.

During the day, 6000 people an hour converged on Roosevelt Field, sensing an imminent take-off. At one time, the crowd was estimated to be in excess of 40,000. They came from New York City, Long Island, and some from as far away as Connecticut and New Jersey. With his brother Tom, Commander Byrd stayed at the Wheatley Hills home of Robert Daniel. The remainder of the crew, with the exception of Acosta, spent the day at the Garden City Hotel. Acosta came to the field, where he wandered about, avoiding the crowds and fidgeting nervously. He'd said good-bye to his family the night before, when a departure had seemed likely. A take-off during the day was rendered impossible by the soft and muddy field, kept so by recurring showers.

Monday the 27th and Tuesday the 28th were passed in similar fashion. Crowds kept coming in large numbers, though they were lighter than over the weekend. From time to time, members of the crew showed up. "Doc" Kinkaid tinkered endlessly with his beloved engines. Commander Byrd issued a statement saying that *America* would fly across at 15,000 feet, but would return at a much lower altitude. This caused some eyebrow lifting, for it was the first indication that he was contemplating a return trip.

Late in the morning of the 28th, word reached the crew of the Maitland-Hegenberger flight over the Pacific. The crew wished them well, although aggravated, obviously, by having another march stolen on them.

In the afternoon of June 28 "Doc" Kinkaid made another check of the oil and fuel systems. The motors were started and run up to full power, and the din echoed throughout the vicinity. The sound was smooth and even. A favorable wind blew from the west toward the incline from which they would make their start. The runway was firm and dry, and, as the crew left for the Garden City Hotel, there was real hope that they might get off early Wednesday.

America's crew was wakened at 3 A.M., Wednesday morning. A light rain was falling, and, as they looked out of their hotel windows, they noted unhappily that a heavy overcast hid the stars. Another day of disappointment and waiting? Not this time! At midnight "Doc" Kimball called Kinkaid at the hotel. He reported that, despite a fog bank over the Grand Banks, the weather over the North Atlantic was generally favorable. Byrd was advised promptly and left instructions that the crew be at the field, ready for take-off, no later than 4 A.M. Kinkaid left at once for Roosevelt. A large mobile beacon had been towed over from Mitchel Field and shone on the plane, which was perched at the top of the incline. The big ship glistened eerily in the dark wetness, while mechanics scrambled all over her. The food was loaded: four roast chickens, sixteen chicken sandwiches, sixteen ham and cheese sandwiches, four quart-sized Thermoses of coffee, and one of tea. This was all in addition to the previously stored emergency rations.

Kinkaid fretted over the excess weight. He prowled through the cabins and disposed of items that he felt were not essential, among which were the comfortable chairs, specially designed for the navigation cabin. The occupants would now have to stand or sit on the floor; but he had reduced the weight from 17,820 pounds to 17,261! He worried about the weight of the radio, but there was little he could do about it. To the commander, it was vital for the flight.

Outside, workmen poured the final drops of 1295 gallons of fuel into the tanks, sufficient for at least 42 hours of flying. It was estimated that the engines would consume 26 gallons an hour and 5-gallon cans of gas were stored in the narrow passageway leading from the aft cabin to the pilot's cockpit. A small crowd under umbrellas stood around in the rain. A mail truck raced up, splashing through the puddles. A bag of mail was put aboard, and the crowd, for some reason, cheered. At 4 A.M. another car drew up to the big plane. In it was Commander Byrd in flying gear and ready to go. He was accompanied by his wife, and brother Tom. He conversed quietly with Kinkaid, Whalen, and others, who stood in a group forward of the starboard motor. Bert Acosta arrived. He's spent most of the night in Byrd's little office off the hangar, after saying good-bye again to his wife and two boys. He talked briefly with the group, and then drove off in a car to pick up Noville and Balchen at the hotel. There seemed to be no end of work for the scurrying mechanics. Some scrambled up ladders which had been placed under the engines, to inspect a propeller, or to test a spark plug; others checked the control system, and the structure—even to the catwalks leading to the outboard engines, to be used by Balchen if emergency in-flight repairs became necessary. The flashes from the newsmens' cameras, and the growing crowd added to the rising fever of excitement.

Otto Noville, the white-haired father of Lieutenant George Noville, appeared and was welcomed by the official group. The crowds were held at a safe distance by Nassau County policemen. Tom Byrd stood next to his slight, dark-haired brother, together with Grover Whalen, Fokker, and Rodman Wanamaker. A mechanic ran up, after making a quick check of the runway, and reported that it was soft but sufficiently firm. The sky began to lighten slightly in the east. Another car drove up, and out stepped Acosta, with Balchen and Noville, dressed in leather flying suits. Photographers lined the crew up in front of the plane and flashbulbs popped by the dozens.

It was after five, now, dark and raining, with heavy clouds hanging overhead. "Doc" Kinkaid climbed into the pilot's seat. He scanned the instrument panel in front of him, dials which showed the rpms, air speed, height, oil pressure, together with a turn and bank indicator, and a rate of climb gauge. Above the windshield hung the earth inductor compass. The port engine was cranked by a mechanic. The propeller turned, and the engine sputtered, backfired, then whirred into action, as Kinkaid moved the long throttle handle forward. The center engine was tried. The propeller turned and turned, but the motor did not catch. Kinkaid frowned as the mechanic cranked away tirelessly. Suddenly, it gave off a throaty roar, while blue smoke poured from the exhaust and drifted over the crowd. The starboard engine caught at once; one by one, he ran them up, with his eyes glued to the tachometer to make sure that they reached full power. Their screeching din filled the air, and the plane bucked against the wheel chocks and strained on her tether on the tail. Then, there was silence again as they idled.

"They're as good as they can be, Commander," yelled Kinkaid from the cockpit.

"I know they are, Doc," Byrd called back.

The farewells were concluded without delay, and consisted mainly of perfunctory handshakes, with the exception of Otto Noville. He rushed over and threw his arms around his son.

They clambered aboard. Acosta went to the pilot's seat, on the left, with Balchen at his right. Noville took his place in the cramped hole behind them, and rested his hand on the dump valve. Commander Byrd, carrying a piece of a flag made by Betsy Ross, pulled himself into the navigator's compartment to the rear.

Acosta opened the throttles. The plane shivered, and the roar was deafening. He signaled. The chocks were pulled, and the tail cable was cut at the same time. The plane leaped down the incline, hit the runway, and started down the field toward the hill leading to Curtiss. *America* gathered speed, and at 1500 feet rose 10 feet off the ground, only to sink back again. At 2500 feet, she lifted again, but to the dismay of the onlookers settled back once more. As the end of the runway drew frighteningly close, she lifted into the air for good, and passed over the incline, leading to Curtiss 50 feet up. The heavily laden plane gained altitude slowly, banked gingerly to the right over Jamaica, Long Island, and headed east, fading fast in the early morning light. The plane had become airborne at 5:25 A.M. after a run of 48 seconds.

On the field, all hands breathed a sigh of relief as the big ship finally lifted off. There was cheering and handclapping from the crowd, until the rhythmic *zoom zoom* from her engines diminished to a faint buzz, and she became but a speck in the distance. The most relieved of the spectators was T. Harold Kinkaid, the tireless engine expert. His engines had passed the fatal test. They had lifted almost nine tons (17,289 lbs.) off the ground.

The now-famous "Doc" started his career modestly enough. At the age of twelve he earned a dollar by memorizing the names of the books of the Bible. With his earnings, he bought a watch, which he took apart and put together again. Spurred on by his success, he graduated to the family alarm clock and rigged it so that it powered his bathtub boat. He started to work at sixteen in an automobile factory, and for the past twenty years had devoted his time to the building and maintenance of airplane motors. He was happy as he went off to breakfast that rainy morning, and was confident that his engines would purr steadily until the final destination had been reached. Furthermore, he was booked to sail for France later in the day aboard the *President Roosevelt*, so that he would be available to care for the Wright engines, *Columbia's* included, on the other side.

Aboard *America*, all went smoothly. The big plane had gathered speed with difficulty as she moved westward on the runway. When she slid off the ramp, there was a heavy "thump" as her wheels struck the hard-packed dirt. Acosta held her steady, as the air-speed indicator showed 40 mph—then 50—and 60. He wanted to make sure of flying speed before easing back on the wheel. Trees, hangars, and field markers flashed by the windows faster and faster. As the needle on the indicator hit 70, there was a brief moment of flight. The wings took hold, but then there was a bump, as the wheels settled back to earth; another brief flight—and another bump—but, this time, it was lighter. Acosta pulled back gently on the control column, and the giant Fokker became permanently airborne.

He turned to Balchen and yelled over the din of the engines, "Whatta helluva take-off that was!" Balchen smiled.

Behind them, Noville, whose hand had been resting nervously on the dump valve, waiting for the dreaded signal from the pilot, relaxed. The take-off had come after a run of 3268 feet.

Acosta held the nose down to gain speed, then eased back again on the wheel. Curtiss Field passed below them quickly. Ahead of them was Jamaica, and, in the misty gloom farther off, the lights of New York City. Acosta banked to the right and pointed *America's* nose into the low clouds, toward Long Island Sound and the Connecticut shore. The wind blew lightly out of the southwest, and favored them as they left Long Island. They hoped that it would add to their registered speed of 85 miles an hour. Balchen sat, quietly, beside the pilot, the picture of concentration, as his eyes focused on the instrument panel. In his cubicle underneath the gas tank, Noville busied himself, now, with the radio, which would keep the world posted on their progress. Byrd pored over his maps, which were spread carefully on the chart table to the right side of the navigator's cabin. The motors droned on, steadily, evenly, and deafeningly. *America*, at long last, was on her way.

The first news from her came at 6 A.M.

EVERYTHING GOING FINE. NOVILLE.

At 6:30 A.M. a report was received from observers at Watch Hill, Rhode Island, to the effect that *America* had been sighted there, flying low under a heavy overcast.

At 7:22 another message was received from the plane: PASSED CAPE COD, TWO MILES WEST OF CAPE COD LIGHT. ALL WELL. BYRD.

At 8:10 *America* reported: WEATHER CLEARING EN ROUTE CAPE

COD TO YARMOUTH. OUT OF SIGHT OF LAND. EXTRA CANS OF GAS CAUSING TROUBLE WITH COMPASSES. BYRD.

Soon after 10 A.M. she was sighted over Yarmouth, and later over Halifax, Nova Scotia.

Three messages were received from her at 1:30 P.M. TELL FLOYD BENNETT WE MISS HIM LIKE THE DICKENS! WIRE CONGRATULATIONS TO MAITLAND AND CREW. They had learned apparently of the safe landing of the *Bird of Paradise* at Wheeler Field; and, WE ARE KEEPING SHARP LOOKOUT FOR NUNGESSER AND COLI. OVER SCATARI (an island northeast of Nova Scotia) FLYING AT 5000 FEET. All were signed BYRD.

Aboard the plane, as they left Cape Cod and headed to sea, Acosta was still at the controls. The weather was dark and gloomy with heavy clouds at 1000 feet together with patches of fog and occasional rain. They flew just under the overcast, over a gray, rolling ocean.

Cape Cod faded quickly behind them in the murky, misty gloom. A light wind still quartered off their tail. Ahead, the sky seemed to lighten perceptibly. The irrepressible Acosta yelled into the communications phone to Byrd for his position. He knew this was one flight he couldn't make by the seat of his pants. From time to time there was a heated exchange between the two over variances in opinion. Balchen studied the instrument panel concentratedly. There was a flurry of excitement when traces of oil were found in the passageway to the aft cabin, but quiet returned when it was discovered that Noville had tripped over a full can, causing a small spillage. There are stories that Noville became airsick, forcing Byrd to take over the radio in addition to his duties as navigator. The plane roared on, with Kinkaid's engines singing a melodious though throaty song.

As they flew over Nova Scotia, the weather cleared suddenly and blue skies and a bright sun covered the rugged Nova Scotian landscape. It was good to see land again, but it would not be for long. Below now, were the lakes, the steep hills, and the rugged timberlands over which the *Spirit of St. Louis* and *Columbia* had flown. At 4000 feet, they seemed to creep by a like a slow-motion kaleidoscope.

At 5:12 P.M., New York time, *America* sent another message: CREW IN GOOD CONDITION. HEAD WINDS ARE BOTHERING US. CAPE RACE IS THE LAST STATION WE WILL RAISE ON THE COAST. REGARDS TO HANGAR CREW. BYRD.

The chivalrous commander forgot no one in his messages. There was no position given with the message, but it was assumed that they were flying over the waters between Cape Breton Island and Placentia Bay, Newfoundland, for at 6 P.M. the S.S. *Nerissa* reported seeing the monoplane off Cape St. Mary's, located on the tip of a neck of land dividing Placentia and St. Mary's Bays. The Chatham, Massachusetts, radio station reported that she was receiving *America's* signals "so loud it would knock your head off!"

The big plane was seen next at Garnish on Fortune Bay, where the weather had begun to close in again; and, shortly after 7 P.M., at Whitbourne, 40 miles southwest of St John's. At 7:20 P.M. she was seen by the citizens of Bellevue, a tiny town on the coast, halfway between St. John's and Cape Race. She was flying very low, and even then was barely visible in the gathering mist and fog. Two hours later she was sighted for the last time by the S.S. *Chalutier*, 200 miles east of St. John's, flying a mere 150 feet off the water.

When *America* left the Nova Scotian coast at Cape Breton in the early afternoon, patches of cloud on the horizon grew fast into an insurmountable mountain of grayish-white. The sun flicked, more frequently, behind fast-moving scuds and soon disappeared as *America* plunged into the gray, swirling mass. The wind had swung further, and blew, briskly now, off their port quarter impeding their progress. Acosta was at the controls, and talked constantly on the intercom with Byrd, seeking guidance; while the latter struggled with the compasses, which behaved erratically. Acosta had little faith in the earth inductor, which peered down at him from over the windshield, though Balchen, doggedly, spun new settings into it.

Outside the cabin windows, there were only fog and cloud. Never had Acosta flown in thicker or wetter weather. The wingtips were hidden from view, and rain streamed off the braces and trailing edges of the wing.

At 6:39 P.M. Byrd radioed: DENSE FOG COVERS ALL NEWFOUND-LAND. HAVE HAD ADVERSE WINDS. IMPOSSIBLE TO NAVIGATE. CAN HARDLY SEE WINGTIPS. RUNNING INTO ANOTHER NOW (presumably another heavy layer of cloud).

Acosta tried to climb over the weather. It was useless. The clouds stretched up endlessly. He dropped down again, almost to the surface, to be comforted by fleeting glimpses of gray, white-capped rollers as they flitted by. Then, for safety's sake, it was back up a bit into the blinding mists. From time to time, they glimpsed a brief snatch of land below—Newfoundland, but it was pure guesswork as to their exact position.

The engines droned on faithfully. Acosta bellowed into the phone, demanding his position and a course. As a civilian, he was not conscious of naval rank and his manner tended to be brusque. Byrd struggled with his instruments and calculations in the rear compartment and tried to oblige as best he could. They were over the sea again. It appeared gray, angry, and endless, as they sped over the foaming whitecaps, while darkness closed in.

At 2:30 A.M., June 30, a message was relayed to New York: AIRPLANE AMERICA AT SEA VIA CHATHAM, MASS RADIO CORPORATION STATION: WE HAVE SEEN NEITHER LAND NOR WATER SINCE 4 P.M. YESTERDAY ON ACCOUNT OF DENSE FOG AND LOW CLOUDS COVERING AN IMMENSE AREA. BYRD. The automatic signals received from the plane indicated that she was 1600 miles from Roosevelt Field, which observers said was good progress. The radio station at Malin Head, Ireland, told of having picked up *America's* signals as early as 11:30 P.M., June 29. Unquestionably, *America* was experiencing bad weather, but it could not be determined if it was radically worse than that which Lindbergh and Chamberlin had met. "Doc" Kimball was puzzled, for his maps had forecast moderately favorable conditions en route. However everyone took heart over the fact that they were still flying, and very close to their planned route.

In the pilot's cabin of *America,* it was a dreary and bumpy night. Acosta struggled with the control wheel, spelled occasionally by Balchen, as the weather pitched the big plane hither and yon. There was no light other than a faint glow from the instrument panel, and outside only the never-ending blanket of wet, dark cloud. Little trickles of water blew around the windshield, as the ship plunged on blindly. Neither sky nor ocean were visible. When Balchen flew, Acosta tried to relax in his seat with his eyes closed, but the careening of the plane prevented much rest. They had been at sea for 8 hours, and there was little change in the weather. Occasionally, they climbed and emerged between cloud layers, only to dive again into more dense and mountainous formations ahead of them. They dropped down quickly and broke out with the dark waves 100 feet below their wheels. At 3 A.M. they ate for the first time. No one was exceptionally hungry, but it broke the monotony. The carefully prepared chicken sandwiches tasted dry, as they washed a few mouthfuls down with luke-warm coffee.

The flight was a new experience for the veteran Acosta. He knew he could fly anything, but previously he had always a general idea of where he was. The hours of blind and strenuous flying began to tell on him, and his comments to Byrd over the phone became less and less polite. But they droned on, with Acosta and Balchen up front, and Noville and Byrd aft of them. Gray cloud engulfed them, and there was no sound, save the even throb of the engines, which seemed less loud than before because they'd become deafened by it. To the east, there appeared a faint lightening of the sky, as the new day started to dawn.

At 6:50 A.M. June 30, Byrd radioed resignedly: WE HAVE SEEN NEITHER LAND NOR SEA SINCE 3 O'CLOCK YESTERDAY. EVERYTHING COMPLETELY COVERED BY FOG. WHATEVER HAPPENS, TAKE MY HAT OFF TO THESE THREE GREAT FELLOWS WITH ME.

The world followed this flight with more up-to-date knowledge than any of the preceding flights because of such messages. The plane had been aloft for 24 hours. The estimated time of arrival in Paris was 5 P.M., June 30, New York time (10 P.M., Paris time). Paris was agog once more with excitement. Early in the day cars moved on Le Bourget by the hundreds. At the field it was damp and rainy and there was a low cloud cover. Levine and Chamberlin interrupted their triumphant tour of Europe, and flew in from Berne early in the day in *Columbia*, to be on hand for the landing. The crowds amused themselves during the long wait by peering into the little monoplane. They were treated to an added spectacle in the afternoon when Chamberlin and Levine dedicated a memorial plaque at the spot where Lindbergh had landed, given by the French Air Veterans Association. The crowd around *Columbia* became so pressing that French police were forced to form a cordon around the ship to protect her. Chamberlin and Levine drove into town to the Ambassador Hotel for a brief rest, until more definite word had been received on *America*.

It continued to pour rain at Le Bourget from a low-hanging blanket of stratus clouds. Smaller and lower puffs skitted wildly across the dark sky. It was a bad day, indeed, for a landing.

Across the ocean, Americans were again on edge, despite the fact that ocean flights were no longer a novelty. Crowds gathered at bulletin boards waiting for the latest word. Others read headline "extras," which were peddled on street corners; still others listened to scanty reports over their radio sets. The air was one of confidence. This was a big, safe, tri-motored plane, which people felt could fly endlessly; the trip had been planned with care for many months by the same man who had planned and executed the successful flight over the North Pole. There seemed little cause for worry, and most Americans waited casually for the news of *America*'s safe arrival at Le Bourget.

At 11:05 A.M., New York time, a message was received from Byrd, saying: HOPE TO SIGHT LAND WITHIN AN HOUR. CREW FINE AFTER A STRENUOUS TRIP.

Locally, it was late on the second afternoon of the flight. They flew still in cloud and rain. The hours passed and there was no sign of the southern tip of Ireland, nor were there any reports of *America* being over Ireland.

A little after 3 P.M., New York time (8 P.M., Paris time), a message, addressed to the Island of Ushant (near Brest) was received from the plane: WE WILL FLY OVER YOU IN A FEW MINUTES.

Sure enough, there were reports of seeing and hearing the big ship over Brest at 8:30 P.M. It appeared now that *America* would have no trouble in reaching Le Bourget close to her appointed time of 10 P.M. (5 P.M., New York time).

It was pitch black outside *America* as she flew on. Balchen had taken over the controls from the exhausted Acosta when they had sighted land, for it was felt that he was more familiar with the European airways. Brest was their first sight of anything except cloud almost since Nova Scotia, and it was welcome. Below, they saw soon the flashing beacon of a lighthouse, surrounded by water, and then suddenly there was more land. They flew into another bank of fog and mist, and the lights below vanished quickly.

Byrd was not certain of his whereabouts due to the faulty compasses. From the coastal maps that he studied, he thought it looked like towns that surrounded Cape Finisterre. They all yearned to find the great peninsula, near Le Havre, so that they could follow the Seine into Paris, but the weather had closed in tight again. The compasses now failed Byrd completely, perhaps from malfunction, perhaps from his own fatigue. He was lost. Balchen, the calm Norwegian, flew on as best he could. He set a course by the doubted compass, hoping to bring *America* to the vicinity of Paris. They all cursed the swirling, dark fog that obscured their view. Balchen squinted through the windshield, mottled by dancing drops of water, into a dark nothingness. Nine P.M. passed. Byrd crawled forward and stood crouched behind Balchen and Acosta. They should have been near Paris by now. All eyes strained for the sight of a light beam or glow, but there was nothing. Ten o'clock came, their scheduled landing time. The murky atmosphere brightened suddenly, then faded.

"We're over the city now, I'm sure," yelled Balchen. Byrd was not so sure. He had lost faith in the accuracy of his instruments. It was now a question of who had the best hunch. Balchen let down, hoping to come out underneath it all, but there was no end to it.

"We don't want to wrap ourselves around the Eiffel Tower," said Acosta half in jest, and Balchen took the plane up to 2000 feet. Byrd squirmed back to the radio and sent a message. It was 10:10 Paris time (5:10 New York time).

I AM FLYING AROUND PARIS. DON'T KNOW WHETHER WE'LL LAND PARIS OR ELSEWHERE. GIVE ME MY POSITION.

It was clear that they were completely lost.

At Le Bourget, at 10 P.M., a crowd that had grown to an estimated 20,000 stood in the wet rain waiting to welcome the flyers. Two powerful revolving lights were beamed skyward, and their spots moved slowly across the low clouds. Every few minutes rockets and red Very lights were fired, only to disappear quickly into the wet mists. Everyone listened intently for the throb of approaching motors, but there was only the sound of the falling rain. Puddles on the field and the wet, parked automobiles shone brightly under the field lights. The crowd was quiet, yet hopeful.

Suddenly they learned of Byrd's message to the effect that the plane was over Paris. They hushed completely and strained to pick up the sound of engines. It was deathly quiet. They waited as minutes, then hours passed. It was after midnight. The crowd remained —wet, but still hopeful. A rumor flew around the field that *America* had landed at Issy-les-Moulineaux, near Versailles. A muffled cheer went up, but soon they learned that there was no confirmation of the report. They quieted. They were used to unconfirmed reports.

At 12:44 A.M. an SOS signal was received at Le Bourget from *America*, followed by another at 1 A.M. Fourteen minutes later there was yet another signal, together with the message: LOST. ONLY THREE HOURS OF GAS LEFT.

At 3 A.M. a final distress signal was received, with a poetic, if poignant addendum: LOST IN THE WIND AND THE RAIN.

5. In New York, it was late in the evening. Hopes were still high, though there was now a disquieting feeling of caution. Earlier in the evening, announcer Graham McNamee con-

ducted a bedside radio interview with Floyd Bennett from St. Vincent's Hospital, and through it all, Bennett had exuded confidence. He was sure the flight would be successful.

What went on in the air, that confusing night, will never be known completely. Tony Fokker was quoted, later, as saying that the reason *America* had been unable to get her position from the ground was that Noville in his excitement had tripped over the radio receiver and automatic transmitter and damaged them both beyond repair. But, Fokker had been opposed strongly to the inclusion of Noville in the crew—only to be overruled by Byrd, who remained steadfastly loyal to his friend.

America continued to fly, blindly. Balchen was convinced that he was flying over or near Paris. According to the course estimated from the faulty equipment, they were making wide circular sweeps over the city, hoping against hope that the light would appear. The irascibility of the crew subsided as their situation became more precarious. The gas supply was dwindling. Byrd, lost, and befuddled by the thick darkness, sent out the first of his distress signals at 1 A.M., closely followed by the others. They were received at Le Bourget, but little could be done to aid the stricken flyers. The weather was too bad to send up a plane to find them and to guide them in. Balchen and Acosta stared blindly through the spinning propeller. There was nothing to be seen but the thick, dark cloud that enveloped the ship. On they flew, their nerves frayed by the incessant blindness of the flight. The needle on the fuel gauge flitted near the final calibration, marked ominously with an *E*. Balchen seemed in control of himself; Acosta was exhausted next to him. Byrd wrote out messages which he passed forward to inquire about the gas supply. He thought desperately about his next move in this dire situation.

As Balchen cruised at 1000 feet, there was a sudden and welcome break in the undercast, and the unmistakable gleam of a lighthouse. Balchen let the ship down to 750 feet, and at last appeared to be under the weather completely. *America* was over the sea. Off her starboard wing the lighthouse loomed clearly, and behind them a length of shoreline. There was no sign of a beach, perhaps because the tide was high. Balchen dropped another 200 feet and banked to circle back. Aft, Noville on the port side, and Byrd to starboard, peered anxiously out the fuselage windows. They could make out the waves lapping against the rocky land. The sea was calm and the friendly gleam from the lighthouse, half a mile away, warmed their spirits. When he was over the lighthouse Balchen banked again and came around for another look. There was no strip of beach on which to land. It had been covered by the tide and there wasn't enough fuel to wait for it to fall. Byrd and Balchen exchanged written notes. Byrd asked whether a landing could be made in the sea without a serious crash. Balchen said it was possible, and Acosta agreed. There was little alternative, for the gas supply was virtually gone, perhaps only enough left for 5 or 10 minutes of flight. It was agreed quickly that they would try to set down in the water as close to the beach as possible. Balchen and Acosta tightened their seat straps while the plane circled, now only 400 feet over the sea.

In the rear cabin, Byrd and Noville were busy. They ripped out the card table which had held the charts and threw it aft; then they tore out the two fuselage windows. The rushing air whistled by. They braced themselves against the rear of the cabin, Byrd to the left and Noville across the narrow cubicle, and stared anxiously out the open windows as Balchen banked over the lighthouse and flew a last, downwind leg before landing. Byrd snatched some flares from a rack and threw them out. They lit up the water below like day.

Balchen, with Acosta again alert beside him, completed the downwind leg, banked, and pointed the big ship down. The sea, lit brightly by the flares, was smooth. The wind was light and in front of them. Lower and lower, the plane glided. Ahead, they could see the gleam from the lighthouse, and to Acosta's right the shoreline. Underneath, and in front, the water came closer, now speeding fast by the cockpit windows as the ship settled. Balchen sideslipped to reduce the speed. The water was 50 feet below—then 40, 30, and 20 feet. Balchen eased back on the wheel to level her off, and they were 10 feet over the water. The moment of truth was at hand. He lifted the nose to stall her slightly. They waited for what seemed like an age as the little wavelets skipped by outside. There was a bump and a crack as the landing gear struck and snapped off; then, another heavier bump, a sloshing spray and a sinking; the nose went down as *America* bobbed heavily to a stop in the shallow water, her tail sticking proudly in the air. She had landed, after a flight of 43 hours 21 minutes, off the little seaside town of Ver-sur-Mer in the Calvados area and not far up the coast from Brest where they had first sighted the continent so many hours before.

Things happened fast as the plane rocked to a stop. Byrd, in the rear compartment, was pitched into the sea through the open window.

Noville, who had been alongside him, was thrown against the forward fuel tank, but gathered himself together and climbed out the other window which was by then under water, and pulled himself up by holding on to the wing.

He called, "Dick, where are you?" until the commander appeared.

In the forward cockpit, according to Balchen, Acosta flew out the window "like a shot" when they hit. In so doing, he suffered a broken collarbone, which he did not discover until hours afterward. Byrd swam around and accounted for Acosta and Noville, but Balchen was missing. Byrd dived to look for him. When he surfaced, he saw the Norwegian swimming nearby, "spouting like a porpoise!" He had been able to squirm out through the submerged cabin window.

The inflatable raft was produced and blown up quickly. Noville crawled back in the fuselage, and returned with the mail pouch; Byrd, too, disappeared briefly. He came back, holding the strong box containing the bit of Betsy Ross's flag.

They were a wet tired crew as they straggled off the raft, at the high water mark of the beach, in the early dawn. They were met by two of the local gentry, Marius Michel and Armand Martin, who had seen the strange-looking craft in the water. M. Cossier, assistant Mayor of Ver-sur-Mer, was notified at once. Meanwhile, Jules Lescope, the lighthouse keeper, took them in and provided them with hot liquids and dry clothes. M. Cossier arrived and took them to his house where they slept for 3 hours, but not before they had rounded up some fishermen to help them drag the mortally wounded *America* to shore, where she lay at low tide like a wounded whale amidst the seaweed. Several days later, with the aid of naval personnel from the nearby Cherbourg base, she was dismantled and taken by truck to Cherbourg for crating and a return to the United States.

Without delay, Byrd cabled Rodman Wanamaker: DEEPLY SORRY WE DID NOT REACH PARIS. WILL REPORT DETAILS. FORCED LANDING. DARK NIGHT. UNAVOIDABLE. AMERICA WILL BE REPAIRED. WILL DELIVER FLAG AND MAIL WHEN WE REACH PARIS.

Wanamaker replied at once: WE ARE ALL REJOICED, AND DEEPLY GRATEFUL THAT PROVIDENCE HAS SPARED YOU AND YOUR SPLENDID CREW FOR CARRYING OUR FLAG WITH THE AFFECTION AND GREAT SPIRIT OF AMERICA TO BELOVED FRANCE.

The crew were guests at a banquet in Caen the night of their landing given by Maurice Helitas, Préfect of the Department of Calvados, and the next morning took the train to Paris where they

19. Lester Maitland *(left)* and Albert Hegenberger before
flight of *Bird of Paradise* to Hawaii.

20. *Bird of Paradise* at Bay Farm Island on take-off for Hawaii.

21. *Oiseau Bleu* landing at Le Bourget after test flight.

22. Captain Hermann Koehl *(left)*, Baron Guenther von Huenefeld and "Fritz" Loose outside *Bremen*.

23. "Bear" Risticz *(left)*, U.S. newsman Hubert Knickerbocker, and Cornelius Edzard with *Europa* in background.

24. Augie Pedlar and Mildred Doran
before Dole Race take-off.

25. Captain Frank Courtney *(left)*,
F. M. Downer, and R. A. Little.

26. The launching of Captain Courtney's *Whale* for
test flight at Farley.

27. Old Orchard Beach, Maine, looking from southeast to northwest, site of many take-offs.

28. *Pride of Detroit* lands at Old Orchard Beach.

29. Bill Brock examines *Pride of Detroit's* J-5 prior to take-off for Harbor Grace.

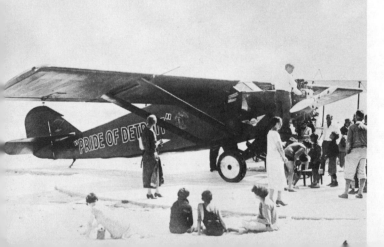

30. Princess Lowenstein-Wertheim in cockpit during summer of 1926.

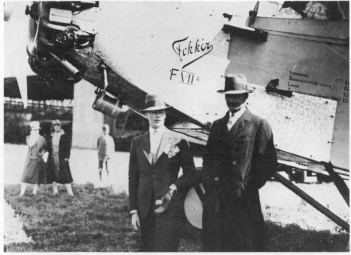

31. Leslie Hamilton *(left)* and F. F. Minchin in front of *San Rafael* at Upavon.

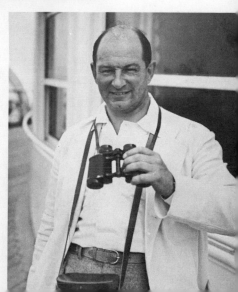

32. "Tony" Fokker.

33. *Old Glory* in front of Harry Jones's hangar.

34. J. D. Hill of *Old Glory (left)*
talks over old times with
Harry Jones.

J. D. Hill *(left)*, Phil Payne, Governor Ralph Brewster of Maine, and
Lloyd Bertaud beside *Old Glory* at Old Orchard Beach.

36. *Old Glory* at Pine Point evening before take-off.

37. *Old Glory* lifts off. Cabbage Island in right background.

38. *Royal Windsor* next to Harry Jones's Stinson at Old Orchard, September 7.

39. At Caribou, Maine, Terrence Tully examines engine of *Sir John Carling* while Lieutenant James Medcalf watches.

were met by a crowd of 25,000 who inundated the Gare Saint-La-
zare. Late in the afternoon they went to the Élysée Palace where
Commander Byrd presented President Gaston Doumergue with the
treasured bit of Betsy Ross's flag, and the President, in turn, made
Byrd an Officer of the Legion of Honor.

Cables poured in from all quarters. President Coolidge cabled from
the summer White House in Rapid City, South Dakota: YOUR
FLIGHT TO FRANCE WILL ADVANCE OUR KNOWLEDGE OF CONDITIONS
WHICH MUST BE MET AND CONQUERED, TO MAKE TRANSOCEANIC
AVIATION PRACTICAL AND SAFE.

Secretary of State Frank Kellogg sent a glowing tribute, and
Secretary of the Navy Curtis Wilbur a brief, but heartfelt one:
WELL DONE, BYRD!

Aviation leaders were equally laudatory in their public statements.
F. Trubee Davison, Assistant Secretary of War for Aviation, said
simply, "It was a perfectly marvelous flight," and Elmer Sperry
commented, "They are all bright minds, and will bring back a fund
of information."

Tony Fokker thought of his airplane. He said: "This demonstrated
that the airplane is not a fragile contrivance"; while Lindbergh, the
pilot, commiserated with the flyers on their unfortunate landing:
"That's too bad. I am sorry it happened that way. Byrd and his crew
are wonderful men and aviators!"

The families of the crew, anxious for so many hours, were exhausted but ecstatic over the news that the men were at least safe.
Mrs. Byrd, in Boston with her four children, said gracefully and
with ill-concealed ecstasy: "I am delighted!" She hastened to add:
"Please say for me how thankful I am for the kindness of the
newspapers who have kept us informed through the entire flight."

Mrs. Acosta, when found by reporters at the Garden City Hotel,
was in tears with joy. She had just told her two boys that "Poor
Daddy's airship fell in the ocean, and they had to swim ashore."

Whereupon, Bert, Jr., asked, "Did Mr. Noville remember to take
off his glasses?"

Mrs. Noville had already received a cable from her husband,
saying: WONDERFUL TRIP. FEEL FINE. DON'T WORRY. LOVE, REX. It gave
little indication of what he and the other men had been through,
and she commented happily: "I think it's wonderful. And they're
all safe. That's the best part of it."

Balchen's family, of course, was in Norway and were not reached
immediately.

During the following week, Byrd and his crew were lavished with a welcome that only Parisians can give. They were wined and dined, both publicly and privately. The climax came when the city of Paris paid an official tribute to the crew before 35,000 people gathered in the small square in front of the Hôtel de Ville. Each was awarded the Gold Medal of the City of Paris amid the cheers of the crowd, and the playing of the *Marseillaise* and the *Star-Spangled Banner*. It was a moving ceremony.

They returned then for a brief visit and farewells to their rescuers at Ver-sur-Mer, and on July 12 sailed for home aboard the *Leviathan*. Also on board were Clarence Chamberlin and his wife—his association with Levine and *Columbia* at an end.

They landed in New York on July 18 and were given a joint and roaring welcome by the city, including the inevitable tickertape parade up Broadway, and articulate words of praise from the past-master of the art, Mayor James J. Walker.

For days after the landing there was speculation over where *America* had flown during her last night in the air. It was assumed that because of the failures of the compasses, she had struck the coast far south of her planned course—at Brest. Most experts surmised that she had then flown in wide circles over Normandy for eight hours, though Balchen disputed this theory vehemently. He was convinced that they had been over Paris and had inadvertently returned to the coast. Strangely, no one reported hearing the plane over either area during the long interval.

Charles Colvin, the embattled president of Pioneer Instruments, found himself again in the storm center of controversy over his earth inductor compass. Once more, his experts were sent over to check with care on why the Byrd instrument had failed. After a thorough examination, they reported that the failure was due either to its proximity to the 5-gallon gas tins or to electrical disturbances in the atmosphere, for they could find no mechanical malfunction.

"Doc" Kimball, too, came in for his share of questioning over the weather. He brushed them off saying it was about what Byrd had expected. However, he was professionally thrilled over the information that he would obtain from the crew.

"Forty-two invaluable hours," he said. "Nothing in meteorological history to compare to it!"

June 1927 passed into history. During the month three hazardous flights had been completed successfully, two over the Atlantic and one over the Pacific. They were the trailblazers for the transoceanic passenger flights that would follow within a few years, and, of more importance, they awoke the die-hard skeptics to the ultimate feasibility and safety of ocean flying, though the skeptics would have a last fling in the tragedies of the months to come.

CHAPTER IX

July 1927

1. With the exception of world-wide demonstrations on behalf of Sacco and Vanzetti, a hot July went by quietly. Ferdinand I, King of Rumania, died in Bucharest, and was succeeded by his five-year-old grandson, Prince Michael, much to the consternation of Crown Prince Carol, in exile in Paris with his red-haired friend, Magda Lupescu. From the Vatican, His Holiness Pope Pius XI warned Europeans against American movies, labeling them as "lethal poison born of dollar superiority." In Guatemala, Dr. Juan Sacasa, the erstwhile Nicaraguan rebel, settled down to a practice of medicine which he had learned at Columbia's College of Physicians and Surgeons in New York, and denied that he had ever been a foe of the United States.

New York's Mayor Jimmy Walker intervened at the eleventh hour in the deadlocked wage negotiations between the Transit Commission and the Amalgamated Association of Street and Electrical Railway Workers, and prevented a crippling transit strike in the city, while auto magnate Henry Ford ended his sponsorship of the anti-Semitic Dearborn (Michigan) *Independant,* and by way of apology to the people of Jewish faith said that he was "deeply mortified" by his association with it.

It was an active month in the world of sport. The New York Yankees and the Pittsburgh Pirates led their respective leagues on the Fourth of July, the traditional halfway mark of the baseball season, and, surprisingly, Lou Gehrig led his illustrious teammate, Babe Ruth in the home-run derby. "Little Miss Poker Face," Helen Wills, salvaged some tennis prestige for America after the defeat of the redoubtable "Big Bill" Tilden at Wimbledon, by winning the

British Women's Tennis Championship, and Bobby Jones ran off
with the British Open Golf title by an astonishing seven strokes.

2. It did not take the freewheeling Charlie
Levine long to stir things up among Parisians after his arrival.
Exhilarated by the receptions he and Chamberlin had received on
their European tour with *Columbia*, he bounded into Paris, fresh
as a daisy, and ready for more, while the exhausted Chamberlin
sought only peace and solitude.

"I'm very tired," the pilot complained at the Ambassador Hotel.
"I'd like to fly back, but the earth inductor is in bad shape, and it
will require three weeks to get it ready for the return trip. Still,
I hate to think of a week aboard ship with the autograph-hunters!"

At official functions they were still seen together, but at all other
times they went different ways with their wives. Newspapers referred
to the coolness between them as "aeronautical incompatibility"—
pilot versus businessman.

They took part in all the festivities which marked the arrival
of the Byrd crew in Paris. The announcement of the inevitable
split-up came at a luncheon given for the commander and his mates
on July 6 by members of the Paris press corps. Chamberlin blamed it
on the telegram that Levine sent to Byrd, in which he offered to
accompany *America* on a return flight to the United States.

Said Chamberlin: "My name was included in that telegram without my permission and I did not know that the message had been
sent until afterward. I have apologized to Commander Byrd and
told him I had nothing to do with sending it." He went on to say:
"If we had time to prepare for the flight in my own way, I'd be
glad to make it, and I am confident that the Bellanca could fly
for 50 hours!"

After the luncheon, Samuel Hartman stood up and read a prepared statement on behalf of his client.

"A short time after his arrival in Europe," it said, "Charles A.
Levine resolved to make a return flight to America, particularly if
no one had flown there before. He has every confidence and belief
that it can be done, and, in the interest of aviation, that it should
be done. He communicated this desire to Clarence D. Chamberlin,
and, of course, invited him to wield the stick. Mr. Chamberlin was
constrained to decline. Accordingly, Mr. Levine had the matter of

another pilot under consideration, and has discussed the situation with several of them."

Chamberlin then rose, and made a brief statement of his own.

"I made it clear to Mr. Levine," he said, "that I did not plan to fly back to the United States in *Columbia*. The fact is, I have made my last flight in her."

Levine, when questioned, said graciously that his selection of a pilot would be made from a number of highly qualified French flyers. By this means, he hoped to win the support of the French people in his venture, but for once his intuition failed him.

The next day came his announcement. His pilot would be Maurice Drouhin, heretofore the pilot of the Farman-built *Oiseau Bleu*, which had been preparing for a flight to New York at Toussus-le-Noble. Though attorney Hartman was sure that Drouhin's abrupt departure from the Farman flight would pose no legal problems, he was totally unprepared for the storm that now descended on his client. The French were up in arms over Drouhin's leaving the French-sponsored flight. The papers castigated both Levine and the unfortunate pilot.

Henri Farman spoke for all France when he said, "We are very disappointed in Drouhin. It will take us at least a month to break in a new pilot."

The Farman Company issued a blistering statement saying that "Levine, with his dollars, has taken Drouhin from us, with the unique object of retarding our imminent voyage in order to be the first to arrive in America by air." It went on: "For the past six months, we have employed Drouhin, and prepared him ourselves for this flight, training him, teaching him to use our maps, and explaining to him everything necessary to succeed in a flight of such importance. Today, when he is completely ready, M. Levine does not hesitate to take him by a coup of dollars."

The papers continued to lambaste *Columbia*'s new crew. They estimated that Drouhin had been bought for $150,000, and both he and Levine were classified as "shameless!" In an effort to mend his relations with the French, Levine announced that he would be glad to use *Oiseau Bleu*, and to pay the expenses of the flight.

"If Drouhin desires to take me aboard *Blue Bird*," he said, "I shall be happy to make the trip in a French airplane, if Drouhin says he is ready and the equipment is in shape to take off. If he prefers to utilize my plane, it is on the condition that I am taken along."

But the damage had been done and the only effect of the statement, which placed the onus squarely on Drouhin's shoulders, was to throw a chill on their relationship at the outset, for Drouhin was fully aware that Farman would not allow *Oiseau Bleu* to take off with the inexperienced Levine as the navigator.

On July 8, Chamberlin relented in his decision to make no further flights in *Columbia*. He agreed to fly Drouhin and Levine to Croydon Field in London, and, on the way, to teach the Frenchman the Bellanca's control system. Though Drouhin spoke no English, and Levine and Chamberlin no French, the three climbed aboard early in the morning and took off from Le Bourget. The flight over the Channel was uneventful. By the use of hand signals, Chamberlin instructed his successor and allowed him to fly the plane a good portion of the trip. Drouhin, an experienced pilot, found the transition from the heavy Farman Goliath to the light, well-balanced Bellanca, easy, and by the time they circled over Croydon Field, he felt completely at home in her.

The flight was Chamberlin's last in *Columbia* for when she flew back to Le Bourget in the afternoon, Drouhin was alone at the controls with Levine beside him. Chamberlin had remained in London to greet his mother, and the next day would journey to Southampton to board the *Leviathan*; the liner would then stop briefly in Cherbourg to pick up Commander Byrd and his crew before sailing for New York.

Samuel Hartman, Levine's faithful defender, was also aboard and he was questioned by reporters on the Levine-Chamberlin break-up.

"Why should Levine not use Chamberlin's name?" he asked, referring to the disputed cable to Byrd. "Levine was always Chamberlin's mentor and inspiration."

Chamberlin made no reply, other than to say, "Well, I will say he was always eager to fly, and, of course, made the flight possible for me."

"Doc" Kinkaid, with *America* permanently grounded, was assigned to tend *Columbia*'s engines at Le Bourget. He was shortly joined by John Carisi who had arrived in Paris, and with the help of French mechanics and sixteen-year-old John Lockwood, the attorney's son, they prepared to overhaul the Bellanca. Levine introduced them to Drouhin, and together they inspected the plane from stem to stern. It was decided to add some gasoline tanks by doing away with the sleeping quarters over the "piano tank" in the fuselage. Kinkaid observed that the new tanks would give *Columbia* an "extra

3 and possibly 4 more hours of flying time" for the perilous westbound trip back home. Carisi had brought with him a new Wright
engine and two new propellers. The plane had been using the
Junkers prop that had been installed after her crash-landing at
Kottbus. Kinkaid thoroughly checked the engine that had carried
them over the ocean, and agreed with Levine that it was entirely
capable of getting them back; consequently, they thought, there
was no need for a replacement. But there was another voice to be
heard from. Mrs. Levine intervened. "Mr. Levine," she said firmly
"does not go to America with my permission unless the new motor is
installed!" There was no immediate reaction however to her ulti-
matum.

By July 18 the new all-metal propeller had been attached to the
old motor, the extra gas tanks installed, and *Columbia* was pronounced ready. With the take-off apparently imminent, the crowds
drifted again to Le Bourget. Worry was expressed publicly that
Drouhin, though an able pilot, was not an experienced navigator,
and everyone knew that for all purposes Levine was little more than
an experienced passenger. Experts were concerned that Drouhin
would have his hands full controlling the aircraft without having
the added burden of plotting and maintaining a proper course.
Bellanca, in New York, re-echoed these sentiments. He said that
Chamberlin would have flown back with a skilled navigator, but
had decided that the task was too risky alone with Levine. He
added, wistfully, that "he [Chamberlin] had no equal in getting
the most out of a plane and engine, and I am certain that the plane
now has a range of 5000 miles."

Levine, unconcerned, was enjoying himself immensely. He and his
publicity manager, Maurice Frankel, flew to London by commercial
aircraft and were the guests at a dinner given by Sir Alan and
Lady Cobham. There was already talk of a possible rift between
Drouhin and Levine, and there were rumors that he was in England
to interview British pilots. On his return to Paris, however, he
quelled these rumors by stating flatly that Drouhin was still his
man.

There was a familiar ring to his words when he said, "I fully
expect him to fly for me. He has a 'tentative' contract, and a firm
one is being prepared by my attorneys. It won't be for $150,000,
though," he added with a laugh. "There are too many pilots around
to pay that price." Drouhin said nothing.

On July 20, a lovely Parisian summer day, *Columbia* made a 15-minute test flight to try out her new propeller. Drouhin was at the controls and Levine rode along as a passenger. Both were delighted with the plane's performance when they alit before a large group of spectators, and it was announced soon after that the return flight would start on receipt of favorable weather reports over the route.

But the days went by with no further sign of a take-off. A new French-designed compass was installed to replace the earth inductor. Drouhin grew impatient over the delays, which were ascribed to the weather. Test flights were continued, as well as a number of flights throughout France to show off the little plane and her owner.

On July 27, Drouhin flew Levine to Nottingham, England, for the King's Cup air races. When questioned there by the press as to his intentions, Levine said, "As much as we want to be the first to take off, we are not going to start prematurely, or rush things."

They flew back to Le Bourget where Levine ordered, of all things, a new earth inductor compass to supplement the French design. Furthermore, he instructed Carisi to install a speed indicator, calibrated in kilometers for Drouhin's benefit, and a magnetic compass for his own.

Drouhin's growing impatience was understandable. Léon Givon, a thirty-two-year-old veteran commercial pilot, with 3500 hours on the Paris to Berlin run, had been assigned as his replacement on Farman's *Oiseau Bleu*. Already, Givon had selected as his co-pilot, Pierre Corbu, another commercial flyer with 1600 hours to his credit, and word from Toussus-le-Noble was that *Oiseau Bleu* was poised and ready to leave momentarily.

On July 31, Drouhin reached the breaking point and blew up at Levine, in a stormy fight at Le Bourget. The French pilot refused to make any further flights with Levine, unless they were solely for test purposes. He informed the irrepressible but startled American, through his interpreter, that he was "fed up with the red tape, delays, and aerial chauffeuring." He was angered additionally by the circus atmosphere that surrounded the flight, with the unsettled money matters, and with the controversy over who would steer on the trip.

Levine had said publicly, "There'd be no fun on the trip if I don't do some piloting."

It came out that the "tentative" contract provided for a 300,000

franc deposit in a French bank for the use of Madame Drouhin
to be paid to her if her husband should die in the attempt; and for
a 100,000 franc forfeiture to be paid to Drouhin in the event his
contract was terminated for any reason. So far, however, everything
was verbal, and nothing had been formalized. The battle raged outside *Columbia*'s hangar, until Levine turned on his heel suddenly
and dashed off to catch a commercial flight to London where, it
was surmised, he would sign up a new pilot. Drouhin calmed down
finally after Levine's abrupt departure, inspected *Columbia* with care,
and drove off to a Paris hospital to visit his wife Georgette who was
awaiting the birth of a child.

3. In July, while Levine and Drouhin sparred
tentatively, three airplanes of French design tuned up at airfields
in the vicinity of Paris and posed a challenge to *Columbia* in her
effort to make the first westbound crossing.

Tarascon's *Oiseau Tango* made test flights from Le Bourget with
her new navigator, air veteran Jean Laulhe, on board, but her
immediate prospects were beclouded by financial troubles.

At Villacoublay, Coste and Le Brix prepared the old green-bodied
Bréguet in which the former had made his famed flight from Paris
to Jask, Persia, the previous year. The plane had been rebuilt so as
to provide an enclosed cabin for the flyers, and further refurbished
with the tricolor of France which proudly decorated her rudder.
She seemed, now, on the verge of departure.

The airdrome at Toussus-le-Noble was also the scene of furious
activity as *Oiseau Bleu* underwent a series of load tests. She was a
familiar sight as she flew around the Parisian skies.

The competition was made keener by the news from America,
where the cities of Cleveland, Philadelphia, and later, Boston, offered prizes of $25,000 to the crew of the first plane to land suc-
cessfully in that city.

The French government on July 28 threw a roadblock at the
French flyers by decreeing that no ocean flights should henceforth
be made by Army personnel in Army aircraft unless the plane was
equipped to land at sea or had more than one engine. The edict
did not stop Coste for very long, however, as *Nungesser and Coli*
by shoring up her fuselage was transformed forthwith into a seaplane with wheels. He flew her then to Le Bourget where she joined

Columbia and *Oiseau Tango*. *Oiseau Bleu* followed soon after, and Le Bourget became to the French what Roosevelt Field had been to Americans in early May.

Levine, while he was there, basked happily in the spotlight that shone on the flyers and was seen frequently with Coste, Givon, or Tarascon exchanging shop talk in front of one of the hangars. There were many "courtesy calls" during these days by the pilots as they eyed one another suspiciously to make sure that no one got too far ahead.

Parisians sensed that a new race was under way, and made daily treks to Le Bourget in increasing numbers. On weekends the field was inundated with people who milled around the various planes as they stood in front of their hangars, glistening under the summer's sun. They gaped with awe at Tarascon's big yellow monoplane, at *Columbia*, or at the little biplane of Dieudonné Coste, which he had named the *Nungesser and Coli* in memory of the lost heroes. Not far away, they looked at the pretty light-blue bodied *Oiseau Bleu* with her bright yellow wings. There was no question as to her designer, for the name *FARMAN* stood out in huge block letters on her rudder, nose, and wings. She was the biggest plane of all, sitting high in the air like a huge heron. She almost came a cropper, though, in her early days at the field, when, with five tons of water in her tanks for a weight test, she collapsed in mid-field, while taxiing for a take-off. Her underpinnings were unable to sustain the weight, but fortunately no serious damage resulted. A few days later, with a reinforced landing gear, she took off after a run of 35 seconds and 700 yards with the same load, flew around Paris for half an hour and came in to a safe and gentle landing. Givon and Corbu got out, satisfied entirely, and, after conferring with Henri Farman, announced that they were ready to leave when the weather was right. It was at this time that Levine and Drouhin agreed to, and executed their "final" contract.

Oiseau Tango was the most spectacular of the waiting ships. She brought "oohs" and "ahs" from the crowds as she flashed around the skies at great speed during her tests. With 800 gallons in her tanks, she took off the day after the *Oiseau Bleu* accident, and whizzed about Paris and over the field in excess of 120 miles an hour, while her powerful motor gave off an ear-splitting blast. Still, Tarascon would not commit himself as to a take-off. He pleaded financial troubles and the need for further tests. He did allow,

however, that when he left his destination would be either Philadelphia or Cleveland.

The tests continued for all planes, but the weather over the Atlantic continued to be unfavorable.

4. During this time, a race was shaping up
among the German aviators. A compact twin-engined Rohrsbach
seaplane neared completion for Captain Ernst Udet's planned late-
summer flight to the United States. The ship featured a detachable
wing, connected to the hull, directly behind an enclosed cockpit.
When the wings were detached, the plane became a seaworthy boat
in which a mast could be stepped and the boat sailed. The idea was
the aviation world's latest in its constant search for over-the-water
safety. Udet was confident. He would leave from Munich, he said,
and added, "I want to take all the romanticism out of ocean flying
and show that a crossing is just a matter-of-fact thing."

The most advanced of the Germans were the Junkers flyers,
headquartered at Dr. Junkers's factory at Dessau. The two, all-metal,
low-winged planes, *Bremen* and *Europa*, were built and thoroughly
tried. Junkers planned to have them fly across together, with *Europa*
pointing for Mitchel Field, New York, and *Bremen* heading for
Chicago. He was anxious, though to test his planes' metal by making
an attempt at Acosta and Chamberlin's endurance mark set recently
in *Columbia*.

On July 22, Fritz Loose and Cornelius Risticz stepped into
Bremen at dawn, and took off from the company field at Dessau.
For twenty hours, they flew back and forth between Dessau and
Leipzig, before a clogged fuel line forced them down. Soon after,
Risticz, with "Bear" Edzard, went aloft in *Europa* and elated the
German public in general, and Professor Junkers in particular, by
staying up for 52 hours and 23 minutes to take the record away
from the Americans by a narrow margin.

There was nothing now to stop the ocean attempt, and final
preparations were hurried. A newly designed pneumatic telecompass,
made by the Askania Works in Friedenau, was installed in both
planes. It was designed to operate mechanically rather than electrically like the earth inductor, but otherwise they were similar. There
were three parts to it—the course indicator, the course setter, and
the compass itself. The compass was placed in the stern of the
ship, so as to minimize the vibration from the engine. The indicator

dial was located in front of the pilot, and to keep on course it was necessary to keep the needle on o, as with the earth inductor. To change course, the setter was altered, and the pilot continued the flight with the needle on o.

Both planes when loaded to capacity weighed four tons, and the Dessau runway was lengthened and paved with concrete so as to provide the planes with a 3000-foot run. The field was bordered by the huge Junkers factory buildings, and at the western end of the strip there was a line of pine trees, but the flyers were confident they would pose no problem.

The route was decided on tentatively, and the course would lead them over Hannover, Scheveningen, Holland, Ipswich (England), and Fastnet Rock (off the Irish coast).

At first Professor Junkers had wanted to fly a third plane, and arrangements reached the point where Franz Schnaebel, an experienced flyer who had toured Mongolia, Japan, and China by air in 1926, was designated as pilot. Lack of adequate finances to cover insurance and fuel killed the idea, despite Junkers's of a free plane and crew.

As the departure time drew near, as in Paris and New York, expectant crowds came daily to the field at Dessau, hoping to see the epic take-off; while, in New York, Grover Whalen was assigned to prepare a welcome for the flyers at Mitchel Field by Acting Mayor Joseph V. McKee. (Mayor Walker was off on a prolonged European tour.) In Chicago Mayor William Hale "Big Bill" Thompson arranged for the same.

5. The British, too, shared in the excitement of the summer months. On June 30, while Byrd was over the ocean, Captain Frank T. Courtney, his wife, and engineer, R. A. Little, boarded the rebuilt *Whale*, at the Dornier plant near Friedrichshafen. She was a huge seaplane, painted a silvery-gray, with the black letters *G-BEQ* showing under her wings, and on the aft of her hull. On her bow, underneath the navigator's cockpit, *DORNIER-NAPIER* and *Whale* were painted.

Courtney, who wore pince-nez glasses which gave him a studious look, took over the controls, with his wife, also a flyer, beside him. They took off, and flew without incident to Farley, England, a little seaside town, 2 miles from an R.A.F. station, at Calshot, and 8 miles from Southampton. Ways had been prepared to pull the big boat out of the water, and, soon after the landing, she was safely high and dry under a shed at the edge of the snug harbor.

They were joined by radio operator and navigator, F. M. Downer, who was to be the third crewman with Courtney and Little on a proposed round-trip flight to New York. They set up headquarters at Calshot after a dispute with R.A.F. officials over their refusal to allow Mrs. Courtney to live on the base. Matters were smoothed over when other accommodations were found for her at a close-by inn in Calshot village.

Immediately, the trial flights commenced. Courtney's plan was to take off from Valencia, Ireland, fly to Topsail, Newfoundland, near St. John's, and after refueling continue on to New York Harbor. There he expected to remain for several days, to tune up the big boat for the return flight. On early load tests, the ship flew easily and well, but as increasing amounts of fuel were added to her tanks in the fuselage she experienced more difficulty in rising from the little harbor.

The take-off was scheduled for July 13, but a series of little troubles delayed her. After riding out a night at her moorings, it was discovered that there was a leak in her starboard float, through which 15 gallons of water had seeped. No sooner had this been repaired than Courtney was faced with the reluctance on the part of the radio experts to fly on *Whale* because the radio in the pilot's cabin was located next to some gas tanks, and they feared that an electrical spark would set off an explosion. After he had calmed their fears, and the radio had been adjusted, Courtney, on a 45-minute test hop over Southampton, detected a malfunction of the front engine. After landing, however, he made light of it.

Said Courtney: "This is a distinct improvement on my earlier trials. We got into the air in nine seconds, and the controls worked well. The front engine is still a bit stiff, but further tuning will soon put that right."

He told bystanders that he would leave for Valencia on July 20. On July 18 the compasses received a final adjustment by means of placing the big plane on a revolving contrivance similar to a railroad turntable.

Excitement mounted in the environs of Southampton and crowds moved on the little town of Farley. In New York, the Mayor's Committee on Receptions was again hard at work. They were advised that Courtney would land near the Statue of Liberty, and a strip of water southwest of Governors Island, half a mile long, and half a mile wide, was cleared and marked off. A beacon aimed at the strip was installed on Governors Island and another was placed on the crown of the Statue. Arrangements were made to have the crew picked up by the city's official boat, *Mecom*, and reservations were made for the captain and his crew at the Hotel Commodore. Despite the excitement over the city's reception given the Byrd crew and Chamberlin on the 18th, the hard-working committee was ready to do it all over again for the British flyers.

Mechanics worked all the night of July 19 on *Whale*, for the British Air Ministry's weather prediction was that the plane would be pushed along by a 40-mile tail wind as she left the Irish coast. Courtney made a final check of his collapsible boat and retired for the night. He arrived at harborside at 4 A.M. the next morning with his crew. R.A.F. volunteers from Calshot Airdrome poured 650 gallons of petrol into the fuselage tanks. Though the tanks had a capacity of 1100 gallons, Courtney decided to make only one take-off with a full load, and that would be the big one from Valencia. It was a gray day, drizzling, and low clouds skittered across the sky. The little harbor was choppy from a brisk westerly, and little boats bobbed up and down at their moorings. When the fueling was completed *Whale* was taken down the ways into the water. Navigator Downer got into his little cockpit in the extreme bow, while Courtney and Little climbed into the pilot's seat, aft of him. Courtney started the two engines, which were arranged in tandem and located above him on the upper wing. The plane roared down the harbor into the wind and lifted off with ease. For over an hour it flew, disappearing for minutes into the clouds, and then, as suddenly, reappearing overhead. The crowds below would be satisfied that *Whale* was on her way, only to see her bank in under the low-hanging stratus layer and circle the harbor. Finally, they saw her make a turn into the wind again, and descend, slowly, and splash in for a landing. In that it was low tide, no attempt was made to bring her into the ways, and she tied up to her special mooring, 300 yards from shore. The crew was fetched quickly by boat and brought ashore. Courtney reported that the bad weather, combined with slight radio trouble, had forced him to return, but he assured everyone that he'd be "ready to go back again at the first sign of good weather." In addition, he twitted the Air Ministry with good humor for its questionable wind forecast.

For days thereafter, New York, Newfoundland, and England waited for news of the take-off. A large cache of fuel awaited *Whale* at

Topsail, and New Yorkers were ready with their welcome. Interest faded, however, as postponement followed postponement, with the weather, troubles with the radio and compass, and a leak in the gas tank given, successively, as reasons for the delay. *Whale* remained at her moorings for the most part, as her flights became less and less frequent. Courtney, discouraged by the weather over the North Atlantic, later announced a revision in his plans. He would fly to Newfoundland, but he would go via the Azores, and then proceed on to New York.

CHAPTER X

August 1927

1. The world devoted its main attention in August to the fate of Nicolai Sacco and Bartolomeo Vanzetti. After reviewing the findings of his Blue Ribbon commission, Governor Fuller of Massachusetts said: "As a result of my investigation, I find no sufficient justification for intervention."

He granted them a ten-day reprieve, 39 minutes before the time of execution, to enable Attorney Arthur D. Hills to make a last-minute plea on their behalf to the Supreme Court of Massachusetts. World-wide demonstrations, including riots and bombings, protested the governor's decision. Walter Lippmann, Sinclair Lewis, and Norman Thomas were among a long list of American intellectuals who espoused the cause of the condemned men; and, Nicolai Sacco conducted his own protest by staging a 21-day hunger strike at Charlestown State Prison in Boston.

With the execution scheduled for August 22, the Massachusetts Supreme Court denied the final plea on the 19th. Supreme Court Justices Oliver Wendell Holmes and Louis D. Brandeis denied a stay on the 20th, and lawyer Hills's hurried trip to Isle au Haut, Maine, the summer home of Supreme Court Justice Harlan F. Stone, met with no better success. At midnight, August 22, while poetess Edna St. Vincent Millay and thousands of Bostonians picketed the jail, Sacco and Vanzetti died in the electric chair.

Before being strapped in, Sacco shouted defiantly: "Long live anarchy!" While Vanzetti said quietly: "I wish to tell you I am an innocent man."

President Calvin Coolidge picked the height of the uproar to drop a bomb of his own. On August 2, he summoned reporters to his vacation White House in Rapid City, South Dakota, and read one typewritten sentence from a small slip of paper, which said: "I do not choose to run for President in nineteen hundred and twenty-eight." When asked if he had any other comment, he replied characteristically, "None," and left forthwith to go fishing, while the flabbergasted Republicans of his party did the same in their quest for a new candidate in 1928.

Otherwise, Americans enjoyed a pleasant month. The directors of General Motors approved a two for one stock split; Eddie Cantor opened at the New Amsterdam Theatre in the *Ziegfeld Follies*, Bobby Jones defeated Chick Evans, 8 and 7, for the National Amateur Golf Championship, and Harry Payne Whitney's *Vanitie*, won the Astor Cup from *Resolute* on the New York Yacht Club's annual cruise at Newport, Rhode Island.

2.   On August 2, when Levine returned from London, the argument with Drouhin flared up again. The forfeiture clause of the contract was the main issue, though Drouhin insisted, too, that the agreement should specify that he be left alone to carry out the preparations for the flight. Levine exploded and threatened to replace Drouhin. Drouhin, in turn, raged, and demanded that Levine sign a contract with him forthwith, or he would sue. Their respective attorneys were summoned in an effort to smooth out matters. Besides the forfeiture and preparation clauses, Drouhin demanded that he be paid 50 percent of the "ancillary rights" accruing from the flight together with a substantial annual wage. Snarling discussions, reminiscent of the Bertaud days, took place at lawyers' offices, the hangar at Le Bourget, and at Levine's headquarters at the Hotel Continental in Paris. Levine played it with his usual aplomb. He wondered aloud to newsmen "if the French will make an international incident if I change my mind [about the pilot]."

While the battle continued, so did the test flights of *Columbia*. On August 5, Drouhin took her off with Carisi and Kinkaid aboard, and with her tanks filled to two thirds capacity. She rose quickly from the field and flitted about the sky, with ease and speed, for thirty minutes. When she rolled to a stop in front of her hangar, the three men leaped out smiling, pleased with her performance. Levine, who was at the field, was questioned about a possible take-off time.

He said with a grin: "Maybe, tomorrow," and he sped off to Paris to keep a social engagement. His flippant answer aroused a group of Drouhin's friends who had begun to accompany him to give him moral support in his dispute with his employer, and before Levine could get away, there was a loud exchange. Most of them shrieked at the little American in excited French, accompanied by wild gestures. Drouhin's interpreter, a M. Mathis, spoke in English. The gist of the argument seemed to be that if Levine was serious about his take-off intentions, he should remain at the field. Levine was unperturbed, however, shrugged his shoulders, and stepped into a waiting car, leaving the angry Frenchmen to be calmed by "Doc" Kinkaid.

On Sunday, August 7, spectators numbering in the thousands gathered at Le Bourget hoping to see *Columbia* go. Levine turned up at the field briefly and only long enough to stir things up again. It was soon obvious that he had no intention of leaving, for no orders had been given to fill the plane's tanks. In an effort to assuage Drouhin, he gave the pilot 20,000 francs as a binder on his contract, and, contrary to his wife's wishes, directed that the new Wright motor be crated at once and shipped home as soon as *Columbia* took off.

Mrs. Levine was not the only one upset over the last order. M. Mathis, the interpreter who stood nearby with Drouhin's friends, took exception to it and told Levine so in no uncertain terms. Levine, in full view of the crowd, charged wildly at Mathis, who, now raging with anger, grabbed Levine by the coat lapels and shook him vigorously. Drouhin and Carisi, tending to *Columbia* inside the hangar, heard the uproar and rushed to the scene. They pulled the two men apart before any serious damage was done. Levine straightened his clothes, announced that the flight was postponed again because of the weather, and returned to the gaieties of Parisian life.

A few days later, Levine and Drouhin appeared together at the field, arm in arm, and apparently in fine spirits. Levine was dressed from head to toe in a new garish all-white flying suit, including white helmet and shoes. He presented a colorful picture as he posed smilingly for photographers. They made a joint announcement to the effect that their problems had been resolved, and Levine produced a signed contract which Drouhin allowed was "entirely satisfactory." In addition to long-term arrangements, an equitable forfeiture clause, and the preparation stipulation, it included a provision for a generous insurance payment to Georgette Drouhin in the event of her husband's death.

Almost at once, there was a flurry of action in the hangar as instrument experts busied themselves removing all the compasses for a final correction.

Levine entertained the reporters. He said they would leave as soon as weather permitted. He described his course as the Great Circle, and added that it would take *Columbia* over Trouville, Cherbourg, Plymouth, Cape Clear, Ireland—over the ocean to Cape Bonavista, Newfoundland, Prince Edward Island, Nova Scotia, Boston, and New York. He was jaunty and cocky, and to those who listened, it seemed that *Columbia* at long last would get away before long. The harmony, however, lasted only a few days.

Levine arrived at the hangar late one afternoon, obviously upset, and astounded even his own followers by ordering Kinkaid to remove the "breaker points" from the engine, thereby disabling it. Rumors were again rife about a new rift between owner and pilot. The Paris press, heretofore equally critical of Drouhin and Levine, sympathized openly now with the French pilot and denounced Levine for his antics. There were headlines about that "menace" Levine, and stories of his prior crew troubles in America, which seemed to them to constitute a pattern in his relationships with people.

Not without reason, Drouhin was enraged when he learned that Levine had disabled the motor, because he feared the Frenchman would steal the plane and try to go alone.

Through his interpreter, he made an understatement of sorts. "Apparently, Mr. Levine has no confidence in me." He went on: "I see no reason why he should have done such a thing. It was uncalled for!"

Bystanders recalled the excited pilot saying a lot more, but the now-tactful M. Mathis censored his irate statement, thoughtfully.

Levine answered Drouhin promptly. "I have a perfect right to take such precautions," he said. "It is my plane and I don't intend to permit anyone to run off with it."

The French press was up in arms. They sided strongly with Drouhin, and advised him to quit the expedition forthwith. One paper charged that Levine was entirely without *savoir faire*, and hinted strongly that he was no longer welcome in France. The uproar continued for the remainder of the month. The flight was postponed and postponed again. French papers grew more vicious in their criticism of the maddeningly unconcerned American, who, on the surface at least, shrugged off his detractors.

L'Auto headlined a story M. LEVINE BEGINS HIS CHICAN-

ERIES AGAIN. *Le Journal* led off with "WHAT DOES M. LE-VINE WANT?"

One morning Levine and Carisi arrived at Le Bourget to find *Columbia's* propeller dented badly. It looked as though it had been struck repeatedly with a heavy wrench. Levine called the police, and to them and attendant reporters complained bitterly over the lack of protection for his plane. Further, he criticized harshly Le Bourget officials for their failure to give his hangar adequate protection. His complaints and demands were met with hoots of derision from the Paris press.

His mounting problems in France did not go unnoticed in the United States, and there were frequent editorial demands that he return home. One well-known editor recommended that the Marines be sent abroad to escort him back by force before Franco-American relations were permanently damaged.

Meanwhile, the weather ostensibly kept *Columbia* on the ground. Levine and Drouhin avoided each other assiduously though when local conditions permitted, Levine allowed Drouhin to make short hops, with either Carisi or Kinkaid aboard, to try out the propeller, and to check the new instruments, but, always after the landing, the breaker points were removed from the ship.

Mrs. Levine attempted a peace-making gesture. When Georgette Drouhin gave birth to a baby girl, she sent baskets of flowers to her at the hospital. But the gesture was futile, for the damage had been done. From time to time, there were further rumbles of discontent. Drouhin's lawyers demanded that Levine deposit the life insurance money in a French bank, pursuant to the contract terms. When Levine refused, the French press, quieted temporarily by the uneasy truce, resumed their attacks on the embattled American.

The final open fight between the two took place on August 28 at Le Bourget. Levine arrived at noon and found Drouhin in the hangar, working on the plane. He demanded that the pilot fly him, at once, to Deauville where he had an important social engagement. Drouhin refused angrily saying that he was "no chauffeur." Levine, thereupon, ordered the tanks emptied, so that no one could fly her. He had forgotten apparently that her engine was without breaker points. He then hired a private plane to fly him to his destination.

The news of the dispute traveled fast, and reporters were soon at hand, surrounding the harassed French flyer.

"I'm no lawyer," said Drouhin. "I'm an aviator, and when the weather is good, I'll show him! I'll go!—and maybe, alone!"

The next day, Levine came to Le Bourget bright and early, having returned from Deauville late the previous evening. There were the usual crowds present, as Le Bourget was also the home base for three other planes awaiting an Atlantic take-off, *Oiseau Bleu*, *Oiseau Tango*, and Coste's Bréguet. Drouhin was not present as he had gone to the hospital to visit his wife. Levine ordered *Columbia* filled with gas. Spectators, hearing the news, began to cluster around, wondering what he was up to now. After lunch, they saw him climb into the pilot's seat. The engine was started, and Levine opened the throttle. To the amazement of the spectators, the little plane hurtled away from the front of the hangar in a cloud of dust, swung down the field at top speed, and took off in a dizzying climb that was so steep that veteran flyers feared a fatal stall. The last those on the field saw of the little yellow monoplane was as she disappeared to the north, flying uneasily at 500 feet.

At Croydon Field, London, personnel were forewarned by the French authorities that *Columbia* might be on her way there, so when she appeared overhead at 4:30 P.M., teetering unsteadily, there was no great surprise.

Everyone on the ground knew that Levine was not a licensed pilot, had never before flown alone, and rarely if ever had made a landing. Emergency measures were taken with lightning speed as the plane circled overhead with her wings dipping back and forth. Crash trucks and fire equipment raced to the runway. Passenger planes were warned to stay clear of the field. Sirens screamed. Mechanics pushed parked aircraft as far from the landing area as possible, as *Columbia* maneuvered crazily in the sky preparing to land. A little de Havilland biplane took off, quickly, in hope of being of assistance to the Bellanca's owner in his latest travail.

British pilots who saw it say to this day that there has never been a landing like it. The first try was unsuccessful as *Columbia* roared in too fast and too high with first one wing and then the other dropping uncertainly. Somehow, Levine got the little ship to climb, and then he made an overly deep, banking turn, but righted the plane in the nick of time, and she flew to the leeward end of the field for another try. Officials looked up helplessly, with horror etched on their faces as *Columbia* banked, and started down fast— much too fast—and once again roared up in the air like a rocket.

She almost stalled, but "Lady Luck" was with Levine. Around the plane came again. There was nothing that those on the ground could do. Even the little DH in the air was forced to stay at a respectful distance. Pilots shook their heads, and spectators covered their eyes. *Columbia* started down in her third approach. She still traveled at break-neck speed. Down she came, dropping almost like a stone. Her wheels hit hard, and she bounced thirty feet in the air. Then she came down again, bounced high, and, in leapfrog fashion, slowed and rolled ultimately to a stop, miraculously unharmed. Field officials rushed to the plane, where they found a jaunty Levine stepping out of the cockpit."

"Oh, hello," he said unconcernedly. "You know, I think I need a shave."

When questioned as to why he had made the flight, he blamed it on French harassment . . .

"The French were watching me," he said, "and I saw my chance, and took off."

He admitted that he had carried no map, but he remarked blandly, "I knew London was north of Paris!"

He arrived without clearance papers, passport, baggage or hat, and he had violated the customs laws of both England and France, but he was not fazed, nor were the British. He was kind of a lovable oddball to them, and soon was the toast of London. The papers called him "plucky but lucky," and one spoke warmly of his "hairbrained courage."

That very night, he and "Doc" Kinkaid attended the theater, accompanied by Lieutenant Walter Hinchcliffe, a well-known commercial flyer. Levine was greeted with wild applause, and called to the footlights for a speech.

"I'm certainly glad to be on British soil," he told the audience diplomatically and obviously, sincerely.

The following day, the hapless Drouhin was fired officially and succeeded by Lieutenant Hinchcliffe, a tall, slender, one-eyed combat veteran with 8000 flying hours to his credit, and known to all as the "Storm Wizard" for his experience in bad-weather flying.

In Paris, Drouhin raged over Levine's coup.

"If I saw him, I'd kill him!" he screamed. He allowed though, as how he would not follow him to London. Mrs. Levine assuaged Drouhin's feelings partially by paying him $6000 in forfeiture money before following her gallivanting husband to London by ship. However, the unfortunate Frenchman was now left with no plane to fly. Unhappily, he was to die the following summer in the crash of a plane that he was test-flying, prior to an attempted Atlantic flight.

For Lieutenant Hinchcliffe, it would be an unforgettable and stormy autumn and fall. From the time that Levine approached him with, "As you know, Hinchcliffe, I am tired of fooling around over here, and want to get home by the same route I came," the reserved and distinguished-looking Imperial Airways Ltd. pilot, was sold on an ocean flight. His employers warned him about Levine and tried to dissuade him from his new association. He replied that he would make the flight during the three-weeks leave that was due him. The airline then tried to get Levine to pay them 2000 pounds for the use of their pilot, but Levine would have none of it. Finally, Hinchcliffe put the decision up to his wife, and when she gave her OK with a simple, "Fly it!" (the Atlantic), Levine had a new partner.

Hinchcliffe, through his service connections, obtained permission from the Air Ministry, for *Columbia* to make use of the R.A.F. field at Cranwell, and *Columbia* once more seemed set for her return trip.

Levine appeared as determined as ever to go, but "Doc" Kinkaid, now on his way home, after an unforgettable summer in Europe, pleaded, "Help me stop him! My advice is given because I think that conditions to make the attempt are suicidal. The machine is all right, and I'll guarantee the engine, but it is impossible to carry sufficient petrol to buck strong head winds all the way across. The weather, at this season in the Atlantic, is absolutely impossible to foresee six hours in advance. Levine might have a favorable report one hour, and find himself in the midst of a terrible storm before he was many hours out."

3. The tests continued for all planes—even for *Columbia*—when the running fight between owner and pilot allowed, but the weather over the Atlantic continued to be unfavorable. Coste summed it up for all, when he said disconsolately, "There is nothing to do, but wait. There seems to be some evil spirit in the weather."

French meteorologists reported continual heavy winds blowing from the west across the Atlantic, and they all waited for the miracle—a favorable easterly flow of air for, at least, part of the trip. Meanwhile, the Belgian pilots, Medaets and Verhaegen, at the field since April, gave up, and returned to Brussels to plan another adventure.

There was brief excitement, in early August, when *Oiseau Bleu* made what was rumored to be her last test—a flight to Cherbourg and back. A large throng was on hand when Givon brought the plane in in the late afternoon and they remained all night, for it was said that he would take off for New York in the morning. It was a lovely, clear moonlit night, and Farman mechanics worked continuously under the hangar lights, on the forward engine.

Dawn came and went with no sign of the flyers. Late in the day, however, Givon and Corbu arrived and climbed into the cabin. The engines were started, and the plane raced down the runway while the crowd cheered. Suddenly, three-quarters of the way down, the onlookers were stunned as *Oiseau Bleu's* power was shut down and the ship rolled to a stop. Givon and Corbu, without a word of explanation, got out of the plane and returned to Paris. Later, it was learned that they had discovered a leak in the main tank, and that the troublesome forward engine was not generating full power. Moreover, the spectators learned that they had waited in vain for the attempted take-off was merely for the purpose of a further test of the motors.

There was still more excitement when Coste, after announcing that his destination was Philadelphia, took off in *Nungesser and Coli* in what was supposedly his last flight test—a round trip to Cherbourg to check out his radio. Late in the evening when he had not returned, fears grew for his safety. The weather was socked in, and searchlights tried to pierce the gloom at Le Bourget. The Mount Valerian beacon, dark since Byrd's memorable night over France, flashed through the fog and drizzle. After hours of anxious waiting, the happy news arrived that *Nungesser and Coli* had put in safely at Villacoublay.

The days went by. It was always the weather that held them back—adverse winds, fog, and cloud layers. After a test flight, Tarascon announced that *Oiseau Tango* still needed work and would not be ready for at least two weeks. He added, though, that when she went, he expected to reach the New York or Philadelphia area within 29 hours. The waiting flyers, during these days, were not harassed by the press as were Nungesser and Fonck, simply because the unfortunate Drouhin and Charlie Levine, with his chicaneries, took up all available space. Nevertheless, the pilots became edgy with the endless waiting, and it was to their credit that they controlled the urge to leave, regardless of the weather, for the North Atlantic during that summer was covered by a succession of violent storms.

4. Ernst Udet still worked on his seaplane at the Rohrsbach factory, and in any case did not plan to leave until September, but Captain Otto Koennecke took up the challenge of the Junkers crews. His plane had been tested to the ultimate at Travelmuende. He was dissatisfied only with the low horsepower of the engine, and he ordered another from the Junkers plant which had an extra fifty horses. The question was whether it would arrive and could be mounted on time.

Koennecke and his crewmates, 105-pound I. A. Wall, the radio man, and Count Solms-Laubach, supervised the installation of a radio and telephone, thereby providing the plane with the most sophisticated communications system yet used by ocean flyers. The telephone was for the purpose of talking directly with ships at sea.

He tentatively scheduled his take-off for August 13, from Cologne's airfield, following a short stopover at Tempelhof Airdrome in Berlin. Financial problems still plagued his venture. The Caspar Company had not been paid for the plane, and were reluctant to let it leave. Koennecke promised, however, that he would raise the money, by charging admission at Tempelhof and Cologne.

He made a last flight over Travelmuende on August 10. The machine with its new engine performed perfectly, except for a slight malfunction in the tachometer. It was fixed quickly and on August 11 he flew to Tempelhof, where he was greeted by a large, but not large enough, crowd of paying spectators. The plane was given a final overhaul by Lufthansa mechanics, and Koennecke flew *Germania* to Cologne on August 13, where he landed at 9 P.M., before 10,000 cheering Germans at Butzweller Hof airdrome. The crew was welcomed with a colorful torchlight parade down the streets of the city. One might have thought that the flight had been successful, already. There were speeches and bands, and they were banqueted by city officials. Representatives of the American Consul presented them with a United States bill of health, so as to avoid a $500 fine when they landed in America. Koennecke announced that he would take off at 6 A.M. the following day, but he did not go. The airport collections had been insufficient to pay for the plane, and it wasn't until August 21 that funds to cover the deficit were made available by the city of Cologne—and paid over to the Caspar Company. By the time that the plane was released to him, free of encumbrances, a hurricane developed off the southern coast of the United States and its swift northerly movement caused a postponement.

During this time, a comfortable seat was built in the cabin for tiny I. A. Wall, but, until he had pumped gas from the tins that surrounded it, he would be forced to stand. U.S. visas were obtained from the American Consul, J. Klahr Huddle. *Germania* was, at last, ready.

But Otto Koennecke never did get off on his Atlantic flight. At first it was the weather, then mechanical difficulties, and finally changes in his crew. Several times, in the days following *Bremen*'s and *Europa*'s attempts, *Germania* was rolled to the end of the specially built concrete runway at Butzweller Hof airdrome, gassed up, and provided with such tasty items as bananas, pineapples, and brandy. On one occasion, Frau Koennecke and the captain's three children were present, giving credence to rumors that *Germania* was at last on her way, but the large crowd waited for hours, and in vain. The big plane merely stood at the end of the strip. Her engine was never started and there was no sign of her crew. Subsequently it was announced that low pressure areas dotted the Atlantic, and Koennecke, decided wisely to wait. At the end of August, Wall, his diminutive radio expert, left the expedition after a disagreement over money, and after a time was replaced by Johannes Hermann.

5. Meanwhile, in Dessau, Risticz and Edzard in *Europa*, and Fritz Loose, Koehl and Baron Guenther von Huenefeld in *Bremen* awaited favorable weather. The planes were pronounced fit by Junkers mechanics and stood side by side on the edge of the field. They were silvery in color, and on the low wing of *Bremen* the number D-1167 was painted in black, while *Europa* bore the license D-1192. The crowds were ever-present, but were held at a safe distance by a rope barrier and hard-working police. The planes were identical in appearance, bearing a distinct resemblance to the low-winged sports planes used by private flyers

today. The only modern feature that was missing was the retractable landing gear, and Bellanca, in America, was already at work on the idea.

The flyers' food, sufficient for three days, was prepared and loaded. Salami sausages, cakes, chocolate, zweibach, hard-boiled eggs, bananas, and lemons were the principal staples. Unlike the French, there was no liquor aboard that could be seen. An alarm was rigged to wake the crew member who happened to be resting in the hammock behind the cockpit. It was the timeless string, attached to the hammock, and leading to the pilot's seat. Three tugs on it by the pilot was the signal to summon the sleeper back to the controls.

The schedule called, first, for a joint take-off on August 12, but there were reports of a bad storm in mid-Atlantic, and Baron von Huenefeld was called away from Dessau to attend the funeral of his father. The next day was out because of the objections of Frau Edzard and Loose's fiancée against a take-off on the 13th. Professor Junkers assigned Schnaebel to fly a large Junkers tri-motor to the coast with *Bremen* and *Europa*, so as to give the press a comprehensive coverage of the start of the trip. The crowds grew so thick during the day that extra police were rushed from the city to guard the little planes. It was decided that *Bremen* would be the pilot plane, because of Captain Hermann Koehl's experience and ability as a navigator, and it was hoped that the two planes would remain within sight of each other on the flight across. The planes were equipped with radio receivers, but, strangely enough, were without transmitters.

On Sunday, August 14, the decision to go was reached by Junkers officials at 3 P.M. The flyers were called at the hotel, and told to report to the field no later than 4:30. Together with their wives and friends they ate a final and substantial meal, and then rushed to their planes. Last minute weather checks over the route were made, and maps of the course, which lined a little office at the edge of the strip, were studied intently. The flyers smoked cigarette after cigarette, while the wives, Fraus Risticz, Edzard, Koehl, and Loose's fiancée, paced nervously about. Baron von Huenefeld was alone. Edzard and Risticz sent a thoughtful message to Madame Nungesser, in Paris.

At 5:15 P.M., they changed into khaki flying suits, and after tender good-byes to friends and relatives, and handshakes with the members of the ground crews, they stepped aboard their respective planes.

Fritz Loose took over the controls of the *Bremen*, while Risticz sat behind the wheel of *Europa*.

The motors were started and run for ten minutes while the hordes of spectators looked on eagerly. A little after 6 P.M., *Bremen* moved to the easternmost edge of the runway and faced down the concrete lane which ended with the row of pines. She was followed closely by *Europa*. Both sat there, for what seemed like an eternity, with their propellers turning over, idly. There was little or no wind. Suddenly, a full-bodied roar came from *Bremen*'s engine. She moved down the 3000-foot strip, her tail held high by a specially constructed wheel designed to drop off after take-off. She looked so small as she speeded along, ever faster. She rose, for a trice, to ten feet at the halfway point, and then sank back again. At 2000 feet, she rose once more only to fall back. Finally at 2500 feet she was off, and climbing, with her silvery body silhouetted against the dark green trees at the end of the field. She passed over them with ease and faded quickly into the reddening, western sky. It was 6:20 P.M. A minute later, *Europa* swung onto the runway, and, with her engine wide open, screamed down the field, in pursuit of her sister ship. She lifted off, after a run of 1750 feet, climbed more easily, and surely than *Bremen*, and headed after her, straight for the Atlantic.

The world learned, at once, of the departures. New York's Mitchel Field was ready to receive *Europa*, while Chicago, *Bremen*'s destination, added extra lights to the existing ones at Maywood Field. *Bremen* was expected there late in the evening of the 16th, or early on the 17th. Mechanics and field personnel rushed about, testing the latest rockets and flares, so as to be ready if the weather was bad.

In New York, Grover Whalen reserved a suite for *Europa*'s crew at the Garden City Hotel, and Clarence Chamberlin announced that he would fly up the coast and meet them. Lloyd Bertaud, who had set an endurance record in a Junkers ship with Eddie Stinson, commented, "I know it's a good plane. I wish them luck."

Observers on airfields, and other coastal points in the Nova Scotia and Newfoundland areas, were alerted to be on the lookout as the American continent awaited not one but two transatlantic planes.

Originally, an alternate course was planned for the planes, leading over Bremen, Heligoland, and the Orkneys, and to be used if the weather was bad to the south, but early reports on *Bremen* indicated that the more southerly route was being followed by her. At 7:30

P.M., she was seen flying over Hannover at 300 feet, and, at 10 P.M., over Scheveningen, Holland. At midnight, she was heard over London but the report may have been inaccurate as there was no sighting, and subsequent sightings found her farther to the north; at 1:40 A.M., over Wakefield, Yorkshire, and later over Formby, 11 miles north of Liverpool. The final report from *Bremen* came when she flew over Dublin, Ireland, at 5:15 A.M., August 15.

There were no sightings of *Europa*, which was supposed to remain close to *Bremen*. Fears began to rise for her safety, but early in the morning it was learned that she had landed at the city of Bremen's airfield soon after midnight—after five hours in the air. She had been severely damaged while landing. Pilot Risticz, at the controls, was for some reason unable to close the throttle, and was forced to fly her in at cruising speed. When he got over the end of the strip, he cut the engine off. He avoided a ditch, but the plane settled down hard. The undercarriage snapped off, and *Europa* skidded to a stop, but not before the fuselage had been torn clear of the engine, and reduced to a mass of twisted metal. Fortunately, the flyers were able to walk away from the wreckage, unharmed.

Risticz told of encountering first fog and then engine trouble over the North Sea. He and Edzard described flying into a thick black cloud bank when they reached the West Friesische Islands, in which they were buffeted about by high winds and heavy rains. Four times, they said, they tried to fly into the weather, and were balked by its fury. After the last try, both agreed that it was useless to go on, particularly when the motor began to act up. Risticz said that the engine ran smoothly only when the throttle was wide open. When the power was reduced, it sputtered, and at times nearly stopped. They turned back to land and crossed the coastline between Bremerhaven and Bremen, and decided to put down quickly.

Risticz was visibly upset by the landing, but he said that it was unavoidable due to the faulty engine and the heavy load aboard the plane. He described the touchdown as "hard," and said that the wheel-less tail plowed deeply into the field, causing the fuselage to shake violently and then to fall apart. Sadly, the two flyers boarded a private plane for Dessau, to give their report on the flight to Dr. Junkers.

After Dublin, *Bremen* vanished for twelve hours. It was presumed that she was well out over the Atlantic, when she suddenly reappeared over the Dessau Field at 4:15 P.M., on August 15. She landed safely, and her exhausted crew crawled out, and were taken into the little fieldside office.

There, they told their story of a 22-hour battle with the elements. No sooner had they left the Dutch coast than they ran into stiff head winds of gale force, which reduced their airspeed to 60 miles an hour. By dawn, they had covered only 600 miles, and the weather and winds continued to plague the little plane. Ten hours of valuable gasoline was gone, and they were not yet over the ocean. From Dublin they headed for the southern coast of Ireland, in the hopes of finding better weather, but there was no improvement. They, too, decided that it was suicidal to go on after they had been forced by a low ceiling to an altitude of thirty feet. Fritz Loose turned the ship around reluctantly, and headed for home. The disappointed flyers avoided the big cities on the way back, for they wanted to conceal their failure until after they landed. They were borne home swiftly by the heavy winds and to their satisfaction were not identified anywhere until they glided in safely at Dessau.

Americans had an inkling of the weather that *Bremen* ran into, for "Doc" Kimball stated after the planes' take-off that they would face severe storms all the way across from the English coast to Newfoundland, and Bellanca commented, "They are plucky to start in weather like this." In Paris, the crews of the waiting planes at Le Bourget shook their heads in disbelief when told of the take-off, but at the same time wished the Germans "all the best."

Bremen was readied at once for another try, and a new Junkers plane was assigned to take the place of the wrecked *Europa,* but storms over the Atlantic caused delay after delay. Finally in early September, the Junkers flights were postponed until the following spring. The reasons given were the bad weather, which did not figure to improve during the fall and winter, and a threatened government ban on ocean flying, after the rash of tragedies that occurred in late August and early September. *Bremen,* however, with Captain Koehl, Baron Von Huenefeld, and Irish aviator Major James Fitzmaurice, would become the first plane to complete successfully a westbound Atlantic flight when she flew from Dublin, Ireland, to bleak, Greenly Isle, Labrador, in the spring of 1928.

6.   Two other planes in England made preparations during the summer for the Atlantic crossing. At Bristol Airdrome, a giant, golden-winged Fokker, with a sky-blue body, was

tried out by Captain Leslie Hamilton and Captain F. F. Minchin. She had been built in Amsterdam and was named *San Raphael*, after the patron saint of flying. She was an impressive-looking, single-engined plane, as spectators viewed her in front of her hangar. She had the huge, thick wing so typical of Fokker designs, and a massive fuselage. A large, block G was painted on her rudder, and her registration letters, *G-EBTQ*, were prominent on her body. Her name, SAN RAPHAEL was inscribed in small letters, just below the aft cabin window.

There was no publicity given to her owner, the Princess Lowenstein-Wertheim. When the announcement was made of *San Raphael's* intended flight from Ireland to Newfoundland, and back across to Vienna, it was signed by Hamilton and Minchin, alone, and it was assumed by the British people that they were her only crew. The Princess was never seen at the airdrome as tests were conducted in July, and it was Hamilton and Minchin who flew by themselves to the Galway coast, to seek out an adequate hopping-off spot. Later, when the plans were revamped to provide for a non-stop flight from England to Lindbergh Field, Ottawa, and return again, there was no mention of the Princess. However, she would turn up in time, as we shall see.

At the same time, at Bristol's Field, there was yet another giant, single-engined Fokker, a sister ship of *San Raphael*, and built, also, at Fokker's Amsterdam factory. She was a large, blue-bodied aircraft with brown wings, and had been designed for Captain Robert H. McIntosh, and his crewmate, W. H. Johnson-Wreford. Her destination was Philadelphia, and that city's $25,000 prize, which they needed desperately to pay off obligations that had mounted alarmingly since the death of an original backer. The money straits reached a point in midsummer where it became necessary to put the flight off. Fortunately, McIntosh came up with an "angel" in William B. Leeds, an American sportsman. His wife, a Russian Princess named Xenia, equally sports-minded, was at the time in America, testing out a new, high-powered speedboat in the waters off Oyster Bay. It was only natural that the plane be named after her.

McIntosh's plan was to take off from Dublin's Baldonnel Airdrome on his Philadelphia trip, and to this end, he had already requested the removal of a formidable stone wall which marked the end of the runway, so as to provide a longer and safer take-off area for his big plane.

Throughout the summer, the two Fokkers made test flights, and along with *Whale* kept aviation interest alive in Great Britain as the English awaited their attempts with eagerness.

7. The Pacific had been conquered twice in less than a month in June, but this was not a deterrent to ambitious promoters, thrill-seekers, and flyers who needed more money in the monthly kitty. James D. Dole, president of the Hawaiian Pineapple Company, had provided an incentive. He was a member of the National Aeronautical Association and he issued a statement saying, "Believing that Charles A. Lindbergh's extraordinary feat in crossing the Atlantic is a forerunner of eventual Transpacific air transportation, I offer $25,000 for the first flyer and $10,000 to the second flyer to cross from the North American Continent to Honolulu in a non-stop flight." Hollywood showman Sid Grauman followed Mr. Dole's notice by posting $30,000 with the Los Angeles Chamber of Commerce which was to be awarded for the first Los Angeles to Tokyo non-stop flight, and the San Francisco Citizen's Flight Committee proposed an extension of the Dole "race" to Australia, and began to raise a purse of $50,000 to entice the flyers.

While the promoters hoped that the glamour of their work would entice the heroes of the Atlantic, they were quickly disappointed. Lindbergh, Chamberlin, and Byrd announced forthwith that they were not interested. The consensus seemed to be that there was not sufficient time to prepare for such an undertaking. Wanamaker, speaking for Byrd, said that he "did not look with favor on entering a race for any of these special prize offers."

Entrants, nevertheless, flocked to the lists. War ace William P. "Lonestar Bill" Erwin registered his green and silver monoplane *Dallas Spirit*, and Major Livingston G. Irving, another war ace from Berkeley, California, entered his bright orange monoplane *Pacific Pablo Flyer*; there was Arthur Goebel, the famed upside-down stunt flyer of the West Coast in Phillips Petroleum's sponsored, *Woolaroc*; and Flint, Michigan, sent the biplane, *Miss Doran*, piloted by John A. "Augie" Pedlar with a lovely, twenty-two-year-old Flint schoolteacher, Mildred Doran, as his mascot. George Hearst, publisher of the San Francisco *Examiner*, entered a speedy new Lockheed Vega, *Golden Eagle*, to be piloted by John W. Frost, and there was a swift monoplane called *Aloha* to be flown by veteran flyer Martin Jensen. These were only a few who jumped at the chance. There were British flyers, Captain Arthur V. Rogers, twenty-nine, married, with a baby daughter, and Captain Frederick A. Giles, who strove to get his plane from Detroit, Michigan, to the starting line in time. In all there were over fifteen entrants.

The entries were closed on August 2 and the take-off was set for August 12 at noon from Bay Farm Island. The Race Committees, one from Honolulu and one from Oakland, agreed that the order of take-offs would be determined by the drawing of lots, and that the planes would leave at one-minute intervals.

Troubles began almost at once. The War Department said that they could not guarantee the operation of the beacons sending out from Crissy Field and Maui, and would not be responsible for their failure. On August 10, two days before the scheduled start, Navy Lieutenants George Covell and Richard S. Waggener, rushing to get to the starting line, crashed on take-off from San Diego's North Field and were killed. The tragedy made the other crews at Bay Farm Island stop and think. They voted to postpone the start of the venture until August 16 to allow them to better prepare. While the Oakland Race Committee thought the pilots' decision was laudable, and sought a two-week postponement of the flight, the Honolulu Contest Committee thought otherwise. They said by wire: THE COMMITTEE DISAPPROVES POSTPONEMENT OF ZERO HOUR FOR STARTING TIME. THE CONTESTANTS HAVE ALREADY BEEN GIVEN SUFFICIENT TIME TO PREPARE.

On August 12, a third contestant was killed. Captain Arthur V. Rogers, the British ace, died when he leaped from his stricken plane at 150 feet. "Thank God, he left me a beautiful daughter," said his wife, Arma, an eyewitness.

There was an attempt by the Department of Commerce to legitimize the contest. Inspectors were sent to approve the planes for the flight. Extra gas tanks were prescribed, along with hours on the azimuth circle to orientate compasses—most of them earth inductors. They talked about lifeboats, sails, emergency rations, and the like. But there wasn't that much time. Only four of the entrants carried radios and only two of the four were equipped to receive.

On August 16, at noon, the race began. Two of the entrants crashed on take-off, and two returned to the field soon after leaving because of mechanical difficulties. Of the four who headed west for Honolulu, only two made the crossing safely. *Woolaroc*, piloted by Arthur Goebel, won by finishing the flight in 26 hours and 17 minutes, and *Aloha*, flown by Martin Jensen, landed two hours later.

Golden Eagle, the George Hearst plane with John W. Frost at the controls, and *Miss Doran*, the red and black biplane piloted by "Augie" Pedlar and carrying the stunning twenty-two-year-old Mildred Doran as a passenger, were never heard from again despite long and frantic searches of the enormous and enigmatic Pacific. The search resulted also in the death of war ace "Lonestar Bill" Erwin. Previously disqualified from the race, he took off in his *Dallas Spirit* to look for the missing flyers and dropped out of sight into the ocean. There were no clues as to the fate of *Miss Doran* and *Golden Eagle*, and the only clue to Captain Erwin's fate was a desperate radio message sent from 500 miles out: AM IN A TAIL SPIN!

The race was a tragedy. Mr. Dole at once declared that it was not his intention to race. Nevertheless, the search for the missing flyers cost the Navy $125,000 worth of fuel, $40,000 in provisions for 8000 men involved in the search, and there was $60,000,000 of naval equipment used to scan the Pacific for the lost flyers.

The New York *Times* in an editorial entitled "Imprudent Flying," said, "The Dole competition took on the aspect of a diversion. The hazards seemed to be completely forgotten. It came to be regarded as a sporting event in which the more entries the merrier. It is time there was federal supervision." The Honolulu Starting Committee now agreed. In a statement they said that the preparation was too brief. "The planes were not fitted for such an adventure, and rashness in understanding it is palpably the cause of what was a disaster." But, it was over, and something had been learned.

8. American born, Eddie was the third of the famous Flying Stinsons. His celebrated older sisters, Katherine and Marjorie, instilled an interest in aviation in their younger brother from the time they had all built and flown kites together in the back yard of their home in Jackson, Mississippi. After his sisters had left home to pursue their careers, Eddie, then thirteen, amused himself by building gliders with his brother John in the family woodshed. Only partial success resulted from the flights, and the last one at home was disastrous, resulting in a crash that reduced their creation to kindling wood. Eddie was undaunted though. He heard that two men were building an airplane in St. Louis and needed someone to fly it. So he packed up and left home, arriving in St. Louis penniless. He convinced the owner of the plane, who was also the proprietor of a local roadhouse, that he could fly

anything with wings—and he was given room and board. It was pure bravado, of course, and his bluff was soon called. With fear and trembling, he climbed aboard the frail pusher, with its tiny engine which had been built by a local machinist. The field was a cow pasture behind the roadhouse. While his new employer's friends stood around smirking, Eddie hurriedly tried to absorb the unfamiliar controls. His left hand went to the elevator, his right to the wing-warping device. There was still another small lever on top of the elevator control for the rudder. "Well," he thought, "I'll figure that one out when I get her up—I've only got two hands!"

He got the craft off the ground and up to 60 feet, when she started down inexplicably. Nothing he tried would reverse the trend. He barely missed a tree; bounced high off the ground like a frog leaping, and came down hard again, as parts of the plane flew off in every direction and were strewn all over the field. The roadhouse owner, enraged, told Eddie to get off his premises pronto and take the wreck with him. Fortunately, a sympathetic farmer was standing by and took pity on the youngster, giving him room and board and the use of another cow pasture on which to practice.

Eddie decided finally that it might be wiser to get a more formal type of training, and he enrolled at a flying school in Dayton from which sister Marjorie had been an early graduate. He was an excellent student and proved quickly to be a natural flyer with a built-in "feel" for the air—a vital asset for pilots of old-time aircraft.

On graduation, he set out for San Antonio, Texas, where Marjorie had opened a school and was known already as the "Flying School Marm." On arrival, he chose to land, unfortunately, on a level field which turned out to be the parade grounds for an Army base. The marching soldiers were goggle-eyed as his strange-looking plane came in. The commanding officer was not, and charged up to the young flyer demanding that he "Get the hell out of here, and now!" Stinson, thoroughly chastened, had no sooner gotten off the ground and away from the base, when a bolt, acting as a pivot for the elevator control, sheared off. The joystick wobbled uselessly in his hand, and he was forced to land without delay. This time, the open space he picked turned out to be a cemetery, some distance from the nearest town. How to repair the elevator? he thought. After a search, he came upon an old coffin, removed a part from one of the hinges, made it into a makeshift bolt, and was off again.

During World War I, Eddie was commissioned a lieutenant, having made peace with the military authorities for his prior indiscretions, and was assigned to Kelly Field in Texas as an instructor and final test pilot. While there, he became noted for his stunts. At Kelly, atop every structure including the flagpole, there was a red warning light. Eddie would bet—$50 for a building light, and $100 for the light on the flagpole—that he could break the bulbs with his wingtips while in flight. It was not long before he had considerably more income than his fellow second lieutenants.

Stinson left the Army following the Armistice, and in financial straits despite his gambling successes. With nineteen other pilots who were in a similar situation, he ordered twenty planes from the Curtiss Company plant in Mineola, to be delivered in three months, and he paid for them with postdated checks. With old planes, the pilots then covered the checks by flying debarking troops home from Newport News, Virginia.

He barnstormed for the next two years. It was a profitable business. Any field would do and the intervening years had made the pilot seem less a maniac bent on suicide, and more of a daring soul whose skill could be trusted to get one up and down again with safety. With his earnings, he joined his brother Jack, now an aeronautical engineer, in the construction of a two-seater plane. After a highly successful series of demonstration flights in New York, it was demolished sadly in a crash on a flight to Dayton, Ohio, thus wiping out the investment from his hard-earned savings. He returned to New York where he got a job as a pilot-mechanic. With his new earnings, he bought a secondhand Junkers monoplane, and achieved notoriety by making a non-stop flight from New York to Chicago with a paying passenger. Soon after, in the same plane, and with Lloyd Bertaud as his co-pilot, he took the world's endurance record from Germany by staying aloft for twenty-six hours and 19 minutes in freezing weather and a snowstorm over New York's Roosevelt Field.

In 1925, his reputation as a skilled pilot and imaginative designer secure in aviation circles, he was backed by a group of Detroit businessmen, and formed the Stinson Aircraft Corporation with factories in Northville, Michigan. He was still only twenty-five years old, and within two years his Stinson Detroiter cabin monoplane was to make this curly-headed, smiling young man world-famous by his breathtaking long-distance flights.

His latest plane was 32 feet long, with a wingspread of 46 feet. The pilot's cabin was enclosed behind a Wright J-5 Whirlwind engine, which drove the plane at a top speed of 131 miles an hour, and a cruising speed of 110.

Two Detroiters were entered in the annual Ford Reliability Tour, sponsored by the Ford Motor Company, and held in the first weeks in July. The tour covered 4000 miles, and the planes were judged on a number of counts, including speed, maneuverability, rate of climb, stability, and performance in bad weather. At the tour's end, a Detroiter, piloted by Eddie Stinson himself, was found to be the over-all winner by a wide margin. The plane was named *Pride of Detroit*.

Also on the tour, together with his wife and nine-year-old daughter Rosemary, was a well-to-do, thirty-nine-year-old Detroit businessman, Edward F. Schlee. He was president of the Wayco Oil Company, which, as a result of diversification, had entered the aviation field. He was so impressed by the performance of the Stinson plane that he made arrangements to buy it from the Stinson Company for an attempted Round the World flight. He hoped to break the existing record for such a trip, set in 1926 by Edward S. Evans and Linton Wells, in which they made use of varied transportation facilities over a period of 28 days. Schlee's trip would be by air alone.

Schlee enlisted the help of thirty-one-year-old William F. Brock, a veteran Western airmail pilot, who had most recently been employed by Wayco's air subsidiary, and on August 6, *Pride of Detroit* was flown to Curtiss Field, New York, from Teterboro, New Jersey, to undergo final renovation. Schlee's itinerary called for a trip of 22,067 miles in 240 hours. The logistics were complicated by the need for the storage of oil and gas, and the arrangements for competant servicing at twenty-two different stops around the world.

The longest over-the-water flight would be from Tokyo, Japan, to Sand Island in the Midways, a flight of 2480 miles, slightly longer than the 2350 mile trip from Harbor Grace, Newfoundland, to Croydon Field, London. Among the stops scheduled after London were those at Stuttgart, Belgrade, Constantinople, Baghdad, Calcutta, Rangoon, Bangkok, Hong Kong, Tokyo, Midway, Honolulu, San Francisco, Cheyenne, Chicago, Detroit, and New York. Her tanks were designed to hold a capacity of 565 gallons—200 in the fuselage, 235 in the wings, and 130 gallons, in 5-gallon tins stored in the rear of the fuselage.

Outside Harbor Grace, Newfoundland, finishing touches were being put on the new Bennett Field, named after Sir John Bennett, a prominent Newfoundlander and Colonial Secretary of the Newfoundland government. Stores of fuel and spare parts were dispatched to it, earmarked for Brock and Schlee. Fred Koehler of the Stinson Company was sent ahead to prepare to service the *Pride of Detroit* prior to her first ocean hop of the trip.

Bryce Goldsborough of Pioneer Instruments spent the interim days at Curtiss, working on the all-important instrument panel. He installed an earth inductor compass, and, to preclude the troubles of the earlier flights, he attached an extra reading dial, encased in a shock absorber, to a cross tube of the fuselage. It was hoped that this innovation would reduce the problems caused by engine vibration. For added safety, he put in a British aperiodic compass, together with a magnetic compass. The panel, in front of the pilots and under the windshield, was equipped with lights, but hooded adequately to prevent glare. The plane carried a standard tachometer, turn and bank indicator, altimeter, and oil gauge among its instruments. A life raft was stowed aft, complete with oars, and two bottles of air for inflation purposes. The plane carried, also, fifteen days of emergency rations, a gallon of water, disinfectants, stimulants, a dozen flares for drift correction, two flashlights, six friction ship flares, and a Very pistol for firing distress rockets.

Pride of Detroit made a test hop to show herself off in her home city, and returned to Curtiss Field on August 22, after a speedy, six-hour flight from Michigan. Brock, the pilot, was overjoyed with her performance, and Schlee pronounced them ready to go. Ed Mulligan, the Wright expert who had helped with Lindbergh's engine, tuned up the *Pride of Detroit*. The little Stinson was housed in the same hangar with a big Fokker, named *Old Glory*, then getting set for a flight to Rome. Eddie Stinson, the young designer, was on hand and offered last-minute suggestions. The pre-flight publicity and coverage was less than that given to the earlier flights, and consequently the crowds at the field were smaller. There were always, however, a number of curious aviation fans, who wandered about, gaping at the aircraft—of which there were now five at Curtiss, preparing for Atlantic flights.

On August 25, *Pride of Detroit* was wheeled out of the hangar at 9 A.M. and her motor started and warmed by Mulligan. Brock and Schlee jumped aboard, after farewells to their wives and to the ground crew. Schlee, the sponsor, was fully aware of the rising public protest against meaningless ocean flights, and he denied to reporters that his trip was a stunt.

Said he: "We are seeking to demonstrate, by a series of long hops, that aviation has now reached a practical service position from which it will never be shaken."

He announced, further, that the trip to Harbor Grace would be broken up by an overnight stop at Old Orchard Beach, Maine, a beach which at low tide provided hard-packed sand, and probably the finest runway in America at the time.

As a young boy, I was lucky enough to spend summers at the Beach, and I was there during this historic summer. I can remember the little yellow monoplane with the red trim appearing overhead in the early afternoon. It had been an exciting summer for us. Lindbergh had flown in a few weeks before in his silvery *Spirit of St. Louis*, and had circled for a landing 75 feet over our house. I can remember the unbelievable roar that came from his powerful J-5. We had run a quarter of a mile down the beach to the hangar where Harry Jones, the local flyer, kept his plane.

Harry Martin Jones's aviation career had started on Labor Day of 1912 at Narragansett Park outside his home town of Providence, Rhode Island, where he promoted an air meet featuring the incomparable Lincoln Beachey, the daredevil aerobatist and his female counterpart, diminutive Ruth Bancroft Law. Young Jones, a motorcycle racer, was intrigued by their dazzling and breathtaking exhibition in the flimsy little planes, and weeks later when a racing competitor learned to fly, he made up his mind. "I could ride circles around the guy," he recalls now, "and if he could learn so could I."

He bought the remains of an old Wright biplane; patched it up and taught himself to fly. Soon he was famous. He landed on Boston Common in January 1913 in quest of a prize offered by the Boston *Post* to the first aviator to do so. Unfortunately, the prize offer had expired at the end of the year, and all he got for his trouble was a $25 fine and orders to remove himself and his plane forthwith. This did not daunt him, however, and soon he was off on a flight to New York with the first aerial parcel post in history. Fifty days and three crashes later he landed in Brooklyn, near the Flatbush Insane Asylum, to be greeted by a streetcar conductor brandishing a club, and insisting he was an escaped inmate.

During the war, he served as a civilian air instructor at Brooks Field, San Antonio, Texas, after which he bought a de Havilland biplane, and with his wife and infant son settled on lovely Old Orchard Beach with its 2½-mile-long strand. There he began a career of passenger flying, and, at his retirement in 1937, he had carried 100,000 passengers safely on short hops over the seaside resort. It was there in 1927, and in the years thereafter, he would find himself as host-pilot to countless ocean flyers who wanted to take advantage of the natural runway afforded by the hard-packed sands at low tide, for their take-offs. There the smiling Lindbergh, on the balcony of a house, acknowledged the cheers of the crowd. A few days later, Clarence Chamberlin came, and he obliged smilingly when I crowded through to get his autograph (which I still possess and cherish).

When we saw *Pride of Detroit* overhead, once again we headed posthaste for Harry Jones's! As we were so doing, the plane banked over Prout's Neck and Pine Point, at the northerly end of the 2½-mile-long beach, and touched down lightly on the sand behind us. She taxied by, up to the hangar, and, with a vividly remembered blast from her J-5, turned, and drove well up beyond the high-water mark, into the sand.

A small crowd gathered. Brock, a short, dark-haired mustachioed man, climbed out, followed by Schlee, tall, slender, and sandy-haired. They were greeted by Harry Jones, and our friend, Mr. Robert P. Hazzard, a prominent shoe manufacturer, who was Governor Ralph O. Brewster's personal representative. He was our friend, because he allowed us to use his lovely oceanside, salt-water pool.

For the remainder of the afternoon, we ogled at the little Stinson, though kept at a safe distance by police. *PRIDE OF DETROIT* was painted in huge block letters on her side, and her number NC-857 (all kids remembered numbers of planes then, starting with Lindbergh's NX-211), was in black, on her wings. She was trimmed with red, and *WAYCO* was painted in red on her fuselage. All the rest of her was a bright yellow. It is a vivid memory, and, after seeing her, you may be sure that we followed the rest of her flights with an avid interest.

We found out that she was to leave early the next morning, and, much to the distress of our grandparents, we were up and about at 4 A.M. in the pitch black, seashore dampness of the predawn. No sooner had we reached the beach, than we heard the engine being warmed up. There was only the faintest sign of light in the east, when she taxied up within 100 yards of our house, turned to the south into a whisper of air and took off. About all we could see of her, as she circled over Biddeford Pool and pointed on her northeasterly course, was a dim trace of light in her cockpit. It was a lovely and clear early morning, and the buzz of the Whirlwind faded quickly, and we were left, after our brief thrill, with only the noise of the little waves of low tide as they slapped idly on the beach.

It was August 26, and in the Portland *Press Herald* that morning, we read the exciting news that twenty-seven-year-old Paul Redfern had taken off the day before in another Stinson Detroiter, *City of*

Brunswick, from Glynn Island Beach, Georgia, on a 4600-mile non-stop flight to Rio de Janeiro. Sadly, despite rumors over the years from the South American jungles, that he had been found alive, neither he nor his plane were seen or heard from again.

9. As the days went by, we read better news about the *Pride of Detroit*. In perfect weather, she flew to Harbor Grace's Bennett Field, landing soon after noon. Brock and Schlee were greeted by a large crowd, led by Sir John Bennett himself. No time was wasted. Schlee announced an early-morning take-off for England, and gas and food were loaded. Despite Schlee's notorious appetite, they would carry only sandwiches, bananas, and coffee to sustain them on their way over. Fred Koehler, the Stinson man, made a last-minute check of the ship. Brock and Schlee went into town to get a good night's sleep.

"Billy" Brock, the pilot, had done all types of flying. As a youngster, he'd been thrilled by the feats of Beachey, and he learned to fly at the tender age of sixteen, while working for an aircraft company in Utica, New York. He barnstormed for a year, and when the war came, became a civilian instructor. After the war, he resumed barnstorming and thrilled crowds with his stunts. His show-stopper was when he climbed from one plane to another while in flight, by means of a rope ladder. Later, he flew the mails, and presently he was chief pilot for Schlee's newly formed Wayco Flying Service.

On August 27, 1927, the two flyers were up at 4:30 A.M. and break-fasted heartily on orange juice, cereal, bacon, eggs, toast, and coffee. They rode to the field with Sir John Bennett.

The field was built on a plateau at an elevation of 300 feet. It had a 4000-foot runway which was graded down 3 degrees from the eastern end, to facilitate a take-off into the prevailing westerly winds. Once they were at the field there was little hesitation. Koehler started the engines with the help of a mechanic, climbed out, and Brock and Schlee got in, with Brock sitting behind the controls. A few minutes passed, as Brock opened the throttle, closed it, and then reopened it. The mighty roar from the engine reverberated throughout the field. Brock signaled from the cockpit, and Koehler pulled the wheel chocks free. *Pride of Detroit*, with her full load of 5050 pounds, started down the runway into a light, westerly wind. She gathered speed quickly, and to the wonderment of the spectators, left the ground after a run of only 1500 feet. Brock held her close to the ground for another 500 feet, then pulled her up to 1000 feet, banked gently, and disappeared into the east. She was off the ground at 6:14 A.M., New York time.

There were few reported sightings of her as she sped across the ocean for London. At 9 P.M., local time (4 P.M., New York time), she was seen by the S.S. *California*, 400 miles off the Irish coast, and at midnight over Valencia, Ireland. There, she disappeared from sight for many hours.

Aboard, the take-off had been easy, considering her full load. She lifted at once when Brock applied pressure to the control column, and climbed speedily to 1000 feet. Only half of the runway had been used. The weather was clear and blue for the first 60 miles, and then increasing cloudiness began to surround the plane. The air became squally and bumpy, and the little ship lurched about. They were fortunate, though, for they were being helped on their way by a strong tail wind. Five hours out, they saw below them a little tramp steamer plowing to the east. It was their last glimpse of life over the ocean. Like the flyers before them, they tried to climb over the weather as it closed in. Up and up they flew as rain beat on the fuselage and streamed off the wings. They reached 10,000 feet. It was cold. The outside temperature dropped to 29, and little beads of ice began to stain the windshield. Down they dropped, quickly, to avoid the icing—back into the turbulent air for another 6 hours of bouncing flight in the blinding storm. They were consoled by the fact that the tail wind continued to waft them ever faster toward London.

It was early the following morning when they caught a brief glimpse of a lighthouse. The beam of light, as it probed the darkness, was a welcome sight to them. They hoped it was Fastnet, off the Irish coast, but they could not be sure, so long had been their blind flight. They flew on and soon after daylight (3:30 A.M.) they saw in the distance what looked like a long stretch of snow. Later, they found out that it was the sand on a beach near Plymouth, England, but, at the time, they were at a loss. They circled low as the beach slowly loomed up in front of them. Schlee scribbed a note on a piece of cardboard, *What town and country are you?* and threw it out the cabin window.

It floated down, but blew out of the reach of two or three early risers, who saw it and tried to chase it. It was gray and cloudy as they flew trying to get their bearings. They were in and out of the clouds as the land appeared, and then quickly was hidden. The hours passed. Through a break in the clouds, they saw a railway station below them. They dropped down, but were unable to make out the name on the station sign. Soon after, they found themselves over a beach again, headed for the sea. They circled, and Schlee wrote out his question on a piece of paper, this time weighted it and threw it out. Two lifeguards on the beach saw it drop, ran over and picked it up. One of them scratched SEATON, DEVON in the sand, while the other hurried to a nearby flagstaff, and ran up the Union Jack. From then on, it was a piece of cake.

At 10 A.M., local time, "Doc" Kinkaid, at Croydon Field along with a large crowd, quieted his companions and said, "I can hear her!" His well-trained ear had not betrayed him, for, in a few minutes, out of the southwest appeared a small sliver of gold in the gray overcast. A great cheer went up from the crowd, held back by guard ropes and a cordon of bobbies. *Pride of Detroit* flew straight down the field at 500 feet, circled into the wind, and made a three-point landing. It was 10:23 A.M., London time, and she had been in the air for 23 hours and 9 minutes. The two men jumped out, doffed their flying gear, and were rushed to the Savoy Hotel in London. Brock teased Schlee about his constant eating during the flight, but Schlee showed the pilot that he had room for more when he arrived at the Savoy, as he consumed a melon, a bowl of clam chowder, ham and eggs, ice cream and cake! Both flyers described the trip as routine. Their only amazement was at the millions of stars they saw in the sky when they flew during the night over the weather.

The Round the World flight continued at once. After a night's rest, the flyers took off for Munich, then Belgrade, and, on August 31, arrived in Constantinople. On September 2, they flew 1075 miles from Constantinople to the Royal Air Force airdrome in Baghdad, and the next day covered 885 miles to Bunder Abbas, Persia. On September 4, they took off for Karachi, India—a distance of 710 miles, and on the following day flew from Karachi on an 825-mile hop to Allahabad, India. They had flown through all kinds of weather, from the frigid cold over the Atlantic to the steaming heat, as they passed over the Near East and India. Both raved over the performance of the engine and the plane, and were grateful for, and enthused by the competent service afforded *Pride of Detroit* at her stopovers. The flight had become a truly international effort.

From Allahabad, they took off on September 6 on a 485-mile flight to Calcutta, after having been provisioned by officers of the

Allahabad brigade. They had still 14,377 miles to travel but the flight thus far had gone with unbelievable smoothness, with only troubles of a very minor nature to impede them. They arrived, safely, in Calcutta in the evening and, after a night's rest, left on September 7 for Rangoon, Burma, where they landed in the early afternoon. On September 8, they took off on a 350-mile trip to Bangkok, Siam. It was a short flight but a hazardous one, as the route lay over a mountain belt, and Bangkok's field was nestled among the mountains in the valley of the Menan River. Instead of risking such a landing, they flew on to Hanoi, French Indochina, and the next day they continued to the R.A.F. field at Hong Kong in a flight that lasted 8 hours. On September 10, they flew 780 miles up the Chinese coast to Shanghai, where they landed after battling stiff head winds for 11 hours.

Mrs. Schlee, back in Detroit, commented to reporters: "I hope they'll take the boat home to Vancouver," for, by this time, three planes had been lost within a few days over the Atlantic, and the public was aroused. Nevertheless, the *Pride of Detroit* kept on going. She took off on the 1200-mile flight to Tokyo on September 11, and many hours later, after being lost in a storm, made a forced landing at Omura, Japan. The landing caused international repercussions, for they had landed in a restricted naval zone where only authorized Japanese personnel were permitted. Japanese police and government investigators rushed to the scene, and for a while it seemed that there might be a serious incident, but after a thorough investigation, and pleas by American Embassy officials, the flyers were cleared to take off for Tokyo the next morning. They were forced to return, however, by a violent typhoon in the Tokyo area, and were not able to complete the 600-mile flight until September 14.

When they arrived in Tokyo, they found themselves in the center of a world-wide debate on the feasibility of further ocean flights, in the light of recent disasters. Government officials in Washington, London, Berlin, and Paris were incensed over "stunt flights," and many recommended legislative action to prevent them. The Assistant Secretary of the Navy cabled the flyers, beseeching them not to try the Pacific flight home. The pressures on them to quit were overwhelming and unending, and Schlee, wisely though sadly, bowed to them.

At a press conference in Tokyo on September 15, he announced that he was abandoning the flight.

"This is one of the great disappointments of my life," he said, "but we couldn't fight public opinion, which is unanimously against us."

The world applauded his decision, and the aviation world marveled at the wondrous accomplishments that he and Brock wrought in the *Pride of Detroit*.

CHAPTER XI

Old Glory

1. When *Pride of Detroit* left Curtiss Field
for Old Orchard, she left behind her besides a hangar mate, a big
Fokker named *Old Glory*, three other planes housed nearby, which
were tuning up for assaults on the Atlantic.

In the next hangar, there had arrived recently from the glass-roofed
Sikorsky factory at College Point, Long Island, a big white, snub-
nosed biplane the *City of Paris,* in which René Fonck hoped to make
a new attempt to reach Paris by air. The expedition was sponsored by
Mrs. Robert Dodge of Oyster Bay and other members of her family,
and Igor Sikorsky had been given carte-blanche by them to design the
best possible airplane for the try. He built a twin-engined ship with
his characteristic rounded bow and twin rudders attached to a
broad tail assembly. Two cigar-shaped motors (bearing the designer's
name) were suspended between the wings on each side of the fuselage,
and were reputed to be capable of driving the ship with 21,000 pounds
of fuel aboard at a top speed of 135 miles an hour. Sikorsky predicted
a minimum range of 5000 miles, ample for Fonck's adventure. The interior was vast, and on later test flights, as many as eleven passengers
were carried in addition to her crew of four. Lieutenant Lawrence W.
Curtin, on leave from the U. S. Navy, rejoined the French ace and
brought along with him another young naval flyer, Ensign Stephen V.
Edwards. Both were given permission by the Naval Department to
join the flight, as a courtesy to Fonck, and as a gesture of good will
toward the French people. The crew were busily making the vast
preparations for the trip.

Sikorsky, mindful of the 1926 crash, had taken pains to strengthen
the undercarriage, and had placed the wheels farther apart to ease the
strain on the landing assembly, and visitors to Curtiss Field during
the days of early August were rewarded by watching the big plane

taxied around the field as she tested her motors and landing gear. The sharper-eyed spectator might have noticed that she bore the coat of arms of the City of Paris on the fuselage under her name, together with the Latin inscription *"Fluctuat nec Mergitur,"* which translated roughly means, "It floats, but it never sinks."

In another hangar was a Stinson Detroiter with the name SIR JOHN CARLING written boldly in script on her fuselage, and LONDON TO LONDON, on her nose. In early July, the London (Ontario) *Advertiser* offered a prize of $25,000 to the first British or Canadian crew to make a successful non-stop trip from London, Ontario, to London, England. The rules were amended subsequently to drop the "non-stop" requirement, but it was necessary that the flight originate in the Canadian city and terminate in London, England. The airplane was provided by the Carling Brewery, and named after its founder, Sir John. Two veterans of the Royal Flying Corps, both of whom had served in France and been wounded in action, were selected as crew. The pilot was Captain Terrence B. Tully, a tall debonair Irishman from Ontario, who was the superintendant of the Ontario government air services and stationed at Sault Sainte Marie. Lieutenant James D. Metcalf, also a member of the government air services, was chosen as navigator. Both men were well seasoned by a number of varied aeronautical experiences and both were members of the Professional Flying Corps of Canada.

Sir John Carling's sojourn at Curtiss Field was brief, and was for the express purpose of having her instruments checked and adjusted by the now-famed Pioneer Company. This task was performed by Maurice Titteringham, and the plane took off on August 25, one hour after the *Pride of Detroit,* and flew to London, Ontario, where she landed, safely after a five-hour flight.

There followed three days of preparations and loading, and on August 29th *Sir John Carling* flew off to the east amid the cheers of thousands of Canadians. Five hours later, she returned and landed, after having run into what were described by the flyers as "impossible weather conditions."

They began all over again. Mechanics inspected the ship from stem to stern. Gas was drained from the tanks, strained through a piece of chamois, and reloaded. Tully announced that he would take off at daybreak on September 1, on the first leg of the trip, to Harbor Grace, Newfoundland.

A crowd of thousands, having been alerted by the prearranged signal of three flash bombs and the city's sirens, streamed to London's airfield before daylight on September 1. At 5 A.M., Tully and Metcalf climbed aboard *Sir John Carling*. Outside the plane stood Tully's worried wife, holding their two young children by the hand. With the roar of the motor drowning out the cheers of the crowd, the Stinson took off easily after a one-half mile run, and headed for Bennett Field, Harbor Grace.

Soon, however, the weather grew thick and the air turbulent, and they became unsure of their position. At 1:30 P.M., through a break in the clouds, they caught a glimpse of a town, and a field which seemed suitable for an emergency landing. After a quick pass over it, they decided to fly on, still hoping to reach their destination.

They pointed northeast, over what they thought was New Brunswick. They found themselves again surrounded by thick cloud. For hours they flew on blinded and lost completely. They carried no radio equipment with which to check on their position, and try as they might they were unable to get over or under the weather.

In the late afternoon they gave up and headed southwest in hopes of finding another field, for their fuel supply was running low. At 7 P.M., after having been in the air for over 12 hours, they broke into the clear, and, believe it or not, found themselves over the little town and pasture-like field they had left five hours before.

The landing was smooth and the plane rolled to a stop, undamaged. The flyers jumped out, exhausted by the long flight and deafened by the engine noise. They were greeted by Henry Mitton, on whose farm they had come down. The farm was located outside the little town of Washburn, Maine—6 miles from Caribou. They described heavy rains and fog over the St. Lawrence River which had forced them to swing south, but they had run into the weather again as they flew over New Brunswick.

They spent the night at the nearby Vaughan House, hoping to complete the flight the next day. But several days of rain followed, which kept them grounded. It did not stop the sightseers, though, for they swarmed over Mr. Mitton's little field to ogle at *Sir John Carling*. To protect her from the overly curious, a detachment of state police were summoned and kept the spectators at bay by roping her off.

Tully and Metcalf were treated as heroes by the natives. They were guests of honor at a number of dinners. On Sunday, September 4, they attended Mass at the Holy Rosary Church in Caribou, and afterward were luncheon guests of Father L. D. Willis, the rector. In the afternoon, Father Willis took the flyers on an outing to

Madawasha Lake in Aroostook County, 20 miles from Caribou, where they enjoyed the wilds of the State of Maine. It was an almost unhappy event for the flyers, when, during the afternoon, the rain stopped, and the skies cleared. Their sojourn had been a happy one.

At 10:30 the next morning, September 5, they returned to *Sir John Carling*, which sat waiting for them in the field in Washburn. With the help of well-wishers, they pushed her to the eastern end of the field, climbed in and took off into a fresh westerly breeze. It was a clear, bright autumn day. Though they encountered some heavy cloud and rain over Cape Breton, the flight to Newfoundland was in the main uneventful. They landed safely at Bennett Field six hours later, where they were welcomed by Harbor Grace's Mayor Casey. The ebullient Tully was the spokesman for the crew and replied graciously to the mayor's greeting. Later in the evening, while *Sir John Carling* was being refueled for the Atlantic flight, the flyers had a scare. One of the mechanics, carrying a kerosene lamp, accidentally ignited some gasoline which had spilled out of a barrel and there was a flash fire. Tully and Metcalf rushed to the rescue and pushed the plane out of the danger area before any damage was done.

Sir John Carling was poised to go on September 5. She awaited only good weather.

There was yet another Stinson Detroiter, tuning up at Curtiss Field on the day *Pride of Detroit* went to Old Orchard. She was the *Royal Windsor*, a sister ship to the planes of Schlee and Tully.

Not to be outdone by the Londoners, a committee of Windsor, Ontario, citizens formed a syndicate to back a Windsor, Ontario, to Windsor, England, non-stop flight and offered the crew a prize of $25,000 if it were made. Like the London flight, the rules were ultimately relaxed to permit the flight to be made in stages.

A Detroiter plane was decided on, and within ten days after the order was placed, the plane was delivered. The syndicate was thrilled, for an air rivalry was springing up between the two Canadian cities, and they envisioned a spectacular race across the ocean which would bring glory to both.

Clarence A. "Duke" Schiller, a twenty-eight-year-old Iowa-born aerial swashbuckler, was named pilot. He was a dapper man with a black mustache and patent-leather colored hair which he wore slicked down. Though an American, he had spent most of his life in Canada, and had been taught to fly by the Canadian Air Force.

Now he made his home in Toronto and was a pilot with the Canadian Forest Patrol.

Phil Wood, thirty-one, was selected as navigator. He was the younger brother of Gar Wood, the American speedboat racer, and also a pilot. He was born in Duluth, flew with the United States Army Air Force during the war, and subsequently became successful in a number of business enterprises. In addition to his navigational duties, Wood found use for his business acumen as the director and promoter of the flight.

They, too, had flown into Curtiss Field for an instrument check before returning to Windsor for the final take-off, and Maurice Titteringham of Pioneer attended to the compensation of *Royal Windsor*'s compasses along with those of *Sir John Carling*. After a series of short hops over Long Island to test them out, *Royal Windsor* returned to Walker Field, Windsor, to take care of her last-minute needs. The crew learned that *Sir John Carling* was planning to leave on September 1, and spurred on by the feverish interest of the citizens of Windsor, they scheduled their departure for England on the same day. It was a publicity man's dream, and Canada, England, and the United States excitedly awaited the take-offs and the race.

Early in the morning of September 1, a crowd of over 5000 gathered at Walker Field. Among them were Helen Wood, Phil's wife, Gar Wood, and Ada Greer, "Duke" Schiller's fiancée. Provisions were stored while the ship was fueled under the direction of Ed Mulligan who had been sent to Windsor by the Wright Company. A dense fog blanketed the field until 7:30 A.M., but as the sun rose the fog thinned and disappeared. Schiller and Wood, in flying suits, said good-bye to family and friends. They carried aboard with them a wreath which they would drop in mid-ocean, in memory of Nungesser and Coli. As he closed the cabin door behind him, Wood noticed a piece of paper taped to the inside.

Don't forget me. Helen, said the poignant note.

Ed Mulligan turned the propeller and the engine roared. The crowd spread out along the dirt runway to get a better view of the take-off. Schiller, at the controls, headed *Royal Windsor* down the field between the lines of spectators. Behind them, Gar Wood sped along in a car with Helen Wood alongside, following his brother's plane. Quickly *Royal Windsor* was airborne, despite the 500 gallons of gasoline in her tanks. They hoped that the fuel supply would be sufficient for 45 hours of flight.

The plane took to the air at 9:17 A.M. As they disappeared to the east, the people of Windsor were confident that their plane would win, for it would fly non-stop whereas *Sir John Carling* planned to lay over at Harbor Grace. *Royal Windsor* was seen only once during the day, at 1:15 P.M. as she flew, east and low, along Oshawa's lake front.

Like her sister ship, she ran into weather trouble as the day passed. The flyers battled low clouds, heavy rains, and a series of line squalls which tossed the little plane hither and yon. As evening approached, and it became evident that they could not go on, Schiller spotted a hay field below him which seemed smooth enough. Its smoothness was deceptive from the air, for when they touched down, it was to a jouncing landing which sheared off the tail skid. In addition, a mysterious fire broke out on the left section of the wing, but the alert Wood leaped out and extinguished the flames with his jacket before any serious damage was done.

It was 7 P.M. and they had been forced down in the little town of St. John's, Quebec, 27 miles southeast of Montreal. With local help, repairs were made on September 2 and the field was evened out for a take-off. They planned to fly to the recently built Portland, Maine, airport, or to Old Orchard Beach but the rains had made the little hay field too soft for *Royal Windsor* to get off with the amount of gasoline that remained in her tanks.

Conditions improved by the next day, and with the help of bystanders, the flyers were able to turn the plane around and push it into take-off position. At 2:35 P.M. they left for Maine, and 2½ hours later flew over the spanking new Portland Municipal Airport at Scarboro, only a few miles from Old Orchard Beach. From the air, as they circled, the field appeared well-constructed and in perfect condition. A large hangar towered at the western end, facing the landing area. They dropped in for a landing just before 5 P.M. and the plane rolled to a stop. When they tried to start up again, to taxi toward the hangar, they found that they were mired in thick mud and no matter how much power Schiller applied to the Wright engine the plane rocked helplessly with its cargo of gasoline and would not budge. There was little to do other than to leave the plane where she was until the field dried. They drove into the city of Portland, where they spent the night at the Eastland Hotel, but they were determined to move on to Old Orchard Beach the next day for a take-off on their Atlantic flight.

They learned, when they got into Portland, that the giant Fokker

Old Glory had arrived at Old Orchard that day from Curtiss Field for her attempted flight to Rome, and Schiller and Wood were struck immediately with the idea of taking off with her, and accompanying her, at least part of the way across.

2. Lloyd Bertaud, on leaving *Columbia's* crew, returned to his old job on the Cleveland to Hadley Field, New Jersey, mail run. The spectacular flights of *Columbia* and *America*, together with Lindbergh's roaring welcome home, took most of the headlines and he became temporarily the forgotten man of aviation. His name appeared briefly in the papers in early July when on a mail flight he spotted a house on fire over Milesburg, Pennsylvania. Circling the burning building, he jazzed his engine until the occupants were awakened and escaped.

He still yearned for a try at the Atlantic and his turn was soon to come.

In June, the publisher William Randolph Hearst ordered a single-engined plane for his private use from the Fokker factory in Hasbrouck Heights, and construction was begun on a sister ship to the *San Raphael* and the *Princess Xenia*.

She was a big monoplane, with a thick 60-foot wing, inside of which were four brass tanks, each with a 96-gallon capacity. A 9-cylinder, 480-horsepower, air-cooled Jupiter engine, capable of producing a cruising speed of 110 miles an hour, was ordered from the Bristol factory in England.

Philip A. Payne, the flamboyant managing editor of Hearst's New York *Daily Mirror*, convinced his boss that it would be good publicity and news for his papers if he entered the new plane in the Atlantic Ocean sweepstakes that was the craze of the western world. Hearst readily agreed. It was decided that a flight to Rome (never attempted before) in the interest of furthering Italo-American relations would fill the bill. Without delay, a Hearst representative contacted Bertaud and he agreed at once to serve as pilot. His contract was described as "generous," and the announcement of the flight was made officially on July 7.

Payne, the entrepreneur, was a Canadian by birth and a graduate of St. Michael's College in Toronto. After graduation he turned to journalism and served a brief apprenticeship as a sportswriter for the Toronto *Chronicle*. He came to the United States, and, at twenty-one, was the editor of the Hoboken (New Jersey) *Dispatch*. After a short postwar stint in Chicago with the *Herald-Examiner,* he arrived in New York and became assistant city editor of the *Daily News,* and, a few years later, city editor. In 1925 he resigned to become managing editor of the *Daily Mirror.*

He was a short, dark-haired dynamic man, who wore glasses. His chief claim to fame, in recent months, was, that after attending Earl Carroll's notorious "bathtub party," he was responsible for a series of stories that led Mr. Carroll to the Atlanta penitentiary for a jail term.

While Payne drummed up the publicity, Bertaud began his flight preparations. He announced that he would make the flight with one other man whom he would choose promptly from a list that he had under consideration. He visited the Fokker plant where he and Tony Fokker mulled over the needed design changes in the plane. It was decided to place a large brass gas tank, with a capacity of 820 gallons, amidships in the fuselage between the cockpit and the small radio cabin. It was expected that the plane when loaded would weigh close to 13,000 pounds, or not much less than the three-engined *America* did when she left for Paris, but the fuel, which would account for much of the weight, would be needed to fly the extra miles to Rome. Bertaud hoped for a take-off between August 10 and August 15, and to speed up construction, Fokker added an extra shift so that work could be maintained around the clock.

There was much speculation as to who would fly with Bertaud. The rumors centered around his old friend Commodore Herbert Hartley, now master of the liner *Leviathan.* Hartley was an old friend, too, of Payne's, and besides being a skilled navigator was up on all the latest aerial navigation aids. Mrs. Hartley, however, ended the speculation promptly when she put her foot down publicly and firmly against the idea, and the commodore was out.

In mid-July, Bertaud announced that James De Witt Hill, a forty-two-year-old bachelor and veteran airmail pilot, would fly with him. He described Hill as the "best flyer in the airmail service today," and added that he had been entrusted recently with flying airmail pouches to President Coolidge at the Summer White House in the Black Hills.

Hill was born in Scottdale, Pennsylvania, and at an early age showed a distinct, if imprudent, interest in aeronautics. He made a parachute out of the family's largest linen tablecloth, and jumped confidently with it from the stable roof. Despite his invention, little "J.D." plummeted to the ground, breaking his arm. While he re-

covered, he fretted over his error of design and decided finally that
the failure was due to the fact that he was too heavy. Whereupon, he
volunteered his lighter and younger brother, Frank, strapped him
into the harness and pushed him off the same roof with no better
result. Frank broke his leg!

Hill spent a year at Lafayette College where he studied civil
engineering, then transferred to Cornell for an advanced course, but
was forced to drop out because of ill health. He recovered in time
and went to the West Coast as the representative of a group of
Eastern engineers, but his health failed him again and two years of
outdoor work were required to restore it.

Aviation entered his life when he joined the Glenn Curtiss Flying
School in San Diego; there he took pilot training. After being
licensed, he worked in experimental aeronautics, specializing in seaplane motors.

He became a civilian instructor during the war, and served at
Brooks Field, in San Antonio, along with Harry Jones, now the
pilot at Old Orchard Beach. After a short postwar stay with an
engineers detachment of the Army Air Services at McCook Field,
Dayton, he entered the airmail service and became one of the earliest
night mail pilots on the Cleveland to Hadley Field, New Jersey, run.

"J.D.," as he was known to all, was a tall lean man, studious-
looking, with thinning hair. His selection by Bertaud was applauded
by the flying community, for though he was a man of few words, he
was universally respected as a pilot.

Together, Bertaud and Hill began preparations. They made a trip
to the New York Weather Bureau where Bertaud reacquainted himself with "Doc" Kimball and arranged to get daily weather reports
covering the 4200-mile route to Rome. Bertaud at this time was
unsure of his course. He talked of the Great Circle route, but considered also a course which would lead them due east from New
York, and then over the ship lanes in a modified great circle to
Europe. Meteorologists Kimball and Scarr said they would do their
utmost to provide them with the most comprehensive weather coverage possible.

The flyers applied for passports and visas to Italy, and spent
what was left of their time with the work crew at Hasbrouck Heights
putting together their Fokker FV-11 model. They discussed carrying
a radio. Bertaud was for it strongly; others connected with the
flight, including Fokker, were against it because it meant extra weight.

When Smith and Bronte landed in Hawaii, after using their radio to send SOSs, Bertaud carried the day.

"The radio showed what it could do," he said. "I am completely sold on the radio, and would not dream of making the flight without one."

The die was cast and A. C. Cardwell & Co. designed a set for them. It included a 100-watt transmitter which would broadcast the plane's call letters continuously, so that her position would be known at all times. It would operate on 600 and 800 meters and was assigned the call letters WRHP. Much to the satisfaction of the Fokker people the complete unit weighed but 82 pounds.

The big plane took shape rapidly. A 52-gallon oil tank was placed directly behind the pilot's seat, and another, with a capacity of 45 gallons, was installed forward of the radio cabin. Commander Byrd telegraphed Bertaud a courteous offer of advice and assistance. The Bristol engine, off the *Berengaria*, arrived at the Fokker factory on July 18, and was mounted promptly. On July 20, the big yellow ship with the huge golden wing stood completed in front of her hangar at Hasbrouck Heights. Workmen painted the stars and stripes underneath the wingtips and the Department of Commerce registration number NC 703 on her wingtop and rudder. Her name, *Old Glory*, stood out in bold letters along the side of her fuselage. She was ready to fly.

Captain Eric W. Densham of the Bristol Jupiter Company tuned up the engine until the howling sound was smooth and satisfied him. There were days spent taxiing her around the field at Teterboro testing her controls and the strength of her undercarriage. C. F. Egge, Superintendent of the Eastern Division of the U. S. Air Mail, dropped into the field and Tony Fokker proudly showed off his newest creation. Egge described it as the perfect plane. Fokker told him that he had great hopes to use the design as a passenger plane ultimately, substituting seats in the area now taken up by the fuselage tank. "J.D." Hill was on hand, too, while Bertaud traveled to Boston to discuss problems of navigation with his old friend Commodore Hartley. Everyone looked for the take-off for Rome within two weeks.

Bernt Balchen, back with Fokker as a test pilot, took *Old Glory* up on her first flight on July 29. When he landed, after circling the field for thirty minutes, he raved over her performance.

"She flies herself," he said. "She's a fine plane! I couldn't put her into a spin."

Later in the day, with Philip Payne and Bertaud aboard, Balchen took her off on a second hop. Bertaud handled the controls briefly during a quick trip over the Jersey meadows and was equally impressed. It was a satisfied and happy crew that alit from *Old Glory* early in the evening. The plane was more than they hoped for.

The next day Bertaud and Hill flew her from Teterboro to Curtiss Field. It was planned to put her through a series of load tests prior to leaving for Rome. On board with them for the short hop were Commodore and Mrs. Hartley; a mechanic, and Russell Birdwell.

On July 31, the christening took place. A crowd of more than 2000, which had gathered around *Old Glory* was scattered by a sudden downpour of rain, and the ceremony was postponed from 2 to 4 P.M. It was still raining slightly when Representative Fiorello H. La Guardia opened the proceedings. Umbrellas were prominent among the slimmed-down crowd of 750 who remained. Among the other notables present were: F. Trubee Davison, Assistant Secretary of War for Aviation, Baron Giacomo de Martino, the Italian ambassador; and Austin Clark, representing William Randolph Hearst. La Guardia read a laudatory telegram to Hearst from Secretary of State Kellogg. Bertaud and Hill were introduced and spoke briefly. Major General James H. McRae of the Second Corps Area spoke, as did representatives of the Third Naval District.

Young Theresa Tassoni, a Hunter College graduate of Italian descent, stepped up and broke a bottle of sparkling water on the exhaust pipe, saying, "I christen thee 'Old Glory.'" The damp crowd clapped while the band played *Giovinezza*, the Fascist anthem, and the *Star-Spangled Banner*.

After the ceremony La Guardia, General McRae, and Austin Clark climbed aboard with Bertaud and Hill. The engine was started and the big plane slammed across the muddy field and took to the air for a quick spin over Long Island. Soon, she was back. In the meantime, the crowd had been "treated" to some excitement when a little Jenny biplane caught her tail in the telephone wires while landing and crashed. No one was hurt though the plane was wrecked. When *Old Glory* was wheeled into her fieldside hangar in the early evening, the spectators disbursed slowly. They had had a thrilling day.

The following days were taken up with trial and change. Bertaud flew a series of speed and load tests and then announced that within a week *Old Glory* would fly a "shakedown trip" to Cleveland and back. For some reason the trip was never made.

3. On August 5, a near-tragedy befell *Old Glory*. A small crowd on hand gasped when a little Jenny, taxiing on Curtiss Field, was caught in a sudden gust of wind, was spun around and blown into the Fokker, coming to rest under her big wing. Pieces of wooden veneer from the underpart of the wing fell off, but the damage proved minor and was quickly patched up. The next day, with Captain Densham aboard, *Old Glory* was flown by Hill and Bertaud, in an effort to gauge her fuel consumption. They had decided to carry a total of 1180 gallons on the Rome trip, and it was necessary to find out how far this would carry them, at cruising speed. They took off with 8000 pounds, after a run of 20 seconds, circled the field, and flew out over Long Island Sound. Bertaud flew the plane at 1450 rpms, and the air-speed indicator registered 91 miles an hour. He opened the throttle slightly revving up to 1500, and, later to 1550, while the needle inched up to 95, and then 97 mph. Hill calculated that, at the rate of gas consumption, she should be able to fly for 4996 miles, which would provide them with a safety margin of nearly 700 miles. He noted, also, that she burned 7 pints of oil an hour!

Two days later they tested another propeller at various speeds as they flew across Long Island Sound to Greenwich, down the coast to New York, and back to Curtiss Field. They covered 200 miles and the plane performed flawlessly. The radio checkout followed. It was a compact set, and, as promised, the weight, including transmitter, receiver, batteries, and wind-driven generator, came to 82 pounds exactly. Bertaud operated it, while Hill flew, and picked up signals clearly from as far off as Cape Race, Newfoundland.

On August 12, with a load of five tons, *Old Glory* took off easily piloted by Hill, and climbed quickly to 1000 feet. She circled over Westbury, Long Island, dropped 500 pounds of sand ballast to protect her landing gear and returned to Curtiss. It was time to try out the plane with a take-off from Byrd's old, artificial ramp at Roosevelt Field. After flying over from Curtiss, the plane was hauled to the top of the "hill" and tied securely by the tail. Hill, in the cockpit, opened the throttle, and, at his signal, a mechanic cut the tether. *Old Glory* plummeted down the incline and hit the runway at 30 mph. She weighed 11,500 pounds. Hill held her on the ground for nearly one-half mile, then eased back on the wheel. Slowly the golden-winged monoplane lifted off. She climbed, steadily, and, at 3200 feet, Hill leveled her off and throttled back. He flew north over Long Island Sound, while Bertaud in the radio cabin operated the transmitter. After 30 minutes, Bertaud dumped 1500 pounds of ballast. The big plane banked over Curtiss and came in for a landing. She had passed another load test with flying colors.

There were only minor adjustments needed now before they'd be ready. While Anthony Fokker worked on the load distribution, Captain Densham tinkered with the engine, which would be asked to lift more weight off the ground than any other single engine had done. Mrs. Bertaud busied herself at the Garden City Hotel with menus for the flyers. Bertaud and Hill went into New York and made out wills, Bertaud leaving his estate to his wife Helen, and bachelor Hill, to his sister Mrs. Walter Stauffeur and his cousin Ethel. The crowds, sensing that a departure was imminent, grew, and cars again clogged the roads leading to Curtiss and Roosevelt Fields.

The German planes *Bremen* and *Europa* had flown off from Dessau, and reporters crowded around Bertaud to get his comment.

"I flew a Junkers plane with Eddie Stinson, once, to set an endurance record," he said, "and it's a good plane being flown by fine pilots."

Accessories were loaded aboard *Old Glory*, now roped off from the horde of curious bystanders. Flares, smoke bombs, a Very pistol, two flashlights, a hunting knife, a rubber boat, and life preservers were stowed neatly away. All that remained to be done was to put on the gasoline and food. Bertaud kept in close touch with "Doc" Kimball, who advised that the weather over the North Atlantic was clearing.

On August 16, a test flight was made over Long Island to try the radio transmitter. The test was made with the help of Station WNY, RCA's transmitting and receiving station located at Bush Terminal in Brooklyn. After the flight, they returned the plane to Roosevelt Field from where the final take-off would be made. Bertaud was dissatisfied with the radio's performance and ordered the generator removed from the plane for inspection.

Mechanics scurried around, going over every moving part of *Old Glory*. They attached a piece of wood shaped like a heel over the metal tail skid, to prevent sparks on the take-off. Some 13 gallons of castor oil were spread over the Byrd incline as an added safeguard. Payne announced that *Old Glory* would carry a small wreath of mountain laurel which they would drop in mid-ocean as a memorial to Nungesser and Coli. The wreath would have an inscription attached, "You lead, we follow," and bits of it would be preserved and sent to Madame Nungesser and the Mesdames Coli after *Old Glory* arrived in Rome. Bertaud, at the Garden City Hotel, plotted weather charts including wind currents, from the information received from Kimball. He told reporters that he would announce his departure promptly at noon on the day decided on, and that *Old Glory* would take off on the dot of 5 P.M. that day. He said that he would leave in the afternoon, so as to arrive over Rome during the daylight hours.

For a time, it looked as though they might get off on the afternoon of the 17th. The weather over the Atlantic was perfect, and a steady westerly breeze, essential for their heavily loaded plane, blew straight down the runway at Roosevelt. By midafternoon, thousands had made their way to the field. The tanks were partially loaded. During the morning mechanics had substituted new lightweight British wheels to cut down on the total weight by over 100 pounds. Chief mechanic George Eliot climbed aboard and the engine was started. Police cleared a lane through the mass of spectators. Eliot opened the throttle and *Old Glory* moved toward the ramp at the eastern end of the field. It was then 3 P.M., two hours before the scheduled take-off time. After a run of several hundred feet, the big monoplane slowed and came to a stop. Mechanics hurried across the field. They found that the wheel bearings had overheated and were too hot to touch. The ground crew, led by Tony Fokker himself, pitched in to repair the damage, but by the time the work had been completed, it was too late to go. The crowd, disappointed, wended its way home.

News arrived at the Garden City Hotel during the evening of the Dole Race tragedy, in which two of the four starters for Hawaii had disappeared. One of the missing planes was the *Golden Eagle*, piloted by John W. Frost, and owned originally by William Randolph Hearst; and Mr. Hearst, wary of public criticism and saddened by the apparent loss of plane and crew, ordered Payne to keep *Old Glory* on the ground until every precaution was taken. Curiously, Payne picked this time to make the announcement, wholly unexpected by Fokker, Bertaud, and Hill, that he would make the flight to Rome as a passenger if the pilots felt that the plane could bear the extra weight.

The next day, there was more wheel trouble. Bertaud was at the controls, taxiing the plane for a take-off, when over the roar of the motor he heard the screech of the bearings in the left wheel. Mechanics again rushed to the scene and this time found that a floating bushing had been forgotten when the wheel was put on, and it had frozen to the axle. Once again the take-off had to be postponed.

On the 19th, the undercarriage problems had been solved. Kimball reported a low over the Gulf of St. Lawrence, but strong winds from the west off the Newfoundland coast. Rain during the night had, however, left the field soggy, and by the time it had dried and been rolled, the hour was again too late. Nevertheless, Bertaud, with Mrs. Hearst as a passenger, took *Old Glory* up for a half-hour spin over Long Island and New York City, and turned the controls over to her, for a time, during the flight. When they landed, there was every indication that they would leave within 48 hours. Weather predictions called for favorable winds during the two-day period, from mid-ocean to the European coast. There was an area of rain over southern Ireland, but conditions were ideal over the rest of Europe. From Newfoundland to mid-Atlantic, the reports showed some cloudiness with fog, but with strong northwest winds, increasing at higher altitudes. Payne, always anxious to keep the flight in the public eye, announced that *Old Glory* would carry a Cornell banner, since Hill was a member of the class of 1902, and Bertaud had trained at the school's ROTC aviation camp early in the war.

The big crowds, gathered for the long-awaited take-off, were sorely disappointed over the weekend of the 21st and 22nd, for *Old Glory* did not leave her hangar either day. A muddy field and cross winds on the runway were given as reasons. Also, on Saturday evening, mechanics, while jacking up the big plane in the hangar to get at the wheels, misjudged the height of a protruding beam, and one of the ailerons struck it. The crumbled section was removed, and the damage was repaired by Sunday night.

For the next few days, the local weather—low clouds, rain, and continuing cross winds on the field—delayed the take-off. *Old Glory* was returned temporarily to Curtiss Field, where she was housed with *Pride of Detroit*, then preparing for her memorable flight. *Sir John Carling* and René Fonck's *Ville de Paris* were there also, in nearby hangars, and they would be joined in a day or two by *Royal Windsor*.

These were golden days for the aviation buffs, who wandered from hangar to hangar, staring at, comparing, and taking endless snapshots of the assortment of planes. Commander Byrd and Fonck dropped by to look at *Old Glory*, and chatted with Bertaud and Hill. Three Italian balloonists, in America to compete in the annual Gordon Bennett balloon race, also visited the hangar. Bertaud showed them over *Old Glory*, and they, in turn, gave him valuable information and descriptions of the Italian topography and airfields.

On August 25, Bertaud, Hill, and Payne watched *Pride of Detroit* take off for Old Orchard Beach in the morning, and soon after saw *Sir John Carling* leave for London, Ontario. The two departures, combined with their long wait, had its effect on them. No sooner had *Sir John Carling* left the ground, than *Old Glory* was wheeled out of her hangar. She was partially loaded with gas, and, at 4 P.M., Payne, Bertaud, and Hill hoisted themselves into the cockpit through the little trapdoor under the fuselage. The engine was started and she took off quickly, alighting at Roosevelt Field moments later. The crowd at Curtiss moved quickly by foot and automobile up to Roosevelt, sensing yet another historic take-off. The fueling was completed and the plane was towed by means of block and tackle to the top of the incline where she was securely tied by her tail skid.

The sun was setting and they seemed ready to go, but fate intervened again. The westerly wind, which had been blowing straight down the runway all day, dropped to a whisper. The crew and crowd waited and waited, watching the windsock on the hangar roof hoping to see it blow erect again. To the disappointment of all it continued to hang limply. They lit cigarettes as if the smoke might encourage the wind to blow but it curled idly into the dead air.

Payne was anxious to go, but Bertaud realized that with 12,000 pounds aboard *Old Glory* would need a strong head wind to get off the ground.

No one yet knew for sure if Payne would go.

Bertaud joked with bystanders, saying, "It'll take a good gale to get my 200 pounds off the ground."

Hill added significantly that every pound counted, especially during the initial take-off.

It was obvious that both thought it unwise to include Payne's extra weight, but after all he was in charge of the flight.

A westerly wind of at least 15 miles an hour was needed, and when the flat calm persisted at 7 P.M., the flight was postponed once more. Floyd Bennett and René Fonck consoled the flyers before they left the field to return to the Garden City Hotel for the night.

Rome was excited by the prospect of *Old Glory's* arrival. The daily papers were filled with a description of the plane and her crew. Readers were kept up to date on the minute details of the last-minute preparations, and all Italy awaited eagerly the news of the take-off. The Ministry of Aeronautics ordered Italian airfields to take every measure to help guide the flyers to their destination. New York's Mayor James J. Walker, in Europe, rearranged his itinerary so as to be at Rome's Ciampino Airfield to welcome them.

The big golden-winged monoplane remained at the top of the incline, fully loaded and ready to leave, all the next day. Head winds extending from Halifax to Long Island, tricky cross winds at Roosevelt, and fog over Newfoundland caused another postponement. Nerves became frayed and the flyers began to show the strain of the long wait.

Rain started falling during the night and fell all day of the 27th. The field was boggy with mud. A tarpaulin covered *Old Glory's* engine and she was tied down to keep her from being blown off her perch by a gust of wind. Talk at the field turned to young Paul Redfern, long overdue and unreported, on his flight from Georgia to Rio de Janeiro. There was an unconfirmed report that he had been seen flying over the Caribbean, but his fuel supply by this time was exhausted. Everyone hoped that he had somehow gotten down safely somewhere.

One hundred gallons of gasoline were drained from *Old Glory*, lightening her load, but at the same time reducing her range by 500 miles. Payne's apparent insistence on making the flight posed a problem. Without him the experts felt that *Old Glory* could get off the ground with no wind, or a cross wind. Fokker and members of his organization were openly critical of the excess weight that he would mean.

Tony said with customary candidness, "There is a difference between an airplane and a truck. The last 50 pounds on an airplane may be just 50 pounds too much!"

Whereupon Philip Payne charged that Atlantic Aircraft Corporation had delivered the plane 540 pounds over the specification weight. R. B. C. Nordwyn, General Manager of Atlantic, speaking for Fokker replied hotly that if the plane was overweight it was due to the owner's requested alterations and additions in equipment while the plane was being constructed. The original contract had called for a weight of 4150 pounds with an added 150 pounds for equipment. Nordwyn said further that no one knew really the present weight of the plane for there were no scales big enough to accommodate the whole machine. He scoffed at Payne's unorthodox weighing methods, in which, first one wheel, then the other, and, finally, the tail, had been placed on the scales and the weights totaled.

Payne replied that the additions he had requested were for essential navigational equipment, an added oil tank and a feed-pipe line. The argument continued for a while but was strangled finally by long and confusing charges and countercharges. The fact remained, however, that *Old Glory* was too heavy to get off Roosevelt Field with a full load, sans a strong head wind.

The wait continued through August 29, as a wet field and southerly winds combined to hold the flyers up. The 30th looked promising in the morning for a moderate westerly blew down the field but by the time they were ready in the afternoon it had backed around to the south.

Tony Fokker was plainly worried and again warned the flyers about overloading. The inclusion of Payne in the crew he felt was foolhardy.

Said Fokker: "The take-off can be affected by many factors— condition of the runway, winds and temperature, among them. It is up to the pilots to know how much of a margin of safety to leave." He added acidly: "I cannot judge to what degree their judgment is being influenced by the identity of the passenger. It is best to have a safety margin of 500 pounds. Byrd had one of 1500!"

The last day of August was the same. The flyers and spectators waited at the field all day, watching the flag at nearby Meadowbrook Polo Field, which fluttered in a northerly direction, indicating another brisk cross wind. The flyers dared not chance it. They waited at the field until 7 A.M. and then sadly gave up for the day.

At Curtiss Field, below, another crowd amused itself watching the white Sikorsky biplane *Ville de Paris* as she was flown about by Fonck and Curtin. It was now conceivable that she would get away before *Old Glory*.

The exciting news, though, came from England, for word was

received that *San Raphael, Old Glory's* sister, had taken off in the morning for Ottawa, Canada.

4. During the month of August, Captains Leslie Hamilton and Frederick F. Minchin tested their new Fokker *San Raphael* with repeated flights throughout southern England, from Bristol's airfield. The English followed the tests avidly in the newspapers, but there was never an inkling that *San Raphael* might take a passenger. Thousands of words were written about the boyish-looking, twenty-eight year-old "Flying Gypsy," Hamilton, and his co-pilot, the tall, reserved Minchin, but nary a word about the sponsor of the flight, Princess Lowenstein-Wertheim.

A steady stream of people beat a path to the field to take a look at the pretty sky-blue plane with the bright yellow wings. They knew her registration letters, G-EBTQ, by heart, and were accustomed to the loud roar of her Bristol Jupiter motor. She was so big and powerful that few who saw her doubted that she would make the ocean crossing with ease.

On August 21, Hamilton announced that he would fly *San Raphael* to Upavon Airdrome, on the Salisbury Plains—100 miles from London, the following day, and would leave for Ottawa within 48 hours if weather permitted.

In the late afternoon of the 22nd, he and Minchin took off and soon after settled the big blue ship onto the turf at Upavon, where she was wheeled quickly into a hangar for a final overhaul. Hamilton, the spokesman, announced that they would carry 800 gallons of gasoline, sufficient it was estimated for 44 hours of flight. Their route he said would take them over Bath, England, the Irish Sea, Cahore Point, Ireland, and they would leave the Irish coast in the vicinity of Clifden, Galway. They would carry no radio, but would take along a collapsible boat.

On August 24, the news was broken that Princess Lowenstein-Wertheim would go and a storm of controversy broke out, not only in England and among her immediate family, but in Europe and the United States as well. There were frequent comments both public and private questioning her sanity and suggesting that senility might have visited her early. Her relatives, particularly her brother, were wild, but there was little they could do for she was nowhere to be found. They searched her house in London and her favorite haunts in the city. They scoured the hotels and inns in the vicinity of Upavon to no avail. Uncannily she had dropped from sight.

While the storm raged Hamilton and Minchin proceeded calmly with their preparations. Frequent short hops were made from Upavon, watched by throngs of excited onlookers. Hamilton noted that the compasses behaved erratically and they were removed at once and replaced by new instruments.

On August 27, there were reports of bad ocean weather from the Air Ministry, and the flight was postponed; Hamilton and Minchin took this opportunity to make a flight with a correspondent from the London *Times* in hopes of easing the rising public opinion against their trip. They wanted to prove that the sixty-two-year-old Princess would be as safe aboard *San Raphael* as she would be aboard the *Aquitania*. The correspondent obligingly wrote a glowing report on the performance of *San Raphael*. The crowds still flocked to the field hoping for a glimpse of the notorious Princess but she remained in her well-secreted hiding place.

For the next three days *San Raphael* was grounded by continued reports of head winds of gale force over most of the North Atlantic. Hamilton and Minchin chafed at the bit. The plane was ready and they wanted to go. They were convinced that nothing could down their powerful Fokker. Finally, on the evening of the 30th, the impatient Hamilton announced that *San Raphael* would take off the next morning, regardless. The announcement came in the face of a warning from Wing Commander Dernon Brown of the Air Ministry that they would have to battle stiff head winds all the way across. Hamilton was determined to go nevertheless. The Princess's relatives searched frantically for her all during the night in a hopeless attempt to stop her, if necessary by force, but there wasn't a trace of her whereabouts.

Bright and early the next morning, a car drew up alongside *San Raphael*, and out stepped the Princess after a drive of 100 miles from the London flat of a conspirator-friend who had hidden her out. She was excited but bright and alert. The crowd that gathered early cheered the dauntless lady and she waved back at them, smiling broadly. She didn't look her age. Her dress was as colorful as her background. She wore a black toque hat, a bright-blue suede jacket, blue riding breeches, black silk stockings, and high-heeled yellow furlined boots. In her hands she carried two attaché cases and two hatboxes.

She chatted amiably with the newsmen.

"I am proud to be the first woman to attempt the crossing," she said. "It is a great adventure."

Minchin talked calmly with members of the ground crew. He was dressed in a dark tweed suit and looked as though he might be a bank executive on his way to work in the City. Hamilton in a double-breasted brown suit stood silently beside the Princess as she quipped gaily with reporters and well-wishers.

Mechanics crawled over *San Raphael* in a final inspection. One of them teetered unsteadily on a ladder set up by the nose, as he checked the motor meticulously. The food was loaded—sandwiches and Thermos flasks of coffee, sufficient for two days.

The Princess's quarters were in the main fuselage of the plane aft of eight cylindrical gas tanks which separated her from the pilot's cabin. A wicker chair was fastened by one leg for her to sit in and an Army cot was placed next to it if she wished to sleep.

The skies were gray and there was a light rain falling as the Most Reverend Francis Mostyn, Roman Catholic Archbishop of Cardiff, stepped forward from the crowd. A chilling wind blew his robes. He sprinkled holy water on the plane and gave it his blessing. He went up to the Princess who knelt and kissed his episcopal ring. They were old friends and they conversed in low tones. The Princess was always smiling. She showed no signs of nervousness. Spectators crowded around them, some holding umbrellas to protect against the fine blowing drizzle that fell intermittently.

Hamilton and Minchin walked out of the large hangar door toward the group, both dressed now in heavy flying suits.

It was a little after 7 A.M. and Hamilton gave the signal that it was time to get under way. He helped the Princess get into her rear cabin where she secured herself in the wicker seat. Hamilton and Minchin pulled themselves into the pilot's cockpit through the trap door under the fuselage. Minchin sat at the controls, with Hamilton beside him. A mechanic on a ladder turned the starting crank and the propeller turned with little jerks. With a burst of smoke from the exhaust the engine caught and roared. For minutes Minchin warmed it up. Spectators could see the two little helmeted heads high up in the cockpit behind the glass windshield. Their faces looked so pale on the gloomy day.

The wheel chocks were pulled clear and the big ship moved slowly to the eastern end of the runway. The crowd followed, but stayed at a safe distance as dirt and dust was blown back furiously by the spinning propeller. The deafening noise was awesome. Minchin gave her full power and there was a tremendous din as the big ship turned into the wind and faced down the field. The tall grass behind her was bent flat by the stream of air. All was quiet now as the blue-bodied plane sat poised with her propeller barely turning over. Ahead of her was a stretch of level dirt runway—a little over a mile in length. At the end of it there was a road, but there were no other obstructions thereafter save for rolling meadowlands beyond the road. The wind had died perceptibly in the last minutes and the sock on the hangar roof moved only slightly. The motor sound increased until it was deafening and *San Raphael* moved lurchingly. The crowds 50 yards away lined the first quarter mile of the strip and watched intently. The blazing yellow wings of the plane brightened an otherwise dull morning as they moved slowly downfield. The plane picked up speed, but there was no sign of her leaving the ground.

It was nerve-wracking to the spectators as the big plane filled to the brim with highly-inflammable gasoline sped nearer to the road that marked the end of the field. The engine thundered and some protected their ears from the noise. With 100 yards to go, daylight appeared under her wheels and *San Raphael* was off—not by much, but airborne at least. She passed over the road with less than three feet to spare and, for what seemed like an age, flew at grasstop level, barely skimming the slight rises in the landscape. Then slowly she rose, circled the field under the gray overcast, and disappeared gradually into the west, being swallowed up fast by the heavy mists. The take-off had come at 7:32 A.M. (12:32 A.M., New York time), August 31.

In Canada, preparations were in high gear to welcome the doughty Princess and her crew, and to help in every way to speed their return. Lindbergh Field in Ottawa, their destination, was a veritable beehive as special lighting equipment was installed on the runway and the latest rockets and flares were assembled to aid them if the weather closed in. Experts predicted their arrival between 4 and 8 P.M., on Thursday, September 1. Lord Willingdon, the Governor General, left orders that he be notified as soon as they were sighted over the American continent, so that he could make arrangements to be at the field. Detachments of Royal Canadian Mounted Police were alerted to be ready to handle the expected huge crowd.

Elsewhere, lookout posts, though it was still much too early, had men scanning the eastern skies hopefully. Harbor Grace's airport, Bennett Field, commandeered automobiles voluntarily to stay during the night with headlights playing on the landing area. Radio lookouts at Belle Isle off the northern tip of Newfoundland and at other stations on the north shore of the Gulf of St. Lawrence readied themselves for a long vigil.

In New York, Captain Densham was ordered by the Bristol Jupiter Company to proceed forthwith to Ottawa so as to be ready to care for *San Raphael*'s engine. It was the Princess's intention to take off on her return trip to England, as soon as possible after landing.

Hamilton's wife awaited him anxiously in an Ottawa hotel, while in London his elderly mother fretted, as did the Princess's unnerved family.

Lighthouse keepers along the Newfoundland coast were warned that the plane should reach their area, by 7 A.M. on September 1. Experts felt that 29 hours of flying time in their fine ship should see them across the Atlantic.

After her take-off, *San Raphael* was seen at St. Anne's Head, Wales, 150 miles from Upavon, at 9:30 A.M., and at 10 A.M., she passed over Barty Castle at 500 feet. She was described as flying "slowly." Sometime later she was sighted flying at 1000 feet over Thurles, Tipperary. In the early afternoon the big plane flew over Inverin on the northern coast of Galway Bay, 370 miles from her take-off point. Again, she was described as flying very low, and slowly, as though she was having trouble with head winds.

The world was amazed by the news of the Princess's departure. There was adverse comment, at first, but gradually it was replaced by a feeling of admiration, sympathy, and strong hopes for her success. In London, Charles A. Levine, who was making his own flight plans, wished her well, and added, "If the present flight is successful, there'd be no fun in it for me, as I wanted to be the first to make an east to west flight." He, and his new pilot, Hinchcliffe, agreed that if *San Raphael* made it they would schedule a new flight returning to the United States by the Far East.

At Upavon Airdrome, the early progress reports from *San Raphael*, were hardly encouraging, and had her ground crew worried. Her airspeed average over the first hours was calculated at a little over 70 miles per hour and was well below the cruising speed of 100 mph that they had hoped for and planned on. They prayed for more favorable winds as the plane got farther out over the ocean, though they were realistic enough to know that to get such winds would be in the nature of a miracle.

There was no further news of the plane during the remainder of the day or night, but this fact did not cause much concern for the chances of a ship sighting them over the ocean were not great. As September 1 dawned all eyes on the Newfoundland coast were pointed skyward hoping for a sight of the big Fokker. The weather was not good. Harbor Grace reported a low ceiling, less than a mile of visibility, and a northeast gale. Up and down the coast, it was the same—a low overcast with fog. Look-outs strained their eyes and ears. Occasionally someone would think he heard the sound of a motor, but it turned out to be a car, a motorboat, or a wishful imagination, for others could hear only the whistling of the wind and the screech of seagulls as they swooped low over the shore.

The hours passed slowly without a sign of or a report on the plane. As the day went on without word Newfoundlanders' hopes were bolstered by the thought that the plane might have skirted the island, and gone inland, undetected. At Lindbergh Field, crowds waited throughout the day under dark gray skies and occasional rain showers. They, too, kept their eyes glued on the eastern sky, hoping to glimpse a dark speck that would mean the safe arrival of *San Raphael*.

Early evening came. The field lights were turned on and searchlight rays played on the low-hanging clouds. From time to time a rocket was fired which lit the sky like daylight, and then flickered out. The crowd knew that *San Raphael* was long past due over Newfoundland, still they clung to a fading hope that she would somehow appear; but there was no sound of an engine. All was silence, cold, and damp.

At Harbor Grace, though the time had long since passed for the plane to come over, rows of automobiles still circled the field, with their headlights ablaze. The optimists in the crowd, now bundled up to protect against the rain and the fog, remained vigilant while buoying their lagging spirits by exchanging possible reasons for the delay.

At 11 P.M., September 1, those at Lindbergh Field, Ottawa, heard a report that a monoplane resembling the *San Raphael*, had been sighted an hour before flying in a westerly direction over eastern Quebec. A cheer went up and life returned to the heretofore quiet crowd. Again, they became alert for the sound of an engine as field attendants fired signal rockets more frequently.

Their hopes were dashed in a short time when it was announced that the reported plane had been identified as a privately owned Fairchild on its way to Montreal. The gloom returned to the patient throng and sat on them even more heavily. The Fokker was now four hours overdue and her fuel supply by all calculations was dwindling, if not already exhausted; and there wasn't the faintest clue that they had reached this side of the ocean.

In response to a message from a coastal station, the S.S. *Mauretania* radioed from 400 miles east of Ambrose Light that she had seen no sign of the missing plane. Other ships at sea sent similar word as well as the lookouts up and down the coast.

In London, reporters reached Lady Mary Savile, the Princess's sister, at her home. She said that her family though very worried had by no means abandoned hope and felt sure that the plane had come down safely somewhere. Mrs. Hamilton, in Ottawa, was certain also that her husband was safe and she continued her vigil in her hotel room.

All during the night of September 1, and the early morning of September 2, northeastern Canada and the United States waited, watched, listened, and hoped in vain. There was no engine sound, and no plane—only the sounds of violent winds and torrential rains which swept the eastern coastline.

The next day, September 2, the *Mauretania* docked in New York, and the ship's officers told of "terrible weather" at sea. It was so bad, they said, that even had *San Raphael* flown directly over them they might not have seen or heard her. In the early afternoon, the first report was received from a ship at sea who had seen the plane. The oil tanker *Josiah Macy* sent word that a plane had passed over her at 9:44 P.M., on the evening of August 31, while she was steaming approximately 900 miles west of Ireland.

The days and the weeks passed, and no more was heard of *San Raphael*; no wreckage or oil slick, not even a bottle with a note in it. Like *Oiseau Blanc* before her, the inscrutable Atlantic hid the secret of her fate.

Ottawa gave up hope on September 3, and throughout Canada there arose a mighty outcry from the public against further ocean flights. Editorials in newspapers and magazines called for immediate governmental action against further "stunt" or "suicide" missions, but the outcry was mild in comparison to what could come within a few days.

5. On the continent, the French pilots awaited their turn, but the weather still thwarted them.

Several days after Levine left on his careening flight to London,

Oiseau Bleu was made ready. In the early dawn of September 2, Givon and Corbu arrived at Le Bourget, bundled in flying gear, and determined to take off, though the weather reports from over the ocean were far from ideal. It was a gray misty dawn, and the field lights were on. A smallish crowd of 500, many in tuxedos, crowded around the plane which stood outside the hangar. Irene Bordoni, the actress, was among the notables. It was a smaller crowd than the one that had watched Nungesser and Coli, but the announcement came unexpectedly and late in the evening, so that few Parisians were aware that *Oiseau Bleu* was about to leave.

Mechanics worked feverishly on the plane. Her wings were wrapped carefully with a paper-like material to keep out the dampness. Corbu, only twenty-five, was accompanied to the field by his wife and tearful young sister. Two of the Farmans were present, Maurice and Henri, and they talked intently to Givon. Photographers snapped pictures of the flyers, and the flash of the bulbs annoyed them visibly.

The ship had been rolled out at 3:15 A.M., and it stood, huge, under the lights. Supplies were loaded. The food was sumptuous, and consisted of one pound of white chicken meat, one pound of ham, one pound of cakes and cookies, six bananas, one pound of sweet chocolate, 125 grams of sugar, two gallons of water, two pounds of coffee and tea, a pint of champagne, a flask of calvados, kola drinks, caffeine, and aspirin! There was, also, a fireless cooker aboard. There was plenty of food and drink, and a remedy for overindulgence, too! In addition, each flyer wore a parachute and a rubber life belt, to which was attached an aluminum box, containing biscuits, alcohol, a medicine kit, and fishing lines. A pneumatic raft was stowed behind the pilot's seat, together with a bottle of air capable of inflating the raft in four seconds.

At 4 A.M., a tractor towed the big plane into take-off position at the end of the runway, where the fueling was completed by 4:35.

There was much emotion displayed by the Corbu family, as first Mademoiselle Corbu broke down and sobbed, closely followed by her sister-in-law. The tears were soon dried and the good-byes finished, and shortly after 6 A.M., Givon and Corbu climbed into the enclosed cockpit, after last words of advice from the Farmans.

The engines were started and run up. They would be required to lift twelve tons off the ground, and both pilots and ground crew listened for any false sounds. Within minutes, Givon was satisfied and waved from the cockpit window. The wheel chocks were pulled clear, as he

40. *Sir John Carling* headed down runway at Harbor Grace.

41. Edward Schlee *(left)* and
Bill Brock in Tokyo at
the end of their flight.

42. Captain Robert McIntosh *(center)* and Major James Fitzmaurice before take-off at Baldonnel Airfield, Dublin.

43. Dieudonné Coste *(left)* and Joseph Le Brix.

44. *Dawn* arrives at Old Orchard Beach to prepare for her flight.

45. Harry Jones greets Mrs. Grayson.

46. *Dawn's* designer Igor Sikorsky *(left)* with Harry Jones at Old Orchard

47. Bryce Goldsborough *(in white shirt)*, Mrs. Grayson and Bill Stultz *(extreme right)*, Old Orchard Beach, Maine, October 1927.

48. *Dawn* on test flight at Old Orchard.

49. *Dawn* threatened by seas at Old Orchard.

50. *Dawn* survives with Mrs. Grayson's help.

51. Motor expert Fred Koehler with designer Eddie Stinson.

52. *Royal Windsor*, on Byrd ramp taking off for Spokane in fall of 1927.

53. Ruth Elder bundles up.

54. Ruth Elder climbs aboard *American Girl*.

55. Ruth Elder debarks in Azores
after rescue at sea.

56. Mrs. Grayson with new pilot Lieutenant Oskar Omdal,
at Roosevelt Field, December 1927.

opened the throttles. The big blue plane started slowly down the runway, as the first rays of daylight appeared in the cloudy sky. The roaring engines echoed over the field. Thick, wet brown dirt flew up behind her, as she inched along at first, and then moved faster. Streaks of blue and yellow flame jetted from the exhausts. It was a long run. The seconds and the yards passed swiftly. The Farmans eyed their watches with intent and concern, while shooting quick glances at the moving plane. After a run of 90 seconds, and at the extreme end of the two-mile runway, *Oiseau Bleu* lifted off, heavily. She made an instantaneous but shallow bank to avoid some trees, and cleared them by an eyelash, for she was barely twenty feet off the ground. Painfully, she gained altitude, and then disappeared into the mist, only to reappear minutes later overhead, having by now struggled to 300 feet. The fire engines, which had raced down the field after her when disaster seemed imminent, returned to the hangar line. *Oiseau Bleu* continued to circle in and out of the low cloud, straining ever for altitude. Nine minutes after the take-off, she disappeared on course for Brest, at an estimated 1200 feet.

Many in the small crowd left for home, having been up all night. Those who remained to see if *Oiseau Tango* or *Nungesser and Coli* would follow in pursuit were surprised when, at 10 A.M., the big Farman biplane emerged, suddenly, out of the mist from the west, and glided down lightly to a landing. She rolled quickly to a stop, turned, and taxied to the Farman hangar. The two flyers scrambled out of the cockpit. They told of a harrowing two hours of blind flight to the coast.

"It was like cotton all the way," said Givon expressively.

He told officials that, because of the weight of the plane, he wasn't able to climb over 1000 feet in an effort to get over the weather. Moreover, he added, the increasing head winds had slowed the progress of the plane, which had never been known for its speed. It became a hopeless cause, and they decided to turn around. They flew about the countryside, spraying out their enormous gas load so as to lessen the landing dangers, a procedure which took two hours; found Le Bourget again and landed. Givon remarked, also, that flames from the exhaust had resulted in a near fire at the time of take-off.

Their wise return was applauded universally. There had been considerable doubt among those who knew, since the test flights, as to whether *Oiseau Bleu* should try at all, because of her slow cruising speed, which they knew would be slowed, further, by the head winds over the Atlantic. On her final test flight to Cherbourg in comparatively still air, she had managed to average only 85 miles an hour.

6.   In New York, the crew of the *Old Glory*
paused to think things over in the face of the public criticism. They
met at the Garden City Hotel late in the evening of September 1,
when it became apparent that *San Raphael* was lost. After the meeting, Payne told reporters that the flight had been postponed temporarily so that *Old Glory* could be used to search the North Atlantic
for clues to the fate of the missing Fokker. He said that they would
leave at once for Harbor Grace and that he hoped that a supply of
gasoline (a special mixture of ether, benzol and gasoline) being stored
for *San Raphael's* use at Ottawa, could be shipped to Bennett Field,
Harbor Grace, for *Old Glory's* use on the search.

There were questions as to whether *Old Glory* would be able to get
off Roosevelt Field, which had been muddied by recent rains, J. D.
Hill made light of the concern, and said they would use the grassy
portion of the field, alongside the runway and that, in any event, he
anticipated no problem with the light load of gas they would need for
the Newfoundland trip.

The change in plans did not last long, however, for the next day
they received word that Ottawa would not release *San Raphael's*
gasoline, and the aerial search was canceled. The crew resumed preparations for the Rome trip. The tanks, which were partially emptied
for the flight to Newfoundland, were refilled, and the crew stood by,
hoping for a shift in the southerly wind that blew across the runway.
They remained oblivious to the adverse editorial comment on their
pending flight. The cross wind persisted stubbornly and the crowd,
hopeful of seeing them off, had to settle for Igor Sikorsky taxiing
the *Ville de Paris* around the field, testing her motor, controls, and
landing gear, until automobiles on the field blocked her path and
forced him to quit for the day. Bertaud worried over the advanced
state of preparations of the Fonck ship. He was bound that *Old Glory*
would not again be left at the post.

During the evening, J. D. Hill placed a telephone call to Harry
Jones at the latter's oceanside home at Old Orchard Beach, Maine.
Jones was an old wartime acquaintance of Hill's while they were
civilian instructors together at San Antonio, Texas.

Hill inquired about the Beach as a take-off point for *Old Glory*.
Jones told him that at low tide, the 2½ mile strip of hard-packed

sand provided the best natural runway in the United States. Hill asked pertinent questions, connected with the prevailing winds, tides, and weather outlook, which Jones answered as best he could. Jones told him, that if *Old Glory* came to Old Orchard, he would turn over all his facilities, including the hangar, to her crew, and help them in any way he could. J.D. thanked his old friend, and returned to meet with Bertaud and Payne. All three were now convinced of the futility of a take-off, with the heavy plane, from the comparatively short runway at Roosevelt. The days of cross winds seemed endless. It was decided at once to go to Old Orchard for the Rome take-off.

Hector Alexander, a mechanic, was summoned and sent on an all-night ride to Maine so as to report back on his findings as soon as possible. Eric Densham rushed to Roosevelt Field in the middle of the night and supervised the transfer of 500 gallons of fuel from *Old Glory*'s tanks to steel barrels. The barrels were loaded onto a hastily-obtained truck in the wee hours of the morning, and the truck drove off on its way to Harry Jones's hangar at Old Orchard Beach. The crew until now thoroughly discouraged over the long delay went to bed at Garden City Hotel convinced that they were, at last, on their way to Rome.

Old Orchard Beach, situated 13 miles south of Portland, has been a well-known vacation spot for surf-lovers since long before the turn of the century. It runs along the ocean in a gentle arc from the Scarboro River at Pine Point for a distance of over three miles to the south, though it is interrupted, 2½ miles down, by a pier which juts 100 yards out into the ocean from the little town of Old Orchard. The pier is the focal point of a Coney Island-type amusement area, and a dance hall at its end echoed for many years to the sounds of the "big-name" bands.

To the aviators of the day it presented an obstacle, 50 feet high, that had to be cleared. Beyond Pine Point and the Scarboro River, the land circled like the top half of a crescent moon, terminating with the Checkley House, on the tip of Prout's Neck. On the other side of the pier, the coast curled around to the other end of the crescent, Biddeford Pool, on those rocks was the Wood Island lighthouse. Between Prout's and Biddeford Pool, two miles offshore, were two islands, which we children referred to collectively, for some reason, as "Cabbage Island."

We lived in the center portion of the beach, halfway between Pine Point and Old Orchard, which was known as "Grand Beach," three houses down from the white, frame house of Mr. Boston, and six, from Mr. Hazzard and his salt-water pool. One quarter of a mile down the beach, toward the pier, was Harry Jones's hangar in which he kept his brand-new, Stinson cabin biplane. The plane was used to take vacationers up on 10-minute flights, and watching them was a constant thrill to us as we frolicked on the hot sand and dived into the sparkling breakers. Harry Jones was our hero. He had flown thousands of passengers since his arrival at the beach in 1919 and to us there was no greater pilot in the world. Day after day, we would delight in watching him roar off the beach and minutes later glide in to a three-point landing, a feat that was then the epitome of flying ability. Though it was better swimming when the tide was high because of the bigger surf, we were always delighted to see it go out because it meant that Harry would be flying soon again.

It was late in the evening on Saturday, September 3. We had been allowed to stay up, when someone found out that an airplane was due to arrive from New York, to take off on an Atlantic flight. The tide was low, and as we stood on the boardwalk in front of our house, you could hear the distinctive "slap" of the quiet evening breakers as they collapsed on the sand. It was a warm night, and the last pink of sunset had faded. Suddenly out of the southwest came the sound of an engine which increased rapidly to a fearful noise. There appeared in the dark sky, the silhouette of a huge airplane, huge in comparison to the little *Spirit of St. Louis*, which had visited us earlier. We watched excitedly as the big plane flew over us, banked over Pine Point, and flew down the length of the beach. Over the pier, she banked again and flew out over the ocean toward Prout's Neck. I can remember being worried that perhaps she had decided not to land after all and that I wouldn't get a chance to see her.

Down the beach near Harry Jones's hangar we could see lots of activity. There were two or three searchlight beams playing in the sky, which was already well-lit by the lights from the pier, and the roller coaster in Old Orchard. There was also a bonfire burning brightly and we knew that they must have been signals to the airplane. My fears were allayed when I saw the big winged shadow bank again and start to lower over Pine Point. As she passed our house the plane was only 50 feet in the air. She was so close that I felt I could reach out and touch her. There was a faint light in the cockpit and the noise wasn't as loud. She settled easily on the beach near the bonfire. The last thing I can remember before being sent reluctantly to bed was a screeching blast from her engine as she was driven up into the soft sand, well above the high-water mark. *Old Glory* was with us and the names of Lloyd Bertaud, James Hill and Philip Payne were burned indelibly into the memory of a child during the ensuing three days.

After the plane had been backed up to its wing in the hangar (Jones, graciously, left his own plane outside), the flyers went to the Hotel Brunswick, a surfside hotel at Old Orchard on the far side of the Pier. On its ocean-front piazza, seated in wooden rocking-chairs, Jones and the crew engaged in a typical airman's gabfest and swapped tales about mutual friends late into the evening. Jones told the crew that he had talked to "Duke" Schiller, whose *Royal Windsor* was stuck in the mud at the new airport in Scarboro. Schiller wanted to fly over to Old Orchard the next day, Sunday, so as to be able to leave with or soon after the *Old Glory*, but Jones had advised him against it because of the large Labor Day weekend crowds that were expected to be on the beach. Two ocean-going planes would be too much.

Jones, who has confessed to me that he thought the ocean flyers of the day were "out of their heads," talked at length to his old friend "J.D." whom he hadn't seen since San Antonio days. When he learned that *Old Glory*'s Jupiter engine had never undergone a 40-hour block test, he was astounded, and told "J.D." so; but, Hill said confidentially that they would not fly non-stop but would land in Newfoundland before tackling the ocean. He added that if there were any problems with the engine they would not go at all.

All day long, mechanics in white suits puttered inside and outside the plane, while we looked on in a state of excitement and wonder, and bathers in long bathing suits, milled around the plane, gaping. There was no attempt however at a take-off.

It announced that the delay on Sunday, September 4, was due to the failure of the gasoline truck to arrive from New York. True, the truck had broken down in Boston, but there was a more serious reason.

William Randolph Hearst, smarting over the loss of *Golden Eagle* in the Dole Race, and upset by the public criticism of "stunt flights," became more concerned by flyers' outspoken worries about *Old Glory*. There was a strong undercurrent of feeling among them that she was too big and heavy for a single engine—no matter how powerful. There is also evidence that Bertaud and Hill felt the same way, for I have been told by old residents of the Beach, that neither of them thought the plane could make it, particularly with Payne in the crew. In any event, Hearst was determined that *Old Glory* should not take off until government authorities had fully approved both plane and equipment. He communicated this determination by telegram to Payne in Old Orchard. Payne replied at once saying that Assistant Secretary of War for Air F. Trubee Davison, together with a representative of the Department of Commerce, had looked over the plane at Roosevelt Field and had pronounced it fit for the flight. Hearst was not satisfied. Perhaps it was to cover his publications in case of disaster, but he wired Payne again:

DEAR PHIL. PLEASE THINK OF MY SITUATION. HAVE HAD ONE AIRPLANE LOST AND TWO FINE MEN DROWNED. IF ANOTHER SUCH DISASTER OCCURRED THE EFFECT WOULD BE TERRIBLE—NOT ONLY TO MY PEACE OF MIND BUT ON PUBLIC OPINION. I TELEGRAPH YOU ALL THIS AND HOPE YOU WILL TRY TO GET THE PILOTS TO AC-CEPT THE PRIZE MONEY AND GIVE UP THIS DANGEROUS ADVENTURE.

The cocky Payne answered promptly with a DEAR CHIEF wire, and explained that the plane and crew were ready, and that he was certain that the flight could be completed easily, and would reflect glory on those who participated in it.

Besides the Hearst-Payne exchange, the weather caused problems, as reports showed heavy fogs lying over Nova Scotia and Newfoundland. Payne told reporters that the delay (which he attributed solely to the failure of the gas truck to arrive) would be beneficial to them in the long run, for a westerly wind was predicted in the Maritime Provinces, which he felt sure would blow the fog out to sea.

The flyers late in the day were joined at the Brunswick Hotel by Mrs. Bertaud, Bertaud's mother, Mrs. Francis Callaghan and Mrs. Payne, who had made a hurried train trip from New York. In the evening Payne announced that the take-off would be made between 1 and 2 P.M. the next day, Monday. At that time, the tide would be low, and a departure then would get them over Newfoundland seven hours later while there was still some daylight, and would enable them to check their position and lighten their gas load, before venturing over the Atlantic. Payne told reporters that he expected the flying time to Rome would be in the neighborhood of 45 hours.

Talk then reverted to the fate of the *San Raphael*. A man in Belle Isle, Newfoundland, testified that he had seen a plane fly over him, and then turn out to sea on Friday, September 2. The flyers shook their heads. The Princess's plane could not have stayed in the air that long. They talked of *Sir John Carling*, then sitting in a field in Washburn, Maine, waiting to fly to Harbor Grace. They were joined by "Duke" Schiller and Phil Wood, who drove over from Scarboro.

Hill said that he was a little worried over the valve guides and stems which had been sticking in his Jupiter motor, but Densham assured him that the trouble could be fixed easily. The talk went on again into the night as the flyers relaxed in the heavy maple chairs that decorated the austere ocean-front lobby.

Monday, September 5—Labor Day—was another cloudless, bright day. The ocean was calm, ruffled only by a breath of air from the west. The water was icy cold, as always, when there was a land breeze. It shortened our swimming time, and we hurried down to the beach to Harry Jones's so as not to miss any excitement.

The plane was surrounded already by a huge holiday crowd. Everyone seemingly had a camera and snapped pictures from all angles. The plane was unprotected by guards or rope barriers, and curious bystanders patted it and touched it as if to make sure it was real. A few mischievous children threw sand on it. *Old Glory* struck us again, with her ungainliness—like a big whale with a wing attached.

At 11 A.M., a white-suited mechanic, who we thought must be Densham, pulled himself into the cockpit. Another mechanic cranked on the starter outside. The powerful engine kicked, and then roared and sent a storm of white sand shooting out behind. For a period of minutes, the engine was run up to full throttle, idled, and then run up again. We had never heard an engine make such a noise before. It was frightening. Someone volunteered that they were testing the radio generator, which operated off the propeller shaft. Suddenly the engine was shut down, and all was quiet, until Harry Jones took off in his Stinson, carrying another load of holiday passengers.

The breeze picked up as the morning passed, and we learned that, because of the west wind at the beach, *Old Glory* would not leave this day. We were not disappointed, for it meant an added day of excitement for us.

At noon, the large crowd basking under the warm sun had a quick thrill. A little Curtiss biplane with a pilot and an International News Service photographer started to take off toward Pine Point in the cross wind. On her run, the pilot got too close to the surf, lost control in the soft sand as the wind edged him into the shallow water. His wheels caught in the sand, and the little plane turned turtle in the breakers, leaving her occupants hanging upside down, just above the water. We started to run toward the accident, but were held back, while the two men were extricated from their seats, and led soaking wet up the beach to the hangar. We asked if they had been hurt, and were told, "Oh, they're just skinned up a little."

Harry Jones was furious though because he felt that the accident, no matter how minor, would affect his passenger business and Labor Day was a big day for him.

"Damned fools!" he said. "They ought to have known better than to take off toward Pine Point in this wind."

The accident must have taught the *Old Glory* crew something, for, late in the day, both Bertaud and Hill turned up at the hangar, and gave orders that *Old Glory* be towed up to the northern end of the Beach, at Pine Point. An open touring car was produced, and a stout rope was attached to the landing gear of the plane and to the rear axle of the car. The procession moved down the beach slowly. We followed on foot and were delighted to see them stop about eight houses above ours. Hill climbed into the plane, the engine was started, and he turned her, with a wild wail coming from the engine, and drove her way up into the soft sand, beyond the high-water mark. The engine was shut down, and the plane was turned around so that it faced the sea, with its tail resting in the edge of the beach grass.

When we got there, the fueling of the big plane was well under way. We thought that perhaps they were going to leave after all, but then we noticed that the tide was coming in fast, and now covered a large portion of the 2¼ miles of hard sand to the pier; and, behind us, to the west, the sun was beginning to sink in back of the pine trees. Nevertheless, we stayed on, as drum after drum of fuel from the recently arrived truck was poured into the tanks. One mechanic stood on a ladder at the nose, and worked on the engine.

Our friends at Grand Beach, who had been watching with us, began to wander off as evening approached, and soon we reluctantly returned to the house for supper.

After supper we dashed back to the plane. There was no sign of the crew or mechanics. We had the plane to ourselves, almost, for only an occasional evening beachwalker stopped by to look at her now. I remember wanting desperately to climb up and look into the cockpit, but it was too high and the ladder was gone. We dared though to get close to her and look at every part. I tried to move the elevators with my hands, but they were too heavy. I can still recall the oily smell that surrounded her, for she was now fully loaded and ready to go. We ran home, as darkness came, for tomorrow would be a big day, and we'd have to be up early.

It was a busy evening for the crew and their families at the Hotel Brunswick. The wives bustled about, preparing food for the flight. Dozens of sandwiches were made, chicken, ham, and cheese. There were stuffed eggs, several loaves of bread, a huge slab of cheese, and seven gallons of water, all packed neatly in a container together with a large Thermos of Bertaud's favorite pea soup. Bertaud chatted calmly with newspapermen and visitors, including Mr. Hazzard, again representing Governor Brewster, and Father James Mullen, the ruddy and genial pastor of St. Margaret's Church. He told them that *Old Glory* might make a return trip via a southern route from French Morocco to Florida. It was 800 miles longer, but Bertaud felt that they would be helped along by the favorable trade winds. The tall, quiet Hill, the only one without a relative present, retired early. Payne and Bertaud, with their wives and Mrs. Callaghan, sat up talking until a late hour.

It was sparkling and clear the next morning. The Checkley House on the end of Prout's Neck, across the shimmering bay, looked close enough to touch, and the coastline, leading to far-off Biddeford Pool, was like a purpled pencil line against the blue water.

Crowds gathered around the plane early, though it was known that she couldn't leave until low tide, shortly after noon. Soon our little portion of the beach was packed with a sea of people. There was almost no wind, and the sun was hot.

With their wives, Bertaud and Payne attended a special Mass offered by Father Mullen at St. Margaret's, the little church at the top of Old Orchard's main street. Dr. James H. Scarr of the New York Weather Bureau, who had interrupted his vacation to come up to Old Orchard Beach, after studying his maps, assured Hill of good weather over the ocean. Hill studied a chart he had been given, pinpointing the position of all the ships at sea, which would be within 200 miles of *Old Glory* on her way across. Though he reserved the right to change his mind, he told a reporter from the Portland *Press-Herald* that he expected to head for Bordeaux from the Newfoundland coast. He realized that it was a longer course than the now classical circle, but he felt that there would be less icing and sleet. Scarr checked with "Doc" Kimball in New York for the most up-to-date observations. Kimball predicted favorable westerly winds along their course—which approximated the 44th parallel. He said there were no storms in *Old Glory*'s path, and at worst they would run into cloudiness with a little mist and light rain. Payne said that they would cross the ocean from Sable Island, and after striking the coast at Bordeaux, would fly over the Rhone Valley, Marseilles, the northernmost tip of Corsica, the Tyrrhenian Sea, and on into Ciampino Airfield in Rome. Bertaud added that the plane would be in continuous radio touch with ship and shore, by means of the automatic transmission of her call letters, and by actual message transmissions. He confessed that his biggest worry was the take-off. If he could get 1179 gallons of gas and a total weight of nearly 13,000 pounds into the air, the battle would be 75 percent won.

Payne and Hill drove up to the *Old Glory* at 10:30 A.M. Well over a thousand people now surrounded her, despite the fact that the holiday weekend was over. The tide was receding, but had not reached the low-water mark. Payne, with his black hair blowing in the breeze, chatted with his wife. "Duke" Schiller and Phil Wood, from *Royal Windsor*, arrived, and talked with Hill.

"J.D." turned suddenly to Payne and said, "Name the hour."

Payne replied, "How about one?"

"O.K." said Hill quietly.

Word was sent to Bertaud, who was still at the hotel with his wife and mother. He joined them, within minutes.

At 11:30 A.M., *Old Glory* was pushed down from the high-water mark to the hard-packed sand and faced toward Old Orchard and its menacing pier, 2¼ miles off. The tide was dropping fast, and soon would be at dead low; National Guardsmen held the crowd at a safe distance from the plane. Motorcycle police sped down the beach to clear it for take-off. It was so exciting for us as we wriggled under and around the spectators so that we wouldn't miss anything. Eric Densham stood on a gasoline barrel and worked on the engine while other mechanics went over every nut, bolt, and spar with care. The noontime sun beat down hotly on the big Fokker and her giant golden wing glinted under its rays.

Not far from where we stood, Bertaud and Hill tossed an orange idly back and forth. Hill flung it suddenly to an unsuspecting third person, and laughed when it burst in his hands. Thirty feet below, the waves billowed up, and collapsed in a spew of white foam.

Bertaud and Payne joined their wives, while Hill joked with a friend. You could see his shoulders, now and then shake with laughter. For the most part, Mrs. Bertaud, Mrs. Callaghan, and Mrs. Payne seemed cheerful enough, but from time to time, they looked away from their men and stared wistfully. Mechanic Alexander, sent by Payne to get a half dozen bananas, stepped through the crowd with a paper bag full, which he had obtained at young Bob Longfellow's grocery, across the main road.

Mrs. Payne and Mrs. Bertaud had written notes to their spouses, to read on the way across. Mrs. Callaghan saw "J.D." standing alone, without relative or girl. She scribbled a note, hurriedly, on a piece of scratch paper, folded it, and handed it to him.

It said, "*You are a grand fellow, and we all like you.*" Then, she threw her arms around Hill and kissed him. He smiled shyly.

Mr. Hazzard, Mr. Fred Boston, and Father Bob White, residents of Grand Beach, joined the small group around the plane, together with comedian Fred Allen, and wrestler Stanislaus Zybysko. They shook hands with the flyers. Schiller and Wood stepped through the crowd to say good-bye, followed by our friend Father Mullen, wearing a surplice and stole. He smiled broadly as he chatted with the flyers. He clambered up to the top of the empty gas barrel which Densham had vacated, blessed the ship, and sprinkled it with holy water.

A mechanic cranked on the engine starter, as Densham sat in the cockpit. The motor gave off a lusty roar as it whirred into action. When he opened the throttle *Old Glory* trembled against her wheel chocks, and the loose sand sprayed out behind her in clouds. It was a fearful roar, and we plugged our ears. There were parting handshakes and tearful embraces.

Payne started to flip a coin to determine who would fly her. He dropped it in the sand as both men laughed. He picked it up, and flipped it again.

"The ship's yours, J.D.," said the burly Bertaud.

"Just like another airmail flight," laughed Hill.

They climbed in the hatch under the fuselage. I had a sinking feeling when one of the mechanics sealed the hatch. How'll they ever get out? I thought. It become the subject of nightmares. We looked up at *Old Glory*. I could see Bertaud's head at the right cockpit window. Hill was hidden by him as he sat at the controls to his left. In the fuselage cabin Payne sat looking out the window, his glasses giving him an owl-like appearance. He sat in a chair beside the chart table, and alongside was the 82-pound radio set on which they relied so heavily. I remember taking a last look at the plane— the flags under her wings, the number NX 703 on her rudder and her wonderful name along her fuselage. It may have been talk which I had overheard, or it may have been the frighteningly, bulky body of the ship, but I recall a distinct premonition of disaster.

There was a violent roar from the Jupiter engine, as Hill opened the throttle, and the plane started to move down the beach. We shielded our eyes from the blowing sand. *Old Glory* seemed so heavy and so slow. I heard many comments, and watched many heads shake.

"She'll never get off," they said, or, "I hear they didn't want to go," or even, "Someone told me Bertaud said they don't have a chance!"

Motorcycles raced down alongside *Old Glory*. Harry Jones followed her in his Stinson, and took swiftly to the air, while *Old Glory* trundled along. The seconds passed. She grew smaller as she went farther away from us, but there was no sign of her lifting. The crowd was tense and quiet, fearful of a dreadful crash. It looked as though she had reached Harry Jones's hangar. There was only a half mile left to the pier, and she was not yet airborne.

"Please get up," I can remember praying.

Still, they stayed on the ground, with the protesting wail of her motor echoing the length of the beach.

Suddenly, she was off—only a little yet off, but the pier was closing in on her fast. She'd never clear it! At the last minute, we saw one golden wing dip as Hill banked gingerly around the edge of the dance pavilion and open air movie at the end, still only twenty feet in the air. As she flew out over the Saco coast toward Biddeford Pool, she gained little or no altitude. We could see her struggling. We held our breaths. As she neared Wood Island Light on Fortune's Rocks, *Old Glory* began to climb. Harry Jones, who followed them in his plane, said that a puff of air had sprung up from the southeast just at the right moment and had helped to lift her to a safer 500 feet. We watched her, spellbound, as she banked gently over Biddeford Pool and headed to the northeast. She flew so slowly. We watched her for fifteen minutes as she struggled over Cabbage Island and Prout's Neck, and finally disappeared from sight.

It was a letdown after three days of such excitement, but the letdown did not last long. *Old Glory* left the ground at 1:25 P.M. At 5 P.M. we heard a roar over our house. Thinking it was *Old Glory* back again, we ran out onto the beach in time to see the trim blue monoplane *Royal Windsor* slide in for a landing and taxi to Harry Jones's hangar. You may be sure that we were up at 4 A.M., the next morning to watch Schiller and Wood take off for Harbor Grace. They arrived at Bennett Field at noon, only hours after *Sir John Carling* had left for London, England. They hoped to take off, themselves, the next day.

Meanwhile, *Old Glory* was flying smoothly. At 2 P.M. she was sighted over Monhegan Island at the entrance to Penobscot Bay, 500 feet up. At 3:55 P.M. the Canadian freighter, *Empress,* 10 miles off Digby, Nova Scotia, reported her overhead, and, at 4:15 P.M. she was seen flying low over Harborville, Nova Scotia. The next report of her came at 5:30 from Truro, Nova Scotia, followed shortly by another at 6 from Arisaig. There, the people said, she flew over so low that they could make out her markings, plainly. It was apparent that Bertaud had followed the Nova Scotia shore of the Bay of Fundy to Cape Split, crossed over the Minas Channel to Parrsboro, and then followed the northern shore of Cobequet Bay, into Truro. From there, he followed the main highway to New Glasgow, turned east, and headed for the Bras d'Or Lakes, where the plane was spotted by many. At 7 P.M. *Old Glory* flew over North Sydney, and minutes later was reported by residents of New Waterford, Cape Breton, to have left shore, flying in a northeasterly direction. All seemed to be well with her when two and a half hours later, she passed over Buren, Newfoundland, at 1000 feet.

In addition to the sightings, there were frequent radio reports throughout the day and evening from *Old Glory.* The radio station at St. John, New Brunswick, picked up a message at 4:20 P.M.: SHIP IS TAIL HEAVY. WILL SEND LATER. LOVE TO ALL. WE ARE MAKING 100 MILES AN HOUR.

It is thought from this that Bertaud was back in the radio cabin with Payne, giving him operating instructions. Within a half an hour, a message was received that Bertaud had relieved Hill at the controls. At 5:51 and again at 6:10 P.M. there were messages from the plane received by the operator on St. Paul Island to the effect that all was well. Her progress and speed reports were encouraging to those close to the flight.

At 6:30 P.M. a radio message was sent by the S.S. *George Washington:*

WE ARE ABOUT 860 MILES EAST OF AMBROSE LIGHT. PLANE JUST TWO DEGREES OFF OUR PORT BOW.

At 8:30 P.M. *George Washington* sent another message:

HEARING RADIO OF PLANE OLD GLORY BUT CANNOT GET PLANE TO ANSWER. APPARENTLY, ALL GOING WELL.

At 9:25 P.M. the S.S. *Berlin,* 1200 miles east of New York, reported that she had heard the plane but had not been able to communicate with her; at 10:33 P.M. the wireless station at Cape Race, Newfoundland, heard from *Old Glory.*

ALL O.K. MAKING GOOD TIME. BEST REGARDS.

The message was unsigned and no position was given. There was no further word for two hours, when, at 12:41 A.M., September 7, the S.S. *California* radioed that, at 11:57 P.M., 350 miles east of St. John's:

MONOPLANE OLD GLORY ON TRANSATLANTIC EASTBOUND FLIGHT PASSED OVERHEAD AT 300 FEET FLYING WELL. The *California* reported further that it was a foggy night with a fresh westerly wind making the ocean choppy.

There followed four hours of silence. This did not give cause for alarm, for it was thought that the inexperienced Payne in all likelihood was struggling to learn the set.

At 4:03 A.M. the radio operators aboard the S.S. *Carmania* and S.S. *Lapland* were horrified when a message crackled over their receivers:

OLD GLORY! SOS! SOS!

No position was given. They strained their ears, trying to pick up further details, but six minutes passed in dreadful silence, during which their frantic calls for a position went unanswered.

Suddenly, their radios crackled again with the desperate message:

OLD GLORY SOS! SOS! FIVE HOURS OUT FROM NEWFOUNDLAND BOUND EAST!

That was all. It was surmised that the distress call came from Payne, for Bertaud, the experienced navigator, would have had the exact position at his fingertips.

Navigators aboard all ships in the vicinity went to work in a flash, calculating rapidly. The last known speed of *Old Glory* was 100 miles an hour, and, adding 15 miles to it for the tail wind, would place them approximately 600 miles east of Cape Race. Radio operators tried in vain to reach the plane again, and, ominously, there were no further reports of the automatic "WHRP" signals.

Captain David W. Bone of the S.S. *Transylvania* estimated that he was 80 miles from where the last SOS had been sent.

At 4:28 A.M. he radioed: HAVE ALTERED COURSE 150 DEGREES TO SEARCH AIRPLANE OLD GLORY, HER SOS INDICATES POSITION ABOUT 49 DEGREES 50 MINUTES NORTH, 41 DEGREES 15 MINUTES WEST. FRESH WESTERLY WINDS AND SEA. The message added that *Old Glory's* signals were very strong at the time of her last distress call.

The S.S. *Carpulin*, in the area, also, raced to the scene. One minute after *Transylvania's* message, she radioed:

RECEIVED SOS FROM PLANE OLD GLORY GIVING POSITION AS FIVE HOURS OUT OF NEWFOUNDLAND BOUND EAST. AFTER, ALL COMMUNICA-

TION CEASED. PLANE MUST BE ON SURFACE OF WATER. HAS NO AERIAL NOW. SEARCHING ACROSS ATLANTIC.

At 4:40 A.M. *Transylvania* radioed again:

FRESH WINDS AND SEA. TRAVELING FULL SPEED. HAVE ALTERED COURSE TO SEARCH FOR OLD GLORY. IT IS PITCH DARKNESS. NO MOON, WILL BE DIFFICULT TO FIND SHIP.

At 5:30 A.M. she sent another message:

PROCEEDING TO ESTIMATED POSITION OF PLANE. NO FURTHER SIGNALS HEARD. AM CONTINUING SEARCH. FRESH WEST BY SOUTH WINDS BLOWING AND ROUGH SEAS. CAPTAIN DAVID W. BONE.

She reported again at 10:30 A.M.:

HAVE SEARCHED AREA FOR THIRTY MINUTES AROUND POSITION WITHOUT RESULT. NOW PROCEEDING TOWARD POINT IN WHICH AIR-PLANE WAS SEEN BY SS CALIFORNIA EARLIER.

Transylvania radioed her final message at 3 P.M.:

HAVE SEARCHED AREA WITHOUT RESULT. LITTLE HOPE SURVIVAL IN VIEW OF ROUGH SEAS. CALIFORNIA SEARCHING NORTH, AMERICAN MERCHANT TO EAST. AM PROCEEDING ON VOYAGE.

At 3:15 P.M. S.S. *Carmania* radioed from the vicinity of *Old Glory*'s final message.

ROUGH BREAKING SEA. TEMPERATURE 59. WATER TEMPERATURE 62. CONSIDER LITTLE CHANCE OF SURVIVAL OF COLLAPSIBLE BOAT IF OLD GLORY WAS PREPARED WITH SAME.

At 5:20 P.M. she radioed again:

NOW NIGHTFALL AND QUITE DARK. REGRET SEARCH FOR MISSING PLANE OLD GLORY WITHOUT RESULT.

When the *Transylvania* docked in New York, Captain Bone said that he had zigzagged across the estimated area of the SOS call for eight hours, with fourteen lookouts scanning the sea with binoculars, but had sighted nary a clue. The passengers aboard the *California*, the last to see *Old Glory* in the air, described her as a dark shadow with a flashing light at an altitude of 300 feet. They added that the shadow had disappeared quickly off the ship's port bow.

The flyers' wives and Mrs. Callaghan boarded the *Bar Harbor Express* at Union Station in Portland for the return trip to New York. They were optimistic over the planes' chances for success, for according to all late reports, everything was going well aboard her. They were told the bad news when their train stopped at New Haven, Connecticut, in the early hours of September 7. An Associated Press reporter advised them that an SOS had been received from *Old Glory*. He described them as being stoical, and hopeful that, somehow, their men had survived. When they arrived in New York they checked in at a hotel, then hurried off to St. Patrick's Cathedral where a special Mass was being offered for the flyers' safety.

Speculation over what happened aboard *Old Glory*, after fourteen hours of normal flight, filled the air during the next days. Tony Fokker was convinced that the overload on the plane had placed too much of a strain on the engine. He noted that the weather was moderately good, the winds were in their favor, and that only engine trouble could have brought the plane down. Other experts theorized that the trouble might have been caused by a defective spark plug, or a leaking gas line. Harry Jones recalled Hill's complaint about "sticking valves." Densham, however, put in a quick rebuttal to the theories. He said that a complete new set of spark plugs had been installed the day before the trip to Old Orchard. He added that the feed lines were made of copper, enclosed in rubber, and bound at danger points with tape to guard against leakage caused by engine vibration. Furthermore, he said, the valve trouble that had bothered Hill had been rectified completely before their departure.

Hope was expressed that the plane, or her inflatable boat, was still afloat, despite the ominous reports of a heavy sea on the fatal night. It was pointed out that if the engine had been the problem it had not been a sudden stoppage, for there had been a six-minute interval between the distress signals, giving them plenty of time to open the dump valves and empty the tanks so as to make the plane buoyant. It was also disclosed that the plane carried a rubber boat big enough for three, which was equipped with signal rockets, emergency rations, and a tiny radio transmitter, with a range of fifty miles.

Throughout September 7 and 8 steamers in the area continued to search the rough seas for a trace of the plane or her crew. Captain Hartley, due to sail with *Leviathan* on September 10, a personal friend of Bertaud and Payne, promised to keep a careful lookout as his ship passed through the waters where *Old Glory* was thought to have gone down.

William Randolph Hearst, disconsolate, released now after the fact a copy of the telegram he had sent to Payne telling him of his uneasiness over the flight. He announced, also that the mail steamer S.S. *Kyle* had been chartered by the *Daily Mirror* in St. John's to search for the plane, but her speed was only 12 knots, and she was not expected to reach the suspect area until dawn September 11.

The S.S. *Republic* radioed that she was scouring a 75-mile area in legs of five miles, but thus far had nothing to report. The *Carmania* and *Lapland* docked in New York after extensive but futile searches. All hands agreed that the plane's failure to pinpoint her position had hampered their efforts seriously and that *Old Glory* should have carried, instead of a passenger, a competent navigator-radio operator.

Captain Bone of *Transylvania*, when interviewed, was gloomy. He said that the plane could not have survived more than one hour in the heavy seas, and that he doubted that the life raft, had there been time to launch it, could have escaped immediate swamping.

Captain F. G. Brown, Royal Naval Reserve, of *Carmania* said that his ship was 180 miles south of the estimated crash position when he received the SOS. He changed course, at once, and steamed to the area at 18 knots arriving two hours before darkness. His search, too, was fruitless.

Charles Kaidd, second radio operator of *Lapland* commented, expressively, on *Old Glory*'s last radio signals. Said he:

"It sounded as if an amateur was operating the radio, and testing his set. He was just putting his hand on the key and taking it off at regular intervals, and kept it up for more than an hour. Each time I heard long dashes that were getting stronger, which meant the ship was getting nearer. Then suddenly I got an SOS followed in a few seconds by the words, '5 hours east of Newfoundland.'"

September 11 came and went without any hopeful word. The S.S. *Kyle* reported that she had searched the supposed crash area, and had found no evidence of plane or crew. Mrs. Bertaud and Mrs. Callaghan at the hotel and Mrs. Payne in her New York apartment clung to the hope that the flyers were safe in the collapsible raft but only negative reports were received from *Leviathan* and *Republic*, and other ships passing through.

The *Kyle* reported that she was proceeding north from 48 degrees, 34 minutes north, 44 degrees, 48 minutes, west, to continue her search.

On the afternoon of September 12, *Kyle* flashed the somber, though exciting news that she had located the wreckage of *Old Glory*,

100 miles north of the estimated position. There was little further
news from *Kyle* as to the possible fate of the crew until late in
the evening when a more detailed message was received from her.
They described hauling aboard a huge section of wing, made of
heavy box beams and ribs of wood, which was typical of Fokker
designs. It was fastened to a small part of the fuselage by four
bolts. No mention was made of identifying markings, but, the
message added sadly, that a thorough search of the area had turned
up no trace of either rubber boat or crew. Despite the news, the
wives and Mrs. Callaghan refused to give up hope. There was always
the possibility that, like Harry Hawker, they had been picked up by
a small, radio-less boat.

When the *Kyle* reached port, a few days later, she had aboard
a 34-foot section of wing together with three gas tanks. Portions
of the undercarriage were attached and the left wheel was intact.
A part of the instrument panel containing the gas gauges survived,
along with bits of feed pipes connected to the tanks. Experts
were astounded that so much of the wreckage had remained afloat
for five days. Reporters who examined the wreckage at Bay Roberts,
Newfoundland, said that the Stars and Stripes and a part of the
lettering were clearly discernible on the wing, and that there was
little doubt that it came from *Old Glory*. What was left of the
steel wing struts, which were 3 inches in diameter, were smashed
as if by an ax, and the ribs had been chewed to bits. The plywood
forming the covering of the wing was splintered, and the spruce
wood framing, 3½ by 2 inches, was snapped off like matchwood. It
had not been a gentle ditching.

The master of the *Kyle* said that the first sign that they were
closing in on something was when the ship sailed into a large
greenish field of lubricating oil. For fifteen minutes they cruised
slowly along the edge of the mass. Suddenly, a lookout shouted,
"Wreckage two points off the port bow!"

A boat was lowered and the salvage operation begun. The large
piece of wing containing the gas tanks was secured and hoisted
carefully to the deck, but not carefully enough. The tanks were full
when the wing was recovered from the water, but as it was being
hoisted aboard, the contents spilled out, and it was never determined
whether they were full of sea water or gasoline.

During the night, the *Kyle* continued its search, plowing in a
northeasterly direction in hopes of coming upon some trace of the

flyers in the rubber boat. They found nothing, only the endless swells of the dark ocean.

The next day a heavy fog rolled in and slowed their search. For 48 hours it lasted, then a shortage of fuel forced them back to port at Bay Roberts. A few days later *Kyle* sailed to St. John's, where the wreckage was transferred to the Red Cross boat *Nerissa* for the voyage to New York. From the looks of it, eyewitnesses at St. John's reported that *Old Glory* appeared to have hit the water at flying speed, head on, with a slight list to starboard. The cockpit was gone, except for the fuel gauges and a speaking tube, and there was no sign of the fuselage or tail assembly. Despite the findings, the families of the flyers clung tenaciously, and for weeks, to the belief that somehow they had managed to survive, but it was not to be. No trace of them was ever found.

In time, the wreckage was returned to New York, in a large, plain pine box, and it reposed for weeks in a warehouse of the New York *Daily Mirror*. Ultimately, the remains were moved to the Museum of West New York, New Jersey, where the left wheel of *Old Glory* may be seen to this day.

What really happened to her, we shall never know. The provable facts are scanty. It is known that Bertaud relieved Hill at the controls, 3½ hours after the take-off. It is also known that when she was seen by *California* 4 hours before her frantic SOS, she was well out over the Atlantic and flying normally; and it is assumed from the caliber of the radio messages that the inexperienced Payne was the operator during the last, fatal seconds. To this day, Hill's friend Harry Jones believes the disaster resulted indirectly from the failure to block test the Jupiter engine, and guesses that the direct cause was the faulty engine valves. Unanswered is the question of why Hill and Bertaud changed their minds and started over the ocean without landing in Newfoundland.

The tragedy affected us deeply at the beach, for we had come to feel that we knew the crew well. It was at this time that we added their names to our evening prayers, and even today, before going to sleep, I find myself saying, "and God bless the poor men who went down in the *Old Glory*."

7. At Harbor Grace's Bennett Field, *Sir John Carling* stood, filled to the brim with gas and ready to go. The debonair Irishman, Terrence Tully, and his navigator, James Metcalf,

were hosted in regal fashion by Mayor Casey and other prominent citizens while they waited for favorable weather over their route to Croydon Field, London. While they waited, they worked on their little Stinson, checking her from stem to stern. The inevitable group of curious onlookers peered at them and their ship; precocious children tried to sneak aboard for a look, only to be chased off good-naturedly by the ever-smiling Tully.

Finally, Tully announced that they would leave at 8 A.M. on Wednesday, September 7. That morning, they were up at 5 and breakfasted heartily; it would be a long time before their next hot meal. They left for the field at 7 A.M. already suited up in their heavy flying clothes. The news of the distress signal from the *Old Glory*, three hours before, was known to some in Harbor Grace, though it had been received too late for the morning paper. Care was taken to keep it from the pilots for fear of upsetting them, but to make sure they would keep an eye open for the stricken plane, a note was slipped into the map case so that they would find it as soon as they took off. What they would do if they came across *Old Glory* was another question, for *Sir John Carling* carried no radio equipment other than an emergency transmitter with a range of fifty miles.

There was the usual bustle of mechanics on and about the plane, which was ringed by a swarm of people. Last-minute supplies were loaded, while Tully and Metcalf exchanged last words with friends and members of the ground crew.

At last it was time to go. Tully stepped into the ship, followed closely by Metcalf. The engine was started and for nearly one half hour Tully warmed it up as intermittent roars burst from the powerful J-5. The crowd dispersed quickly, and took up positions on both sides of the runway. They were a quiet and tense crowd, many of them aware that *Old Glory* was down. Tully, at length satisfied with the sound of his engine taxied to the eastern end of the runway and headed into the wind. There was a moment of stillness as the plane sat with her engine idling; then the noise increased to a screaming wail and *Sir John Carling*, a little monoplane that was no bigger than Lindbergh's or Chamberlin's, started briskly down the field in front of a tornado of dust. At the half-way mark, the spectators were surprised to see her lift easily into the air and climb sharply to 500 feet. She banked and headed off on an easterly course toward the Atlantic. It was 8:25 A.M. When last seen by Newfoundlanders she was flying speedily to the east over Cape St. Francis, 30 miles from Harbor Grace, at an altitude of 2000 feet. After she disappeared from view most of the crowd at the field left quickly. Those who remained however were rewarded for four hours later another little Stinson "Detroiter," the blue *Royal Windsor*, flew in over the field. After circling once it settled to a soft landing, and taxied up to the hangar just vacated by *Sir John Carling*. They had completed a fast morning flight from Old Orchard Beach.

"Duke" Schiller and Phil Wood hopped out to be greeted by the mayor who had been given advance word of their arrival. He escorted them to town for some food, after which they retired to their hotel. They told reporters that they intended to leave for Windsor, England, as soon as the weather permitted. Like Tully and Metcalf, they were unaware when they landed of the fate of the *Old Glory*, which they had watched take off only yesterday. They were shocked and visibly depressed when told the news. At once they announced a change in their plans. They would postpone their own flight to make a search for the downed plane. Events during the next 24 hours would affect deeply their plans and hopes.

It was expected that *Sir John Carling's* flight to London would require at most 24 hours depending on the following winds, and it was expected that they would arrive at Croydon Field, London, around 2 P.M., London time, September 8. During the day, there were no reported sightings of the plane from ships at sea, but no one was surprised or disturbed as their course would lead them north of the heavily traveled ship lanes. The night also passed with no news.

In the morning, crowds streamed out to London's Croydon Field as the English prepared to welcome their second transatlantic flight. It was still too early to expect them but the crowd nevertheless was excited and eager.

The morning went by speedily as spectators amused themselves by watching the arrival and departure of commercial planes. The skies overhead were gray and a damp wind blew out of the west, which had a foreboding of rain. Two o'clock, the estimated time of arrival came. People scanned the horizon, not only to the west, but to the north and south as well for they remembered that *Pride of Detroit* had fooled them by sneaking in from the southern coast. They cocked their ears for the faint buzzing of an engine that would mean *Sir John Carling* was approaching. There was nothing. There was a murmur of excitement as a plane appeared out of the southwest, but as it came closer and glided down it turned out to be only a little DH biplane.

The day went on without a sign of that hoped-for speck in the distant sky that would tell them that the flyers were safe at last. What was more ominous, there were no reports of her from any point in the British Isles, though lookouts in Ireland, Wales, and even as far north as Scotland, had been alerted. Surely, the people thought, they should have been sighted somewhere by now. As the afternoon slipped by the weather worsened and rain began to fall. The visibility was reduced to a mile. Despair crept over the crowd as evening came, and there was still no word of *Sir John Carling*. The field lights were turned on and shone dully through the misty rain. A searchlight pointed its moving beam on the low clouds overhead and an empty silence hung over the damp and gloomy field.

At 11 P.M., her gasoline supply long since gone, *Sir John Carling* was reported, officially, as missing. Oddly, at the same time word was received in London that *Pride of Detroit* was long overdue in Bangkok on her flight from Rangoon. It was a saddened London that retired on that dreary, wet night. Fortunately, however, they awoke the next morning to learn that Brock and Schlee had bypassed the Siamese field and had landed safely at Hanoi. *Sir John Carling*, though, was still missing.

Mrs. Tully, in Windsor, Ontario, with her two children, was distraught, though friends tried to encourage her not to give up hope. They pointed out that the plane had a life raft aboard which was equipped with an emergency radio transmitter and the men might well be safe on the sea. It was also possible, they said, that they might have flown on to the continent and landed in some out-of-the way field.

Mrs. Patrick Tully, sister-in-law of the pilot, and a war widow, bubbled with confidence in Roscommon, Ireland, when questioned by reporters.

"They called him 'Wild Irish' Tully," she said, "and he's a marvelous flyer. I'm sure he's landed somewhere in Ireland!"

The ships at sea, including the S.S. *Republic*, already scouring the eastern Atlantic for *Old Glory* were notified at once of the latest tragedy, and widened their areas of search to look for *Sir John Carling*, too, but, despite an extensive and lengthy search by ships from all the maritime nations, the plane was never seen nor heard from again.

The Atlantic had claimed another victim, and the only clue she yielded as to the flyers' fate was days later. At a beach in Newquay, England, a 6-foot piece of wing, similar in color to the silvery-gray of *Sir John Carling*, and a piece of an airplane rudder, were washed ashore by the tide. It was impossible to establish definitely whether the wreckage came from the missing plane.

At the same time, oddly enough, other wreckage was picked up off the French coast. A fisherman claimed to have recovered a large yellow wing from the ocean, 250 miles off the Brittany coast, which was said to be from the *San Raphael*, but neither the fisherman nor the wing was ever presented for verification; and a week later some flotsam that looked like airplane wreckage floated ashore at Cape Gris Nez thought to be from *Oiseau Blanc*. It was a gruesome time, indeed, for transatlantic aviation.

At Harbor Grace, when it was learned that *Sir John Carling* was missing also, Schiller and Wood were disconsolate. They were determined to go and search for the two planes though Schiller admitted, in a variance of the old adage, that it would be "like looking for a needle in a 'bunch' of hay." Nevertheless they prepared *Royal Windsor* for the mission. Their sponsors in Windsor, Ontario, however, intervened. Along with the rest of the world they had been sickened by the "senseless" tragedies of recent weeks. They telegraphed the flyers suggesting that they give up the flight and followed up soon with another wire ordering them to do so. Schiller and Wood acquiesced reluctantly, but requested permission to hunt for *Old Glory*, and *Sir John Carling*. The Windsor syndicate refused them and ordered them back to the United States.

They were mindful, perhaps, of the fate of Captain Irwin, in his search for the missing Dole flyers. The flyers announced the cancellation of their plans at Harbor Grace, but at the same time disclosed they would return at once to New York to prepare for the non-stop race from New York to Spokane, Washington, scheduled to begin on September 21. For the record, *Royal Windsor* piloted by Schiller, started the race but never finished. She was forced down by motor trouble and later was severely damaged in a take-off accident at Lowry Field, Denver, Colorado. She never flew the ocean.

We at Old Orchard saw her once more, in mid-September, as she stopped briefly en route to Curtiss Field from Halifax, but she had lost her glamour and we barely took notice of her arrival and departure. The excitement and the sadness over the *Old Glory* had jaded us, and at an early age we had become worldly wise, aviation-wise that is. *Sic transit gloria.*

CHAPTER XII

September 1927

1. In September the passions of the world cooled slowly from the steaming readings at the time of the Sacco and Vanzetti executions, and though in Europe and America there were sporadic riots to protest their innocence, the fate of the two men was soon just a memory.

On the world scene, the recently retired Chinese Nationalist General, Chiang Kai-shek, announced his engagement in Japan to a young, Wellesley College (Massachusetts) graduate, Miss Meiling Soong, and preparations were begun for an early wedding in the city of Kobe. Premier Benito Mussolini and New York's Mayor Jimmy Walker got together in Rome, and the Duce spoke glowingly of "His Honor": "He is a man of great talent," Mussolini said, "young in looks and in spirit, and a practical idealist."

France welcomed the American Legion, but after a few days of celebration by the ex-servicemen Parisians were heard to say wearily, "Americans are all grown-up children!" The Soviet Union provided the international eyebrow-lifting of the month when Leon Trotsky was ousted from the Communist Internationale after a dispute with Joseph Stalin. Said Trotsky, "Bureaucratic discipline, founded on false political precepts, offers no weapon for unity—only disorganization."

At home, Al Smith gained support in his quest for the 1928 Democratic presidential nomination, while Herbert Hoover and Charles Evans Hughes were mentioned most often as Republican standard bearers. Wayne B. Wheeler, the National Prohibition Administrator, died, but the event gave no hint of relief to opponents of the 18th Ammendment. Erwin M. Griswold of Harvard's *Law Review*, announced the election of honor students, Alger Hiss, Abraham Feller, and Lee Pressman, to its editorial board. There was a sharp attack on cigarette smoking by the medical profession. Doctors offered statistics to prove that 60 percent of the babies born of cigarette-smoking mothers died of nicotine poisoning before reaching the age of two!

The entertainment world mourned the death of dancer Isadora Duncan in a motor accident. Thousands of New Yorkers enjoyed the music of Paul Whiteman's orchestra at New York's Paramount Theatre. Theatergoers were thrilled by the performance of young Muni Weisenfreund (Paul Muni) who starred in only his second English-speaking role in *Four Walls* at the John Golden Theatre. Ed Wynn opened at the Apollo Theatre on 42nd Street in one of his happiest musical comedy hits, *Manhattan Mary*.

In sports, Gene Tunney retained his heavyweight boxing title by surviving the "long count" before a crowd of 105,000 at Chicago's Soldiers Field in his bout with Jack Dempsey. The United States Davis Cup team lost the challenge round to France's "Four Musketeers," Lacoste, Cochet, Borotra, and Brugnon, but the nation was recompensed when Tommy Hitchcock led America's polo team to a victory over Great Britain for the International Cup.

The weather was unusually warm in the East and the heat was not lessened by the controversy that followed the stream of aviation tragedies of the past summer.

2. It was only natural after *San Raphael, Old Glory*, and *Sir John Carling* disappeared within eight days, that the rising resentment against ocean flying should erupt into loud and angry protests. Government leaders, editors, and private citizens thoughout Western civilization rose up in their wrath. The losses of Noel Davis, Wooster, Nungesser and Coli were recalled along with the missing Dole Race flyers and Paul Redfern, now being sought in the Brazilian jungles. The "near misses" were remembered also: Fonck in 1926, Commander Byrd, *Bremen* and *Europa*, Givon's *Blue Bird*, and Courtney's *Whale*. Was it all worth the loss of fine pilots and expensive machines, they asked, and where was it all leading to? Even now, Brock and Schlee were in Tokyo, preparing for a hazardous flight across the Pacific, and *Royal Windsor* at Harbor Grace, Fonck at Roosevelt Field, and Koennecke, Udet, Coste, McIntosh, and Tarascon in Europe were poised for a late autumn try at the stormy Atlantic.

Léon Givon, in *Oiseau Bleu*, awaited again favorable weather for his new attempt, and, of course, there was always the un-predictable Charles A. Levine, at Cranwell Airdrome, who was de-termined to be the first to make a successful eastbound crossing.

The newspapers were filled suddenly with cartoons of Poseidon-like characters emerging from rough seas to pluck tiny airplanes from stormy skies. Editorial writers referred to ocean hops as "Death Flights."

IT IS TIME TO HALT THE FOOLHARDY, cried the Brooklyn *Eagle*, and Chicago's *Evening Post* appeared with a banner headline, LET US HAVE AN AVIATION HOLIDAY!

Many campaigned for congressional legislation, but the Newark *Evening News* commented with restraint, "Hasty legislation dictated by hysteria is unwise."

President Coolidge was drawn into the fray. He doubted the "efficacy" of legislation, and said that any limitation on the flights must be wholly voluntary. Nevertheless, the strong protests con-tinued both here and abroad.

In England, King George V put himself on record as disapproving further ocean flights. Curiously, he was joined by veteran long-distance flyer Sir Alan Cobham, who said, "There is no scientific value [to them] that is commensurate with the loss of life of skilled airmen."

Lord Thompson, the former British Air Secretary, criticized the emulation of the flights.

He said, "If it's been done, why do it again?"

Sir Sexton Branches, a vice air marshal, took the other side. He pointed out that the English Channel was flown, first in 1908, and added, "Now, we buzz it every day." Prophetically, he predicted that it would be the same with the Atlantic.

The French government took a position short of a legislative ban, saying, "The government would prefer no further efforts to fly the Atlantic."

In Canada, the Air Board said that it would ask for special powers from Parliament "to prevent suicide in the air," while, in Australia, the government decreed a limitation: "No aircraft," the edict said, "except seaplanes, flying boats and amphibians, will, in the future, be permitted to be used in sea flights of more than fifty miles."

The matter was the subject of widespread debate in the United States. Pressures were put on President Coolidge to institute an investigation, with an eye to developing practical recommendations for governmental supervision. However, Coolidge remained firm in his stand against any form of legislative intervention, saying, "It might have the effect of throttling the development of aviation."

Secretary of Commerce Herbert Hoover sided with his chief, when he said, "Though aviation is perilous, I do not believe we should attempt to stifle the spirit of youth."

F. Trubee Davison, the Secretary of War for Air, said, on the other hand, that he opposed further ocean flights at this time because the aircraft were not up to combatting the weather that they had to face.

"However," Davison added, "the day will come."

The Department of Commerce's Director of the Bureau of Aeronautics, William P. MacCracken, Jr., who would be charged with the administration of any legislative limitations, commented, "The Department will be glad to assume such regulatory powers as Congress may wish to confer on it—but it will not end the loss of life in these pioneering enterprises."

Harry Guggenheim, president of the Daniel Guggenheim Fund for the promotion of aviation, tried hard to get to the heart of the matter.

"Stunt flights," he said, "and the men who back them financially for the sake of publicity, should not be countenanced. By stunt flights, I mean any flight that does nothing for the advancement of aviation. A flight that merely accomplishes what another flight has done, with the same or inferior equipment, is a stunt flight."

The first flyers to make the Atlantic crossing jumped to the defense of the aviators, to stifle any possible legislative action.

Lindbergh stated reasonably: "To totally restrict hazardous flights would be placing a ban on scientific progress. The flight of the Wright brothers was more dangerous than flying is today. Hazardous flights should not be prohibited, but they should be attempted only after careful study, by experienced personnel, with the best modern equipment, and for a scientific purpose."

Chamberlin said flatly: "I am against government regulation, suggested by well-meaning, but ill-advised people; it will retard the advancement of aviation."

Byrd phrased his comments guardedly: "The situation is well in hand now through the airing of public opinion." He went on: "Newspapers, which have so particularly helped aviation, are now the means of curbing the pioneer flights, and, thus, preventing more tragedies."

The debate continued for weeks. The calls for federal legislation grew louder, but the government turned a deaf ear and declined to interfere with one notable exception.

On September 9, Acting Secretary of the Navy Theodore Douglas Robinson, addressed a letter, "My dear Captain," to René Fonck at Roosevelt Field. It went on to say, that after mature consideration, the Secretary, on behalf of the Navy Department, had decided to cancel the leaves of Lieutenant Curtin and Ensign Edwards, thus necessitating their withdrawal as members of Fonck's crew. Furthermore, Robinson, in his letter, outlined limitations on ocean flying by U. S. Navy personnel. Henceforth, they would be permitted to take part in ocean flights only when they were made in seaplanes. Though Fonck continued for a short time to test *Ville de Paris* at Roosevelt, he was forced soon to give up his plans.

At a luncheon, given at New York's Ritz-Carlton Hotel, the French war ace told the gathering gallantly, "Being a soldier, I could not ignore the attitude of the Navy Department."

For a time, he toyed with the idea of using *Ville de Paris* as a passenger plane. He planned to fly six passengers from New York to San Francisco in 22 hours, at the fare of $1000 per person—the fare to include three meals and a berth. Curtin and Edwards were regranted their leaves for the trip, but public interest did not materialize, and the idea was dropped. Ultimately *Ville de Paris* was dismantled and stored away in crates, while Fonck, in October, sailed home to his native Paris. He would never try again.

The world-wide protest had an effect on other crews and their backers, too. It was the same in Europe, as flight after flight was canceled or postponed until spring. In the face of a threatened government ban, the trips of the Junkers' land planes, *Europa* and *Bremen* were deferred and their crews scattered quickly with the exception of Captain Loose, and later, Johann "Bear" Risticz, who joined the tri-motored seaplane, D-1230, which was then preparing for an Atlantic crossing via the Azores.

Ernst Udet did not drop out at once, but continued to prepare the Rohrsbach flying boat. The combination of public pressure and a crash-landing in Copenhagen's harbor on September 28 forced him to quit a few days thereafter. In France, Coste and Le Brix, after playing with the thought of a crossing to New York by the southern route, abandoned the plan on September 29, to prepare for their illustrious flight over the South Atlantic to Buenos Aires.

Tango Bird dropped out of the running on September 10, after her long summer of testing. Tarascon said simply, "The weather is too miserable. I would not think of trying to cross the ocean under these conditions." He added decisively, "The American Navy is quite right!"

Poor Léon Givon, who, with Pierre Corbu, had been trying to get *Oiseau Bleu* off again, had more troubles. The French press, prior to the outcries against ocean flying, had taken editorial swipes at him—first, for not leaving sooner, and, after his take-off, for giving up the flight too soon. The bad press made him somewhat of a scapegoat for the French failures of the summer, and one evening, as he returned to his hotel from the field, he was set upon by a group of jeering thugs. In the fight, he was hurt, seriously enough to force him to drop out, and the Farman brothers soon withdrew the plane.

The English plane *Whale*, down in Coruña, Spain after an attempt to reach the Azores, became a casualty of pressures from the British public. Lord Thompson roused feelings with a fiery statement that "Something must be done to end this mass suicide," though he qualified it somewhat by adding that, for the time, he was against legislation. Courtney, aware of the temper of his people, and deluged with pleading wires from home to quit, dropped out on September 11 and returned to England. He would come back next summer and achieve a partial success.

Early in September, the cities of Boston and Philadelphia withdrew their $25,000 prize offers, in the wake of the public outcry against stunt flights, and though Cleveland's offer still stood, Koennecke of the *Germania* saw the handwriting on the wall.

He called in the press and said, "I have definitely and finally given up the idea of a transatlantic flight." He added that he now planned a flight to the east for *Germania* which would terminate, he hoped, in San Francisco.

On September 20 he took off from Cologne on the first leg of his trip. Eighteen hours later, Germans heard the thrilling news that he had landed safely in Angora, Turkey. He continued on, a few days thereafter, to Baghdad, and, by stages, reached Karachi, India, in late October. Unfortunately, his hopes were dashed when, on a flight from Karachi to Allahabad, India, on November 6, he was forced down 177 miles short of his goal, in the little town of Etahwah. During the forced landing, the tail assembly on his plane was demolished, and it was there that the attempt was given up. The expedition by now was without funds, and Koennecke himself was seriously ill. With the aid of German Consular officials, the crew, at length, returned home. Captain Koennecke did not try again.

By the middle of September, in Europe, the number of flights waiting to go had been reduced drastically. It is conceivable that some of the crews, fearing the autumn weather over the Atlantic, and lacking confidence in their planes, welcomed the public outburst, for it gave them an honorable means of quitting. In any event, only Captain McIntosh, in *Princess Xenia*, remained in the running for the North Atlantic, while the two German seaplanes, "Fritz" Loose's Junkers, and Horst Merz's Heinkel seaplane, D-1220, were poised to fly to New York by way of the Azores.

3. The relationship between Charles Levine and his new pilot, Hinchliffe, during the first days of September were surprisingly harmonious. The tall, suave Britisher and the volatile American agreed, at first, on everything.

"No," they had chorused. "If *San Raphael* is successful, we will not try the Atlantic, but, in all probability, will fly to the east."

When it was learned that *San Raphael* was lost, they waited beside their loaded plane at Cranwell for favorable winds. There was a flurry of comment on September 5 when Levine announced that he might take the well-known aviatrix and heiress, Mabel Ball, along as a passenger. Mrs. Levine was told of the idea as she boarded the *Ile de France* in Southampton for the trip home.

"No he will not!" she said firmly, before disappearing into her stateroom.

On September 6, both flyers arrived at the R.A.F. field at 6 A.M., dressed in flying suits, apparently ready to leave. *Columbia* was pushed out of her hangar and what appeared to be last-minute preparations were started, as mechanics swarmed over the little plane. At 8 A.M., however, with a small crowd standing around waiting, the flight was postponed until the next day. On September 7, it was put off once more at the last minute with Levine making the announcement while Hinchcliffe stood by with his mustache twitching perceptibly. It was obvious that the pilot was tired of waiting.

The weather over the ocean was bad, and the Air Ministry meteorological office suggested that he postpone his flight until May. On September 11, Levine told reporters that he was definitely out, as far as an Atlantic crossing was concerned, but that he and Hinchcliffe would depart soon on a non-stop flight to the east. The long-suffering Hinchcliffe still said nothing.

Mrs. Levine, in the meanwhile, had returned home to New York, and now enlisted the aid of her family to get her husband to return to the United States by ship. His nineteen-year-old daughter, Eloise, sent him a touching note saying, "Daddy, please come home on the *Leviathan*."

Levine, in London, gave no evidence of heeding, but neither as the days drifted by did he give any indication that he was about to fly east. Finally, Hinchcliffe, his British reserve tested sorely by the delays, was able to get Levine to agree to a take-off for Karachi, India, on September 17. "Doc" Kinkaid, about to return to the United States on the *President Roosevelt*, gave a last overhaul to the J-5 motor, while John Carisi attended to the rest of the plane and oversaw her fueling. Levine announced an 8 A.M. departure. Both men were up at 4 A.M. Levine breakfasted heartily, but for some reason decided then to return to his bed. Hinchcliffe, his reserve now completely overdrawn, raced to Levine's room; routed him out of bed, and dragged him to Cranwell. They looked over the plane. Suddenly, Levine had disappeared, leaving word with attendants that he had to pack. The hours passed, and there was no sign of the unpredictable American. The staid Hinchcliffe exploded, at last.

He told the reporters who stood by, "Levine is packing his toothbrush, and making sure that each bristle is straight!"

At last, Levine returned, bag in hand. He looked at the field and told Hinchcliffe that it was too wet for a take-off.

Hinchcliffe retorted hotly, "Poppycock! And besides, we have a perfect take-off wind!"

Levine would not be pressured, and a violent argument broke out between the two men, which lasted intermittently for four hours. At one point, the loyal Carisi ruffled the already-snarled feathers of Hinchcliffe, and the Englishman started after the ground crew chief, with his fists up. Calmer heads separated them before any serious damage was done. By the time the battle waned, the wind did likewise, and the flight was put off once more. The crowd wended its way home after an exciting day. When he regained his aplomb, Hinchcliffe faced the reporters and explained patiently that Levine had ordered the postponement because of "personal business." As the British press began to chide Levine, "Doc" Kinkaid took his side. As he boarded the *President Roosevelt*, he said, "Levine is as square a proposition as I've ever seen in aviation," but, at this point, it would take a lot more to return Levine to the affections of the British.

If Hinchcliffe was angered by Levine's previous didoes, it was nothing compared to his rage on September 19 when he arrived at Cranwell Airdrome hoping to leave, only to find that his employer had left, himself, on a trip to Paris.

"Look at the weather today," he shouted to reporters. "If he doesn't go by Thursday, the 22nd, the SOB will get himself a new pilot!" This was no idle threat, for Hinchcliffe's leave from the airline was coming to a close.

In Paris, Levine encountered more trouble. He arrived as usual without passport, health clearance, or identification papers. Authorities, by now familiar with his unorthodoxies sped him protestingly vigorously to Police Headquarters where there ensued a three-hour bilingual harangue. Levine took loud exception to his treatment, in English, while the authorities defended their laws with equal vehemence in French. According to bystanders it was a noisy affair.

Finally, no doubt to get rid of him once and for all, Levine was released provided he return at once to London. This he did and when greeted by British reporters at Croydon, explained that he had been in Paris regarding his plans to build a 50-passenger airship to fly the Atlantic.

At the same time, he announced that he hoped to be off in *Columbia* on September 21. So did the R.A.F. personnel at Cranwell. To a man they felt that the colorful Levine had worn out his welcome.

Charlie took no cognizance of the furor that was building up around him. By now, he was used to it. It was his airplane, he reasoned, and he'd leave only when it suited him.

At last, on September 24, both flyers appeared at Cranwell at the crack of dawn. There was only a handful of spectators at the field, as a flight over land to the east apparently did not have the same appeal as a long ocean trip. Most of them were curious to see Hinchcliffe and Levine, about whom they had read so much of late.

The plane was taken from the hangar at 7:30. She had been ready and fully fueled for many days, and there was little left to do to her. Levine, dressed in his fancy white flying suit, chatted pleasantly with the few reporters present for the take-off. Hinchcliffe, tall and distinguished, with a patch covering his missing left eye, climbed into the cockpit. The engine was started and warmed for minutes, while the faithful Carisi listened to its "music" with a critical ear. Levine jumped in, after shaking hands with Carisi and everyone else in the vicinity. He was smiling and excited.

Columbia roared down the runway with Hinchcliffe at the controls, and took to the air at 8:06 A.M., headed for India. Their troubles began within the hour. Hinchcliffe found that the plane was making only 85 miles an hour, far below its normal level, with the throttle at the cruise setting.

Levine blamed it on an inefficient propeller, and cursed Carisi who remained safely at Cranwell. During the day, as they flew over Western Europe, trouble developed in the feed line and with the fuel pump, and it became necessary for Levine to pump gas manually into the engine. This time it was Kinkaid who was the target of Levine's wrath, as perspiration poured off his brow. To add to their woes, the weather worsened as the afternoon wore on. The combination of lack of speed, faulty fueling system, and bad weather made it obvious to both men that they could not go on much farther.

At 6 P.M., they circled Vienna's Aspern Airport, after having flown 900 miles in ten hours. Despite bad local weather, Hinchcliffe, the "Storm Wizard," was able to bring *Columbia* in safely.

Levine leaped out of the plane, smiling, and said, "Well, here I am again!"

They were driven into town to spend the night, but, before leaving, Levine announced that he would take off the next day, either for Venice to attend the Schneider Cup Air Races, or for Belgrade, where he had an appointment to discuss the sale of his proposed airplane to the Yugoslav army.

At Belle Harbor, Long Island, Grace Nova Levine breathed a sigh of relief, when the news arrived of his safe landing.

"I hope he'll come home now," she prayed, but her husband had yet a couple of stops to make before he would consider his summer complete.

Columbia took off bright and early the next day, and headed for Venice. Overnight mechanics at the field cleared the feed lines, and the trip was made without incident. Levine, who could be ingratiating when he desired, was at his charming best during his stay, and was the toast of the city—then crowded with aviation people, in for the famed international air competition.

On September 26, he attended the races, won by a sleek, low-winged Supermarine seaplane from Great Britain, which covered the 217-mile course at an average speed of 281 miles an hour!

Then it was off for Rome for Hinchcliffe and Levine on October 1, where again Levine was the center of attention. The now-affable American accepted the plaudits of the Romans with smiles and becoming modesty. On October 3, he had an audience with Pope Pius XI at the Vatican. He dutifully kissed the Pope's ring when it was offered, and admitted, after the meeting, that for the first time in his life he had been struck speechless.

On the day after, there came the crowning achievement of his rollicking summer. He met his long-time idol Benito Mussolini at the Palazio Venezia. After a visit with Il Duce that lasted well over an hour, Levine emerged with stars in his eyes. He spoke glowingly and proudly of the Italian Premier as being "The greatest statesman in the world at present."

The bad came to Levine with the good, however. The same afternoon, on a flight in *Columbia* with Hinchcliffe and Prince Louis of Orléans, the engine sputtered and stopped, soon after take-off. Desperately, Hinchcliffe tried to glide back into Ciampino, but he fell short by a mile. The plane crash-landed in a rough field, the landing gear buckled and she nosed over. The three men scrambled out, unhurt, but were forced to walk back to the airfield for assistance.

There was nothing that could be done for the ship for the damage was so severe that her European flying for 1927 was at an end. She was carefully packed and returned by ship to the United States, but she was not finished. Under new ownership, *Columbia* flew the Atlantic again in another year, from Newfoundland to the Scilly Isles, off England. She then retired and was returned to her maker, Giuseppe Bellanca, to rest peacefully in his new factory at Newcastle, Delaware. There her gallant life came to an end as violently as it was lived in a roaring hangar fire.

Levine left Rome by commercial airline, but not before he made one final gesture to his friend and hero, Mussolini. As his plane flew over the Eternal City, he dropped a watch by parachute for the Premier's new-born son, Romano, and then at last started on his way home.

Hinchcliffe returned to England and to Imperial Airlines, but, sad to say, he perished in the springtime trying to fly a plane, westbound, over the Atlantic.

As he boarded the *Leviathan* Levine was asked about the kind of welcome he expected in New York.

With aplomb he replied, "Any arrangements Mayor Walker may make are O.K. with me."

The mayor did not let him down, for, on Sunday, October 16, he was met on his arrival by the dapper, homburged Grover Whalen with a carnation in his buttonhole. He was later taken in a motorcade up Broadway to City Hall, under a storm of tickertape. Thousands heard the mayor extol his virtues. Afterward, there was a parade up Fifth Avenue, and then to the Hotel Astor, where he, his wife, and daughter, Eloise, were the guests of honor at a luncheon.

U. S. Representative Hamilton Fish presided, and in his remarks, spoke glowingly of the dapper little flyer.

"He typifies courage"; he orated, "one hundred percent, unadulterated courage. He represents what the Jewish people have been doing right down through their history."

The weeks that followed were exciting ones for Levine, as he was wined, dined, and praised by his fellow New Yorkers. It had been quite a summer for the little man from Brooklyn. He had flaunted himself, along with his toy, *Columbia*, throughout western civilization. He had outraged nations, not to speak of his family. He was called incorrigible, stubborn, contrary, and often, insane, but his courage nobody could ever question; secretly, perhaps, he was a breath of fresh air even to his severest critics, and he must have had fun!

4. In early autumn, *Princess Xenia* remained the only land plane in Europe still waiting for a try at the North Atlantic. Throughout the summer months the big blue-bodied Fokker with the brown wings, had been tested thoroughly on flights from the airdrome outside of Bristol, England, and now, in September, awaited a 233-mile trip to Baldonnel Airdrome, outside of Dublin, from where she would take off in quest of Philadelphia's $25,000 prize.

Her crew had watched *San Raphael* leave their midst for Upavon. Her flights continued, oftentimes piloted by Captain Piercy, who though no longer a member of the crew, remained on because of his experience as a knowledgeable aviator.

On September 4, Captain McIntosh and Captain Wreford, the original backer scheduled to accompany McIntosh, stood outside *Princess Xenia*'s hangar at the field. With them were Captain and Mrs. Piercy. They were joined by Mr. Leeds, the American, who had recently supplied the expedition with much-needed financial help. There were also newspapermen. Naturally, the conversation turned to the fate of *Princess Xenia's* sister ship *San Raphael,* then long overdue on the way to Ottawa, and presumed lost, and to the effect that her fate would have on their own flight.

McIntosh was adamant that the flight should go on regardless, and his crew stood solidly behind him despite the protests that were then prevalent in England. As if to prove his point, McIntosh, the veteran Imperial Airways pilot, announced that they would leave for Ireland that afternoon, with a departure for Philadelphia scheduled, tentatively, 48 hours later.

As they stood around, the little group of flyers talked about the latest bottled message from Nungesser, which the papers said had been picked up on the Nova Scotian coastline. It had said according to reports, "We landed 20 miles off Sable Island." They shook their heads with despair, saddened by the pleasures humans get from another's woe.

McIntosh turned to the reporters and told them that he intended to race *Columbia* to the United States and would leave Baldonnel at the first sign of passable weather.

At 3 P.M., the big plane was wheeled from her hangar and the Jupiter engine started. McIntosh pulled himself into the cockpit, followed by Captain Piercy. Mrs. Piercy and Wreford sat in the rear compartment. At 3:45 *Princess Xenia* started down the runway, lifted off easily and faded in the western sky. Two hours and thirty-five minutes later, she circled low over the city of Dublin while Dubliners strolling on St. Stephen's Green and O'Connell Street stared up to see what was making the howling noise. The mighty blue plane turned to the southwest and landed at Baldonnel, 12 miles away, at the foot of the Dublin Mountains. Soon, she was safe in her hangar, and her crew quartered snugly in the Gresham Hotel.

The weather and the loss of *Old Glory* and *Sir John Carling* delayed them for several days. Messages swamped them from the entire British Isles, advising the flyers to give up the flight, at least until next summer. The reasoning was that two Fokker, single-engined planes had gone down within a week, and people thought it would be more prudent if they waited until a multi-engined plane, or a seaplane were available.

McIntosh, however, was oblivious to the advice and pleas. He felt that he had a fine airplane, and it made no difference to him when Philadelphia, their destination, canceled out on their $25,000 prize offer in the wake of the recent disasters. He said he would go there regardless.

He made one concession toward safety. On September 10, he replaced young Captain Wreford, with an Irish military aviator of renown, Major James C. Fitzmaurice. McIntosh felt that an experienced pilot would be of greater assistance on such an arduous flight, than a veteran land soldier, and would thus give *Princess Xenia* a better chance at success. When Wreford was told he was incensed for he had given all of his time and most of his money to the venture. He vowed publicly that McIntosh would not replace him with such dispatch, but, in fact, the young nephew of Britain's Home Secretary was finished. The newspaper stories said that "he had withdrawn because of war wounds."

Fitzmaurice, a handsome Irishman, became a familiar figure to the crowds who visited *Princess Xenia* during her stay at Baldonnel. He appeared always immaculately groomed in his tan Army uniform, Sam Browne belt, and polished leather knee boots. He joined McIntosh on September 11 on a long test flight which took them to Belfast, to Scotland, and back to Baldonnel. It was pouring rain and the ceiling was low when the plane appeared out of the northeast late in the day. She jockeyed in under the low clouds and glided in to a soft landing. Both pilots expressed enthusiasm over the plane's performance and talked optimistically, even cockily, about the pending trip to America.

They waited for the weather from the 12th to the 15th, during which time they suffered editorial abuse for their refusal to quit. Fitzmaurice was a daily target of Dublin's papers for his part in the venture, and both flyers became edgy and impatient to leave. The public pressure on top of the suspense was beginning to tell.

On September 16, though a layer of low cloud hung overhead and the visibility was so poor that the end of the runway was shrouded in mist, they could wait no longer, and decided to take off at once. Workmen had finished lengthening the take-off strip, and had removed the stone wall which marked the end of the old field.

In the morning, McIntosh ordered the ship loaded and 720 gallons of gasoline, sufficient for 41 hours of flight, were poured into the wing and fuselage tanks from large steel casks. They would not carry a radio, but aboard was the usual safety equipment—Very pistols, an inflatable boat with oars and flares—all tucked snugly into the empty cabin aft of the fuselage tanks.

Since the decision to leave was made suddenly and without fanfare there were few spectators at the field. Less than 200, mostly Irish air officers, members of the press, and friends and families of the flyers, watched, as *Princess Xenia* was wheeled from her hangar and groomed for the trip. Major Fitzmaurice's wife and five-year-old daughter drove up before noon after being told by him that this was the day. At 12:30, *Princess Xenia*, the last of the single-engined Fokker sisters, was towed to the leeward end of the field, and faced down the mile-long runway. There was a smell of rain to the air, and the mists gave the surrounding countryside an eerie, pale look. A damp wind blew from the west. At 1 P.M., a mechanic climbed into the cockpit, and sat behind the controls. Another stood on a ladder, and turned the starting crank. The propeller jerked and then spun into action, as clouds of thick smoke emitted from the exhaust.

Another member of the ground crew ran up to the plane clutching a carton containing the provisions for the flight—sandwiches, fruit, and tinned meat. Fitzmaurice, muffled up in leather flying clothes, talked to his little family. He showed them a letter from the recently elected Prime Minister, William Thomas Cosgrave, that he was taking along. McIntosh talked for a minute to Captain Piercy and Mrs. Piercy, while *Xenia*'s engine was warming up. He turned suddenly, waved "Cheerio," and exchanged places with the mechanic in the cockpit. After the mechanic had dropped to the ground, Fitzmaurice picked up his little daughter, and kissed her tenderly. He put her down, and embraced his wife. He ran to the plane and wriggled up through the little hatch into the seat alongside McIntosh.

Reporters noted McIntosh's last statement, of, "With luck, we'll do it."

The Jupiter engine roared deafeningly and the plane moved down the runway. It gained speed quickly, which was surprising to the bystanders. Less than one-half way down, *Xenia* rose into the air, and continued west toward the Galway coast. She was accompanied by an Irish military plane which had taken off minutes before. The time was 1:36 P.M.

At 4:20 P.M., *Princess Xenia* was seen over the Aran Islands, in Galway Bay, flying slowly at 1000 feet. The military plane had been forced back an hour before by the increasing head winds.

After leaving the Aran Islands, *Princess Xenia* plunged into an area of turbulent, swirling clouds, and heavy rains. The 40-mile-an-hour winds slowed her forward speed to barely 60 miles an hour. McIntosh and Fitzmaurice struggled with the bucking airplane as she flew through the stormy skies. They tried to climb above the fierce

weather hoping for a better wind slant, but it was useless. The cloud
bank rose endlessly and the head winds, if anything, grew stronger.
McIntosh then pointed *Xenia's* nose down. At 100 feet, he broke
out into the clear. Below, was a gray and angry ocean. Still lower,
he dropped, until the waves were but thirty feet under the plane, and
the spray from the huge rollers rained on the bottom of the fuselage.

The flyers looked out of the cockpit window on the dark, stormy
scene. The waves passed by them with a tantalizing slowness. *Princess
Xenia* was barely making headway into the teeth of the freshening
gale. Above them was a menacing layer of stratus cloud.

For another hour they battled the elements as the rough air
bounced *Princess Xenia* and her two pilots around without mercy. At
5:30 P.M. McIntosh shook his head sadly at Fitzmaurice alongside him. He couldn't make himself heard over the din of the whin-
ing motor, and he pointed his finger listlessly back toward shore.
Fitzmaurice understood and nodded. It was suicidal for them to continue against these winds, and in the present weather. McIntosh
turned the ship around, while Fitzmaurice moved back, and opened
the dump valve in order to lighten the ship.

The wind was behind them now, and the waves streaked by underneath. The air speed indicator needle reached a peak of 155 miles
an hour, as *Princess Xenia* fled back toward the Irish coast. At
6:20 P.M., the coastline appeared in front of them, together with a
group of small islands. Fitzmaurice identified them as the Mutton
Islands, off County Clare. He clambered back again and emptied
another gas tank, so as to be as light as possible for the landing.
McIntosh dropped the plane once more to 50 feet, while they circled
over the Kerry and Clare coasts, looking for a likely spot to set down.
The rain fell in torrents and the wind whistled still out of the
west. The ceiling lifted slightly, enabling them to ascend to 150
feet and for an hour they circled seeking the refuge of a smooth
field. Bits of low cloud swept over the ship, from time to time, like
puffs of smoke, and blotted out the flyers' vision momentarily. Suddenly, the land and ocean would reappear as if a curtain had been
drawn. At 7:20 P.M. McIntosh caught sight of a beach off his
left wingtip as he banked over the ocean. It was ringed with high
cliffs, but he felt that it would be suitable for a landing. He pointed
Princess Xenia into the wind and glided quickly down from the bleak
skies to touch down on the hard sands of Beale Strand, Ballybunnion,
a beach close to the mouth of the Shannon River in County Kerry,

and 160 miles southwest of Dublin. It was 7:30 P.M. and the flyers had been in the air for six hours.

After a night's rest, Captain McIntosh rushed back to Dublin to announce that despite the failure, *Princess Xenia* would try again as soon as she could be overhauled and made ready. Captain Piercy was dispatched to Ballybunnion, and, with Major Fitzmaurice, flew the plane back to Baldonnel on September 18. It was said that the plane would take off again for Philadelphia within 48 hours but the take-off never took place. Whether the flyers had second thoughts about venturing over the fearsome Atlantic once more or whether they were persuaded finally by public opinion, is not known.

Ultimately, *Princess Xenia* was flown to Upavon Airdrome. On November 14, with Australian flyer Bert Hinkler as the crew replacement for Fitzmaurice, McIntosh took off on a flight to Karachi, India, in an effort to break Chamberlin and Levine's non-stop, distance record. Nothing was heard from *Princess Xenia* for three days, and there was deep anxiety over her safety, though hopes were expressed that as they were flying over land, there was a good chance that they had made it down safely in some isolated community. And so it was, for, on November 18, it was learned that *Princess Xenia* had crash-landed days before, near Lemberg, Poland. The big Fokker had also come a cropper, though her fate was not as severe as that of her sisters. Mechanics of the 6th Polish Air Regiment patched her up as best they could, but her flying was over for 1927.

She was rebuilt during the winter, and in 1928 she regained some prestige, when, with the Duchess of Bedford aboard, she made a spectacular, round-trip flight from England to India, and back.

There was much in store, too, for Major Fitzmaurice, for in the spring of 1928 he would join Captain Koehl and Baron Von Huenefeld aboard Dr. Junkers's famed *Bremen* for the first successful, non-stop flight across the Atlantic from east to west.

5. Princess Lowenstein-Wertheim, though the first, was not the only member of the fair sex to attempt an Atlantic hop during 1927. Strangely enough, at the height of the controversy over the "death flights," two American candidates remained in the running. They were both women, vying to be the first of their sex to make the flight: Mrs. Frances Wilson Grayson in her Sikorsky-built amphibian, *Dawn,* and lovely Ruth Elder in her Stinson "Detroiter," *American Girl.*

Both were at Roosevelt Field preparing feverishly for their trips, despite unending pressure on them from women's groups throughout the country to quit. The female lobby so alarmed Mr. J. J. Lannin, the owner of Roosevelt Field, that he issued his own set of ocean flight restrictions for those who wished to take off from his field:

1. The plane had to be multi-engined
2. It had to be able to land on sea and land
3. It had to carry a navigator, a radio, and pass government inspection

Whereas the amphibian *Dawn* met all these requirements, Miss Elder's plane did not, but the attractive young aviatrix used her charms well and the restrictions were waived for her by Lannin within twenty-fours after they had been imposed.

Mrs. Grayson, the first to announce her intentions, was a wealthy New York real estate operator in her mid-thirties.

She was born in Arkansas, and on the death of her mother moved with her father and brother to Muncie, Indiana, where she was raised. She was a precocious child, with an aptitude for music, and upon her graduation from high school she was sent to the Chicago Musical College to study piano. Music was not enough for this ambitious girl and soon she had transferred to Swarthmore College for a special course in recitation and dramatic art. While there, she met and married John Brady Grayson, twenty years her senior, and a cousin of Admiral Cary T. Grayson, Woodrow Wilson's personal physician. They lived happily for a time in Warrenton, Virginia, where he was the Postmaster, but the life of a country wife finally palled on her. She divorced Grayson in 1923, and moved to New York where she was first employed by a newspaper syndicate. Thereafter, she turned to real estate and in four years had amassed a fortune, estimated at more than four million dollars.

During her spare time in New York, she became interested in aviation and her interest led her to an acquaintanceship with Igor Sikorsky. He gave her flying instruction, and though she had never soloed she was entirely familiar with the operation of an airplane.

In May, as a result of Lindbergh's hop, she was bitten by the ocean flying bug and turned her boundless energies and ample resources to becoming the first woman to fly the Atlantic. She consulted her friend Sikorsky, and made a down-payment on a twin-engined amphibian which would be the first of its kind to make the attempt. Work began on it at once at Sikorsky's College Point factory.

In due time Sikorsky arranged for a meeting between Mrs. Grayson and Mrs. Ange Ancker, a wealthy, Aiken, South Carolina, sportswoman, and a daughter of Pittsburgh steel magnate, Charles H. Sang. The meeting took place next to the information booth in airy Pennsylvania Station, New York. There were a battery of lawyers present, and, as a result of the conference, the Ancker-Grayson Aircraft Corporation was formed, with each party contributing $20,000 of capital. When asked if the new company had other purposes besides the Atlantic flight, both were non-committal.

"That is a long way in the future," said Mrs. Grayson when a reporter suggested the possibility of an airline to Europe.

By early September, the amphibian was completed. On September 12, it arrived by truck at Roosevelt Field where the assembly was started at the Sikorsky hangar. Mrs. Grayson now announced that her plane would be used on a flight to Copenhagen, Denmark, with a stopover in either England or France. She said also that Wilmer Stultz had been engaged as the pilot, and Bryce Goldsborough, on leave of absence from Pioneer Instruments, had signed on as the navigator and radio operator. She made it clear that she intended to share the pilot's duties with Stultz.

Stultz, known to his friends as "Dusty" or "Bill," was a youthful-looking air veteran of twenty-seven. He joined the Army Air Services in 1917, and after two years transferred to the Navy, in Pensacola, where he remained until 1922, retiring from active duty with the rank of lieutenant. He was hired by the Curtiss Airplane Company to deliver forty aircraft to the Brazilian Navy, and his duties included, further, the supervision of their assembly, as well as test flights. Since his return to the States, the wavy-haired Pennsylvanian had been engaged in various phases of commercial aviation.

"Goldy" Goldsborough, as we have seen, was in the midst of a busy year with Pioneer. Prior to helping found that company, he served as a chief petty officer in the Navy, and during the war was in command of an important radio installation in the Far East. Since his association with Pioneer, he lived in Brooklyn with his wife Gertrude and their seventeen-year-old son Fred. "Goldy," who was considered briefly as navigator for *Columbia* never lost the itch to make an ocean flight, and when he was approached by Mrs. Grayson he jumped at the chance. Now, relieved of all other duties, he devoted his time exclusively to his new venture.

Together with Mrs. Grayson, Bill Stultz, and Igor Sikorsky, they oversaw the assembly of the big buff and blue amphibian. In no time, she was ready for testing. She had a wide-beamed hull, with a metal keel, and the hull was covered, and braced, to withstand heavy seas. Underneath her top wing were slung two Whirlwind engines. Tiny pontoons were attached to the tips of her stubby lower wing, to aid the ship when afloat. Her tail assembly—rudder, stabilizer, and elevators—were rigged high in the air so as to keep them clear of the seas in the event of a forced landing. The pilot's cockpit was enclosed in the hull in front of the wings and was equipped with dual controls. Mrs. Grayson's cabin was aft and was well-appointed with a chair, bed, and writing and dressing tables. It was illuminated softly by what then went for indirect lighting. The cabin was typically Sikorsky, for, from the time of his earliest planes, he had stressed a comfortable interior for crew and passengers alike. She was to be named *Dawn,* and the day before her ground tests were scheduled to start workmen were seen painting her name together with a replica of the Danish flag on her fuselage. Despite country-wide pleas to give up the idea, it was apparent that Mrs. Grayson was determined to go ahead with her plans.

6. On August 23, American newspapers carried a small item to the effect that one Ruth Elder and her pilot, George Haldeman, had left Lakeland, Florida, in Haldeman's Waco biplane, on a flight to Detroit for the purpose of picking up a new Stinson "Detroiter" monoplane in which they would make a non-stop hop to Paris. Brief dispatches during the next few days told of the flight back from Detroit to Tampa in the new plane and mentioned also that the proposed trip was being sponsored by a group of Wheeling, West Virginia, businessmen.

Miss Elder and Haldeman climbed into their new plane on September 11 at Tampa's airfield. Since the outcry against ocean flying was at its height, following the week of tragedy, Miss Elder was asked if public opinion would affect her plans in any way.

She answered firmly, "We have no intention of abandoning the flight."

At 7:11 A.M. they took off for Wheeling, but ran into bad weather en route. Heavy winds blew them off course and at 5:30 P.M., they were forced down by a lack of fuel at Holley Field, Portsmouth, Ohio. The next morning at 11 they left again for Wheeling, and landed before 5000 cheering spectators at 1:15 P.M. It was a Wheeling venture and her citizens were naturally aroused. Again, Miss Elder was questioned on the wisdom of flying the Atlantic.

Again, she replied adamantly, "The plane has been purchased, and nothing in the world can stop me now!"

In the afternoon, the big crowd watched as the Stinson "Detroiter" was christened *American Girl of Wheeling.*

New Yorkers had no idea of what was in store for them when the next day at 6:45 P.M. the brilliant yellow monoplane, *American Girl* swooped over Roosevelt Field and slid in for a landing. A small crowd watched, fascinated, as a young and strikingly beautiful girl jumped from the plane and greeted reporters. She was a knockout— with dark hair, large gray eyes, and a dimpled smile. She wore a multi-colored ribbon in her hair, and it was not long before all the young girls in the New York area displayed what came to be known as "Ruth ribbons." As the slim beauty, dressed in tan golf knickers, white open-necked shirt, and with her helmet pushed back on her head, chatted gaily with the goggle-eyed press, the cameras flashed, young men whistled, older men gaped, and wives groaned. Aviation's first sex symbol had come on the scene.

After a press conference, which was prolonged intentionally by staring reporters, Miss Elder was allowed to leave for her headquarters at the Hotel Pennsylvania. Pilot Haldeman was forgotten in the glamour of the moment and he busied himself seeing that the plane was properly housed.

From then on, Miss Elder was front-page news. Rarely did an edition appear without a picture of her smiling prettily in a tantalizing pose. Each day she appeared at the field with a different-colored "Ruth ribbon," and reporters flocked around her wherever she went. She was the darling of the crowds who took little notice now of the amphibian *Dawn*, as it taxied about the field in the preliminary tests.

Haldeman, too, was in the background, but he kept himself occupied working on the plane. He emerged once to deny vigorously that he was engaged to Miss Elder. When asked, in heaven's name why not, he answered simply that he was already married and the father of a boy.

Suddenly, the blow was struck that shattered the hopes of legions of young men. A reporter cornered Miss Elder at the Hotel Pennsylvania and asked her if she was engaged to Haldeman.

She answered, "No, I'm already married, too."

She said that she was in truth Mrs. Lyle Womack, and had

wanted to keep her marriage secret for fear of arousing the wrath of housewives throughout the country. Now, that the secret was out, she went on to give her life's story.

She was twenty-three, and had been born in Anniston, Alabama, where she was raised. Two years ago, she said, she had moved to Lakeland, Florida, where she worked for a short time as a dental assistant, and later married Womack, an advertising man. She became interested in aviation and was taught to fly by Floridian, George Haldeman. Her husband voiced no objections and went so far as to pay for her lessons.

It was Haldeman's turn to tell his story. He was twenty-nine, and a native of McPherson, Kansas. Because of age, he was refused when he first tried to enlist in the aviation section of the U. S. Army Signal Corps. He worked for a year as a bank clerk, and, when the war broke out, he applied again and was admitted to flying school. During the next few years, he served as an instructor and test pilot at Brooks Field, San Antonio, and was discharged with the rank of lieutenant. Among his friends and cohorts at Brooks, were J. D. Hill of the ill-fated *Old Glory*, and Harry Jones of Old Orchard Beach.

He then flew with his friend (and a backer of the proposed flight), Eddie Cornell, on a nation-wide barnstorming tour which took up most of a year. Afterward, he moved to Lakeland, Florida, where his father had a real estate business.

He joined the Waco Aircraft Company and gave flying instruction on the side. He said that though Miss Elder had not yet soloed, she was a promising pilot. Finally, he stressed that his only connection with Miss Elder, at the time, was to be her co-pilot on the Atlantic flight. So, much to the disappointment of the romantically inclined, their relationship was solely one of business.

During the September days that followed crowds mobbed Roosevelt Field hoping for a glimpse of the glamorous aviatrix. They were rarely disappointed, for she was nearly always found in the vicinity of *American Girl*, smiling and vivacious, as she chatted and joked with members of the ground crew. *Dawn*, too, was at the field, as well as Fonck's *Ville de Paris*, but it was Ruth Elder who stole the show.

Haldeman applied himself strenuously to the preparation of *American Girl* for her flight. She was scheduled to carry 520 gallons of gas, to the 450 carried by Chamberlin, and she would weigh 5600 pounds when fully loaded, more than either Lindbergh's or Chamberlin's plane, though she was approximately the same size.

She had been designed originally as a four-passenger plane, but two of the seats were removed to provide room for extra cans of gas. The 46-foot wing of the monoplane was connected to the 32-foot fuselage, above the pilot's cabin, and was braced to the bottom of the fuselage by four (two on each side) semi-lift struts, which were streamlined rather than curved. At the front of her body was the cockpit, with two glass windows facing forward, and two on each side, giving the crew a wide range of vision. The tip of her nose was painted a bright red, and her name *American Girl* was written in black lettering with white edging, along the side of her yellow fuselage. Like her sisters, *Pride of Detroit*, *Sir John Carling*, and *Royal Windsor*, she was equipped with dual controls and her J-5 Whirlwind engine enabled her to cruise at more than 110 miles an hour. She was a trim little plane, similar in appearance to *Columbia*, and those who flew "Detroiters," said they were her equal, in every way.

For the remainder of the month, Haldeman flew *American Girl* on test hops over Long Island, trying her instruments and checking on fuel consumption. Often, Miss Elder would accompany him. They put the ship through stringent load tests, and *American Girl* experienced no difficulty in lifting increasingly heavy weights off the ground. Rarely did she use over half of Roosevelt's mile-long runway, and local flyers marveled at her capability.

A leak was discovered in the gas tank, but promptly a new one was ordered and installed. *American Girl* was ready, but like those that went before her, she was attendant on the weather.

Haldeman announced, that because of the lateness in the season, he would forego the Great Circle route, for a course leading, due east into warmer climes, in order to escape icing. He realized that this would mean flying added miles, but, he, Miss Elder, and the visiting Eddie Stinson, were confident that she could make it across with hours of flying time to spare.

Dawn, which shared the Sikorsky hangar with *Ville de Paris*, was put through her paces by Stultz and Igor Sikorsky. Goldsborough worked tirelessly equipping the ship with the latest instruments, including a Pioneer-made earth inductor which had been the source of so much controversy. Though he had always given his best when working on the instruments of planes others would fly he knew that this time his life would be dependent on their proper operation, and it was a rare day when he was not aboard during the test flights.

From time to time, Mrs. Grayson came over from her residence at the Forest Hills Inn, and joined them on a flight, but more often she attended to the myriad of other details needed for the flight. Occasionally, she would consent to be photographed with the glamorous Miss Elder. They presented a striking contrast—the older, dynamic Mrs. Grayson, wearing a fish-bowl hat pulled down over her eyes; and the pert, lovely Miss Elder, with the inevitable "Ruth ribbon" in her hair.

The crowds loved it—a new race for the Atlantic, and between women.

On September 19, with Mrs. Grayson and Bryce Goldsborough aboard, Bill Stultz took *Dawn* into the air with a load of 9000 pounds, three-quarters of her anticipated weight for the ocean flight. While Sikorsky and his aides watched from the ground, the big amphibian roared off, but not until she had traveled down most of the runway. There were anxious seconds for the onlookers and crew, as the long buff-colored wings drove closer and closer to the incline, over which Fonck's plane had plunged only a year before. When they landed, there was a discussion between the crew and Sikorsky as to whether it might be preferable to leave from the long beach at Old Orchard, Maine.

No time was wasted, and Mrs. Grayson put in a call to Harry Jones at the beach. Though the season was over for him, as the summer vacationers had long since departed, he agreed to remain on the scene and provide them with what help he could. Mrs. Grayson thereupon announced her decision to leave for Maine as soon as the final tests had been concluded.

CHAPTER XIII

October 1927

1. Neither famine, war nor pestilence could have distracted Americans during the first weeks of October, much less the unseasonably hot weather, for it was World Series time. The famous "Sultan of Swat," Babe Ruth, after belting a record-breaking 60th home run on the next to last day of the season, off a luckless left-hander by the name of Jonathan Thompson Walton Zachary, went on, with his cohorts Lou Gehrig, Tony Lazzeri, Earle Combs, et al., to swamp Pittsburgh's hapless Pirates in the autumn classic, four games to none.

The news from abroad provided little that was out of the ordinary. Mexico, in the throes of political and religious upheaval, suffered from a mounting wave of executions and assassinations. Japan smarted under the short end of the 5–5–3 ratio, apportioning naval ships to her, at Washington's recent disarmament conference, but Emperor Hirohito decorated American bankers Morgan, Schiff, Kahn, Mitchell, Baker, and Lamont, for their assistance to his country in the years since the devastating 1923 earthquake.

There was a sidelight from the Soviet Union. World-famous basso, Feodor Chaliapin, won a state divorce, which cost him fifteen cents; when he agreed voluntarily to pay his ex-wife the equivalent of $300 a month in alimony; the government press chastised him for his "lavishness."

At home, the economy continued to boom. On October 5, the stock market enjoyed its fifth biggest day in history, as stocks soared to new highs. General Motors reported a record net profit of $193,758,302 on sales of $1,028,131,492, and directors declared an extra dividend of $2.50 in addition to the regular quarterly payment of $1.25 per share. In Washington, the Supreme Court, on the grounds of fraud, voided a government lease of the Naval

Reserve Oil fields at Teapot Dome, Wyoming, to oilman Harry F. Sinclair, and, in so doing, branded ex-Secretary of the Interior Albert B. Fall "a faithless public officer."

Lovely Grace Moore was signed to sing at the Metropolitan Opera; Wanda Landowska played Mozart on her harpsichord at Philharmonic Hall; *Wings* with Charles "Buddy" Rogers, Clara Bow, and Richard Arlen attracted moviegoers in droves to the Criterion on Broadway; and Al Jolson drew wild applause when he warbled "Mammy," in *The Jazz Singer*, a film that featured a new sound invention called Vitaphone.

As the crisp fall weather came over the nation, football took over center stage among sports lovers. They talked of the deeds of Michigan's Benny Oosterban, NYU's Ken Strong, or Dartmouth's Al Marsters, and debated whether Yale was justified in suspending their star back, Bruce Caldwell, for having played in two games as a freshman at Brown, before his transfer.

Every year has its fish story and 1927 was no exception. When the trawler, *Marjorie Parker*, docked in Boston Harbor, her master, Captain George Perry astounded the fishing community when he exhibited his latest catch—a three-eyed haddock!

2. As October arrived, amidst a sweltering Indian summer in New York, the crews of *Dawn* and *American Girl* waited for good ocean weather. The warnings continued against the proposed flights from all quarters. Perhaps the most significant was from meteorologist, "Doc" Kimball, who said that while fifty hours of clear weather over the Atlantic could be hoped for during the summer months, it would be a rare occasion now because of the speed with which weather systems move during the fall and winter.

The bloom was off the rose, too, for the charming Miss Elder. More and more, she was accused of seeking publicity from her flight. Some went so far as to say that all she wanted was a movie contract, but her beauty belied a stubbornness of purpose, and no amount of criticism or slander could persuade her to give up. Mrs. Grayson, in *Dawn*, was in a less vulnerable position, simply because her plane was an amphibian and was able to land on the water.

During the first days of the month, there remained no doubt that the two ladies were locked in a competition which amounted to combat. They eyed the other's camp and plane warily and at all times. On October 5, Miss Elder was at the field, dressed colorfully in tan knickers and a bright pull-over sweater. She watched intently as Stultz, "Doc" Kinkaid, and tall, hawk-featured Bryce Goldsborough jumped into *Dawn*'s cockpit, and took off on a final load test, with five tons of fuel aboard. Below, on Curtiss Field, Haldeman, who referred to himself as "co-pilot and navigator" in deference to Miss Elder, worked furiously on *American Girl*. The time of truth appeared to be drawing near.

When the big amphibian landed, it was announced by Mrs. Grayson that she would fly to Old Orchard the next day, but storms, raging along the eastern seaboard, held her up and kept both planes hangar-bound for several days. In the meantime, the U. S. Weather Bureau threw up another roadblock in their paths by stating that as of October 10, no more weather reports or meteorological services of any type would be provided for ocean flyers this season. Neither Mrs. Grayson nor Miss Elder seemed perturbed by this subtle governmental pressure. Both maintained firmly that it would cause no change in their plans as they would obtain the necessary information elsewhere.

On October 9, the weather was still bad and both planes stayed under cover, but, on the morning of the 10th, it was clear at Roosevelt, and Mrs. Grayson announced that *Dawn* would leave for Old Orchard in the afternoon so as to arrive on the beach when the tide was low.

At 1 P.M., with a small crowd at the field, the big amphibian was wheeled out of the hangar. She was filled with sufficient fuel for her Maine flight and "Doc" Kinkaid, back from Europe, started the engines. He, and Boris Lebensky, assigned to *Dawn* by Sikorsky, listened carefully as the twin J-5s were opened up. They gave off an even, pulsating beat. Wilmer Stultz appeared on the scene, accompanied by lanky Bryce Goldsborough. The last to arrive was Mrs. Grayson, dressed in a leather flying suit, and wearing the familiar airman's helmet of the day. She told reporters that, while they would go as far as Old Orchard, there did not seem to be a prospect of an immediate take-off because of the weather. Recent forecasts predicted a week of storms with unfavorable winds over the Atlantic. At present, observations showed storms centered off Sable Island, and southwest of Cape Hatteras, with easterly winds blowing over almost one-half of the Atlantic. She added, though, that *Dawn* would be ready when the weather cleared.

Last-minute inspections were made by the crew, while other hands stored the necessary supplies for their stay at Old Orchard. Finally all was ready, and, shortly after 5, Stultz and Mrs. Grayson went aboard—Stultz taking the left-hand seat with Mrs. Grayson alongside of him. She had announced on many occasions that she intended to spell Stultz at the controls frequently. Boris Lebensky, "Doc" Kinkaid, and Bryce Goldsborough hopped quickly into the rear cabin with "Goldy" taking his place at the radio. The ship was assigned the call letters WMU, and the instrument expert had promised that he would keep in constant touch with the ground during the flight. Kinkaid and Lebensky were along for the ride, for their work on the plane and her motors would not begin until they reached the Old Orchard Beach.

The chocks were pulled clear, and Stultz taxied the ship, bouncing on the little wheels that dropped down from the hull, toward the eastern end of the runway near Byrd's renowned artificial hill. Igor Sikorsky, Ruth Elder, and George Haldeman were among the crowd of a thousand, who looked on as Stultz turned the plane into the wind. The engines whined loudly as *Dawn* moved down the strip. The wheels didn't look as though they could keep the hull from scraping the ground. *Dawn* gathered speed, and, at 2:10 P.M., lifted with ease after a run of 2000 feet. She banked to the right to take advantage of the slight cross wind that blew from the northwest. The spectators could see clearly her registration number NX 1282, as her right wing dipped. Stultz took her up to 2000 feet and headed northeast toward Long Island Sound. Five minutes later, she disappeared over the gentle rises leading to Oyster Bay.

On the ground, Sikorsky smiled as his latest creation soared safely away; for once, however, there was no smile on the pretty face of Ruth Elder. As usual, she was surrounded by a throng of reporters and other admirers. After explaining to them patiently that her husband's absence was due to business in the Canal Zone, she said despondently, "If conditions don't clear up by the 15th, it is more than likely that we will postpone the flight until spring. I hate to give it up, but we are not going in the face of the weather."

Aboard *Dawn*, Bryce Goldsborough took the opportunity to practice instrument navigation, and, intentionally, he made no use of familiar land marks as they passed below the ship. *Dawn* flew across the Sound to Greenwich, Connecticut, and then "Goldy" gave Bill Stultz a course for Boston.

Mrs. Grayson, after the take-off, moved out of the co-pilot's seat, and back to her own cabin where she began the story of her great adventure, for which she had already sold the rights. She did however take time, during the three-hour and fourteen-minute flight, to send a radio message to the world:

THE PLANE TOOK OFF BEAUTIFULLY, it said. PILOT STULTZ BEGAN TO LIFT OUR GRACEFUL SIKORSKY SHIP WHEN 2000 FEET FROM THE END OF THE RUNWAY. WE WERE OFF THE GROUND IN 25 SECONDS FLAT AND HEADED OUT OVER THE SOUND. WEATHER FINE FOR THE FIRST LEG OF OUR TRANSATLANTIC FLIGHT. AFTER FURTHER TESTS WITH THE SHIP WEATHER PERMITTING WILL CARRY THE PRO-PROGRESSIVE AMERICAN WOMAN'S GREETINGS TO MY SPLENDID AS-SOCIATE MRS. ANCKER IN DENMARK. GOLDSBOROUGH NAVIGATING AND RADIOING. DOC KINKAID TIMED THE TAKE-OFF AND IS LISTENING TO THE MOTORS. LEBENSKY GETTING MUCH-NEEDED SLEEP. I AM ENJOYING THE TRIP.

It was signed simply: FRANCES GRAYSON.

Over Boston, Goldsborough gave Stultz a new setting, and then began to work the radio equipment himself, testing it with calls to local receiving stations. WMU was heard frequently over the airwaves that afternoon and reports indicated that the reception was "loud and clear."

At 5:10 P.M. *Dawn* circled over Old Orchard Beach, after approaching over Biddeford, and zooming over the pier at 500 feet. The Beach was bare and cold-looking, and the streets of Old Orchard, empty of people. Long gone were the crowds of sun-loving bathers. Over Pine Point the big plane banked with peninsula-like Prout's Neck, jutting off the right wingtip. The wind blew strongly out of the north and the plane skittered in front of it, on its downwind leg. Beyond the town of Old Orchard, Stultz brought *Dawn* into the wind and began his descent. They were 150 feet up, as the pier flashed below them, and then they were down on the smooth, hard sand.

A small, shivering crowd, led by Robert Hazzard and Fred Boston, together with Harry Jones, greeted the flyers as they stepped out. It was cold, with a biting wind whistling down the beach. The lovely, warm summer was now only a memory. The ocean was an icy blue, flecked with whitecaps, and spray streaked off the breaker tops as they fell to the beach far below the hangar.

We, too, were still there, our school opening having been delayed by an epidemic of infantile paralysis. We saw young Stultz, his dark hair ruffled by the stiff breeze, talking to Harry Jones, while angular Bryce Goldsborough stood by quietly. Mrs. Grayson—we, for some reason, called her Lady Grayson—talked to reporters gaily outside her cabin hatch. She was a live wire and took pleasure in sparring with the gentlemen of the press. I looked through the window into the main cabin of the plane. It was a mess, with tools, cans, and soft drink bottles strewn about. I was shocked. I saw Mrs. Grayson's comfortable leather seat and her table, but I was chased away before I could see more. It was freezing, and we soon ran up the beach and home, while Mrs. Grayson and her crew retired to the re-opened Hotel Brunswick where they warmed up in front of a roaring fire, in the oceanside common room.

Lebensky and Kinkaid stayed behind briefly with Harry Jones at the beach. He had placed his hangar, gas tanks, and equipment at their disposal, and the three attended to bedding down *Dawn* for the night, safely above the high water mark. Afterward, they, too, joined Stultz, Goldsborough, and Lady Grayson in front of the fireplace at the Brunswick.

3.   At 7 o'clock on the morning of October 11 a meeting took place in Ruth Elder's suite at the Hotel Pennsylvania in New York. Present were George Haldeman, his old friend, Eddie Cornell, and T. H. McArdle, both of whom were backers of the flight. The weather over the Atlantic, though promising, was far from ideal, but Miss Elder knew that they would have to decide soon, one way or another, for the winter was coming on fast. McArdle and Cornell, mindful of the sentiments of the general public, at first tried to dissuade them against leaving until springtime. Miss Elder and Haldeman, though, balked at the idea and at length won the two men over.

Miss Elder turned to her co-pilot, regarding the take-off time, and said, "It's up to you."

Haldeman replied, "It's now or never."

The die was cast, and the flight would start in the afternoon.

The two flyers set the wheels in motion. *American Girl* was taken to Roosevelt Field, where loading was begun with the utmost speed; 520 gallons of gas were put aboard—200 into the wing tanks, 180 into the fuselage tank, and five 28-gallon cans were stored aft, but within easy reach of the crew. While the tanks were being filled, other workmen scurried in and out of the plane, storing flares, smoke bombs, Very pistols, and a 14-pound emergency radio set, complete with a kite antenna. They would carry no raft, but in lieu would wear waterproof and airtight rubber suits, designed to float for at least 72 hours. The hoods were specially equipped with devices to condense the breath of the wearer, so as to make drinking water.

The food was put on, and was the typical fare of ocean flyers: six turkey sandwiches; six cheese sandwiches; two quarts of coffee; a quart of beef tea; chocolate and oranges. To make sure that they wouldn't get hungry, someone added a roast chicken at the last minute.

The fueling and equipping was not completed until just before 3 P.M. and the plane was then towed, fully loaded, to the "Byrd ramp" at the east end of the field.

Outside the hangar, the enchanting Miss Elder, smiling and relaxed, joked with reporters and her fans. In that the morning papers had been unable to carry news of their departure, the crowd was slim, hardly reaching 500 in number, as take-off time approached. Miss Elder, always the center of attention, was dressed in tan knickers, and a red and green plaid sweater, with golf stockings to match. A broad band of red and green silk, her "Ruth ribbon" for the day, held her dark hair in place.

Haldeman was out at the ramp, working hard on his final check-up of *American Girl*. He announced that they would fly due east after leaving land at Montauk Point, in order to stay in warmer air. He added that this would make it possible to climb over bad weather without fear of icing. Among the bystanders were Eddie Stinson and Bernt Balchen. With Balchen was a young Norwegian friend whom he had brought back from Norway to join Byrd's forthcoming South Pole expedition, Lieutenant Oskar Omdal. Omdal, a pilot, had flown over the North Pole in the dirigible *Norge* and was well-acquainted with the perils of icing. He was questioned by reporters as to the effect it might have on *American Girl*.

"They should have little worry over it," the Norwegian said. "Ice usually forms on metal. When cloth fabric is well doped, it does not seem to accumulate ice very fast."

A late weather advice from Newfoundland was handed to Miss Elder. She smiled as she read it, for it reported clear skies over the Atlantic, with strong westerly winds.

At 4 o'clock, Haldeman returned to the hangar and stepped into a fur-lined flying suit which covered up his neat blue pin-stripe. He helped Ruth Elder struggle into hers. Haldeman, noting that daylight was fading fast, motioned that they should get under way. They returned to the plane, accompanied by the spectators. Haldeman kissed his wife, Virginia, and slipped into the pilot's seat, because, in this instance it would be the co-pilot who would perform the take-off.

Miss Elder, still smiling gaily, kept repeating, "I'm very happy!" as if to ensure the world that she had no qualms about going. Her flying helmet now hid her "Ruth ribbon."

She shouted to the crowd, "Good-bye, everybody!" and, still waving and smiling, climbed in beside Haldeman. T. H. Sorenson of the Wright Company turned the propeller over and over again. The J-5 belched smoke and coughed, but did not catch for long minutes. Finally, as the exhausted Sorenson looked desperately for help, the motor burst into noisy action as Haldeman opened the throttle.

Before getting aboard, Haldeman looked at the windsock on the hangar roof. Its position showed that a southeast wind had sprung up, making a take-off from the mound impractical.

After the motor was warmed, Miss Elder leaned out of the cabin window and blew a kiss to the crowd. The little Stinson moved down off the incline, and taxied slowly the length of the field, to the edge of the ravine which led down to Curtiss. Some of the crowd followed, while others remained on the mound. Behind them were the dreaded telephone wires that had come close to foiling Lindbergh's attempt.

At the far end of the field, the little yellow monoplane turned into the wind, with a loud burst from her motor. The runway was lined now by automobiles, parked airplanes and excited people, but the yellow strip of sand and clay, knifing through the meadow grass, was clear.

The propeller of *American Girl* turned idly, flashing in the setting sun as Haldeman tested his controls. He wiggled successively, the ailerons, the rudder, and, then, the elevators. Everything was in order. He opened the throttle slowly to take-off power, and the plane moved east down the runway as clouds of dust blew up behind her. It was known that he would cut the motor, if the plane were not airborne when they reached a flag, planted at the three-quarter mark. There was no reason for worry, however, as the plane's tail lifted at 2000 feet, and she left the runway after another 750 feet. Haldeman held her close to the ground to gain as much speed as possible. The spectators, who had stayed behind at the "Byrd ramp," scattered fast as *American Girl* thundered toward them at grasstop level. Just before reaching the mound, Haldeman turned slightly to the southeast to avoid it, and to get a lift from the head wind. The wings of the plane were at the level of the top of the mound as she zoomed by. The crowd watched anxiously as the plane approached the telephone wires. *American Girl* skimmed over them, with far more ease than had the *Spirit of St. Louis*. She flew out over the golf course adjacent to the field, climbing steadily, while golfers stared up bewilderedly at the little yellow ship. She vanished quickly in the eastern sky while the sun sank slowly toward the horizon behind her. They had left the ground at 5:04 P.M.

In Anniston, Alabama, Mrs. J. D. Elder, mother of the flyer, said, "We all feel sure she'll make it"; but veteran weatherman "Doc" Kimball was more guarded in his optimism.

"I have great confidence in Haldeman," he said. "He knows what he wants to do and how to do it. If anyone can work his way through the bad weather ahead of him, he can do it, but he'll have rough going."

The country—especially the women—were indignant over Miss Elder's departure in the face of such odds. Again, cries of "stunt" and "Publicity seeker" were heard, in reference to the flight.

Mrs. Franklin D. Roosevelt voiced the average feelings of all the critics when she said, "My personal feeling is that it is very foolish to risk one's life, as well as that of a pilot in the face of contrary advice from almost everyone who knows anything about aviation. All the experts told Miss Elder that she should not try it, but she was determined to go ahead. Of course, there is no denying that she exhibited marvelous courage and, for that, we must pay her tribute.

"Nevertheless," Mrs. Roosevelt concluded, "it seems to me unquestionably foolish for a young woman to fly alone, with only a pilot, over such a long distance."

Her defenders, of whom there were some in the aviation world, pointed out that not only would the plane be flying in the warm air of the southern route, but that her course would parallel, in time, the heavily traveled ship lanes in the event there were trouble. It was also noted that when she neared the European coast she would be on the track of the *Leviathan* (with Levine aboard), which had sailed on the 11th, the *Ile de France*, and the *Homeric*, all of them en route to the United States.

In the late evening of October 11, a radio message was received in New York from Captain H. A. Peterson of the S.S. *American Banker*.

It said: AT 10:35 P.M. OCTOBER 11 405 MILES OFF AMBROSE LIGHT SIGHTED AMERICAN GIRL HEADED EAST AT 1000 FEET AT GREAT SPEED FLASHING LIGHTS. WEATHER IDEAL. BRIGHT MOONLIGHT NIGHT. LIGHT NORTHWEST BREEZE.

For the next 28 hours though, *American Girl* was unseen. There was little worry, for it was thought that Haldeman might be flying over the predicted bad weather in midocean. In that connection, "Doc" Kinkaid had advised him to maintain an altitude of 10,000 to 15,000 feet, to get clear of the clouds and to take advantage of the best winds. The experts felt, too, that barring engine trouble, the plane had sufficient gas to stay in the air for 48 hours.

As darkness fell, on October 12, crowds gathered for an all-night vigil at Le Bourget. *American Girl* was expected the next morning, Paris time, and no one wanted to miss her arrival because of the usual traffic jams. They brought sandwiches, cold beer, and wine, and spread out on blankets in groups all over the field. Le Bourget took on a gay and festive air, as the picnickers prepared to welcome the pretty American girl and her pilot. They were heartened by reports that the weather was ideal, from the French coast into Paris, but sobered by the fact that there was still no word that *American Girl* had been sighted.

When October 13 dawned, without word, concern for the flyers was felt in New York and Paris.

Suddenly, at 11:30 A.M., receiving stations at Horta, the Azores, relayed a message they had just received: LANDED BY S.S. BARENDRECHT WITH BROKEN OIL LINE. BOTH HALDEMAN AND I OK. RUTH ELDER.

It was followed within minutes, by another message from the skipper of the *Barendrecht*: SAVED CREW OF FLYING MACHINE NX1384 FROM NEW YORK TO PARIS. BOTH WELL. MACHINE DESTROYED BY FIRE WHILE SAVING. TRYING TO LAND BOTH AT THE AZORES.

America was relieved while it awaited full details.

Virginia Haldeman, in a New York hotel, broke down and wept with joy.

She cabled her husband: GEORGE HALDEMAN! JUST SO HAPPY! I DON'T KNOW WHAT TO SAY. HURRY BACK. GREAT FLIGHT. LOVE TO RUTH.

Even Lyle Womack turned up, and fired off a cable to his wife: WORLDS OF LOVE FOR THE BRAVEST GIRL IN THE WORLD. ANXIOUSLY AWAITING YOUR RETURN. LYLE.

After the take-off *American Girl* had clear sailing until 6 o'clock the following evening. Haldeman told of a smooth flight in clear skies, with a good following wind. He and Miss Elder alternated at the controls of the ship. As night approached, however, mountainous banks of dark cloud gathered on the horizon ahead of them. They flew bravely in and were wafted about wildly by their currents. Rain swept off the wings, and set their windshield awash. It was blinding as they were pitched about dizzily. The seat straps strained against their bodies as the fury of the gale sought to pitch them through the roof of the plane. For eight hours they fought off the monumental storm. They went down to the surface in an effort to get free—but to no avail. Haldeman then nosed *American Girl* up to 10,000, 12,000, then 15,000 feet. It was hopeless. They were lost in a suffocating sea of woolly cloud, and pounded by sheets of rain. There seemed to be no top to the storm, for no matter how high they flew, and the altimeter at one point read 17,000 feet, they were imprisoned by the thick and bumpy weather. They continued to be flung around mercilessly, shooting up like a rocket for 500 feet—then plummeting down like a stone. They feared for their wings and their tail assembly, but the plane proved sturdy. It was a night of terror, and Haldeman described Miss Elder as "extremely courageous and very helpful with the controls."

All bad things end, at some point, and such was true of the storm, but not until 2 A.M. on the morning of Thursday, October 13. As suddenly as it had come, it vanished, and once more they flew smoothly over a calm sea and in a star-lit sky. Unfortunately though, their problems were not over. The storm had blown them off course and had affected their compass. Neither Miss Elder nor Haldeman were experts at navigation, and they were now lost over a vast ocean. To make matters worse, Haldeman noticed that the engine was beginning to heat up, and that the oil pressure was dropping. He closed the throttle so that the revolutions per minute dropped from 2000 to 1150. The plane limped along at a reduced speed, during the morning hours. Happily, the weather was clear, and from the air, the sea seemed smooth enough for a landing if it became necessary.

At 7:46 A.M., Haldeman was at the controls, and saw a ship steaming on the horizon, almost hull down. He made for it as fast as the overheated engine would allow, and it was not long before they were circling, low, over a tanker.

The boat flew a Dutch flag.

Miss Elder wrote out a message: "How far are we from land, and which way?" weighted it, and dropped it accurately on the tanker's deck, as they flew over her. The sailors painted their position on the deck, together with the information that they were 360 miles northeast of Terceira, Azores, and 500 miles west of Lisbon, Portugal.

The flyers were elated at the distance they had covered in spite of the storm. For almost two hours, American Girl circled the ship in wide sweeps, while they calculated their next move. Haldeman discovered that a broken oil line was the cause of their engine trouble, and since it was impossible to make repairs of this nature in the air they had little choice other than to come down.

American Girl continued to circle the tanker, which was now lying almost dead in the water. The flyers wanted to get rid of as much fuel as possible, and to make careful preparations for the precarious landing at sea.

It was 10:20 A.M. when they started their final ditching pattern. They swooped low over the Barendrecht, flew downwind for a half-mile, turned, and began the descent. The sea, as it flashed below them, was not the mill pond it had seemed from above, but rolled easily with a gentle ground swell. Haldeman brought the plane, lower and lower. The swells were just under their wheels. Through the windshield, the horizon dipped, first to one side and then to the other, as the pilot sought to keep the plane on an even keel. He pointed the nose up slightly to lose speed. They hit, first with a light shock, as the undercarriage snapped off, and then with a heavy jolt, as the fuselage struck the water, sloshed along in a stream of spray, and rocked to a stop, with her engine and nose buried under the surface.

The Barendrecht was one-quarter mile in front of them, and steaming hard in their direction. A lifeboat was lowered. Haldeman climbed out of the cockpit window, and helped Miss Elder up after him onto the wing, where they awaited their rescuers. They were down safely and it was quiet, sunny, and warm, and the lifeboat was only yards away. They had failed, but the two flyers had much for which to be thankful.

In a matter of minutes, they were aboard the Barendrecht, and sailors had already put lines around American Girl. Miss Elder, wearing knickers and a leather jacket, applied lipstick first, and then turned to the captain.

"Thank you very much," she said with a radiant smile.

American Girl did not make it aboard, for, as the seamen hoisted her over the side, she burst into flame, without explanation. Some thought the fire was caused by gasoline spilling from her tanks onto the still-hot engine parts. In any case, the lines were cut quickly to prevent damage to the ship, and the flaming wreckage dropped into the sea, drifted astern, and sank soon, ass Miss Elder and Haldeman watched sadly from the deck.

American Girl had flown them 2623 statute miles, to a position only 520 miles due west of Portugal, and, had it not been for the broken oil line, there is no telling how far they might have gone. The *Barendrecht* changed course for her illustrious passengers and made for Horta.

Though the women in the United States criticized Miss Elder for her foolhardiness, the men were less harsh. The aviation community had mixed feelings about the flight.

Clarence Chamberlin, while praising her skill and courage, said, "They'd have been better off if they'd used a seaplane."

His friend, Bellanca, disagreed, saying, "There is no seaplane built that is capable of making such a flight." He added that in his opinion the effort was meritorious, because much information could be obtained from the off-season flight, made over a new route.

Grover Loening, a pioneer in amphibian design, got into the dispute. He took issue with Bellanca, when he said, "Amphibians should be used, exclusively, now on ocean flights. They are capable of such trips, and there is no point in the use of land planes." As to Miss Elder's participation, he was brief. "The fact that there was a girl aboard is immaterial."

On October 15 it was another exciting day in Horta. Only recently, the German Junkers seaplane had landed, carrying the lovely Lilli Dillentz, another candidate in the race to be the first woman to fly across the Atlantic. Now another beauty, the American, Ruth Elder, was expected.

The entire island turned out to greet her. Long before *Barendrecht* was sighted, the townspeople flocked to the harborside. The docks and the roofs of buildings with commanding views were packed by those wishing a better vista. When at length the ship docked, and Miss Elder sauntered down the gangplank followed by Haldeman, she was greeted by a cheering throng, led by none other than Lilli Dillentz.

She looked radiant. She wore the captain's hat jauntily on the back of her head, with her dark hair curling out underneath. The two girls posed together, and laughed and talked. They were similar in looks and manner, both slender, both dark-haired, and both vivacious.

The people of Horta swarmed around them, trying to get a close look at the glamorous couple, for seldom had two such attractive visitors been in their midst.

Haldeman stood quietly in the background.

For two days, all activity on the island came to a halt, as the Americans were guests of honor at an endless number of receptions. Their visit was climaxed by a festive party at the British Consulate, given jointly for the German and American flyers. For the occasion, Miss Elder discarded her usual costume of knickers, sweaters, and "Ruth ribbons," and appeared at the Consulate, clad in a long, flowing evening dress, which brought stares and murmurs from the bedazzled guests. She was determined not to be outshone by the lovely Miss Dillentz!

On October 17, she and Haldeman boarded a ship for Madeira, where again they were feted lavishly. Special police were need to protect Miss Elder from her thousands of admirers. After Madeira, they traveled to Lisbon for more of the same, and then it was on to Paris, their original destination, for another round of celebration. Though they were treated with warm hospitality in the French capital, they were not extended an official state welcome, because, as the French papers put it, "It was a brave attempt, but it failed."

Nevertheless, Miss Elder charmed Parisians with her beauty and presence. She shopped for clothes, placed a wreath on the Tomb of the Unknown Soldier at the Place d'Étoile, and, like the flyers before her, paid a call on the aged Madame Nungesser. She left with the French, the image of a brave, warmhearted American girl.

She and Haldeman sailed for home aboard the *Aquitania* in early November. Their triumphant tour of Europe had been a happy one, and Miss Elder found herself deluged with enticing offers for stage appearances, and even the movies.

They arrived in New York on Armistice Day, and were accorded the usual welcome. Smiling Grover Whalen, impeccably groomed, cruised out into New York Harbor on the *Mecom* to bring the flyers back to the Battery. There followed a parade up Broadway under streamers of tickertape to City Hall, where they were honored by Mayor Walker.

His Honor said to the flower-laden beauty, as he handed her the keys to the City: "Pulchritude is no bar to courage!"

Thus ended the saga of *American Girl*. So far, the Atlantic had resisted all attempts by women to conquer her. One had died trying, and another saved in a Harry Hawker-type rescue. Only Mrs. Grayson and Miss Dillentz were still in the running, as the fall deepened, and the winds grew colder.

4. At Norderney, in the Fresian Islands, as October arrived, Captain "Fritz" Loose, late of the *Bremen*, was busy preparing Dr. Junkers's low-winged seaplane for a trip to the United States, via Lisbon, the Azores, and Newfoundland. With him were Rolfe Starke, his navigator, Rudolph Fritzler, a mechanic, and Karl Loewe, the radio operator. The cabin of the big tri-motored D-1230 was converted to hold extra gas tanks and the most up-to-date radio transmitter and receiver.

While the final changes were being made it was noted that a pretty young lady was frequently on the scene talking with the crew. No one paid much attention to her other than to admire her natural attributes and there was no mention of her in the German papers as the time neared for a take-off. The flight was being hurried, as it was known that Horst Merz and his crew at Warnemünde, were ready to take off via the same route for the United States in their Heinkel flying boat D-1220. Reports of the impending race between the seaplanes were arousing interest throughout Germany.

At 4:30, on the afternoon of October 4, great excitement prevailed as the crew led by "Fritz" Loose went aboard D-1230 and started the engines. At the last minute a bundled and hidden figure was helped into the cabin. It was a great mystery to the crowd on shore as to the identity of the extra crew member and it wasn't solved for without further explanation D-1230 taxied out into the harbor and took off for Lisbon. Forty-five minutes later, however, heavy weather forced them down at Schellingwoude, near Amsterdam Harbor, and the secret became known to all. No sooner had they come ashore than it was revealed that the passenger was a young brunette actress from Vienna by the name of Lilli Dillentz. She wished also to become the first woman to fly the Atlantic. It was learned, further, that she was the daughter of Carl Mollitzer, a well-known Austrian painter, and that she was married to a Viennese architect, Richard Dillentz. Rumor had it that she had paid the equivalent of $12,000 for her passage.

Throughout the night at Schellingwoude the tanks of the 8-ton seaplane were filled with freshly strained gas as she floated at her mooring. The refueling was done with the aid of searchlights, and despite a heavy rain that fell steadily in the harbor. A large flotilla of little boats floated about all night in the rain watching the procedure.

At 5 the next morning, D-1230 was ready and her engines were started. She taxied to a leeward position in the harbor, turned, and with her engines aroar, headed for a take-off, leaving a foamy path in her wake. After a run of 200 yards, spectators on the shore were surprised to hear the noise from the motors drop, and watched the plane rock to a stop. The trouble became obvious, at once, as a coastal steamer loomed up out of the mist and passed directly in front of the plane. Again, D-1230 was revved up and skipped over the surface of the bay. This time, she lifted off without difficulty, climbed steadily, and disappeared into the gray skies of the southwest, bound for the Tagus River. Aboard, was Lilli Dillentz, the second woman in history to attempt an Atlantic air crossing.

There was no word from the big silvery-gray Junkers until 11 o'clock that evening when a radio message was received in Dessau saying that D-1230 had been forced down in the sea, off Cape Vera Cruz, 80 miles north of Lisbon, on the Portuguese coast. The message advised, moreover, that the plane was under the tow of a fisherman and expected to reach the mouth of the Tagus the next day. Sure enough, the following afternoon at 4 the big plane appeared in the Bay of Tagus at the end of a towline from a small motorboat. There, the plane was cast off, her motors started, and she took off on a short flight to the nearby naval station.

After they had gone ashore, Captain Loose told of the trip. He said they had made excellent time until they were off the Portuguese coast when a blinding fog suddenly surrounded them. They circled for an hour hoping that it would blow off and then decided to put down in the water, rather than risk more serious consequences. The sea was glassy smooth and they landed safely. Almost at once they saw a fishing boat in the distance, made toward it, and accepted the tow.

The plane and crew were healthy, and Lilli Dillentz was calm and radiant. She said that she was "charmed" by the flight and stressed repeatedly how much she wanted to be the first in the race of the ladies. Weather en route to the Azores, however, delayed Captain Loose and his crew for a few days, long enough for the glamorous Madame Dillentz to sweep Lisbon off its feet with her beauty and bubbling personality.

Meanwhile, on October 12 at Warnemeunde on the Baltic coast,

Horst Merz, the veteran Lufthansa pilot, was ready to go in his low-winged Heinkel seaplane. His destination, too, was Lisbon, then the Azores, Newfoundland, and New York. D-1220 carried no glamorous passenger, but had a competent crew aboard, comprised of Wilhelm Bock, who doubled in brass, as co-pilot and radio operator, and mechanic Friedrich Rode. The plane was powered by an American-built, Packard engine. Mechanic Rode, while living in the United States, had worked for the Packard Company, and was familiar with the operation of their motors.

In the early afternoon, as a small crowd lined the shores, D-1220 taxied into the harbor and took off for Lisbon, hot on the heels, they hoped, of their Junkers rivals. The plane developed a leak in the radiator soon after the start and she was forced down at Brusnbuttel, near Cuxhaven, at the mouth of the Elbe River. She remained there until the next day undergoing repairs, when again she took off and headed for Amsterdam for a more extensive overhaul. However, the patched-up radiator acted up, and Merz was forced down after flying less than fifty miles, at Wilhelmshafen, where he stayed until October 15. Once more, D-1220 took to the air and pointed toward Lisbon.

This time, the flight went smoothly for a while, until a broken feedpipe brought her down outside of Viga, Spain. It was not until the morning of October 18 that D-1220 with Merz at the controls, appeared over Lisbon, and settled on the Tagus, with the first leg of her trip over. By this time, though, Loose and his crew, including Miss Dillentz, were safely in the Azores, waiting to take off for Newfoundland at the first sign of tolerable weather.

On October 14, at 6:30 in the morning, despite a low cloud cover over Lisbon, D-1230 had floated away from her mooring in the Tagus, turned into the wind, and roared off to the west bound for the Azores, on the second stage of her flight. The weather at the start was almost "zero-zero," with low cloud and fog, but pilot Loose and navigator Stark combined their talents to keep the ship on course and speeding at better than 100 miles an hour across the Atlantic. Behind them in the cabin, looking out one of the windows that lined the fuselage, was their now-famous passenger, Lilli Dillentz.

Two hours after leaving the Portuguese coast, the weather broke, and the plane emerged from the clouds into an area of blue skies and unlimited visibility. At noon, though, cloud banks loomed again on the horizon. They plunged soon into a heavy overcast, and were flung about the skies by the turbulence and gale-force winds. The weather forced them down from 1800 to 900 feet, where they were able to see the gray and white-capped ocean.

It was not long before they sighted St. Mitchell's Island, the easternmost of the Azores, moving in, slowly, below them. Happily, they thought, they were close now. At 2:30 P.M., Azores time, the big seaplane banked into the wind, and descended into the choppy, gray waters of Horta Harbor, after a flight of 1095 miles in ten hours. Loose taxied the ship behind the breakwater, and they tied up to a mooring which had been prepared for them. They were safe and snug, with the second leg of the trip successfully ended.

The crew was taken ashore and welcomed by the residents of the town, most of whom were employed by the Atlantic Cable Company. Lovely Lilli Dillentz attracted the most attention and drew the most admiring glances, until, at last, they were permitted by the crowd to retire to the privacy of the German Consulate. Before they went to bed, they learned that Dieudonné Coste and Joseph Le Brix, had landed safely in *Nungesser and Coli*, after a non-stop crossing of the South Atlantic, from St. Louis, Senegal, to Port Natal, Brazil.

5. In Horta, Azores, after the departure of Ruth Elder, the carnival-like atmosphere disappeared and the crew of the Junkers D-1230 settled down to prepare for the next leg of their trip—to Newfoundland. Pretty Lilli Dillentz, the passenger, had but one competitor left in her quest to be the first woman to cross the Atlantic by air and she was anxious to press her advantage. Captain Loose, however, was an experienced airman, and would not consider a take-off until weather conditions were ideal. He knew that as winter approached storms would streak across the ocean without a break, and that ideal conditions seemed but an impossible dream. Nevertheless, D-1230 made an effort to leave in early November, but the heavily laden machine was unable to rise off the wind-whipped waters of Horta Harbor. The crew continued to work, wait, and watch as the days went by. Their lives at the Consulate were comfortable, but they yearned to go, and were spurred on by the spirited Miss Dillentz.

In Lisbon, Horst Merz, commander of the Heinkel D-1220, waited too, with his crew, for weather that would permit him to join the Junkers group in Horta. On November 4, with the outlook better than it had been for weeks, they boarded their low-winged seaplane; took off and headed west. During the first hours of the flight, the weather was clear and the visibility unlimited. The sparkling blue ocean stretched out for miles. The inevitable clouds, though, began soon to rise up from the horizon, and in little time D-1220 got a thorough structural test as she was thrown wildly about in a blinding squall. Merz, like the others before him, tried to climb over it all, but, as always, the layer of cloud was too high. He took the other alternative, and nosed the big plane down, breaking out finally at fifty feet. They flew on, skipping the waves, for nearly ten hours, climbing from time to time to a safer altitude when the ceiling allowed them; then the weather would close in again, and they would be forced back down until the pontoons skimmed the angry gray combers. It was tiring for pilot Merz, but he was fortunate, for radio operator Bock was able to spell him at the wheel at intervals, to allow him to rest his aching arm muscles.

The islands appeared at last, and soon the snug sight of Horta Harbor. Merz circled the harbor twice, and bounced his plane in for a landing on choppy waters that looked so calm from the air. At 3 P.M., D-1220 picked up her mooring inside the breakwater, and only fifty yards away the Junkers boat bobbed in the tide. There was a gala, and song-fested reunion of German flyers at the Consulate that night.

Strangely enough, it was the Heinkel crew that made the first attempt to fly on to Newfoundland. Under bright moonlight, in the early morning of November 13, D-1220 was towed, fully loaded, from her moorings behind the breakwater, out into the channel. There, Merz started her engine, turned into the wind, and the plane moved across the water. Faster and faster she sped as her pontoons skipped over the little wavelets; then she was off and climbed slowly. She circled low over the harbor twice, at not over 200 feet, and headed for the open sea, and Newfoundland. Those on shore who were watching heard the loud wail of the motor stop suddenly. Some claim they detected the sound of a splash. In any event, everyone saw the motorboat that was attending the plane roar out of the channel at top speed.

When it arrived at the scene, the crew of D-1220 was swimming around a partially submerged wreck that had been their seaplane. They were picked up, wet, but unhurt, and what remained of the plane was towed back into Horta Harbor, damaged beyond repair. One wing was missing, and the pontoons were smashed to bits. The Heinkel expedition was at an end.

Merz told of taking off normally, and of circling the harbor to get his bearings, and to make sure of his engine before tackling the ocean. No sooner had they flown away from the harbor, than the motor stopped dead, without even a warning sputter. Try as he might, Merz was unable to bring the heavy ship in on a "dead stick." D-1220 dropped fast, and struck the water hard. The pontoons caught in a rising swell and snapped off, and the plane broke up, and nosed over into the sea. Though she was partially submerged, the crew had been able to scramble through the windows to safety, and, like all sound seamen, had stayed with their ship until help arrived. It was a disappointed, well-soaked, and shivering trio that returned to the Consulate for an early-morning breakfast.

Now, it was D-1230's turn to try, and though the end result was not as drastic, she was equally unsuccessful. During her long stay in Horta, her crew had been revamped completely. Johann "Bear" Risticz, co-holder of the endurance record, and pilot of *Europa*, arrived to take over as second in command to Captain "Fritz" Loose. The remainder of the crew consisted now of radio operator Wilhelm Niemann, navigator Alexander von Bentheim, mechanic Joseph Flistner, and, of course, their lovely ward, Lilli Dillentz.

During the long wait of the Junkers expedition, Miss Dillentz became a great favorite, not only of the German colony on the island, but of all the people of Horta; but, despite her popularity, she was anxious to get on with it, and as the days passed after the Heinkel crash, she kept saying that she was confident that her crew would make it, if only the weather would improve.

On the afternoon of November 22, Captain Loose gave the word. The weather had picked up over their route and it was time to leave.

The all-metal seaplane was filled quickly with fuel and supplies, and, a little after 5 P.M., the crew and Miss Dillentz were put aboard. The plane was towed, like the Heinkel, from her mooring out into the channel where her three motors were started. Loose let them run for a few minutes, then opened the throttles, and the plane surged across the water. The shrill scream from her engines could be heard all over the little community. D-1230 rose heavily into the air, and disappeared from the view of those lining the shore, in a northwesterly direction.

There was much excitement in Horta for a few hours, as Miss Dillentz, at long last, seemed to be on her way to success and glory.

At 9 P.M., however, her well-wishers were filled with gloom, for D-1230 loomed up at the edge of the breakwater, on the end of a towline from a motorboat. Soon, she was fast at her mooring, and her passenger and crew, ashore.

Loose and Risticz told sadly of the vain struggle to get the big seaplane, with her heavy cargo of gasoline and people, into the air. Minutes after they lifted off the channel waters, it became obvious that they could not gain, and maintain sufficient altitude for the trip. They were never able to rise above 50 feet, though Loose and Risticz tugged, together, at the controls. Reluctantly they set the plane down on the calm ocean, where they were picked up almost at once by the little fishing boat which towed them home.

They were determined to give it another try. They had grown desperate with frustration, plus the long days of work and waiting. The petrol supply was cut back to the minimum with which Loose and Risticz felt that the hop could be made, and non-essential supplies were discarded in an effort to lighten the ship.

On the evening of November 23, the weather cleared en route to Newfoundland, and the forecasters gave them hope that the favorable conditions would last for at least 24 hours.

Once more, Loose alerted his crew. Mechanic Flistner was put aboard early to tune up the engines, for the fate of D-1220 was still fresh in their minds. At 1 A.M. the mechanic sent in word that the motors were ready. At the dock Miss Dillentz and the crew received a rousing send-off from the members of the German colony and other residents of the town. While the flyers were taken out to the mooring by tender, the spectators, despite the late hour, scurried to nearby promontories around the harbor to get a better view of the take-off.

At 2 A.M. D-1230 cast off from her moorings, and again was towed out into the channel, but a brisk and rare night breeze roughened the water, and Loose decided to wait. They put back in again, but stayed aboard the plane at the mooring.

At 3 A.M. the wind slackened and they were towed out once more. The engines were started, and a beam from a searchlight aboard the tender shone on the ship, giving it a ghostly look in the dark night. Loose turned into the wind and opened the throttle. The silvery seaplane, still in the searchlight's ray, plowed along on her pontoons, leaving a stream of white foam in her inky wake. The noise from her engines was deafening, and she was quickly skimming over the choppy waters. On and on she went, hopping, now, from wave top to wave top. She seemed on the verge of getting off, but her wake was still heavyish. Suddenly, the echoing noise from her engines faded to a whisper, and the plane rocked fast, to a stop. Again, D-1230 had been unable to lift off the water. People on the shore watched, as her tender sped to her side and took her under tow once more, for the long trip back to the mooring. Miss Dillentz's dream had become impossible.

They remained in Horta for another two weeks, hoping for another try. The combination of bad weather and overweighted plane stopped them. Winter storms blanketed the North Atlantic day after day, and Loose dared not sacrifice another gallon of petrol. At last they gave up. D-1230 was dismantled and crated, and along with her crew, sailed for Germany. The saddened people of Horta waved a nostalgic farewell, too, to their charming visitor, Miss Dillentz, who returned to Paris for the Christmas holiday season.

If the Atlantic was to be flown by a woman in 1927, it would have to be done by the off-again-on-again Frances Wilson Grayson, for she was the only one left in the running.

6. When word was received at Old Orchard Beach that *American Girl* had taken off, Mrs. Grayson gave orders to hurry preparations.

"There is plenty of room for two women over the Atlantic," she said with defiance, and then added, "It was a wise sage who said there is glory enough for all."

In the morning, a 10,000-pound ballast of sandbags and water had been loaded onto *Dawn*. The engines were started, and with Bill Stultz at the controls, and Goldsborough, "Doc" Kinkaid and Mrs. Grayson aboard, the amphibian was taxied up the beach to Pine Point, for what they hoped would be the final load test. She turned a quarter of a mile from our house, and headed down the hard, dark sand toward the pier, 1½ miles away. Surprisingly, the ship lifted off after a run of less than 1500 yards, and was well up in the air as she flew over the pier and banked out toward Biddeford Pool. For fifteen minutes, she circled over Cabbage Island, Prout's Neck, and Old Orchard, and then, when over the ocean, we saw a great cloud of spray fly out behind her. "Goldy" had opened the dump valves to release the water ballast and lighten the ship for a landing. She banked gracefully over Pine Point, and touched down lightly, right in front of our house, and taxied back to Harry Jones's hangar.

Dawn was a big plane. Her dark-blue fuselage was shaped like a boat. Her 72-foot-long wing, from which the twin engines were suspended, sat high above the fuselage, and was attached to it, and to a stubby 28-foot lower wing, by streamlined, Duralumin struts. Though she was big, to us she had a fragile look, caused mainly by the upper wing and tail assembly, both of which were so far above the hull that they did not seem to be a part of it.

When she landed, "Doc" Kinkaid said that the port engine had missed fire on two cylinders, and that he would need eight hours at least to tune it up. He set to work at once and found after careful examination that the trouble was the result of water in the carburetor. He ordered the gas tanks drained and dried, and he personally attended to the drying and cleaning of the valves and pipes.

At 5 P.M. a small crowd gathered for the christening. It was a cloudy day with occasional drizzle, and there was a real nip in the salt air. You knew it was no longer summer.

Mrs. Ralph Brewster, the wife of the State of Maine's governor, presided. Mr. Hazzard was there, too, and I think we pleased him when we said we liked his distinctive road-side HAZZARD SHOE signs, even better than the famous Burma Shave ditties. Perhaps it was to thank him for the use of his pool.

He stood beside Mrs. Brewster as she broke a bottle of Poland Springs Water over the propeller while she solemnly named the plane. I can remember the bottle, wrapped in blue and gold ribbon, with bright-colored streamlets attached to its neck.

Mrs. Grayson, wearing a brown and white antelope coat, stood with Goldsborough and Stultz alongside the plane. It had been parked in the soft sand to the right of the hangar.

Mrs. Brewster turned to Mrs. Grayson, and said, "Prayers of women everywhere will go up for your success, if you shall decide it is wise to start." It was hard to hear her over the noise of the surf and wind. She wound up her short speech with a plea, "But Maine people hope you will wait until spring."

Mrs. Grayson remained silent, but not for long.

When Mrs. Brewster had gone, she said to reporters, "In urging me not to go, I feel she has assumed as great a responsibility as if she had advised me to go."

She continued, "The flight of the *Dawn* will bring the women of two continents together, and we have taken all precautions against the so-called hazards of the glorious month of October!"

Mrs. Brewster was not alone in her desire that the flight be postponed. Messages, including telegrams, letters, and even phone calls, poured in to the Hotel Brunswick from inside and outside the State of Maine, urging her to reconsider her decision, but Mrs. Grayson would hear nothing of it. She was set firmly on making the flight in 1927!

Columbus Day was gray and gloomy. A cold wet wind blew out of the northeast. It comes back to me clearly, because we had to return to school, and, though it was sad to leave, it made it easier if the weather was not bright and sunny. To add to our disappointment, we learned that the weather had caused a postponement of the flight, and now we would not have a chance to watch Lady Grayson take off. We did, however, walk down to the hangar for a last look at *Dawn*. Her wings were too long to allow them to fit inside, and she stood in the soft sand outside the hangar, facing the wind-whipped ocean. None of the crew was around, but there were a number of mechanics working on her. Some were filling her tanks with gasoline. I worked up my nerve to ask one of them how many gallons *Dawn* would carry.

Without looking away from his work, he answered laconically, "Eight hundred and fifty-nine."

"Wow," I said to myself, "that's a lot of gas!"

Other workmen were polishing the wings and the hull, to rid them of the dirt, sand, and oil that had accumulated. We stood and watched nostalgically, for inside of us was the aching realization that we would have to leave soon. The time came too quickly, and we walked back up the beach, but our hearts were still with the big amphibian and her crew.

During the day, the crew, with the exception of Mrs. Grayson, remained at the Hotel Brunswick, sitting in the heavy maple chairs in front of a warm fire while the wind whistled and the surf pounded outside.

Mrs. Goldsborough and Mrs. Stultz arrived on the train from New York at midday—the train making a special off-season stop for them. They joined their husbands at the hotel. "Doc" Kinkaid returned from the hangar with the pronouncement that "My work is finished. The J-5s are ready to go."

Stultz told newsmen that weather reports showed cross winds 80 miles offshore, which would reduce the speed of the plane by 20 miles an hour, and make the flight impossible.

Mrs. Grayson left, earlier, to shop in Portland. As she was leaving a young woman stepped up to her and presented a rabbit's foot for luck.

The girl said, "It's the left hind foot of a rabbit that was shot ten years ago in a graveyard at midnight by a one-eyed Negro. (All of which was supposed to contribute to its luck-giving qualities!) Mrs. Grayson laughed, accepted it, and left for Portland where she shopped at Benoit's for heavy-woolen underwear, fleece-lined gloves, woolen socks, and a powerful flashlight to be used for signaling.

Bryce Goldsborough ventured out into the weather, which was worsening, to tinker with *Dawn's* radio. When he returned he announced that on the flight WMU would transmit during the first fifteen minutes of each hour, with the exception of the first two, on 625 and 830 meters. He told his mates also that it was really beginning to blow up at the beach.

The storm that had been brewing all day struck the beach with full fury during the night. There were heavy rains, and winds with gusts up to 60 miles an hour. When Mrs. Grayson, Goldsborough, and Stultz arrived at the hangar the next morning, they found that high tides had imperiled *Dawn*. Her undercarriage was buried in the sand, and her buff-colored wings and her engines were littered with seaweed and dried salt spray. Though it was thought that she was secure in her space well above the high water mark, the tide whipped up by the storm had raged to within feet of the hangar entrance, and engulfed the plane. It was lucky that she had not been carried away for natives said that it was the highest tide in ten years.

Mechanics and crew got busy, for the sea again was surging in. Mrs. Grayson led the way, protecting herself from the driving rain with a borrowed raincoat and knee-length boots. She manned a shovel with the others as the sand was cleared away from the wheels. Wooden planks were laid down to form a temporary runway, and *Dawn*, with everyone pushing and hauling, was moved farther up into the soft sand almost to the main road behind the hangar.

As they worked the tide kept creeping in and soon the angry water swirled around them as they struggled with the big plane. The wind shrieked, and the rain and salt-water spray slanted in their faces. Suddenly, a huge breaker snatched up a 50-gallon can of oil and swept it away. Stultz and Goldsborough dashed into the foaming surf and managed to bring it ashore. The ship was tied down by the wings, and all seemed safe for the moment.

Relief came in the afternoon. The tide went out, the rain stopped, and the skies began to brighten. "Doc" Kinkaid took the tarpaulins off the engines and dried the cylinders. He said that there was no damage, and, more important, that no water had gotten into the gasoline.

Igor Sikorsky arrived at the hangar, having come on from New

York, and he joined Lebensky, Goldsborough, and Stultz in a thorough inspection of the plane. They announced that it was fit and had not suffered from the storm's battering. Mrs. Grayson, soaked to the skin, ducked into the comparative warmth of the hangar and, after powdering her nose, said that she felt better. Soon they were all back in front of the fire at the Brunswick, tired, but happy that *Dawn* was in one piece.

The next day was sunny and lovely. The sunlight danced on the smooth waters, and it seemed as though you could touch Prout's Neck or Cabbage Island, so close did they loom across the bay. It was a typical fall morning in the State of Maine.

Mrs. Grayson was up early. She announced that *Dawn* would take off the next morning at 7, when the tide would be dead low. Though the wind was blowing off the sea, an ideal southwest wind was expected within twelve hours which would assist the heavily fueled plane off the ground.

Before she drove off to Portland, to take her mind off things, she said confidently, "I am going to be the first woman to fly across the Atlantic!"

That evening she hostessed a dinner at the Hotel Brunswick for the entire party, including newsmen, photographers, and local dignitaries. The little wooden tables in the dining room, which faced the ocean, were pushed together so as to make one long banquet table. Lady Grayson sat in the center flanked by her crew. After the main course she made a brief speech telling of her hopes, the difficulties they had surmounted, and the problems that lay ahead. With a touch of humor she said that she had reduced her wardrobe for the trip to one rose-pink negligee, which she'd wear under her flying suit, and a pair of silver, high-heeled slippers. She told them also that she would carry a picture of her mother, a Bible, and a picture of Francis Scott Key, which her godmother, his great-great-grandniece, had given to her. Igor Sikorsky gave her a seventh-century Persian coin which had been dug up on the Sikorsky estate near Kiev in Russia. She promised him that it would be embedded in a little wooden disc and mounted in her cabin.

The crowning point of the dinner came when she gave each guest her autographed picture and received, in turn, from the gentlemen of the press, a necklace of pearls.

The spokesman told her that each pearl was a separate prayer of good luck.

She retired at 11 P.M. and left instructions to be wakened at

6 A.M. Before going to bed, she took one final dig at her critics: "The theory about there being a season for flying the Atlantic is wrong, and I will prove it wrong."

Bad weather reports from ships at sea foiled them the next day. The radio station at Chatham, Massachusetts, reported messages telling of 25 mile-an-hour easterly winds blowing over the western Atlantic. The crew was up at 4:30 A.M., ready to go, but, after a study of the weather systems, decided once again on a postponement, and returned to bed. Later in the morning, Mrs. Grayson drove off to Portland where she bought several cans of dark blue paint. She returned to the beach, and painted over the upper half of the hull, which had been stained by salt water. She was still hard at work, at 4:30 P.M., when a delegation from the Old Orchard Board of Trade, led by chairman George F. Hichborn, arrived at the hangar. They presented the doughty lady with a large bouquet of red roses.

Chairman Hichborn cheered her by saying in the presentation, "Go to it! You'll make it!" It was the only speech she had heard urging her not to quit.

Sunday, the 16th started out as a foggy day. From time to time the fog lifted and the sun shone warmly, but then it would be back again and all would be a ghostly gray. The easterly winds persisted at sea and stopped them once more.

Bryce Goldsborough told of spending most of the night at his hotel window practicing star shots before the fog interrupted him toward dawn.

Bill Stultz began to show impatience.

"Gosh, I hope we'll get away tomorrow," he said to Mrs. Grayson.

There was no Episcopal church in Old Orchard, and Harry Jones offered to fly Mrs. Grayson, in his Stinson, to Portland for services, but after taking off they were forced back by the fog. She then drove to Saco to a little white Congregational church. After the services, the pastor asked his visiting worshiper to come back in a month and help celebrate the 100th anniversary of his congregation. She said that she would try.

She returned to the beach and to *Dawn*. She gave instructions to have the upper part of the plane rubbed with emory board to eliminate "skin resistance caused by the sand." Mechanics, thereupon, scoured every joint and crevice with gasoline. A vacuum cleaner was brought into use to take up the sand which had collected in the cabin. During the work, mechanic Clarence Wood of College

Point, Long Island, was cut badly by a sharp corner of the metal door to the cabin. He was rushed to the local doctor who stitched him up and he returned to the line. *Dawn* was ready. She waited only on her fickle enemy—the weather.

The beach was at its best on the 17th. It was cloudless, and you could see for miles. The crew was wakened at 5:30 A.M. and decided to go, after a breakfast conference. "Doc" Kinkaid rushed to the hangar, where he supervised the final check. He looked over the motors again and pronounced them, "Perfect!"

Miss Mary Hill, employed by Fred Boston, provided the flyers with coffee and soup, while another maid, Mary Madden, prepared a tasty assortment of sandwiches, which were stowed aboard. The crew thanked the girls, and Miss Madden obliged with a farewell serenade of "My Wild Irish Rose."

At 9:30 A.M., mechanics Parkinson and Wood, the latter's hand in bandages, cranked on the inertia starter handles, and the twin engines, after a few smoky sputters, burst to life. Kinkaid ran them up, as spectators fled from the lee of the plane to escape the flying sand granules. He listened carefully to each and then nodded to Bill Stultz, who stood outside on the sand. Mrs. Grayson said her good-byes, the last to Miss Julie Dunphy of Brookline, Massachusetts, a house guest of the Bostons. There weren't many around to see her off, except for a scattering of natives, and a few of the late-staying summer folk.

Stultz climbed into the pilot's seat. Goldsborough took his position next to the radio and prepared to send out the WMU signals. Mrs. Grayson, bundled in heavy flying clothes (with her negligee underneath) was the last to board.

The wind was from the north. Stultz taxied *Dawn* to the southerly end of the beach and turned her in the shadow of the pier. At least he would not have that hazard to worry about. The engines were revved up and the big blue amphibian started heavily down the sand toward Pine Point. After a run of nine-tenths of a mile in 52 seconds, she became airborne directly in front of our now-vacant house. She rose ten feet, and no higher. As she banked gingerly to head for the waters off Prout's Neck, she looked to be nose-heavy. She was barely off the water and appeared ready to settle in at any moment. The spectators watched with bated breath as she continued her valiant struggle to stay aloft. Suddenly, there was a cloud of vapor streaming from her nacelle tanks. Goldsborough had opened the dump valve and released 260 gallons of precious fuel. Now, *Dawn* soared up with ease, but without the gasoline it was useless to go on. Around she came again, banked over the Saco shore, glided in over the pier, and landed gently. It had to be a gentle landing for even without the 260 gallons *Dawn* weighed 9940 pounds.

The flyers jumped out of the plane. They were disconsolate. Bill Stultz, when questioned, said that the plane had, indeed, been nose-heavy because of an error in placing some of the gas load too far forward. He said, however, that the weight could be redistributed without difficulty, and they would be off again in no time. But Bryce Goldsborough stepped in with another problem. When it had seemed that the plane most certainly would be forced to land in the sea, he had tried to retract the landing gear. To do it, each wheel had to be lifted separately by pulling on a shock cord inside the cabin. As the plane started to lose altitude, he yanked desperately on the cord, but succeeded only in getting one wheel up. The cords had been weakened apparently by exposure and his only alternative at that point was to dump gasoline and lighten the ship. Mrs. Grayson decided instantly that *Dawn* would make no futher attempts until the gear problem was rectified. She wired Sikorsky, who had gone back to New York, to return to the beach at once and provide some means of quicker retractibility of the plane's wheels.

Nothing was accomplished the next day, the 18th, for again the coast was lashed by a northeast storm. *Dawn* was tied down securely and weighted with sandbags to protect her from the heavy surf and high tides, and she rode out the gale without harm.

On the 19th, Sikorsky and a mechanic arrived, bringing with them 100 feet of new shock cord. While they were at work replacing the defective line to the landing gear, Kinkaid, Day, and Parkinson drained the gasoline tanks and strained the gas through chamois skin to rid it of impurities. Bill Stultz stood nearby, talking to Harry Jones. He was concerned as to whether the plane could get off the ground with enough fuel to keep his J-5s turning all the way to Europe. Two engines needed twice as much gasoline, he knew if *Dawn* flew with the necessary amount. Sikorsky made light of the problem, as he tried to allay Stultz's fears.

There was a flare-up between Goldsborough and Mrs. Grayson in the afternoon. She berated him for not giving her enough navigational and radio instruction, and he retorted that he already had plenty to keep him busy. Angry words filled the air for a few minutes, but then the two took a walk up the beach, and when they returned, harmony had been restored. The soothing sound of the breaking surf had a calming effect on both. Goldsborough went back to work, and charted three separate courses for *Dawn*—the Great Circle, the ships' lane, and the southern route. He then drove to Portland, where he and his wife were honored by the Lion's Club at dinner, while Mrs. Grayson attended evening services at the little Congregational church in Saco.

On the 20th, it was windy and rainy again. Prout's Neck was shrouded by mist, and Biddeford Pool was obscured entirely. Sikorsky finished the repairs to the landing gear, and, in the afternoon, when the weather lifted slightly, *Dawn* took off on a test hop. They tried out the new retracting equipment, and found that the wheels could now be brought up to within three inches of the hull in 52 seconds, and could be fully retracted in 1 minute. Goldsborough was satisfied with the improvement. It was a busy day, socially, for Mrs. Grayson and her crew. At lunch, they were guests of the Thirteenth Club in Portland. The members, all prominent in the community, gave them a standing ovation, when they were introduced. In the evening, the indefatigable lady addressed a women's group in Biddeford, Maine. She thrived on activity.

It was crisp and bright again on the 21st, but a strong west wind blew across the beach, and prevented a take-off. They were ready, once more, and the forecast was for improved local winds the next day. They lounged around the hotel for most of the day, and in the evening the entire party were guests at a banquet given for them by the Portland Chamber of Commerce at the Eastland Hotel. There were innumerable speeches, toasts, and prayers for the flyers' safe landing. After dinner, they all repaired to nearby B. F. Keith's Theater for the vaudeville and motion picture show, following which they were driven on the thirty-minute trip back to the Brunswick. Mrs. Grayson was desperate to be off, left an early call, and it seemed certain to everyone that tomorrow would be the day.

They were all up early on Saturday morning. Mrs. Grayson looked out her window to see the sun peeking over Prout's Neck, Checkley House, and the bay a-sparkle. The wind was still westerly, but so light that it would not pose a threat to the take-off, though a head wind would have been more desirable with the heavy load.

At 6 A.M., when the great beach was bared by the fallen tide, *Dawn*'s engines were started and warmed by "Doc" Kinkaid. His expert ear detected no trace of dissonance as he opened first one throttle, and then the other. Once more, Lady Grayson, Stultz, and Goldsborough said good-bye to the scattered few early-birds who had gathered. They climbed in, and Stultz taxied the ship down to the pier, turned, and roared off toward Pine Point. After a long, long run, *Dawn* lifted off, but again only slightly. The 910 gallons she carried were a back-breaking load. She turned out to sea, but, as in her first attempt, she did not appear to be gaining altitude. She flew at wave-top level. Her struggle for flight this time was short and spectators on the beach watched her splash into the calm waters off Cabbage Island. She taxied back toward the beach, and in a matter of minutes the big amphibian was flung gently on the sand by the little breakers of low tide. With her wheels down, she returned to Harry Jones's hangar, and three unhappy, angry, but determined flyers, jumped out onto the sand.

Stultz shook his head and said, "She wouldn't lift at all!" Mrs. Grayson ordered 71 gallons drained off to lighten the load, but, by the time the work was done, the tide had come in too far to permit a safe take-off area, and the flight was again postponed.

There was no banqueting or revelry of any sort that night. Goldsborough and Stultz retired early, with their wives, who were, by now in a state of nervous collapse over the false starts.

Mrs. Grayson sat up listening to the pounding of the surf on the beach. The noise was a tranquilizer for her.

Early Sunday morning, despite gray skies and a misty rain, they were off again. This time *Dawn* took off from Pine Point, and was 600 feet in the air as she passed over the pier. She was 310 pounds lighter, and lifted off after a run of one mile, in 63 seconds. It was a little after 6 A.M., as they circled over Wood Island Light, on Fortune's Rocks, and disappeared behind Prout's Neck on a northeasterly course.

For the first four hours, as they flew the traditional route that would take them over Nova Scotia to Newfoundland, everything went like clockwork. The Whirlwind engines roared evenly, and drove the plane through the gray skies at 125 miles an hour. The clouds swirled over them at times but then the gray inscrutable sea would break into view again—bleak, cold, and endless.

Bill Stultz flew the plane, Goldy bent over the radio, and Mrs. Grayson busied herself at her writing table in the rear cabin.

At 10:15 A.M., as they traveled off the eastern coast of Nova Scotia, toward Newfoundland, they flew into a thick cloud bank. The turbulence shook the plane violently, and suddenly and inexplicably, Stultz felt her nose down in a steep dive. He struggled desperately with the controls, for they were only at 600 feet, and there was little time or room. Goldsborough yanked at a dump valve and 110 gallons of gas spilled out. Stultz was able to bring her to level flight a bare ten feet over the sea. Slowly he coaxed *Dawn* back up up to 1000 feet.

Minutes afterward they flew over a freighter which steamed below them in a westerly direction. Goldsborough identified it as the *Coshoma County*, of the American Diamond Lines. It was raining, but the sea was smooth. "Goldy" checked their position, and calculated it to be somewhat to the east of the traditional course, approximately 30 miles south of Sable Island. He informed Stultz, yelling over the noise of the engines, that they had traveled 500 miles, and were headed for the well-traveled ship lanes, which they would intersect, 900 miles out. Both pilot and navigator commented on the lack of fog which usually blanketed the area.

All of a sudden, Stultz saw the port engine give off a series of thick white puffs of smoke. Simultaneously, the engine began to misfire, and the ship, to vibrate. He glanced at the tachometer. The needle was gyrating wildly, and then it dropped to zero. He looked out at the motor. It was smoking, but the propeller was still turning over. The vibrations had damaged the rpm indicator. He saw a great glob of black oil spurt out of the engine. The plane started to settle from the loss of power. Stultz opened the throttle of the starboard engine, while Goldsborough hurried back and dumped more of the gas supply. The plane leveled out at 300 feet, but her speed was down to 90 miles an hour. Goldsborough sent out an SOS while Stultz turned *Dawn* around and pointed back to the freighter. Over the freighter they circled, trying to decide whether to land in the sea. Goldsborough communicated with her captain who told Goldy, that if they decided to come down, they should land on the starboard side of *Coshoma County*, so as to be protected from the wind. Stultz, at length, was satisfied that *Dawn* could make it back to Old Orchard despite the head winds, and Goldy provided him instantly with the proper heading. The big amphibian limped homeward with her starboard motor wide open. The port engine still ran but with little power and her exhaust pipe trailed a plume of smoke. They could see one of the cylinder heads white with heat.

At 3 P.M., Goldy sent a message ashore addressed to his wife and Mrs. Stultz.

It was received at the Cape Elizabeth, Maine, receiving station,

and said: WE ARE ON OUR WAY BACK TO OLD ORCHARD WITH
ENGINE TROUBLE. WEATHER AHEAD TOO BAD TO GET THROUGH WITH
HEAVY LOAD.

Bar Harbor appeared below them through a thickening mist, and
at 4 o'clock the sands of Old Orchard hove into view off the
starboard wing. It had been a harrowing flight back, with the
flyers eying the smoking engine anxiously, fearing a fire, but now
they had made it. At 4:10 P.M., they were safely on the beach, and
Dawn was parked in her niche next to the hangar. Few people were
there to greet them, for the word of their plight was, somehow, slow
in spreading.

Mrs. Grayson was excited and effusive.

She described the flight in her typical, lyrical, almost poetic
fashion:

"For the first thirty minutes," she said, "we all seemed in the
thrall of a spell. None of us spoke. There Bill Stultz sat hunched
over the controls, looking straight ahead. Goldy was lost in concentration at the prospect before us. I never moved a muscle, as
I was in the rear cockpit."

She described how later in the morning she noticed Stultz looking
out at the port motor, and how she felt the plane suddenly slow
and begin to sag, and, finally, how a sheet of black oil had splashed
over her window.

"Then," she said, "we circled over a ship a few times, and flew
back."

She made no mention of how they arrived at the decision to
return, or whether there had been any argument about going on.

Stultz's comments were brief.

"She was puffing white smoke," he said. "That almost always
means a blown piston head." He went on: "Mrs. Grayson was a
brick. She left it to Goldy and me to decide what to do."

There was much discussion during the remainder of the day as
to whether they should give it all up. Mr. Wilson, Mrs. Grayson's
father, sent her a telegram from his grocery store in Muncie, Indiana,
urging her to postpone the flight until spring. Bill Stultz, too, had
serious reservations about going again. He felt that the venture was
too risky, in view of the weather and the heavy load. Though it was
not disclosed at once, he sounded out Mrs. Grayson about the
possibility of being released from his contract. She said that she'd
take it under consideration, but said that she herself was determined
to go on. She fired off two wires—one to the Wright Company in

Paterson, New Jersey, ordering a new engine for immediate delivery
to Old Orchard, and the second to "Doc" Kinkaid in New York,
asking him to return at once. He had left immediately after the
take-off.

The logistics of the operation were complicated further by the fact
that when *Dawn* left, apparently for good, John Hutchinson, owner
and manager of the Brunswick, with the help of his son Hal,
boarded up the hotel for the season and released the kitchen staff.
When the party returned, he tried to recapture the chef, but the
latter refused to postpone his annual deer hunt one day longer, and
disappeared into the wilds of Maine. As a result, the crew and
their wives picked up what food they could at the few eateries that
remained open over the winter in Old Orchard.

7.   On October 24, Kinkaid returned and ex-
amined the faulty engine. After his inspection, he said that it had
come close to exploding in the air. He told of a broken valve in the
head of the number two cylinder, which had fallen on the piston
head. The next upward stroke of the piston had saved matters
miraculously, for it shoved the valve back to its original position,
where it had stuck for the flight home. Had that not happened,
he said, there would have been an explosion and a fire, and the plane
and her crew would have perished in all likelihood.

Kinkaid told the anxious Mrs. Grayson that the new motor was
scheduled to arrive on the morning train, the next day. He added
that the installation would take up the better part of six hours, after
which he would taxi the plane out on the beach and run the engine
for another ten hours, in a thorough test.

The newspapers were filled with rumors of a rift between Mrs.
Grayson and Stultz. There were stories that Stultz had turned back
without consulting her, and there were others to the effect that he
had turned back against her orders. The mongers were stilled temporarily when Mrs. Grayson took the pilot on one of her beach walks,
and, when they returned, they were chatting happily. People close
to the flight though, detected a slight strain, still, between the two,
due primarily to Stultz's reluctance to continue.

The engine arrived on schedule, and was uncrated quickly, cleaned,
and assembled. By nightfall, it had been bolted into place by "Doc"
Kinkaid and his assistants. He announced that the tuning would be
finished, and the plane ready to fly within 24 hours.

More credence was given to unrest in *Dawn*'s crew, when on October 27th Mrs. Grayson journeyed to Boston, and checked in to the Hotel Touraine, where she conferred at length with Clarence Chamberlin. It was reported that she asked Chamberlin to take over the pilot's duties, but that he was reluctant to do so, in that he didn't want to make another ocean flight in present-day aircraft. Furthermore, it was said that he urged Mrs. Grayson, because of the weather, to defer her flight until the spring. His arguments had some effect on her for a time, for after the meeting, she announced that unless the weather improved by October 31, she would wait until the winter was over.

Stultz, when questioned at Old Orchard, admitted that he wanted out, but he said in a public statement, that he would stay on per his contract, if Mrs. Grayson so desired.

"I would be delighted," the young pilot declared, "if Mrs. Grayson would get some other pilot for this expedition, because I do not believe we'll have any suitable weather, and I have other work I'd like to be doing."

Mrs. Grayson announced suddenly on October 29, that *Dawn* would return to Curtiss Field, New York, for further tests, and to give her an opportunity to consult with Igor Sikorsky.

In a flowery statement to the press, which she read in the common room of the Hotel Brunswick, she said, "In my disappointment of today, I can only strive for a bigger, greater success tomorrow." Then she added with a touch of rancor, "I wish to ascertain [from Sikorsky] why the plane gained altitude, then lost 400 feet, according to pilot Stultz, at the end of four hours when the plane was approximately 1000 pounds lighter, causing him to turn about and head west for Old Orchard."

This was the first public indication that she was piqued by the turn of events that day off the Nova Scotian coast. Stultz, however, refused to be drawn into a controversy.

His only comment, when he was questioned later, was, "I do not feel that the tests of which she speaks are needed. We know what the plane will do, but we also know that it cannot be flown in bad weather." The remainder of the day was spent packing for the trip home.

The next morning, a few of Old Orchard's hardier citizens turned out to bid farewell to *Dawn*. Kinkaid, Mrs. Stultz, and Mrs. Goldsborough had left for New York the night before. The papers had hinted of trouble aboard *Dawn* on her fateful morning over the sea, but, as they boarded this morning, Mrs. Grayson and Stultz denied vociferously that there had been anything resembling a mutiny off Sable Island. Harry Jones, who had provided his valuable facilities to *Dawn* and her crew, was thanked with warmth. He admired Mrs. Grayson—perhaps because of her vision of aviation.

He said to me not long ago laughingly, and yet admiringly, "She was a very nice lady." He continued realistically, "At least, she paid me for everything except for the last load of gas she used."

Stultz sat at the controls, and three mechanics followed Mrs. Grayson and Goldsborough aboard. The plane roared down the beach, lifted off quickly, and disappeared into the southwest. It was the last glimpse that State of Mainers had of Lady Grayson and her *Dawn*. Three hours later, Stultz circled her over Curtiss Field, and dropped her in for a landing. The big ship was pushed in at once to the Sikorsky hangar where she was housed.

Mrs. Grayson had nothing to say, except to deny that she had any personnel problems. Stultz was asked once more whether he would fly again in *Dawn*.

He answered, with a quizzical smile, "I hope that by that time, my interest and attention will be otherwise engaged."

It was, and happily, too, for Stultz lived to pilot Amelia Earhart from Newfoundland to Wales, when that pretty, curly-haired girl embarked on her career as America's female counterpart to "Lucky Lindy." As for Bill Stultz, his days of fame thereafter were numbered. In 1929, while stunting a plane over Mineola, Long Island, he crashed and was killed.

The fall was over. The ladies still hadn't flown the Atlantic. They had tried and failed thus far, but one was still trying, and the year was not yet over. Mrs. Grayson, now back at Curtiss Field, thought now about her situation. She did not quit easily and she had her eyes open for a new pilot, so that she could make "one more try from Old Orchard."

CHAPTER XIV

The Year Ends with the Dawn

1. In the words of a Gilbert and Sullivan madrigal, "Leaves in autumn fade and fall, winter is the end of all." And so it was, for just ahead were the snows and the icy winds of that bleak season. The year 1927 had budded, bloomed with its distinctive color, aged, and now was ready to take its place with its predecessors. The people it was leaving, however, continued on, for their time had not yet come.

In China, General Chiang Kai-shek emerged from retirement with his new bride, and took command of the Nationalist Armies of China, after being guaranteed the power to suppress foreign influence within its ranks. His government took note, with some bitterness, of the honors paid to the American bankers by Emperor Hirohito of Japan, and complained of the proposed loan of $40,000-000 to the South Manchurian Railroad, which, they asserted, was already 50 percent Japanese-owned. In Russia, a revolt in the Ukraine was declared ended officially, with a reported casualty list of 5000; and ex-Prime Minister Vincenzo Nitti of Italy criticized British and French leaders for blindness to the evils of Fascism, and accused Benito Mussolini of preparing a war against the West between 1935 and 1940, when he felt France would be weaker. In London, William Ralph Inge, Dean of St. Paul's, shocked some segments of the theological world by advocating the use of artificial contraceptive devices to combat the overpopulation on the earth.

In the United States, it was business as usual. Forty-two-year-old Bernard F. Gimbel succeeded his father, Isaac, as president of the famed retail store bearing the family name, and the Ford Company introduced the Model A as the successor to the Tin Lizzie at the Auto Show held in New York's Waldorf-Astoria Hotel on Fifth Avenue at 34th Street. The new car won instant approval from the public, particularly for its price range—$385 for a rumble-seated roadster, and to $570 for a de-luxe sedan. Washington announced that, despite $42,000,000 paid in fines, and 22,500 jail sentences, people were still drinking in violation of the Volstead law; and New York City declared war on its smoke nuisance. An advisory board was created by the Health Department "to conduct a survey of the evil, and how to fight it."

It was a brilliant season on Broadway. Edna Ferber and George S. Kaufman's *The Royal Family* opened at the Selwyn Theatre on 42nd Street with Haidee Wright and Ann Andrews as Fanny and Julie Cavendish. Noël Coward's *Fallen Angels* with Fay Bainter and Estelle Winwood at the 49th Street Theatre, and George Gershwin's *Funny Face*, starring the incomparable Fred and Adele Astaire was at the Alvin. Of the latter, critic Brooks Atkinson of the *Times* said simply: "S'Wonderful!"

The hits were joined at the tag end of the year by Miss Ferber's and Jerome Kern and Oscar Hammerstein's unforgettable *Show Boat*, at the Ziegfeld Theatre. Theatergoers were raving about Helen Morgan's plaintive singing of "Bill" and Jules Bledsoe's powerful and resonant rendition of "Ol' Man River," not to mention Norma Terris, Charles Winninger, and Edna May Oliver.

Those who were more seriously inclined musically cheered Madame Ernestine Schumann-Heink's farewell performance at Carnegie Hall, or were awed by the talent of an eleven-year-old violinist by the name of Yehudi Menuhin, who made his debut with the New York Symphony Orchestra.

In sports, Army concluded a happy football season by beating both Notre Dame and Navy, with the help of stars Chris Cagle and "Light Horse Harry" Wilson. New York's Rangers, playing at the new Madison Square Garden on Eighth Avenue and 50th Street, shared the lead with Montreal's Canadians, in the National Hockey League race. The sport, a novelty to Americans, was drawing capacity crowds, and the names of "The Edmonton Express," Eddie Shore, and "The Stratford Streak," Howie Morenz, were mentioned already, in the same breath with other athletic heroes of the day.

As Christmas decorations appeared and carols floated in the air, a tragedy marred the season in the United States. On December 17, the U. S. Submarine S-4, with forty men aboard was sunk off the harbor at Provincetown, Massachusetts, when it was rammed accidentally by a destroyer. There followed days of desperate rescue attempts, led by Captain (later Admiral) Ernest L. King, and his trained team of divers. Heart-rending messages from six men, trapped in the torpedo room of the sub, were tapped out. "Need food, water, air. How long will you be? Air is bad." The divers, with what equipment they had, worked tirelessly in the cold waters. Two days later, they heard faint taps. "Last bottle of oxygen gone. Is there any hope?"

Twenty-four hours after, there were only sporadic, and indecipherable sounds from S-4. On December 21, when the rescuers were finally able to pump air into the sunken ship and then make their way in, all aboard were found dead.

2. When she returned to New York, Mrs. Grayson's first order of business was to seek a replacement for Bill Stultz to whom she had granted his requested release. Though Clarence Chamberlin had expressed a disinterest in becoming a part of the expedition, his name re-entered the picture, at least in the eyes of the public, when he turned up at Curtiss Field on November 1 and took *Dawn* up on a 20-minute test flight over Long Island. After he landed he was bombarded with questions from inquisitive reporters. He answered them with a poker face, expressing satisfaction over the performance of the plane, but remaining noncommittal as to his own plans.

Mrs. Grayson did not remain idle while he thought things over. She canvassed the field of aviators who were experienced in winter or arctic flying. At once, the name of Bernt Balchen came to mind and from her Forest Hills Inn headquarters, she phoned him at the Fokker factory in Hasbrouck Heights where he was engaged in testing a new tri-motored design for Pan American Airways. She used all her ample persuasive abilities on the young Norwegian, but he was hesitant and wanted time to think over her offer. Mrs. Grayson, however, was impatient and would not be deterred, and it was announced forthwith that Balchen was her new pilot.

Reporters rushed to question the flyer at Hasbrouck Heights. He laughed when told of the announcement, and commented good-humoredly, "Well, I can't say that the lady didn't ask me, but before I make any decision like that I want to fly the *Dawn*."

His work at the Fokker plant forced him to postpone continually his proposed trial of the amphibian, and at length by mutual consent, he was dropped as a candidate.

Once again Mrs. Grayson turned to Chamberlin.

With an apparent change of heart, he said now, "If I believe the plane is capable of crossing the Atlantic, I may make the trip," and, with Mrs. Grayson on board, he took *Dawn* up on another test spin. When they landed, both pilot and passenger were silent as to any decision, but a few days later it was learned that Chamberlin had determined, once and for all, not to go. Whether his decision was based on the plane's performance, or whether he was deterred by the thought of an ocean flight in midwinter, was never made public.

Thea Rasche, a German aviatrix of note then in America, expressed an interest in the assignment, but was turned down firmly. Mrs. Grayson tried Arthur Goebel, the winner of the Dole Race She had no pilot, and there were indications that Goldsborough, under pressure from his family might leave also. She was tired and despite her seemingly endless supply of energy, she needed a rest.

She announced an indefinite postponement of all flight plans, and said that she would sail for Europe on November 4 aboard the *Majestic*.

"I want to get away from the *Dawn*," she said wearily, "and everything connected with her, for a while, so that I can get a new perspective on things."

She told reporters that she had learned much from her three unsuccessful attempts in Maine, and added surprisingly, that, "There will be no non-stop flights across the ocean for me. It was my idea from the beginning that we should make stops en route, but my pilot overruled me."

Bill Stultz made no comment.

As she boarded the *Majestic*, holding a large bouquet of roses, she said that she planned to confer in Copenhagen with her partner Mrs. Ancker as to the future of *Dawn*, and would also use the trip as an opportunity to broaden her aviation knowledge by talking with the flying leaders of Europe.

The next news of Mrs. Grayson was from Berlin, where she was interviewed at her hotel. She reiterated the fact that she would not fly non-stop, saying that she felt aviation would be benefited more by a flight made in safe, and easy stages.

The winter weather she had seen during her crossing had been an eye-opener, but she said, "It's nonsense to say you can't fly in winter!"

There was an inkling as to her future plans when she let it be known that Lufthansa officials had assured her that their airport in Iceland was fully operative and would be placed at her disposal if she so desired. She concluded the press conference by saying that from Berlin she intended to travel to Denmark and inspect possible landing sites, as well as to confer with Mrs. Ancker.

Following a visit to Copenhagen, where she was treated with affection by the Danes, she moved on to Paris, and talked at length, with a number of French pilots, including Léon Givon of *Oiseau Bleu* and Maurice Drouhin, late of *Columbia*. She gathered meteorological information from the renowned Admiral Delacambre, who had provided forecasts for Nungesser and Coli and other French pilots, and she called on Madame Nungesser. She told reporters that she was convinced that ocean weather was just as good during the winter months, and that she now planned her take-off for February.

When she was asked about the dropping of Stultz as her pilot, she replied with aplomb, "It takes a stout heart and implicit faith to make a trip like ours, and when I discovered my pilot had faltered, somewhat, I felt that it was only fair that I release him."

She anticipated no problem in getting another pilot. "Goldsborough, and whoever goes with us, and I will probably have heated arguments all the time, but we will also remain the best of friends to the end."

Her days in Paris were exciting. She was treated as a celebrity wherever she went. She made a flying trip over the city, and was given an official tour of the now-famous Le Bourget Airdrome. She impressed the French with her style and obvious intelligence, and when on November 23, she left for home on the *Leviathan,* she carried with her the best wishes of the French people.

The trip renewed her vigor and crystallized her thoughts as she had hoped, and when she landed in New York on November 28, she said without reservation that her ocean flight would be made before springtime. She had gained Mrs. Ancker's blessing for the venture, and was convinced by her studies, and from her conferences with the experts, that an Atlantic flight in winter weather was not only feasible, but, in all probability, would be aided by the stronger winds from the west that would be blowing.

From the Forest Hills Inn, she dove into her new project with energy. She ordered the engines of *Dawn* overhauled at once, and Wright expert Ed Mulligan, whose summer began with the *Spirit of St. Louis,* was assigned to the task. Mechanics under his supervision stripped the motors down, and rebuilt them in the cold Sikorsky hangar at Curtiss. Men from the College Point factory checked every structural part of the big amphibian. Mrs. Grayson kept a close eye on the activities, but her immediate need was for a competent crew. She called Bryce Goldsborough in Brooklyn, and after some urging, he consented again to serve as navigator and radio operator. To get her pilot, she sought again the advice of her friends Chamberlin and Balchen. It was through the help of the latter that she found her solution, for he suggested the name of Lieutenant Oskar Omdal, whom he had brought back from Europe to serve as his relief pilot on Commander Byrd's planned flight to the South Pole. Since the flight had been postponed, Omdal was available, and Balchen felt that he might accept an offer. He arranged for a meeting of the two, at which Omdal agreed to go without hesitation.

He was a blond, thirty-two-year-old Norwegian who had made the Norwegian Navy his career. Besides being in the crew of the dirigible *Norge*, he has served as a pilot for arctic explorer, Roald Amundsen, and had considerable experience in flying the Dornier *Whale* (more recently, Captain Courtney's plane) in the severest arctic weather. He was noted as a cold-weather pilot, as well as an expert at take-offs and landings in the snow.

Mrs. Grayson was delighted with her find, for besides his abilities as a winter flyer, he had no fear of icing, as we have seen. He was convinced that ice formed only on the metal edges of the aircraft, and if these danger points were coated with glycerin, there would be no worry about an accumulation.

Mrs. Grayson planned, still, to take off from Old Orchard Beach, and to this end, she wrote to her friend, Harry Jones, in early December, to inquire about take-off conditions at this time of year. Jones, in the off-season the proprietor of a radio shop in Portland, wrote back to her and said that he saw no reason why the beach surface would not serve her just as well in the winter as in the summer, and offered her again the use of his hangar.

Unwittingly, he released the substance of their exchanges to the press, and was quoted as saying, "Mrs. Grayson really means to fly across the Atlantic, and the chances are a whole lot better than when she was here. The snow will not bother them, and as long as the motors hold out, they will keep going. There may be a question about heating the plane, but that's a minor detail."

The news story upset Mrs. Grayson, because, since her return from Europe, she had kept her plans secret in order to keep public discussion and possible criticism of her venture at a minimum. The only stories, heretofore, were small items saying that she would make a winter flight, and that Lieutenant Omdal would act as pilot. She was wary that the government would try to pressure her to quit, and she hoped that the flight would be forgotten by the public until *Dawn* was on her way.

She wrote Harry Jones from the Forest Hills Inn on December 14, as follows:

> *Dear Captain Jones,*
>
> *Thanks for your work, and making arrangements for our return to Old Orchard. First one thing, then another, has delayed us. So today, I am hesitating about going to Old Orchard. It may be best for us to take a night flight, testing instruments, and the pilot's ability in night flying, so we may go to Harbor Grace and look things over there.*
>
> *However, please say nothing about this. Please keep my plans strictly confidential. I regretted the New England papers carried the news about my anticipated return to Old Orchard. You know how uncertain everything is in aviation, and if one could keep all publicity out of the papers until one does something, it would be so much better for everyone.*
>
> *All I can say now is "Thank you," which I do with warmest appreciation.*
>
> *Just what we will do will be determined by today's tests and the weather.*
>
> *Remember me to your dear family.*
>
> *Kindest personal regard to you, and everybody up there, but, to you, in particular.*
>
> *Sincerely, Frances Grayson*

On December 7, the day he was announced as the pilot, Lieutenant Omdal arrived at Curtiss Field in the afternoon with Mrs. Grayson. The two, along with Ed Mulligan and Bryce Goldsborough, took *Dawn* up on a test trip, to familiarize Omdal with the controls. When they landed 30 minutes later they jumped out of the plane, obviously pleased. The engines had purred smoothly, and Omdal had found the ship easy to fly. It was at this point Mrs. Grayson wired Harry Jones that they would fly to Maine and arrive at the beach at low tide, around 3:30 P.M. on Saturday,

December 10. From there, it was her plan to continue on to Harbor Grace, though she dropped hints that if all went well they might conceivably fly straight across without stopping.

Omdal continued to test the *Dawn* during the next two days, flying her with heavy loads, and learning to handle the big ship with sureness while Goldsborough worked with painstaking thoroughness over the instruments and radio on which they would rely so heavily. He fretted over the wintry weather. The U. S. Weather Bureau had discontinued their services to ocean flyers, but he was able to get up-to-date weather information from the Canadian government and the British Air Ministry, as well as direct data from ships at sea. "Doc" Kimball also volunteered help during his spare time. The reports were not encouraging, as wintry storms were sweeping the Atlantic in close succession; Mrs. Grayson, however, was not discouraged, for she was convinced that the strong, westerly flow of air would waft them across safely.

The crew was joined by Fred Koehler of the Wright Company, who took over from Ed Mulligan. Koehler had only recently come over to Wright after eight years with Eddie Stinson. He had worked on *Pride of Detroit* earlier in the summer when she was in Newfoundland, and was thoroughly familiar with Harbor Grace's Bennett Field. Though he, too, was a pilot, having instructed at Langley Field during the war and flown for some years on the Chicago to Omaha airmail run, he had grounded himself for the more sedentary life of caring for planes.

He said frankly, "I've had 4500 flying hours, and that's enough for any man!"

His knowledge of the Newfoundland field was invaluable to Omdal, and Koehler agreed to accompany them to Harbor Grace for this reason, and to prepare them for the big hop to Europe.

Storms lashed the northeast coastline over the weekend of the 10th and 11th, and delayed the trip to Old Orchard. The postponement gave Omdal the opportunity to accustom himself further to the *Dawn*, and he took full advantage of it, flying repeatedly, over the Sound and New York City. He handled her now with complete confidence. Mrs. Grayson was usually on board during the flights, and, from time to time, she would come forward, slip into the pilot's seat alongside him, and take over the wheel. It was being made clear that she intended to share the controls with him on the way over, and she showed him a surprising skill.

The crowds at the field were slim, for Mrs. Grayson had continued her policy of providing the press with a minimum of information; consequently, the stories of *Dawn*'s preparations were limited to one or two sentences in the back pages of the papers. To the public, there was nothing imminent, or particularly interesting about her trip. Besides, the weather was cold and uncomfortable, and there was Christmas shopping to be done.

On Monday the 12th the weather cleared and the flyers were alerted for the afternoon. In the morning, Omdal flew *Dawn* off Curtiss Field for a last test. He had the "feel" of her now, but he wanted to get as much time in as he could. After circling Mineola for half an hour, he banked, and started back toward the field. The wind was blowing from the line of hangars across the regular runway, but the pilot, now at home in the plane, let down confidently, for a cross-field landing. The onlookers were shaken as they saw *Dawn* approach, with great speed, touch down at better than 60 miles an hour, and career across the turf, headed straight at a hangar. They held their breaths as she sped for what looked to be sure destruction. At the last instant, when a crash seemed unavoidable, Omdal put *Dawn* into a screeching ground loop less than a 100 feet from the shed, and the big ship slued around in a swirl of dust, and came to a jolting stop.

Mrs. Grayson was not in the vicinity, but when she heard of the near disaster, she postponed the flight to Old Orchard again. Though the *Dawn* had survived the ordeal without damage, she was unsure at this point whether her pilot was ready for the long flight ahead, and felt that a few more days would make little difference, one way or another.

A new idea occurred to her in the light of the day's events. She thought that perhaps a direct flight from New York to Harbor Grace would be of more value to them, as it would afford the crew a chance to fly at night over the water. While she pondered the decision, Omdal continued to fly the amphibian, though he was balked on two consecutive days by tire punctures from nails on the field as he taxied for a take-off. Though annoying, the damage was repaired quickly both times, and Omdal was able, after minor delays, to continue with his trial spins.

On December 16, Mrs. Grayson made her decision. They would not go to Old Orchard after all, but would fly directly to Harbor Grace, from where they would leave, as soon as possible thereafter, for Europe.

The wheels were set in motion as only Mrs. Grayson could do it.

Quantities of 96-test aviation gasoline, lubricating oil, and spare parts, were rushed to Bennett Field to await their arrival; and preparations were made so that the plane would be serviced speedily, in the event they wanted to take off at once for Europe. Harry Jones was notified of the decision in Old Orchard, and, as requested, made no mention of the change in itinerary.

Such was the extent of her secrecy, that the general public had little idea of what was in the offing. They had read a tiny item on Omdal's close call, but there was little in the papers to indicate that *Dawn* was about to go.

At the time, too, the papers were headlining the lastest exploits of the famed "Lone Eagle," Charles A. Lindbergh, who, on December 13, made a non-stop, solo flight from Bolling Field, Washington, D.C., to Mexico City. When he landed the *Spirit of St. Louis*, after 27 hours in the air, he received as many plaudits as he had from his ocean trip. Government leaders, private citizens, and aviation notables raved over his latest performance.

Mrs. Grayson, thankful that someone else was taking the headlines, said admiringly of him, "His simplicity and spirit of motive have certainly inspired me."

Work continued at Curtiss Field. New propellers were installed on the Whirlwind engines to try and cut down on their voracious appetite for gasoline. The props were tested on a short flight, and Koehler was satisfied with the improvement. Workmen loaded the safety equipment; a pneumatic boat with oars, flares, rockets, and emergency rations. Sikorsky came to the field for a final check and pronounced the ship fit. The tumult over Lindbergh's flight quieted, but Mrs. Grayson's privacy was protected, for the excitement was replaced on December 17 by the country's agonies over the terrible fate of the submarine S-4. News of the *Dawn* was lost in the reports of the Navy's desperate struggle to reach the drowning men.

Late in the evening of Thursday, December 22, as all America grieved over the loss of the 40 men on the S-4, Mrs. Grayson announced that *Dawn* would take off at dusk the next day for Harbor Grace. She explained to reporters that her reason for the late start was to get them over Newfoundland by sunrise, 7 A.M. the next day, so as to facilitate the landing. She added that the night flight would provide the crew, also, with a helpful "shakedown" cruise, which she felt they all needed before tackling the Atlantic.

She was questioned about the weather en route, which was reported as far from good. She answered that it didn't worry her. They would never be far from land, she explained, and she was confident that the twin J-5s, which Koehler had assured her were in perfect condition, would carry them through any kind of storm. Furthermore, she said, as an added safeguard they were carrying a powerful radio capable of being heard at a distance of 800 miles in daytime and over 1000 at night.

It was partly cloudy the next morning, Friday, December 23, and the temperature was in the low thirties. *Dawn* sat atop the Byrd Ramp at the eastern end of Roosevelt Field, having been flown over from Curtiss the night before.

Fred Koehler stood on a ladder alongside the cockpit, with a pocketful of wrenches, and tinkered with the starboard engine. It was cold, working with the metal tools, and, every now and then, he blew on his hands to warm them. Another mechanic sat in the cockpit and worked the controls, while a fellow-worker watched from the outside and yelled, "O.K.!" Still others loaded supplies for the immediate flight, and for the big one across the ocean.

There were no spectators, yet—only the field personnel. It was too early and too cold. The silence was broken, on occasion, by small planes roaring off the runway, or by the noise of an engine being warmed in a nearby hangar.

During the morning, 595 gallons of gasoline, all carefully strained, were poured into *Dawn*'s tanks, filling them to one-half capacity. Though the gas supply would not be sufficient to take her across the ocean, there was ample to get her to Harbor Grace. Also, Omdal would have no problem getting her off the runway, as she would weigh less than 10,000 pounds.

Shortly after noon, two mechanics were seen daubing a thick coat of liquid on *Dawn*'s wings and fuselage, per order of Lieutenant Omdal. There was little left for the ground crew to do, but they still worked inside and outside the plane—partly to keep warm. The sky was now gray, and though the sun would peep through momentarily, it was one of those dully cold December days.

At the Forest Hills Inn, which was festooned with Christmas color, Mrs. Grayson spent her morning cleaning up last-minute details. She wrote letters, talked to her attorney, and attended to other personal affairs, like any traveler on the eve of a trip. She called Bryce Goldsborough, who was at his Brooklyn home with his wife and son. Goldy told her that he had already talked to Bennett Field, and had been told that the weather, there, was fair, with the temperature just above freezing. The wind was light from the northwest, but was expected to back around to the west during the day. Though a temperature drop was forecast for the night, the general outlook for the next 24 hours was favorable. He was told, also, that the field, while frozen 3 inches deep, was even and free of snow and that they should have no landing problems. Mrs. Grayson was satisfied and told Goldy that they would leave as scheduled. She then phoned her pilot, Lieutenant Omdal, who had been living in Brooklyn, with a cousin. His sister had come in from Long Island, and they were breakfasting together. Mrs. Grayson advised him of Goldy's report and told him that the flight was on. He said he would be there.

All three arrived at Roosevelt in the early part of the afternoon. Goldy put in another call to Bennett Field, and learned that the weather was holding up, and that there was no change in the forecast. He inquired about conditions in the harbor and along the coast, and was told that they were all ice-free, and open, if they chose to pull up the wheels and set down in the water. Officials at Bennett Field said that a powerful beacon had been set up on top of Target Hill, not far from the airport, to guide them in if the weather turned bad.

As the afternoon passed, the crowds gathered slowly. They never approached in numbers, the throngs of spring and summer, but they appeared sizable enough as they surrounded the ramp and the plane. Gone now were the straw hats and shirtsleeves—replaced by heavy coats, mufflers, and ear tabs. It was cold, breaths showed, and people stamped their feet to keep warm in the frigid December air.

They were distracted at 4 P.M. by a huge cloud of black smoke that rolled skyward from the direction of Mitchel Field. Sirens screamed as fire apparatus rushed to the scene of the blaze. Many in the fickle crowd forgot *Dawn*, and ran off to follow the latest excitement—which turned out to be a fire in an old Mitchel Field warehouse. By the time they returned, *Dawn* had gone.

The few who stayed with the amphibian, soon saw her crew stride across the field from a hangar, led by the petite Mrs. Grayson. She was laughing and chattering away with her mates, and, though excited, appeared anything but nervous. The flyers were dressed in extra-heavy fur-lined suits, which made them look bulky. They wore fur-lined boots and helmets, and their goggles were perched on their foreheads in the style of the day. The small group of spectators clapped as they neared the plane. Mrs. Grayson smiled and waved back. They were soon hemmed in by reporters at the edge of the ramp.

"When will you leave Newfoundland for Europe?" Mrs. Grayson was asked.

"We hope to be ready for the ocean hop any time after Sunday." She went on without interruption, "Our greatest hazard will be the collection of ice on the wings." Omdal shook his head perceptibly. "But," she continued, "I think we have partially solved this problem by coating the wings heavily with glycerin. We will suffer from the cold, I am afraid, as on the crossing the weather will be ten to twenty degrees below zero. It will be only slightly warmer in the cockpit of the plane. We are equipped with extra-heavy, fur-lined flying suits, and we will also use face masks, which will help."

Omdal then outlined his experience with icing in the arctic, and scoffed at the thought that they would be bothered by it particularly in view of the application of glycerin.

Goldsborough promised reporters that he would be in constant radio communication with land during the flight, and that they would be kept up to date on *Dawn's* progress.

The spectators crowded around as the group was lined up, and the photographers had their turn. Flashbulbs blinked in the twilight that now covered the field. Mrs. Grayson seemed so tiny in the crowd, and yet so dynamic that she stood out from the rest. She continued to answer all questions, pleasantly and incisively. She said that she expected the 1200-mile flight would take them between 11 and 12 hours, and if they arrived over Harbor Grace before daylight, they would circle the area until sunrise, for they had 20 hours of fuel on board. She was asked what they would do if there was snow on the field. She replied that their latest check showed the field in excellent condition, but that if snow fell, they'd simply pull up their wheels and land in the harbor, or a nearby lake that was not frozen.

Koehler sat in the cockpit, waiting for the signal to start the engines, but Mrs. Grayson, after weeks of silence, let the men of the press have their day.

One of them noticed that she was carrying a pistol.

She laughed and said jauntily, "Just a badge of authority for the commander of the expedition."

The talk turned to the S-4. Mrs. Grayson sighed and expressed horror at the suffering of the trapped men while they waited for the rescue that never came.

She would have talked with the reporters forever, but Goldsborough pointed to the western sky. Dusk had fallen, and night was coming fast. Already, lights twinkled brightly in the hangars at the edge of the field. The coldness of the early evening was abetted by a freshening wind that blew out of the west, down the long runway. The breeze was good for the *Dawn*, but comfortable for those who stood by, waiting.

Koehler, in the cockpit, with the help of a mechanic outside, started the starboard motor. It caught at once, and thundered out a smooth sound. The port motor balked momentarily, as the prop moved around, uncertainly, and then, it too roared to life amid billows of smoke from its exhaust. Koehler warmed them both thoroughly, and the noise made talking impossible; some of the spectators shrank away from the din. He closed the throttles, and the engines idled.

Mrs. Grayson and her crew shook hands with the official party of ground crew and reporters who surrounded them. Koehler slid over to the co-pilot's seat, as Omdal, hunched over, crawled to his place behind the controls.

Goldsborough went aboard, followed by Mrs. Grayson, who climbed into her "office" in the fuselage cabin. They seemed calm enough, but there was little reason for anxiety, for *Dawn*'s trip was, after the past summer, routine, and she would never be far from land. Mrs. Grayson had given a course, subject to alteration by Goldy, leading them over central Connecticut, Massachusetts, the southern tip of Maine near Old Orchard, and along the Nova Scotian coast to Newfoundland. The route, as planned, would keep them over land for a greater portion of the flight than that of any of the preceding ocean flyers.

It was getting late. Koehler waved out of the cockpit window. Police cleared the runway and moved the orderly crowd back from the base of the ramp. A mechanic poised himself at the rear of the plane to cut the tether, and another prepared to pull the wheel chocks. Omdal opened the throttles until the engines roared with full power. The noise shattered the still of the evening. The mechanic at the stern, his clothes whipped by the blast from the props, cut the restraining hawser, and the wheel chocks were pulled simultaneously. *Dawn* catapulted down the ramp, hit the field with a bounce, and headed down the runway. She was a shadowy form as she lumbered along in the half darkness. There was only a trace of pink left in the dark-gray western sky. To the surprise of everyone, she left the ground short of the halfway mark, after a run of but 2500 feet. In the dusk spectators could make out her wings dimly as she rose. She was 100 feet in the air as she passed over the incline to Curtiss Field. Omdal seemed to be sacrificing altitude for speed, for without climbing farther, he banked sharply around, and set *Dawn* on her course to the north-east. Within 2 minutes, she had disappeared from view. For a little longer, the spectators continued to hear the humming throb of her motors; then, it, too, faded away and was gone. The take-off had come at 5:07 P.M. EST.

3. There were no immediate sightings of *Dawn* or radio messages from her. Some thought it curious that no one had at least heard the big plane as she flew over Connecticut, but the lack of radio messages was understandable. Goldsborough, from the beginning, had said that WMU would not begin transmitting until they were 2 hours out.

Back in New York, there was some cheer at 7:40 P.M. A radio message was received from Léon Deschampes, an employee of the French Cable Office on Cape Cod at Orleans, Massachusetts, saying that he had seen the *Dawn* overhead at 7:25 P.M., headed out to sea. It was now understood why she had not been seen earlier. Her course had been changed, and instead of flying inland, she had skirted the New England coast to Cape Cod. Everyone was relieved, and the experts were encouraged by the fact that she was averaging close to 100 miles an hour.

Lookouts, from Boston to the Penobscot Bay, Maine, area, kept a sharp eye out for her throughout the entire evening, but had nothing to report. Nor did the radio receiving stations along the coast hear any receptions from WMU. Anxious reporters called Harry Jones, in Old Orchard, as midnight approached. He was not worried by the lack of news. He said quite rationally that the normal course from Cape Cod to Nova Scotia would take them well off the New England coastline, and that Goldsborough was most likely too busy with night navigation to operate his radio.

Harbor Grace's Bennett Field buzzed with activity getting ready for *Dawn*'s arrival. During the evening workmen rolled out drums of gasoline and oil and assembled parts and other materials needed for her inside a hangar which would be the depot where she would be serviced. The field lights burned brightly all night long, and those at the field could see the intermittent flash of the beacon atop Target Hill as it slowly circled the sky. The weather was still clear, and the temperature down a little—to the high twenties, but the cold was not a deterrent to the hardy spectators who had watched Brock and Schlee, Tully and Metcalf come and go and were determined not to miss *Dawn*. Like their counterparts at Roosevelt, they were well bundled, and stamped their feet, drank hot coffee, tea, and more spirited things to keep warm during the long hours.

The fresh westerly that had swept the field since late afternoon dropped in the wee hours of Christmas Eve; though there had been no reports on *Dawn's* progress, all Harbor Grace was confident that she would be over the field on schedule, at sunrise, or shortly before.

They waited and waited. Their watches and clocks at the field pointed first to 5 A.M.—then 6 A.M. The sky in the east grew rosy, and the sun peeked over the horizon, but there was no sound of a motor or sight of a plane. Wise field personnel declared that there was no cause for worry, because *Dawn* carried enough gas to stay up until after noon, and no doubt the winds had slowed her. The radio silence, though worrisome, was explained by a possible failure in the transmitting equipment, or perhaps atmospheric interference with reception; but expert opinion could not contain worries, as first, 1 P.M. passed, and then, agonizingly, minute by minute, the afternoon, without word or sight of Mrs. Grayson's plane.

At 6 P.M., Alex Sutherland, chief wireless operator at the Halifax, Nova Scotia, naval dockyard, checked all government radio stations along the Canadian coastline for any possible news. There was none. Ships at sea in the area were called, but they had seen nothing. In desperation, Léon Deschampes of the French Cable Office was phoned at Orleans to see if he could add anything to his story. He was questioned closely, and admitted finally that he had not seen *Dawn* the night before, but that he and two other co-workers in the sea-front shack, had heard her fly above, very low. He went on to say that at the time the weather was clear and the wind was blowing hard from the west. He then added a bit of fresh information. Ten minutes after the plane had flown over, he said, he heard the sound of the engines return, and judged the plane to be still at low altitude, and about a mile away, inside the outer shore of the Cape. He volunteered his opinion that *Dawn* was down, somewhere, in Long Island Sound, or Massachusetts Bay. It was 10 P.M. on Christmas Eve, and there was still no trace of her.

Christmas Day came without word. In Hollis, Queens, Mrs. Ingebord Jensen, Omdal's sister, remained calm. She said she had every

confidence in her brother, and told of his past landings in rough
waters and bad weather, while serving in the Norwegian Navy.

Gertrude Goldsborough, at home in Brooklyn, was distraught. She
and her son spent most of the day in the house, interrupting it only
with a short visit to a neighbor's. Late in the afternoon, she called
her mother who lived in Woodside, Long Island.

"Is there any hope?" she cried like a child.

"Of course, there always is," her mother answered.

In Muncie, Indiana, A. J. Wilson, Mrs. Grayson's father, was sure
that the *Dawn* was safe.

"I think she's on her way to London," he said confidently. Though
he seemed not worried, he admitted that Christmas dinner would be
held up until they had some definite word.

Late on Christmas Eve, when aviators were certain that *Dawn* was
lost, or in deep trouble, pilot William Winston, an employee of the
Curtiss Flying Service, volunteered to take off early Christmas Day,
with food and medical supplies, and search for *Dawn* along her route,
as far as he could. Steve Parkinson, a friend of Goldsborough's, and
one of *Dawn*'s mechanics at Old Orchard Beach, demanded that he
go, too. There was a question of money, however, for the Curtiss
charge for flying over water amounted to $75 an hour.

Mrs. Goldsborough, steeling herself for a sad Christmas, was told.
She noticed among her Christmas gifts, an envelope marked DO NOT
OPEN UNTIL CHRISTMAS. She opened it, and out dropped a check from
her husband for $500. She called Steve, and despite his objections,
threw her present in the rescue kitty. He and Winston had ponied
up their savings, and now the search could start at once. At the same
time, Mrs. Ange Ancker cabled from Copenhagen that she was leaving for America forthwith, and would organize further rescue attempts on her arrival.

Fred Koehler's brother was found in Paterson, New Jersey. He told
how Fred had given up flying finally, because he felt "his luck had
about run out." He could not believe that *Dawn* was really gone.

Reporters turned again to Harry Jones.

He addressed a statement to the saddened families:

"Don't give up," it said. "They may have headed inland if they
couldn't get across the Bay of Fundy, and they may very well be
down safely somewhere."

Others were not so hopeful. "Doc" Kimball, the weatherman,
thought of their chances, originally, as one out of ten.

Now he said, "I admire Mrs. Grayson's courage, but she made the attempt against almost insurmountable odds."

Wilmer Stultz said that weather caused the trouble, not the motors. He went on to explain that the flyers were the victims of very poor judgment to attempt the flight at this time of year.

For the first time since Old Orchard, he spoke. "The seaworthiness of the ship can be questioned, too. It has a freeboard of only 8 inches, and if the *Dawn* went down in any kind of rough weather, it would be swamped!"

Igor Sikorsky was incensed, and took exception to the remarks of *Dawn*'s former pilot.

"She'll land in any kind of water," he retorted, "and she's now safe in some quiet cove!"

Clarence Chamberlin, when questioned, said that he was never enthusiastic about *Dawn*'s chances, because of midwinter icing conditions. He ridiculed Omdal's claim that a treatment of glycerin would do away with the danger.

"It would wash off at once," he said. "There's nothing yet invented to prevent icing." Chamberlin continued talking about the problems of flying a new plane. "It's a hard job for a flyer to step into a plane that he is not familiar with, as was the case with Omdal and the *Dawn*, and pilot it on a right flight, such as this one to Harbor Grace. I have flown *Dawn*, and the ship handles beautifully, but I would hate to have had his assignment!"

During Christmas Day, speculation was rampant as to *Dawn*'s fate. People hoped for news, but all was silent. Goldsborough's failure to keep in touch by radio, as he had promised, led the experts to guess that something had happened to the plane early in the flight. Meteorologists checked the weather over Cape Cod at the time of the reported sighting, and found that the skies had been clear and the seas calm. The temperature and precipitation charts disclosed no evidence of icing. Men on the street thought that the high-set tail assembly might have snapped off in a squall, or that both motors had quit simultaneously. Professionals and tyros, however, agreed on one thing: whatever happened must have happened suddenly, for there had been no time apparently for a radioed SOS. Veteran pilots backed Stultz in his feeling that *Dawn* would have had trouble making a landing in the open sea. If Omdal had tried to land on a long, flat roller, they felt he would, most likely, have found it gone when he got down, landed in a trough, and been crushed by the next wave that came along. They were unanimous in their opinion that an 8-

inch freeboard afforded little protection in the wild Atlantic. Mrs. Goldsborough clung to the hope that they had headed inland, and were safe in a sheltered cove. She was asked if she was against her husband making the trip.

She answered simply, "I never opposed anything my husband wanted to do. He always showed good judgment, and I always was certain everything he tried would come out well."

As the sun set on Christmas afternoon, Winston and Parkinson returned to Curtiss Field after a fruitless search of Long Island Sound and Massachusetts Bay. They had flown the coastline for 8 hours without turning up a clue. The Curtiss Flying Service, whose amphibian they had flown, announced that they would make no charge, and that Mrs. Goldsborough's money, and other donations, would be returned.

In the late evening, there was an exciting radio message which had been relayed from the Canadian government wireless station, located on Sable Island off the Nova Scotian coast:

AT 9:45 P.M. EST 23RD DECEMBER HEARD AIRSHIP DAWN SAYING THAT SOMETHING HAD GONE WRONG BUT COULD NOT GET THROUGH OWING TO INTERFERENCE. PARTICULARS OF SIGNALS: ICW WAVE LENGTH 625 METERS. CALL SIGN WMU. The message was significant to radiomen as it meant that it had been transmitted on the emergency set, and on the distress wave length.

Dawn's call letters had been properly identified, and, in that the interrupted continuous wave (ICW) on the little set had only a range of 50 miles, it was the feeling that *Dawn* must be down close to Sable Island. Aviators were dubious, though, because *Dawn*, even at top speed, could not have reached the vicinity after 4¾ hours of flight from Roosevelt.

The U. S. Government ordered Coast Guard and Navy ships to join the search from ports along the northeastern coast. The destroyers *Shaw, Monaghan,* and *Downer* put to sea, at once, to scour the area between Cape Cod and Sable Island. The destroyers *Mahan* and *Sturtevant* steamed out of Boston Harbor hours later, after having been diverted from the S-4 salvage operations off Provincetown Harbor.

At 5 P.M., on December 26, the dirigible *Los Angeles* left her hangar at Lakehurst, New Jersey, on an all-night flight to the search area. She was under the command of Charles E. Rosendahl, who had orders from the Naval Department to supplement the ocean search from the air. She carried 48 hours' fuel, and a crew of nine officers and twenty-seven enlisted men, all equipped with electrically heated flying suits.

On December 26, there was word of another radio reception from *Dawn*. Andrew Hillyard, an experienced operator from the Anglo-American radio station at Heart's Content, Newfoundland (30 miles up Trinity Bay from Harbor Grace), reported that between 6:30 and 7 P.M., on Christmas Night, he picked up a message on his home set, saying:

"Where are you? Can you locate us?"

The signature was garbled, but sounded like WHU or WPU, and the message was repeated ten times over a period of half an hour. For verification, he called in a neighbor who was a co-worker at the cable station, and told him the story. Together, they decided that they should report what he had heard to the authorities. If, in fact, the message was from the *Dawn*, it was almost 30 hours after her gas supply had been exhausted.

There were many reports from residents down east, who thought they had heard *Dawn*'s engines. An officer of a local bank was sure that he had heard her over Halifax, at 10 P.M. on Christmas night. Wallace J. Richards of Heart's Content, Newfoundland, said that he had stopped at the Half Way House on his way home from Carbonear and "heard the hum, and, most certainly, the exhaust of an airplane, which I judged to be at 1000 feet, on Saturday night [Christmas Eve] at 10:45 P.M."

The Burresses, proprietors of Half Way House, corroborated his story, except that Mrs. Burress said that she had heard the plane 2 hours earlier.

In the ensuing days, there were rumors that *Dawn* had been seen or heard from Christmas Eve to Christmas afternoon, over the areas of Concepcion Bay, the Avalon Peninsula, and Harbor Grace, but there was still no trace of her. Manager Collum of the Marconi Station at Cape Race was skeptical of the reports that *Dawn* had reached Newfoundland. He said that after she was reported missing, he had signaled her continuously for 24 hours, without response.

On December 30 the Naval and Coast Guard units requested, and were granted leave to return to port. They had hunted over a path 75 miles in width, approximating *Dawn*'s course as far as Newfoundland, and had seen nothing; the dirigible *Los Angeles* returned too to her Lakehurst station, without success, after searching an area of 11,000 miles under hazardous weather conditions. She had flown as far east as Sable Island, without turning up a clue—neither wreckage, oil slick, nor suspicious flotsam. Commander Rosendahl was visibly angry, when he landed.

He proclaimed, "There should be immediate governmental restriction on such foolhardy flights that have no real, only personal value!"

The Navy called off the search, and though a private Grayson Rescue Committee, sponsored by Mrs. Ancker, continued to look for *Dawn* for weeks, in inland lakes and hidden coves, there was no trace of her.

During the days after Christmas, those who waited and hoped in New York, were discouraged further by the ocean liners arriving one to two days late because of storms at sea.

When the *Albertic* from Liverpool docked on December 26, her captain, F. F. Summers, described the preceding Saturday, the 24th, "as one of the worst days I have ever spent in the Atlantic. The winds off Sable Island were blowing at 65 to 70 miles an hour, and the snow was so thick, at times, you couldn't see the bow from the bridge, and it was so cold that the snow froze as it hit the deck." The storm had lasted, he said, from noon on Saturday until 4 A.M. Sunday. "And the rollers were 30 to 40 feet high!" When the Red Cross liners, *Nerissa*, and *Sylvia* limped into port hours later, their crews told the same story. "Doc" Kimball tried to console the grieving families. He said that the liners were to the east of *Dawn's* course, and the storms, in any case, would have had no effect on her, as she would have been past them, if she reached the Newfoundland coast as scheduled.

What happened to her and her crew we shall never know. The evidence is scanty and highly circumstantial. Much of it was obtained from stories told days after her disappearance.

We must assume that the engines that Léon Deschampes and his mates heard at 7:25 on Friday night over Orleans, Massachusetts were those of *Dawn*. Whether the engine noise he heard 10 minutes later was that of the Grayson plane trying to get her bearings, is open to question.

On December 30, a small steamer, the *Oakey L. Alexander*, docked in Portland, Maine. Her radio operator, Jerome Knowles, said that on Friday evening, the 23rd, at 7:30, as his boat plowed up the New England coast, he intercepted a radio message, requesting that the Chatham, Massachusetts, station provide a compass setting.

There was silence for seconds, followed by the indistinct words, "Plane down!"

Simultaneously, came the story of Richmond H. Blake, radio operator on the steam trawler, *Tide*, which put into Boston on the same day.

He told reporters, "We were lying in the South Channel fishing grounds, about 80 miles southwest of Highland Light, Cape Cod, at 7 Friday night, when I picked up a call from the *Dawn*. The radio operator on the plane was trying to get his bearings, and I answered his call and tried to assist him. We exchanged signals for 20 minutes, and then the *Dawn's* signals ended abruptly. I tried to pick them up again for several hours, but was unable to do so."

Blake identified *Dawn's* call letters properly, and said they came in loud and clear. It gave credence to his report. It now seemed likely that *Dawn* had fallen into the sea, soon after leaving the Cape Cod shore.

The last story was told on January 2, 1928, when the schooner, *Rose Anne Beliveau* dropped anchor in Portland, Maine, after a long sail from Turk's Island. At 7:30 on the fateful Friday night, First Mate Louis Thibodeau was on watch as the schooner splashed through a rolling sea in a gale-force, 18 miles off Nauset Beach, Vineyard Haven, en route to Salem, Massachusetts. He said they were reefed down and heeled far over, and shipping water over the lee rail.

"I heard the noise of a motor," he said. "I could not make it out, at first. I went below and called Captain Comeau. He came on deck as did the cook and three seamen. We could still hear the sound of a motor, and then came a splash, and, after at least 5 minutes, the sound died out and no more was heard."

Edward Thibodeau, the helmsman, said that at the time it was all he could do to keep the schooner on the wind, but added, "I was frightened when I first heard the noise. It was so close that it seemed directly under the spanker boom where I was standing. I was on deck the entire time, and heard the motor churning for at least ten minutes."

Captain Comeau gave his version to the reporters in Portland.

"No plane could have existed on a night like that. The wind was strong, and there was sleet falling, which at times turned to snow, making the visibility very poor." He continued: "It would have been impossible for us to render assistance. Our boat was making at least ten knots. We were taking in sail at that time, and it would have been suicide to put out our small boat over the side. There were two steamers a few miles ahead, and we could just make out their stern lights, but they were bound north, and there was no way to communicate with them."

The searching newsmen were not satisfied, and asked him why he hadn't told the story before—perhaps, in Salem, where they had put in earlier. The captain answered directly that no one had asked him about it.

He said, "I talked with the crew, and after listening in on the messages received over the small radio in my cabin, I came to the conclusion that the sound of the airplane was that of the Grayson plane. I read the papers which I bought in Salem, and kept thinking about our experiences off Cape Cod, and the more I thought of it, the more convinced I was that the noise which we all heard might be information of value, so when I reached port, I happened to say something about it, and there you have it!"

The ship's chandler for *Rose Anne Beliveau*, Clifford C. Brown, said of Captain Comeau, "I have known the skipper for fifteen years, and he's as honest as they make them."

Nothing more was heard from or about *Dawn*. She and her gallant crew, like many of her predecessors, were muted by an angry ocean. Lilli Dillentz, Mrs. Grayson's erstwhile competitor, was asked for her opinion of the flight, as she prepared for a trip to the United States with her husband by ship.

She summed it up succinctly: "It was sheer madness!"

Mrs. Grayson explained it perhaps better, and with more insight, with a few words that she wrote during her long wait by the rolling surf, at Old Orchard.

"Waiting.
Who am I? Sometimes I wonder.
Am I a little nobody? Or am I a great dynamic force—
Powerful in that I have a God-given birthright and have
All the power there is if only I will understand and use it.
I will win!
I must not quit too soon!"

EPILOGUE: THEY LED THE WAY

The year 1927 was over, but the upcoming 1928 would bring no peace to the embattled Atlantic. Already, flyers in Europe and America made plans to follow up on the victories thus far gained. In Boston, a curly-haired social worker by the name of Amelia Earhart toyed with the idea of a flight; and, in the Bronx, New York, a former Italian air ace, Cesare Sabelli, talked of a late-winter flight to Rome in Giuseppe Bellanca's new creation—a 140-mile-an-hour monoplane, with a landing gear that folded like the legs of a bird.

Abroad, there was no lack of challengers. A sister ship of *Oiseau Tango* was purchased by Parisian hotel heir, Armand Lotti, Jr., and with a crew led by pilot Jean Assolant and René Lefèvre was readied for a hop. Dieudonné Coste, fresh from his South Atlantic triumph, looked forward to another Paris to New York try; while in Germany, Captain Hermann Koehl was Baron Guenther von Huenefeld prepared Dr. Junkers's *Bremen* again for a westbound attempt.

Despite the public outcries of "Stunt!" "Suicide Mission!" and "Death flights!" which might serve to delay the inevitable, the old ocean was waging a losing war, and within a few years would be brought to her knees.

She did not surrender gracefully, as we have seen. Many brave aviators and expensive aircraft fell prey to her furies. Some, such as Lieutenant Commander Noel Davis and Lieutenant Stanton Wooster, died arming for the battle. Others, like Nungesser, Bertaud, Princess Lowenstein-Wertheim, Tully, and Mrs. Grayson, to name only a few, the Atlantic claimed for herself, together with their fine crews and machines. In the years to come, she would swallow more gallant pioneers, but her days of tyranny were numbered.

To the Ladies and Gentlemen of the skies, who perished in her jealous snares during 1927, modern transportation owes a debt of deep gratitude, and a promise of eternal remembrance, for it was they who led the way.

BIBLIOGRAPHY

American Magazine, May 1932, "Flying Kites Taught Him to Build Trans-Atlantic Planes"

Current History, July 1927

Chamberlin, Clarence D., "Record Flights," Beechwood Press, 1942

————, "Give 'em Hell," Beechwood Press, 1942

de la Croix, Robert, *They Flew the Atlantic,* translated from the French by Edward Fitzgerald. W. W. Norton & Co., 1959

Dutton, William S., "Old Timer of the Skies," *American Magazine,* March 1930

Ellis, F. H. & E. M., *Atlantic Air Conquests,* Ryerson Press, 1963

Fokker, A. H. G. & Gould, Bruce, *The Life of Anthony H. G. Fokker,* Henry Holt & Co., 1931

Green, Fitzhugh, *Dick Byrd—Air Explorer,* G. P. Putnam's Sons, Knickerbocker Press, 1928

Lindbergh, Charles A., *We,* Charles Scribner's Sons, 1927

————, *The Spirit of St. Louis,* Charles Scribner's Sons, 1953

Literary Digest, September 24, 1927, "Comments on Death Flights"

Literary Digest, December 3, 1927

Magoun, F. Alexander & Hodgins, Eric, *Sky High,* Little, Brown & Co., 1935

Miller, J. Earle, "Eddie: 14,000 Hours in the Air." *Popular Mechanics,* April 1929

Mollison, James A., *Sky Riders,* Collins (London), 1939

New York *Herald Tribune,* microfilm edition, New York Public Library

New York *Times,* microfilm edition, New York Public Library

Oughton, Frederick, *The Aces,* G. P. Putnam's Sons, 1960

Review of Reviews, June 1927

Roseberry, C. R., *The Challenging Skies,* Doubleday & Co., 1966

Sikorsky, Igor I., *The Story of the Winged S,* Dodd, Mead & Co., 1938

Whitehouse, Arch, *Decisive Air Battles of the First World War,* Duell, Sloan & Pearce, 1963

INDEX

M